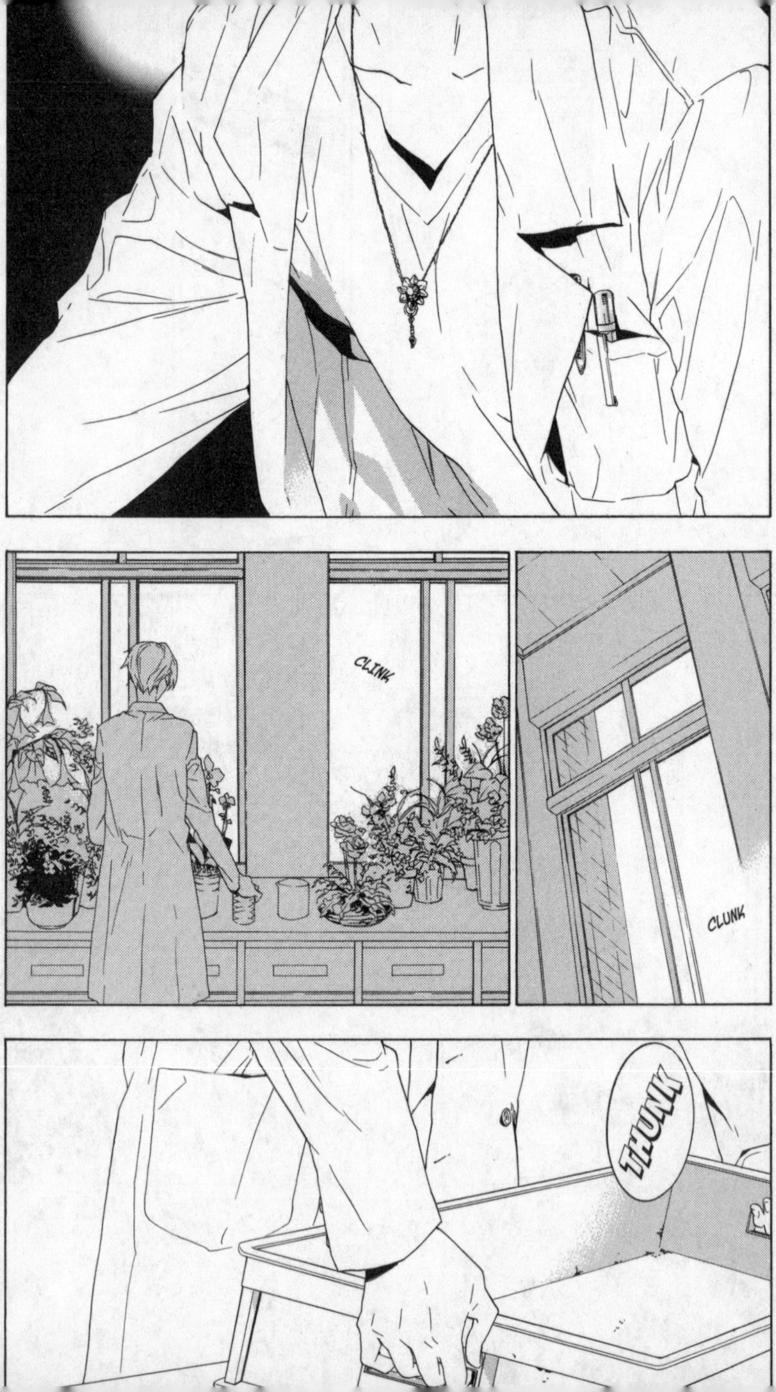
CLUNK
CLINK
THUNK

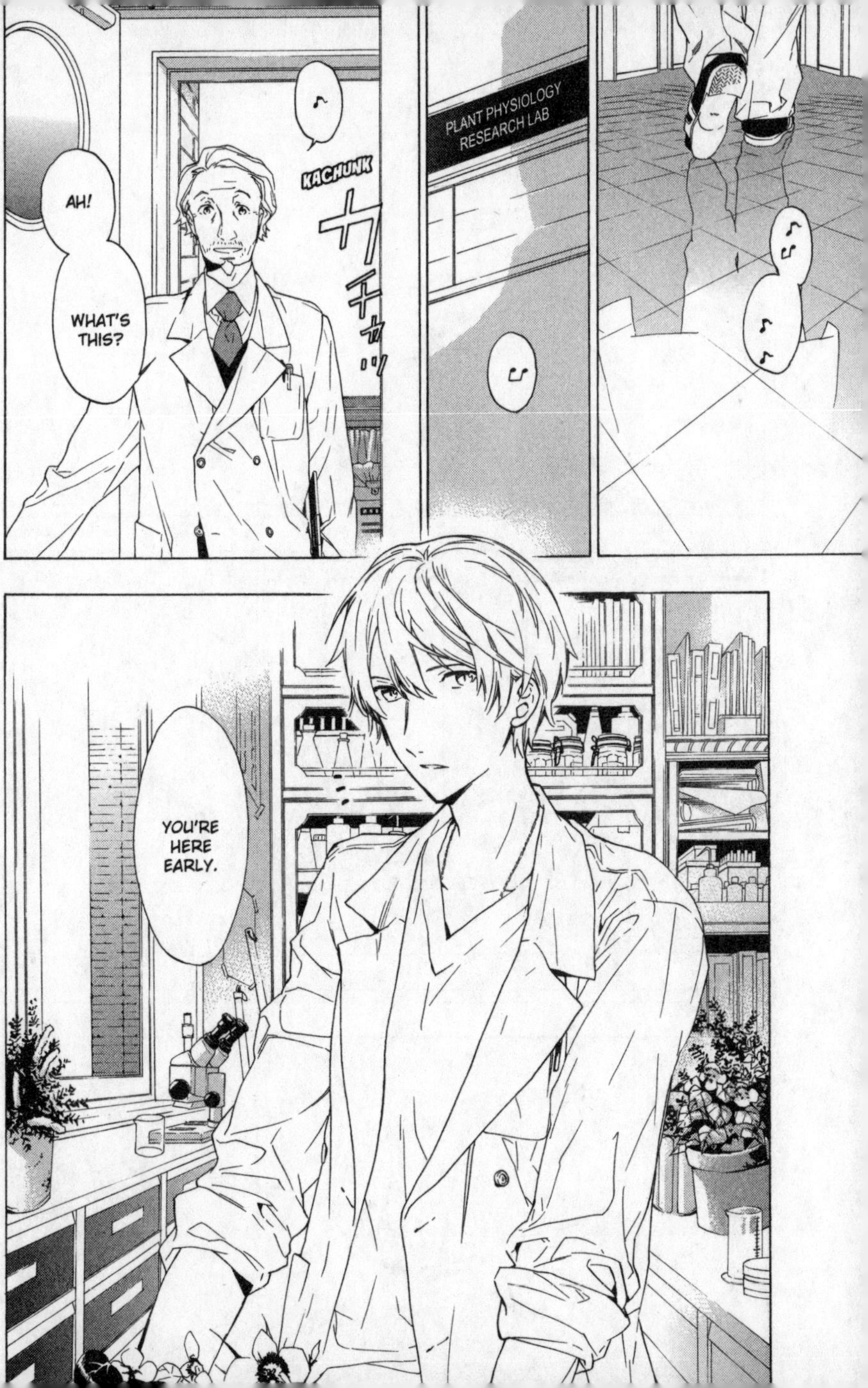
PLANT PHYSIOLOGY RESEARCH LAB
KACHUNK
カチャッ
AH!
WHAT'S THIS?
YOU'RE HERE EARLY.

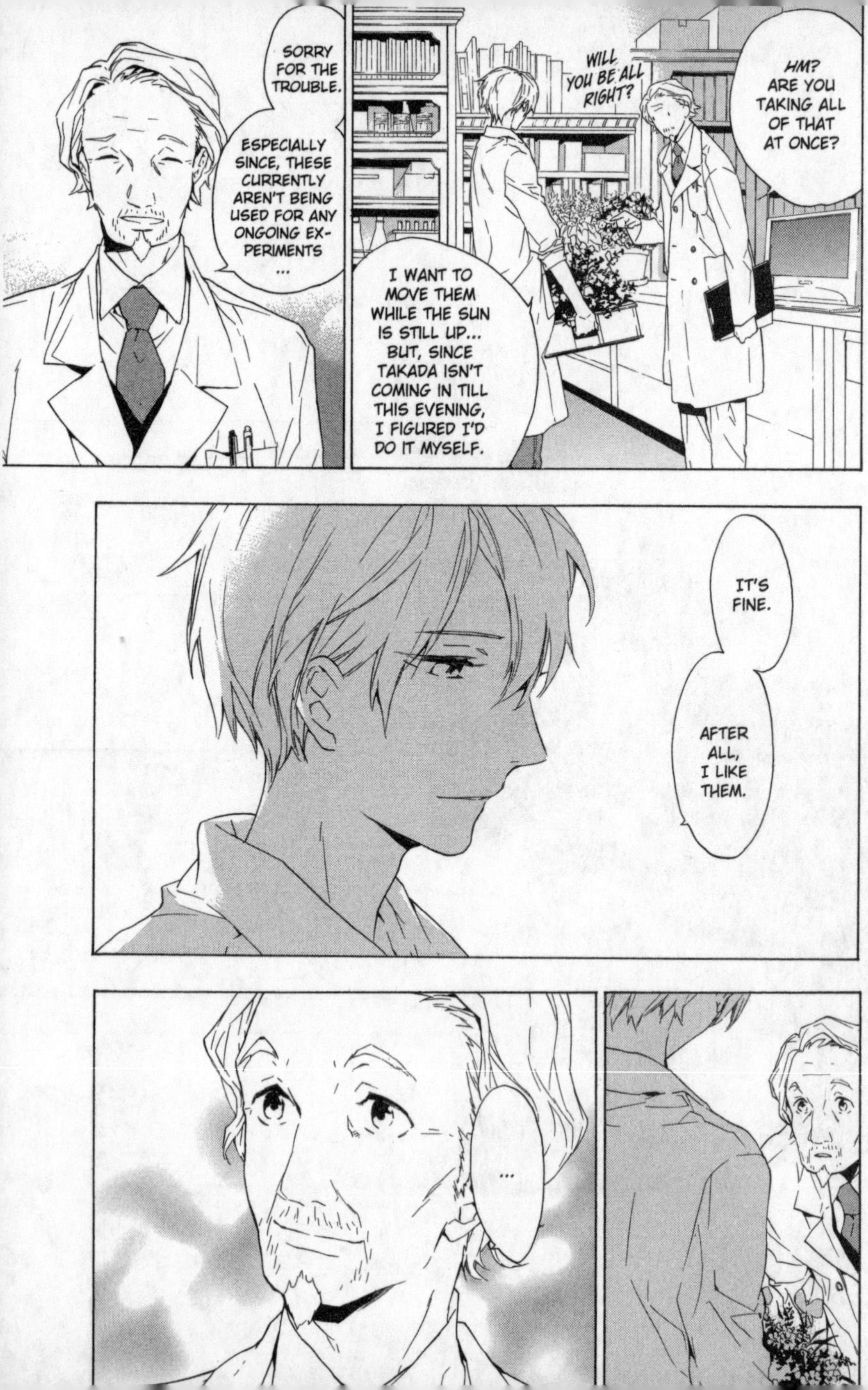
HM? ARE YOU TAKING ALL OF THAT AT ONCE?
WILL YOU BE ALL RIGHT?
I WANT TO MOVE THEM WHILE THE SUN IS STILL UP... BUT, SINCE TAKADA ISN'T COMING IN TILL THIS EVENING, I FIGURED I'D DO IT MYSELF.
SORRY FOR THE TROUBLE.
ESPECIALLY SINCE, THESE CURRENTLY AREN'T BEING USED FOR ANY ONGOING EX-PERIMENTS ...
IT'S FINE.
AFTER ALL, I LIKE THEM.
...

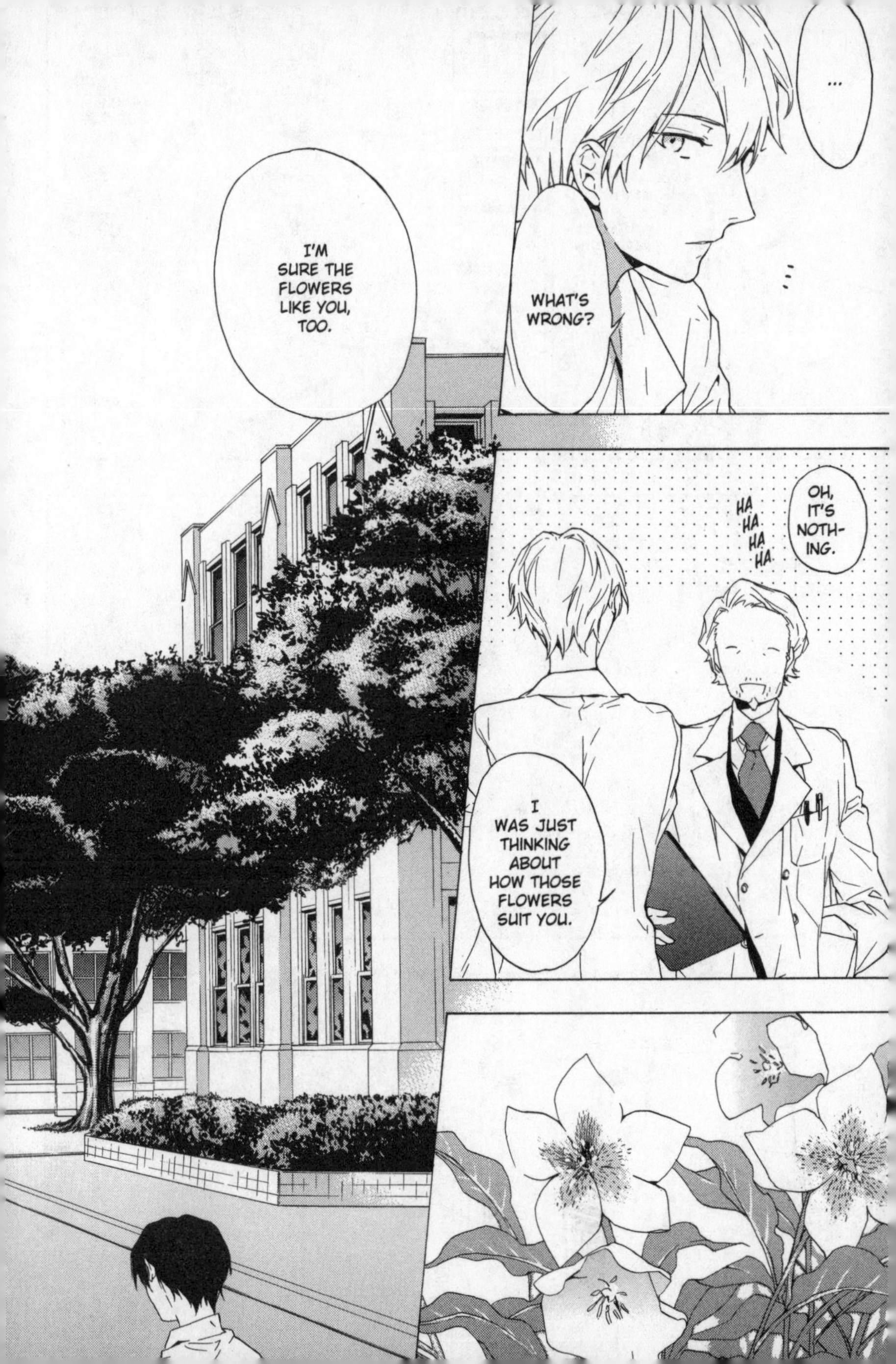
...
WHAT'S WRONG?
OH, IT'S NOTHING.
HA HA HA HA
I WAS JUST THINKING ABOUT HOW THOSE FLOWERS SUIT YOU.
I'M SURE THE FLOWERS LIKE YOU, TOO.

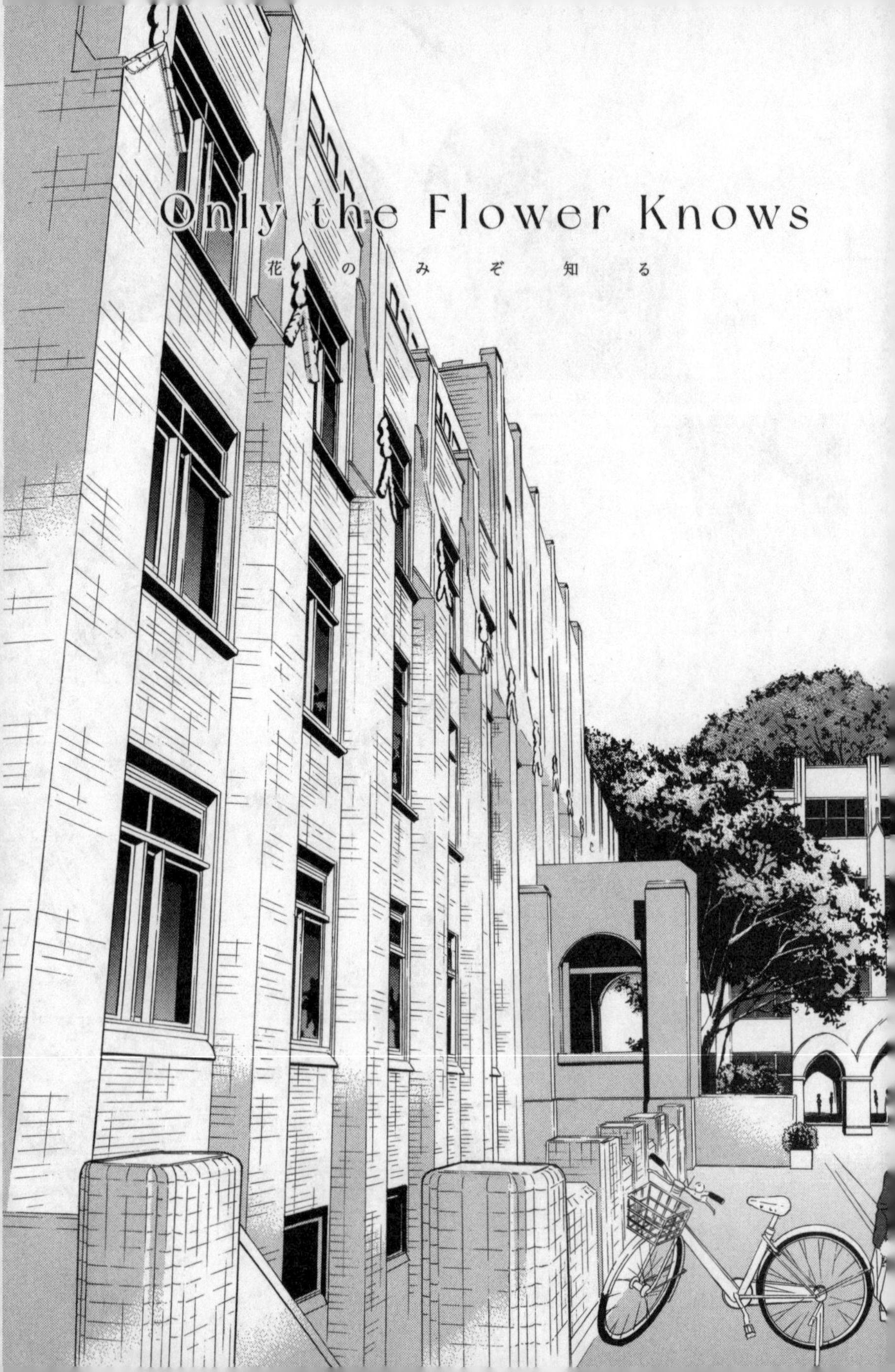
Only the Flower Knows
花のみぞ知る

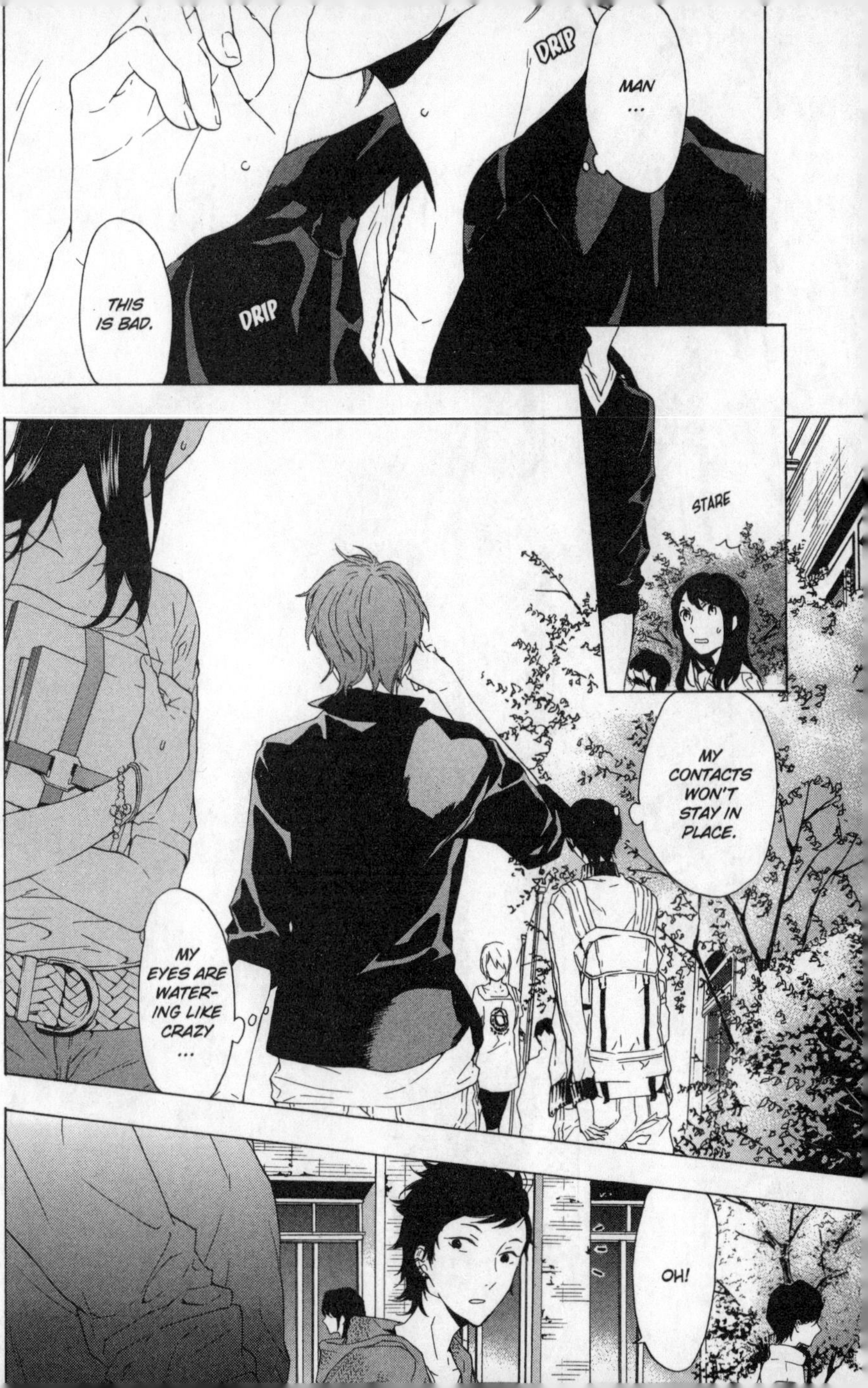
DRIP
MAN ...
DRIP
THIS IS BAD.
STARE
MY CONTACTS WON'T STAY IN PLACE.
MY EYES ARE WATERING LIKE CRAZY ...
OH!

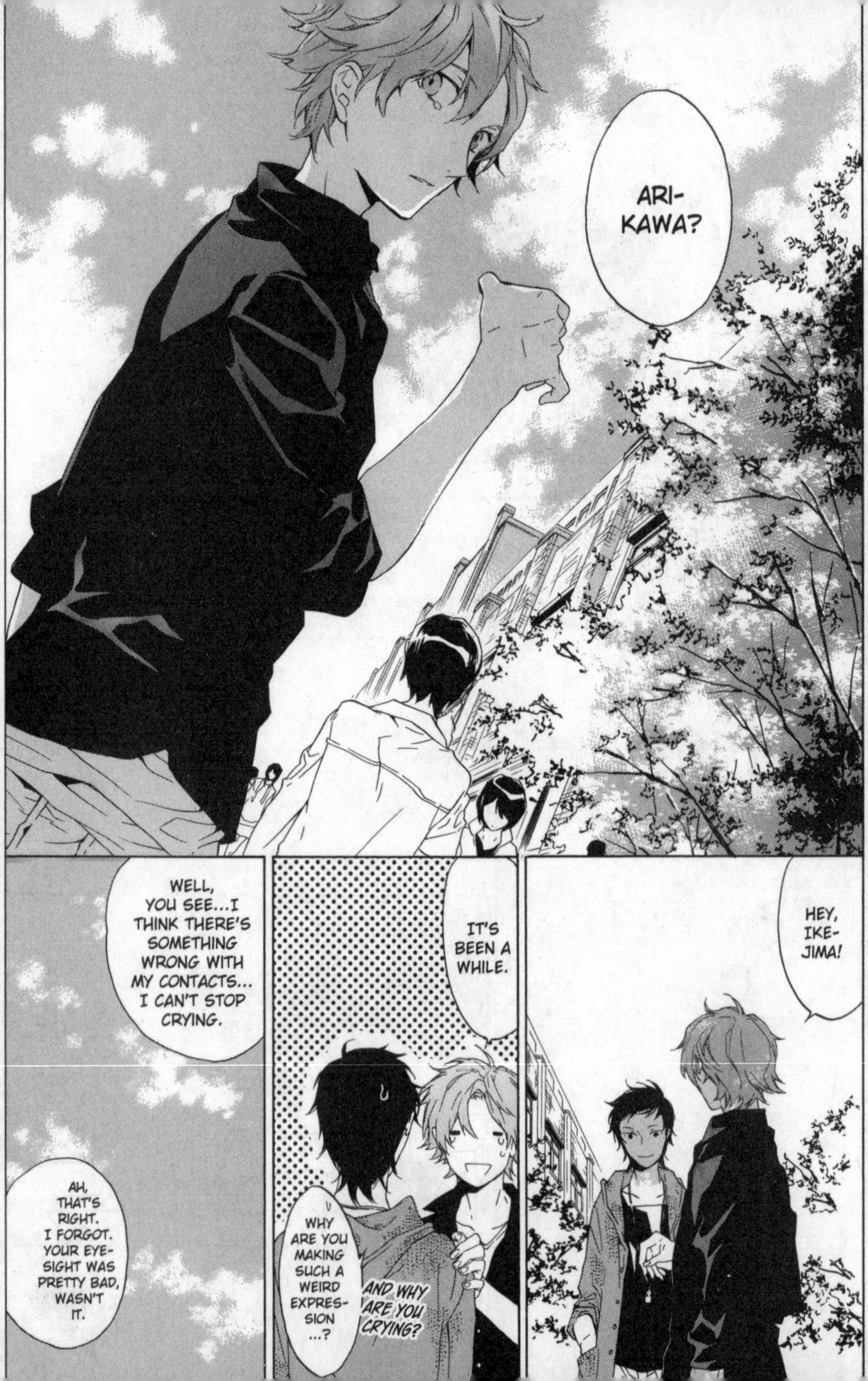
ARI-KAWA?
HEY, IKE-JIMA!
IT'S BEEN A WHILE.
WHY ARE YOU MAKING SUCH A WEIRD EXPRES-SION ...?
AND WHY ARE YOU CRYING?
WELL, YOU SEE...I THINK THERE'S SOMETHING WRONG WITH MY CONTACTS... I CAN'T STOP CRYING.
AH, THAT'S RIGHT. I FORGOT. YOUR EYE-SIGHT WAS PRETTY BAD, WASN'T IT.

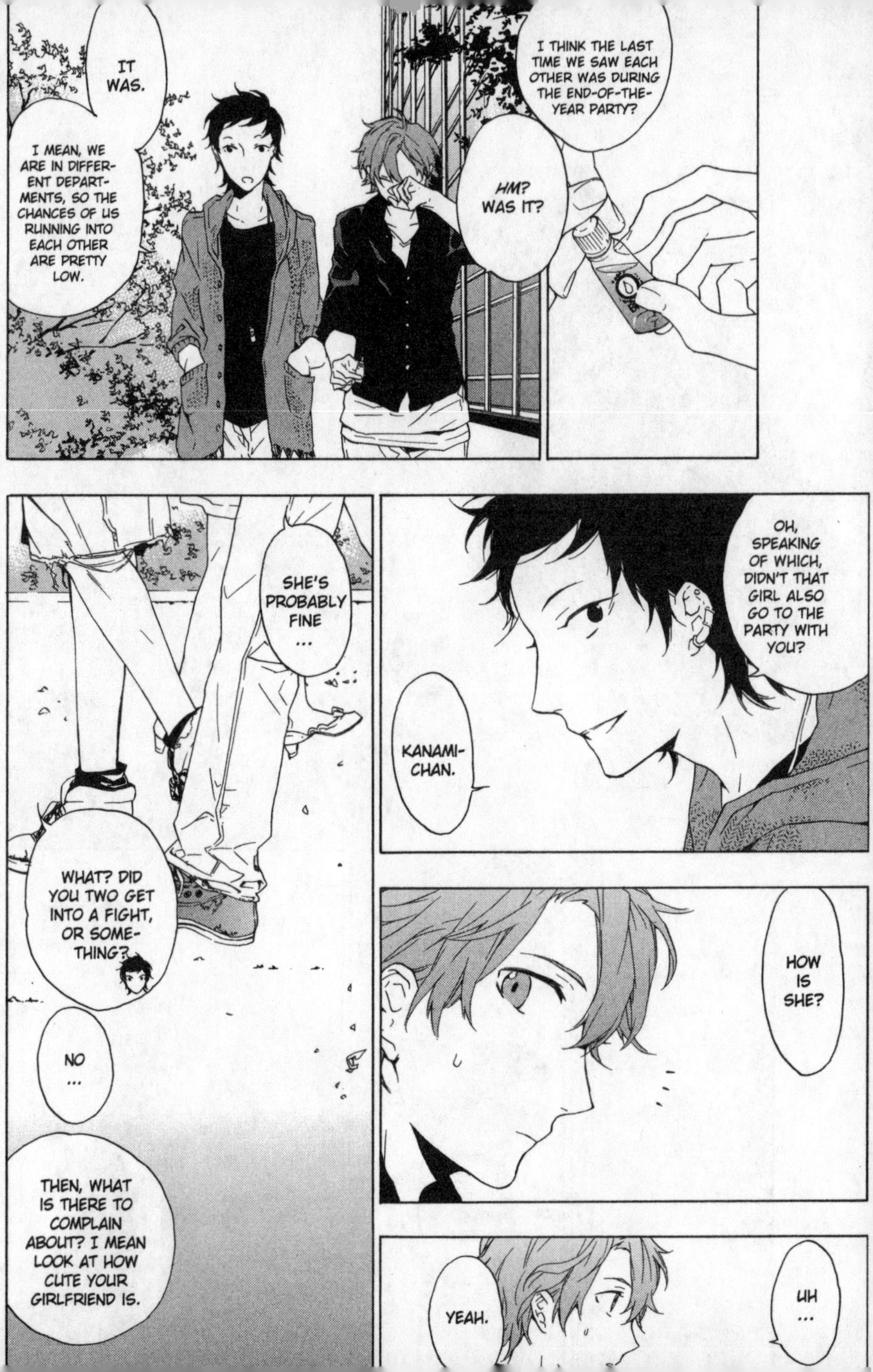
I THINK THE LAST TIME WE SAW EACH OTHER WAS DURING THE END-OF-THE-YEAR PARTY?
HM? WAS IT?
IT WAS.
I MEAN, WE ARE IN DIFFER-ENT DEPART-MENTS, SO THE CHANCES OF US RUNNING INTO EACH OTHER ARE PRETTY LOW.
OH, SPEAKING OF WHICH, DIDN'T THAT GIRL ALSO GO TO THE PARTY WITH YOU?
KANAMI-CHAN.
HOW IS SHE?
UH ...
YEAH.
SHE'S PROBABLY FINE ...
WHAT? DID YOU TWO GET INTO A FIGHT, OR SOME-THING?
NO ...
THEN, WHAT IS THERE TO COMPLAIN ABOUT? I MEAN LOOK AT HOW CUTE YOUR GIRLFRIEND IS.

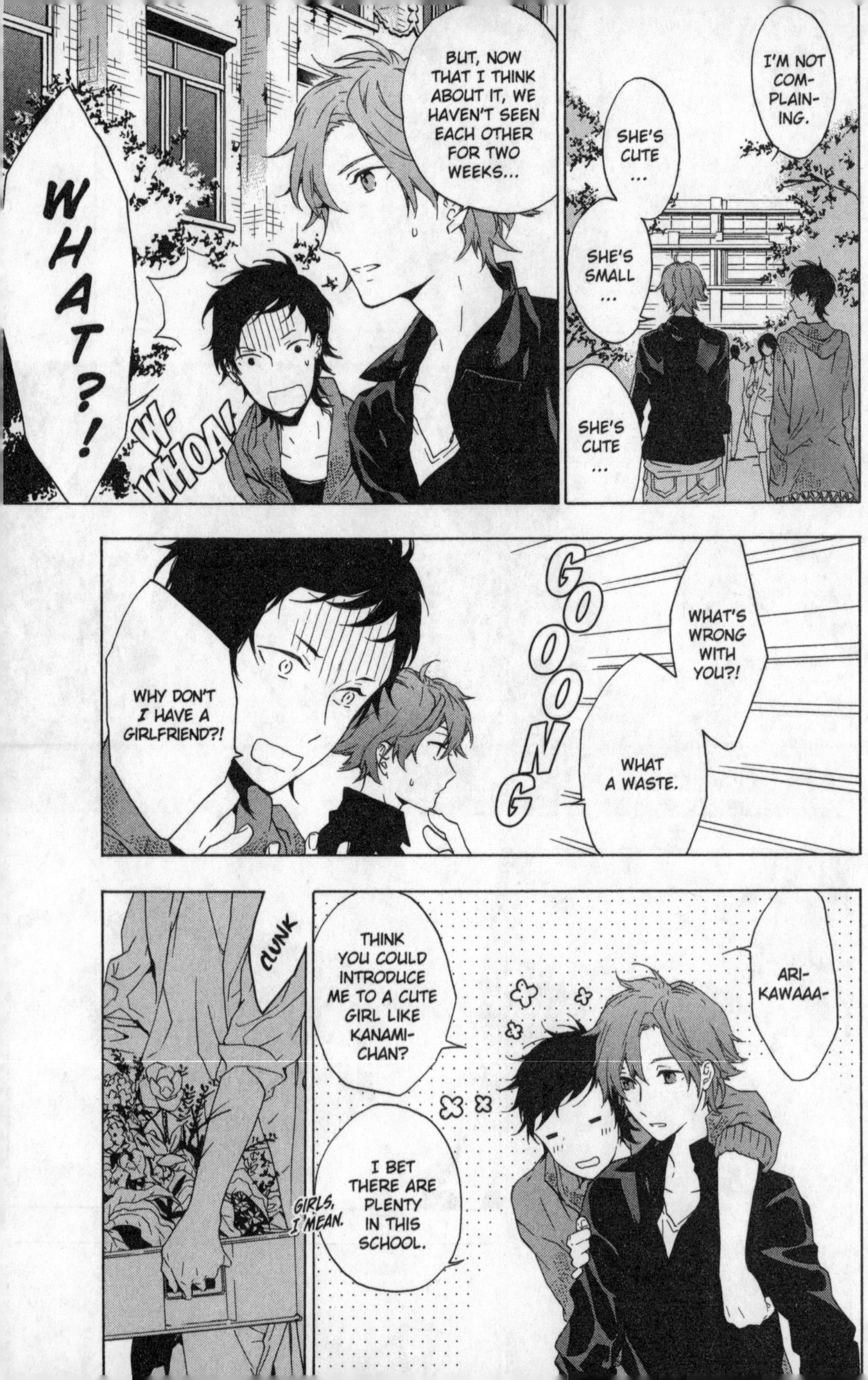
I'M NOT COMPLAINING.
SHE'S CUTE ...
SHE'S SMALL ...
SHE'S CUTE ...
BUT, NOW THAT I THINK ABOUT IT, WE HAVEN'T SEEN EACH OTHER FOR TWO WEEKS...
WHAT?!
W-WHOA!
WHAT'S WRONG WITH YOU?!
GOOONG
WHAT A WASTE.
WHY DON'T I HAVE A GIRLFRIEND?!
ARI-KAWAAA-
THINK YOU COULD INTRODUCE ME TO A CUTE GIRL LIKE KANAMI-CHAN?
I BET THERE ARE PLENTY IN THIS SCHOOL.
GIRLS, I MEAN.
CLUNK

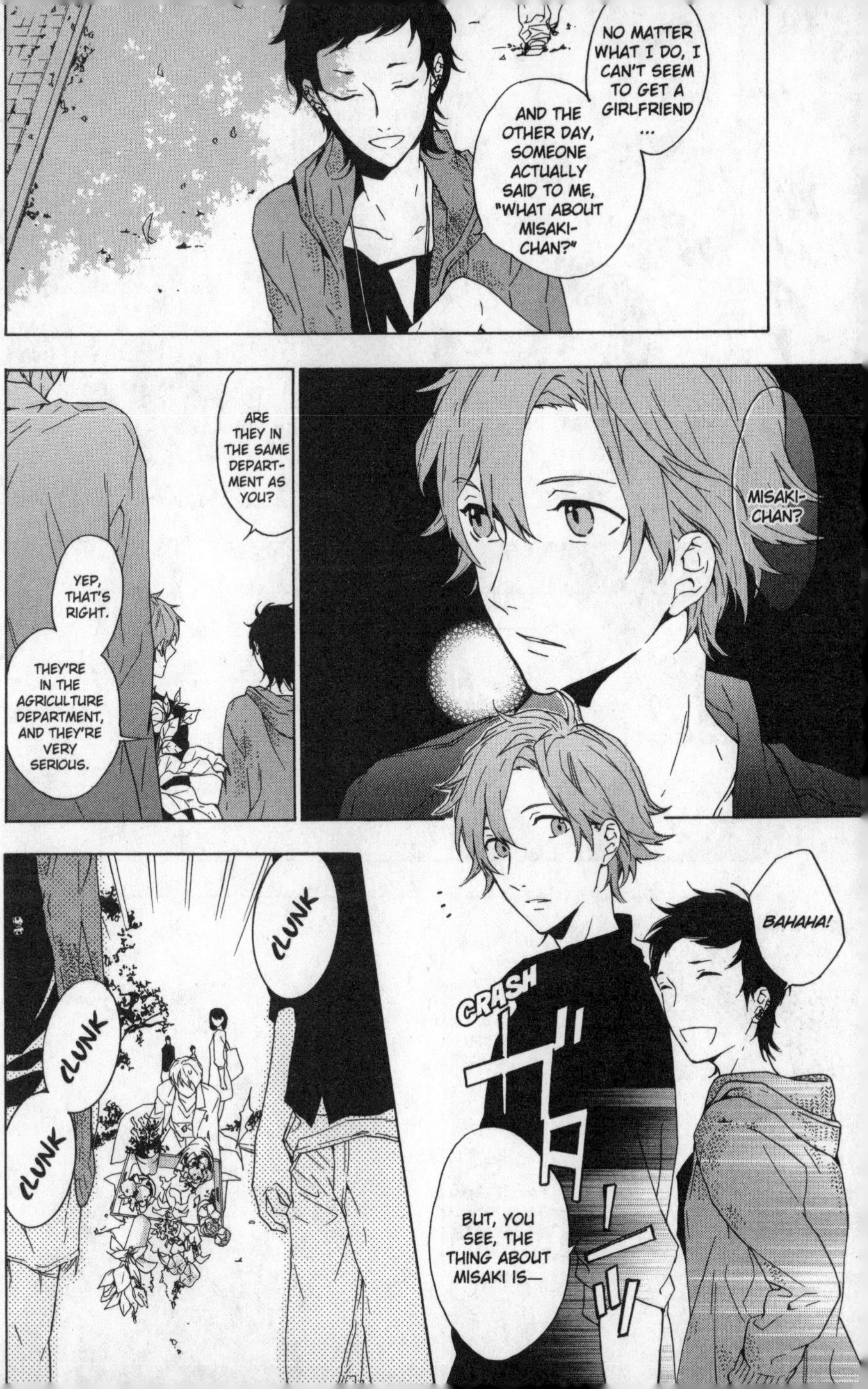
NO MATTER WHAT I DO, I CAN'T SEEM TO GET A GIRLFRIEND ...
AND THE OTHER DAY, SOMEONE ACTUALLY SAID TO ME, "WHAT ABOUT MISAKI-CHAN?"
MISAKI-CHAN?
ARE THEY IN THE SAME DEPART-MENT AS YOU?
YEP, THAT'S RIGHT.
THEY'RE IN THE AGRICULTURE DEPARTMENT, AND THEY'RE VERY SERIOUS.
BAHAHA!
...
CRASH
BUT, YOU SEE, THE THING ABOUT MISAKI IS—
CLUNK
CLUNK
CLUNK
CLUNK

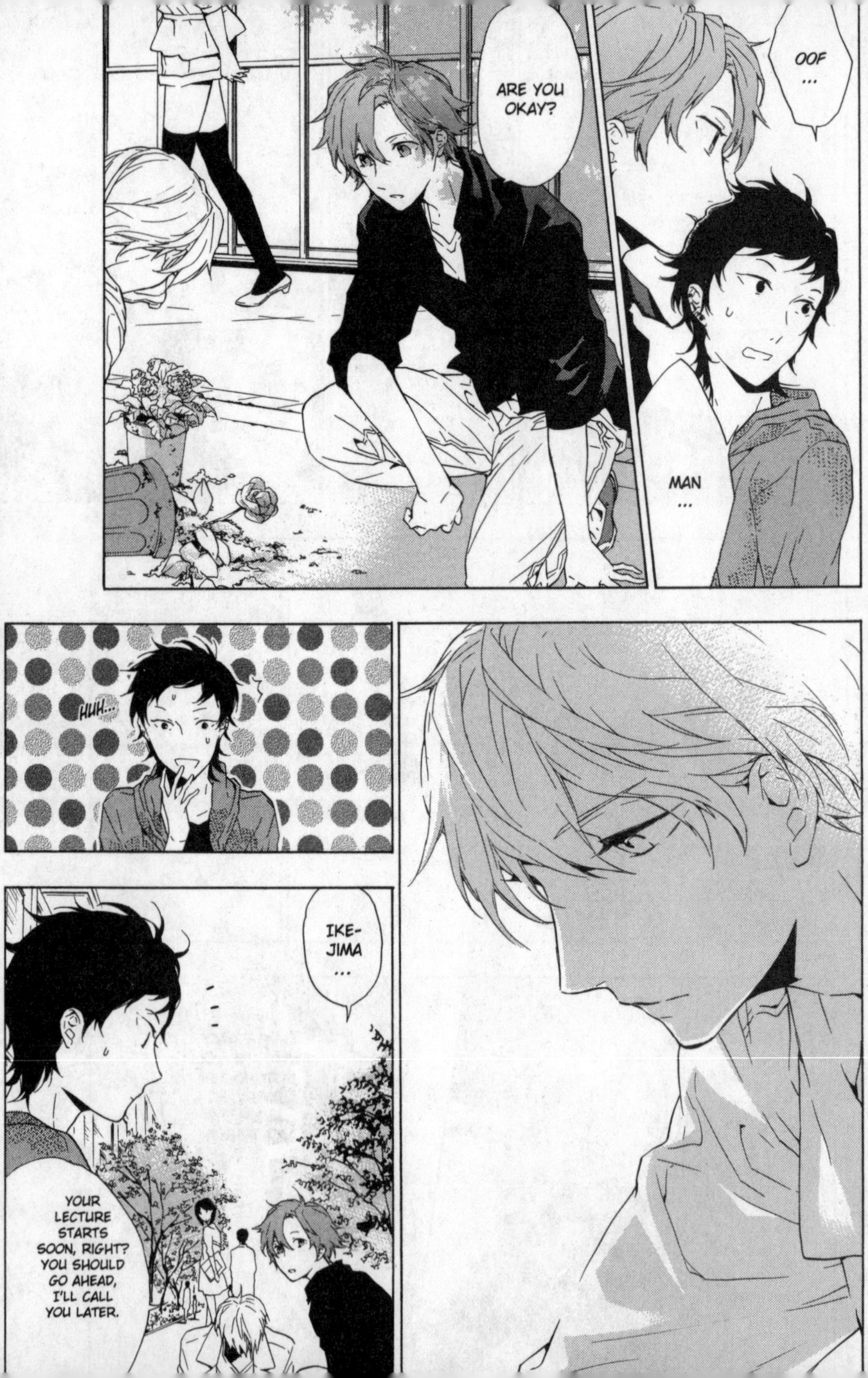

OOF ...
MAN ...
ARE YOU OKAY?
HUH...
IKE-JIMA ...
YOUR LECTURE STARTS SOON, RIGHT? YOU SHOULD GO AHEAD, I'LL CALL YOU LATER.

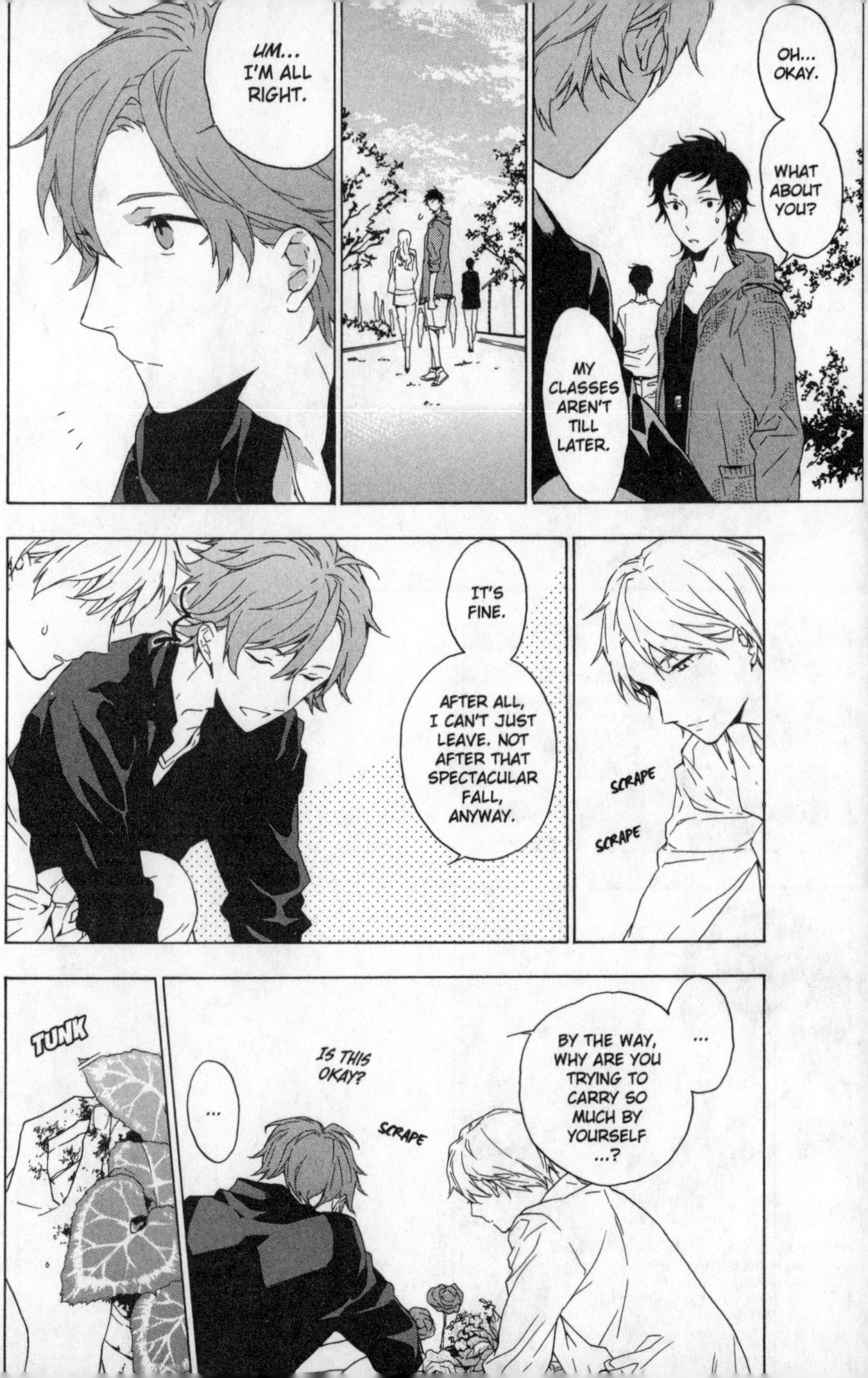
OH... OKAY.
WHAT ABOUT YOU?
MY CLASSES AREN'T TILL LATER.
UM... I'M ALL RIGHT.
SCRAPE
SCRAPE
IT'S FINE.
AFTER ALL, I CAN'T JUST LEAVE. NOT AFTER THAT SPECTACULAR FALL, ANYWAY.
...
BY THE WAY, WHY ARE YOU TRYING TO CARRY SO MUCH BY YOURSELF ...?
IS THIS OKAY?
SCRAPE
...
TUNK

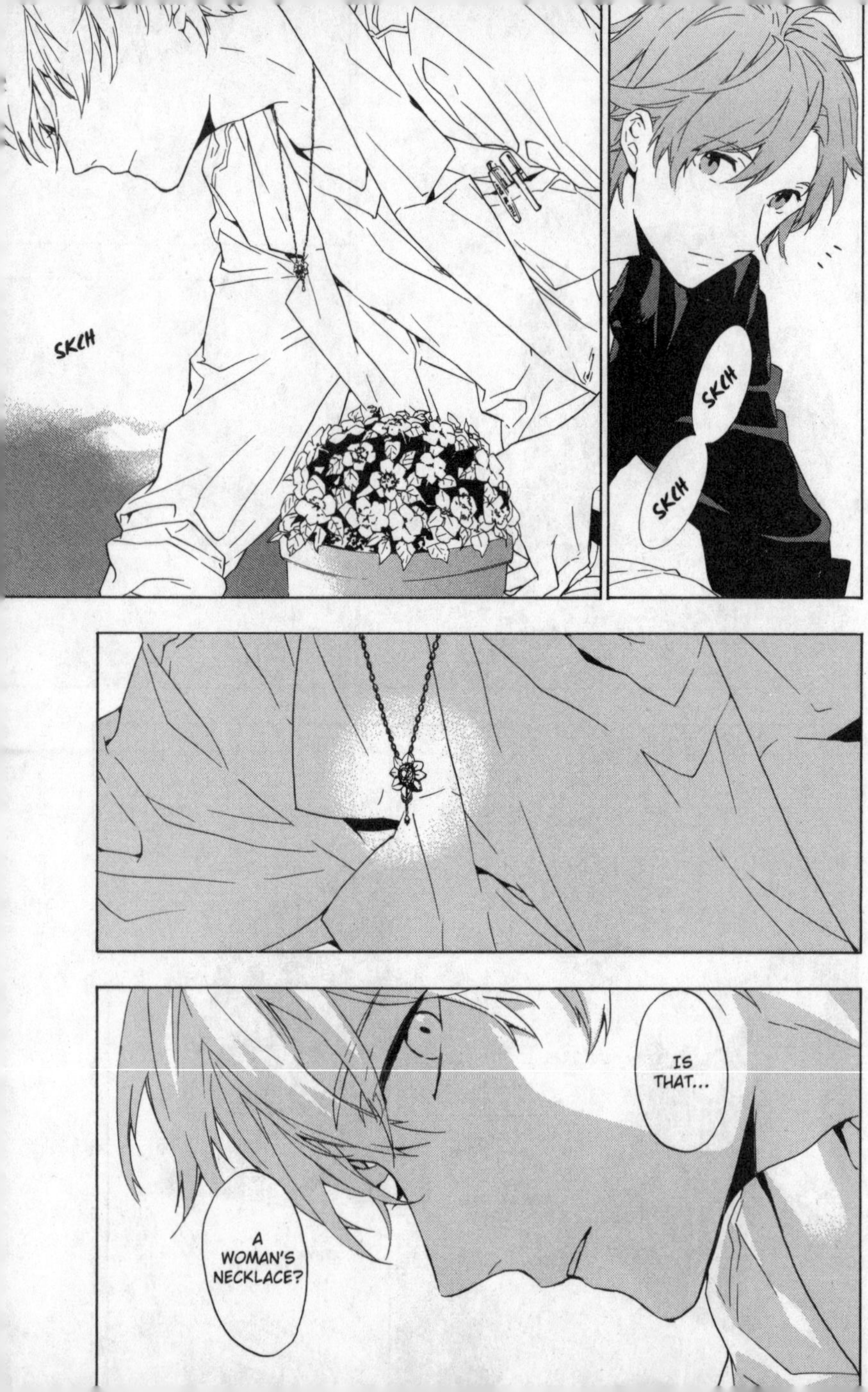
...
SKCH
SKCH
SKCH
IS THAT...
A WOMAN'S NECKLACE?

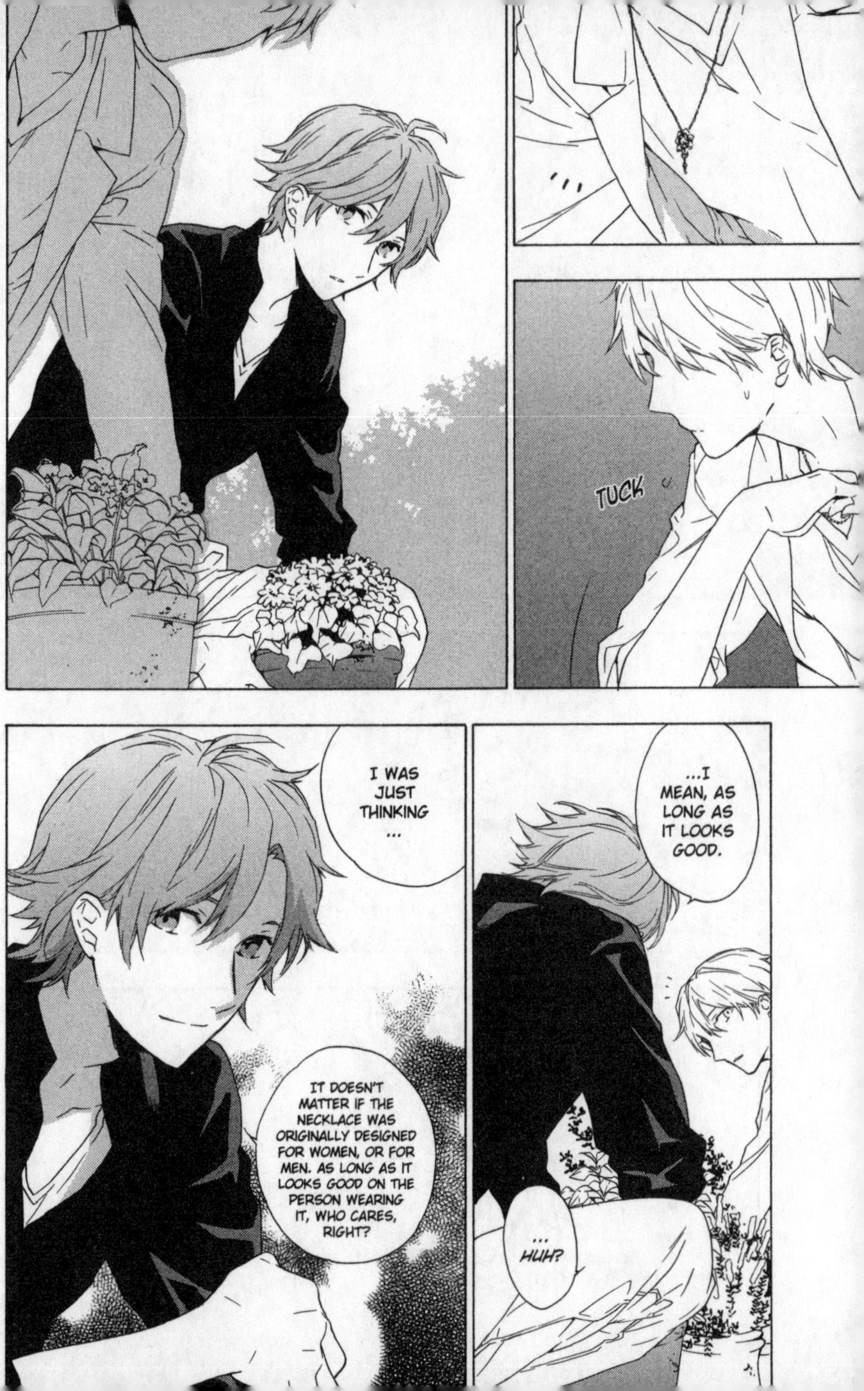
...
TUCK
I WAS JUST THINKING...
IT DOESN'T MATTER IF THE NECKLACE WAS ORIGINALLY DESIGNED FOR WOMEN, OR FOR MEN. AS LONG AS IT LOOKS GOOD ON THE PERSON WEARING IT, WHO CARES, RIGHT?
...I MEAN, AS LONG AS IT LOOKS GOOD.
...HUH?

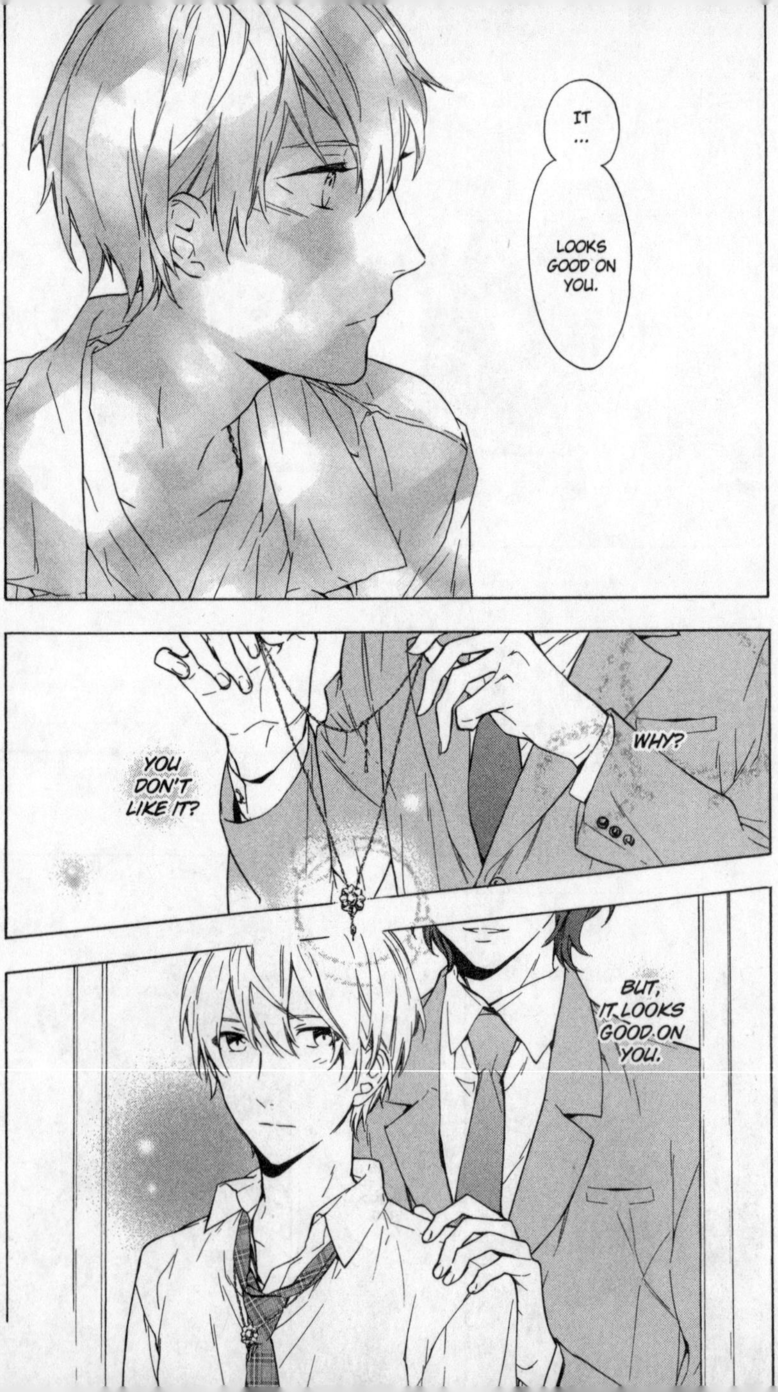
IT ...
LOOKS GOOD ON YOU.
WHY?
YOU DON'T LIKE IT?
BUT, IT LOOKS GOOD ON YOU.

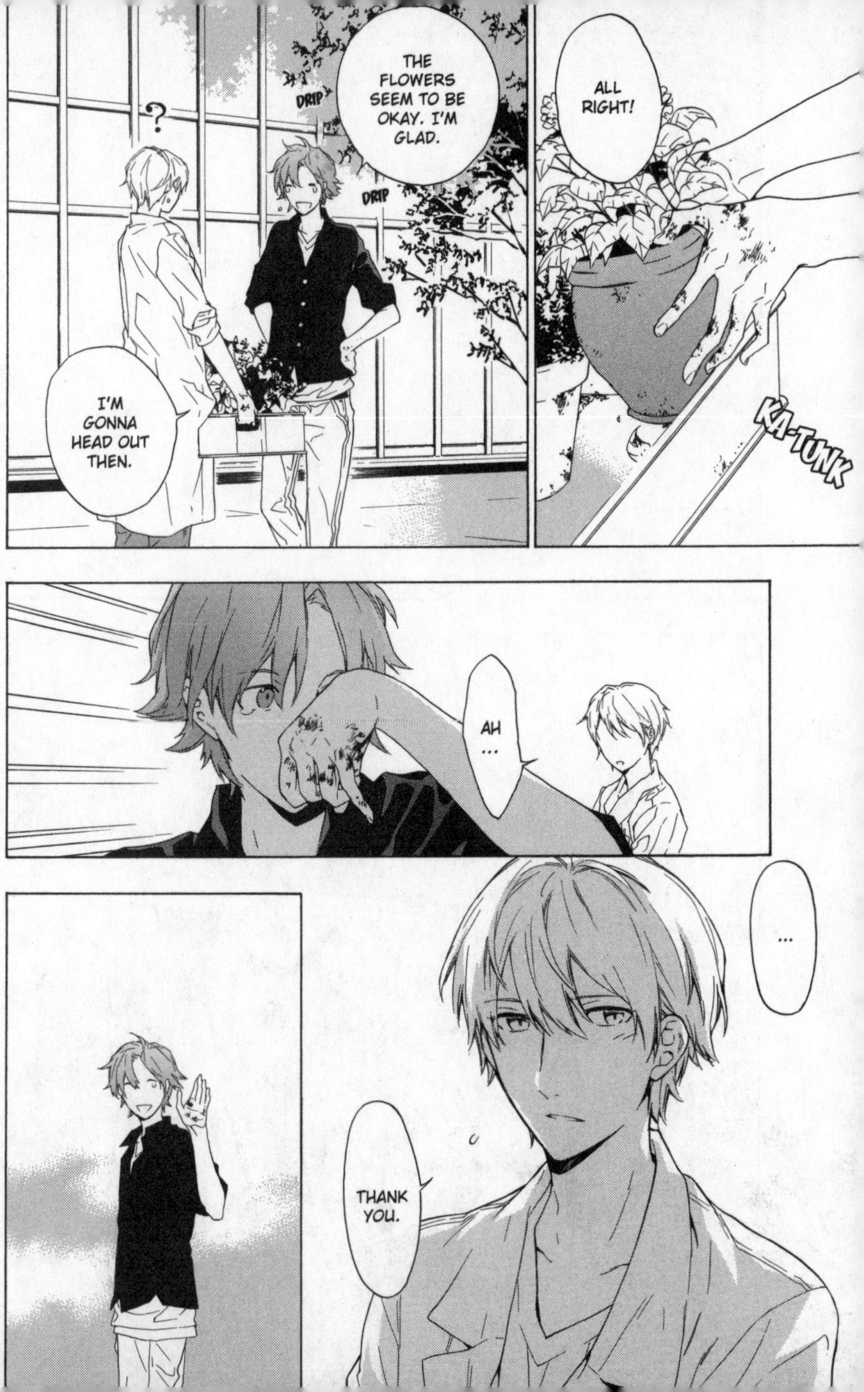
ALL RIGHT!
KA-TUNK
THE FLOWERS SEEM TO BE OKAY. I'M GLAD.
DRIP
DRIP
?
I'M GONNA HEAD OUT THEN.
AH ...
...
THANK YOU.

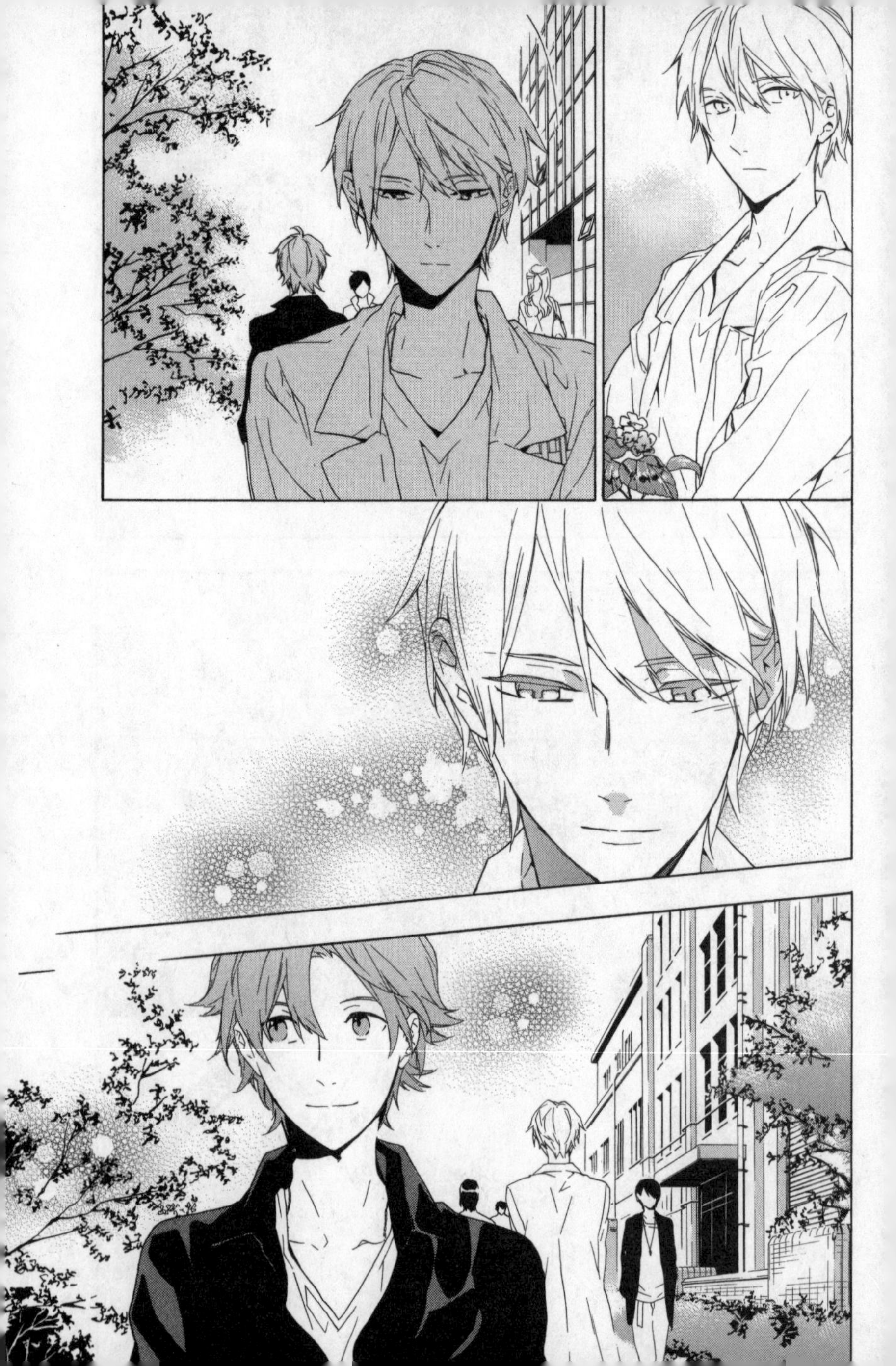

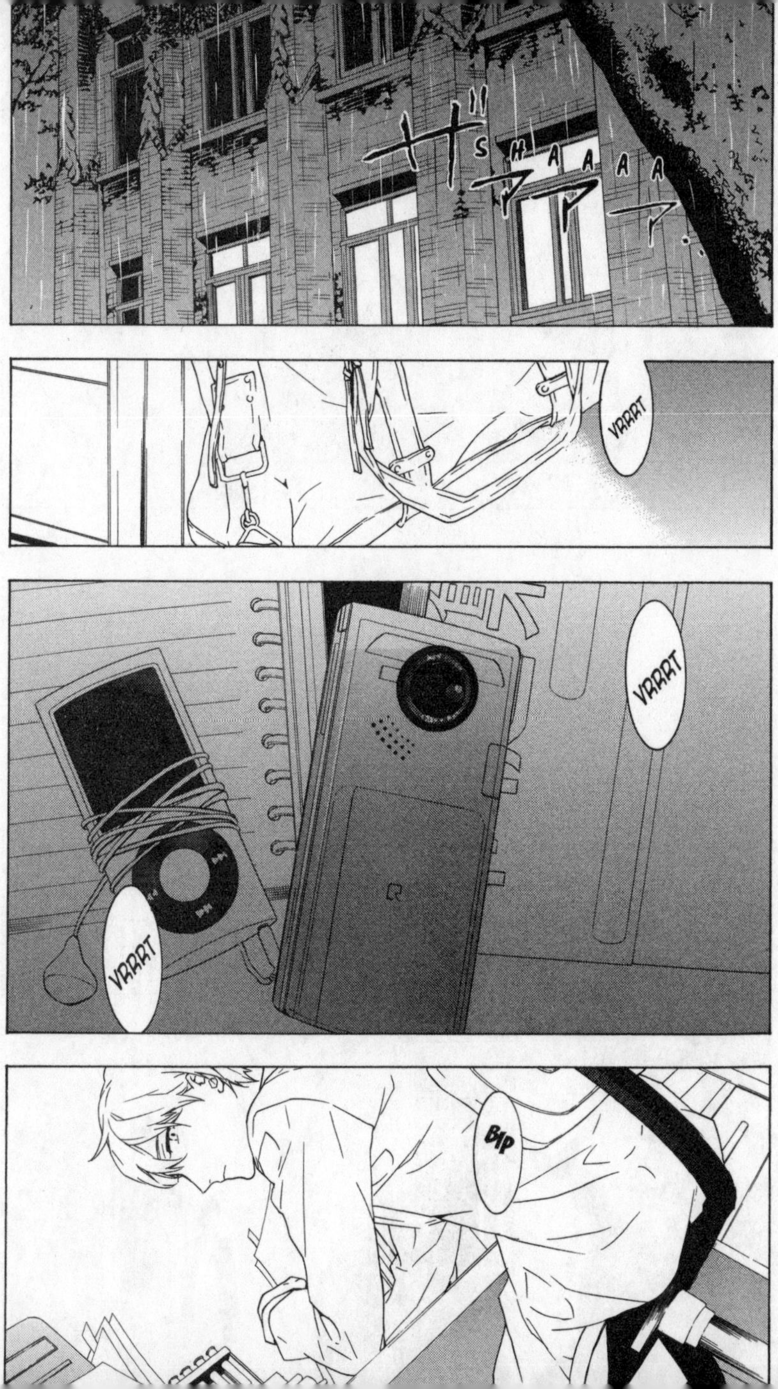
SHAAAA
VRRRT
VRRRT
VRRRT
BIP

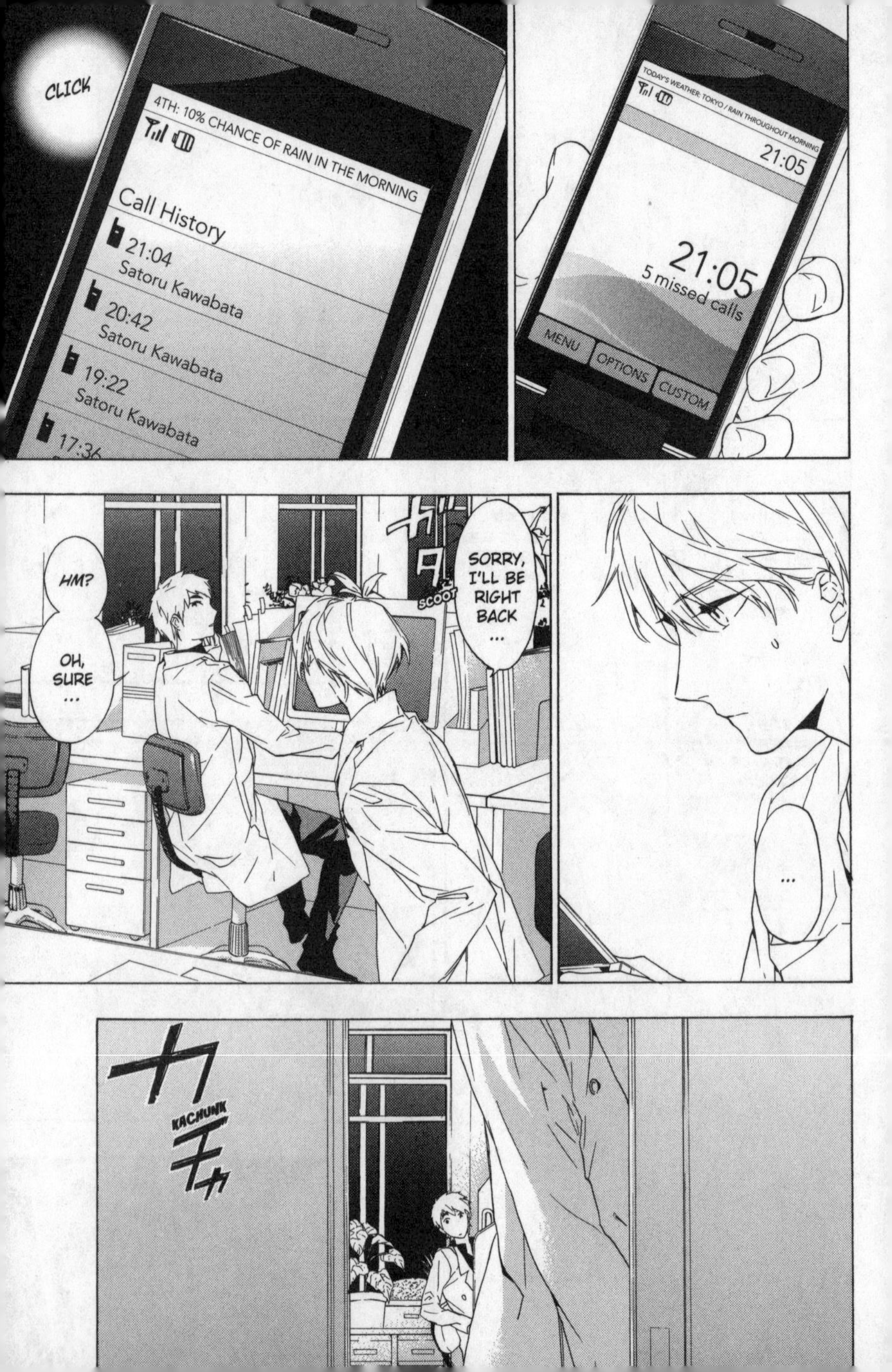
TODAY'S WEATHER: TOKYO / RAIN THROUGHOUT MORNING
21:05
21:05
5 missed calls
MENU
OPTIONS
CUSTOM
CLICK
4TH: 10% CHANCE OF RAIN IN THE MORNING
Call History
21:04
Satoru Kawabata
20:42
Satoru Kawabata
19:22
Satoru Kawabata
...
SORRY, I'LL BE RIGHT BACK ...
SCOOT
HM?
OH, SURE ...
KACHUNK

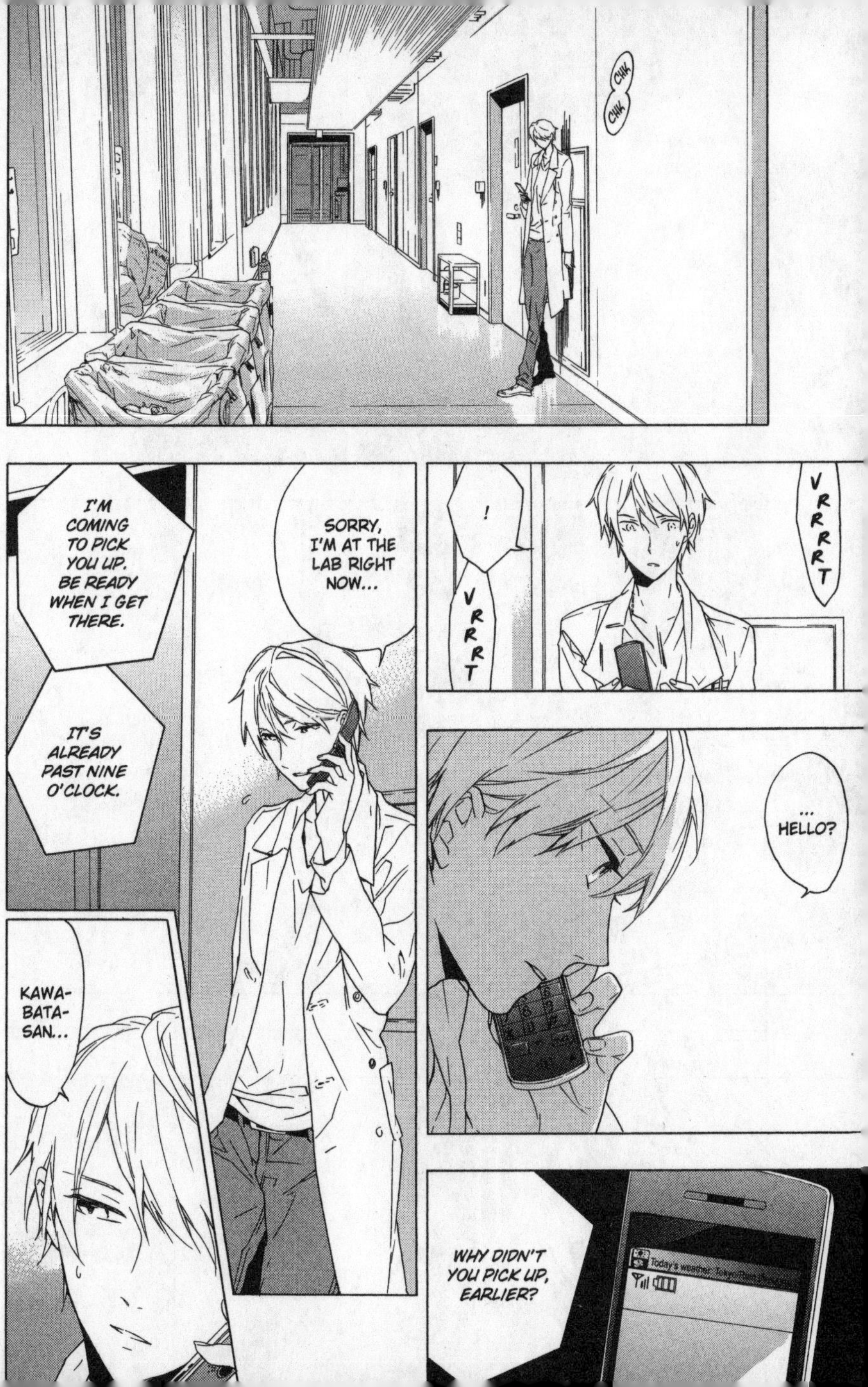
CHK
CHK
VRRRRT
!
VRRRT
...HELLO?
WHY DIDN'T YOU PICK UP, EARLIER?
SORRY, I'M AT THE LAB RIGHT NOW...
I'M COMING TO PICK YOU UP. BE READY WHEN I GET THERE.
IT'S ALREADY PAST NINE O'CLOCK.
KAWA-BATA-SAN...

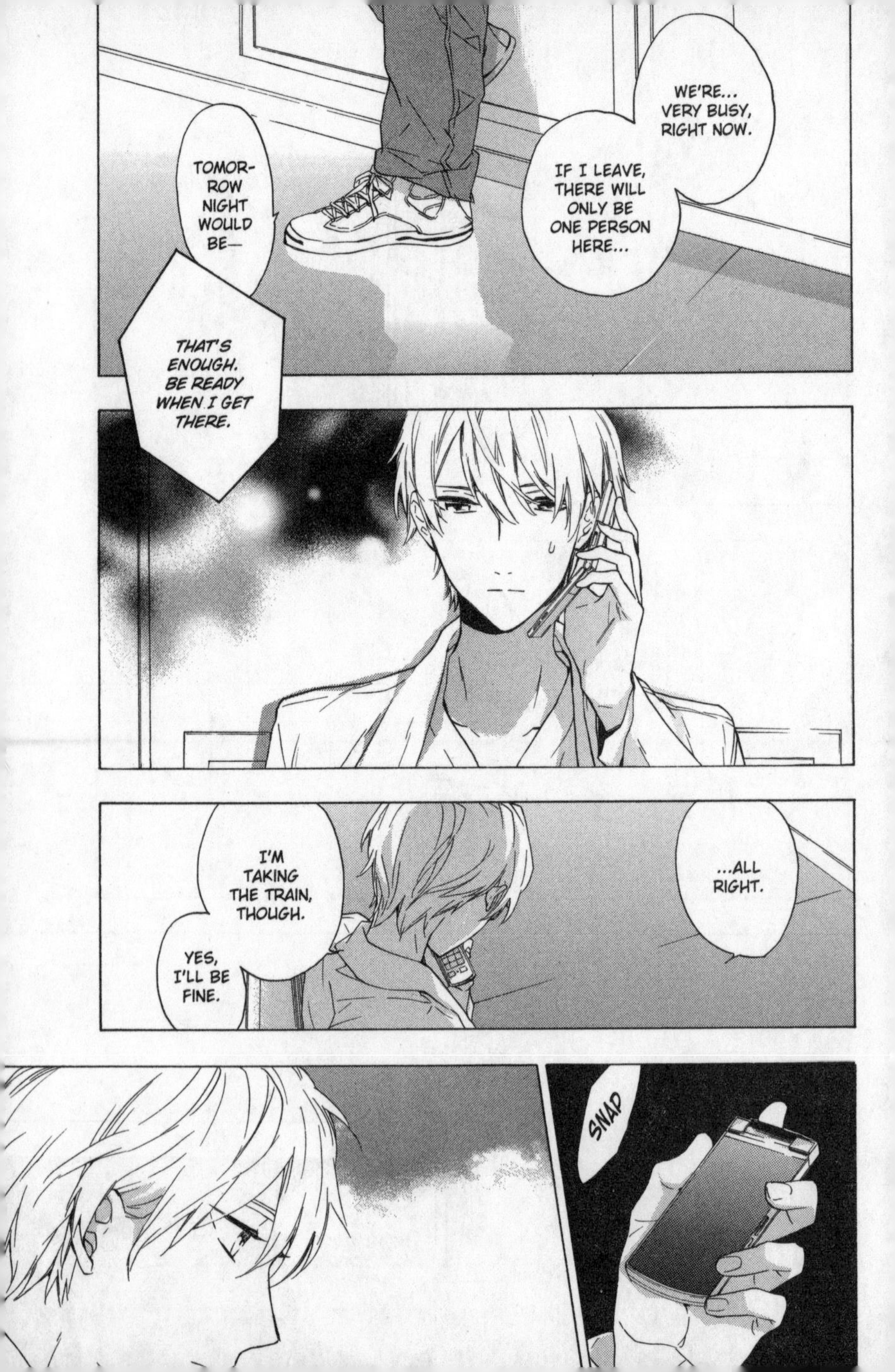
WE'RE... VERY BUSY, RIGHT NOW.
IF I LEAVE, THERE WILL ONLY BE ONE PERSON HERE...
TOMORROW NIGHT WOULD BE—
THAT'S ENOUGH. BE READY WHEN I GET THERE.
...ALL RIGHT.
I'M TAKING THE TRAIN, THOUGH.
YES, I'LL BE FINE.
SNAP

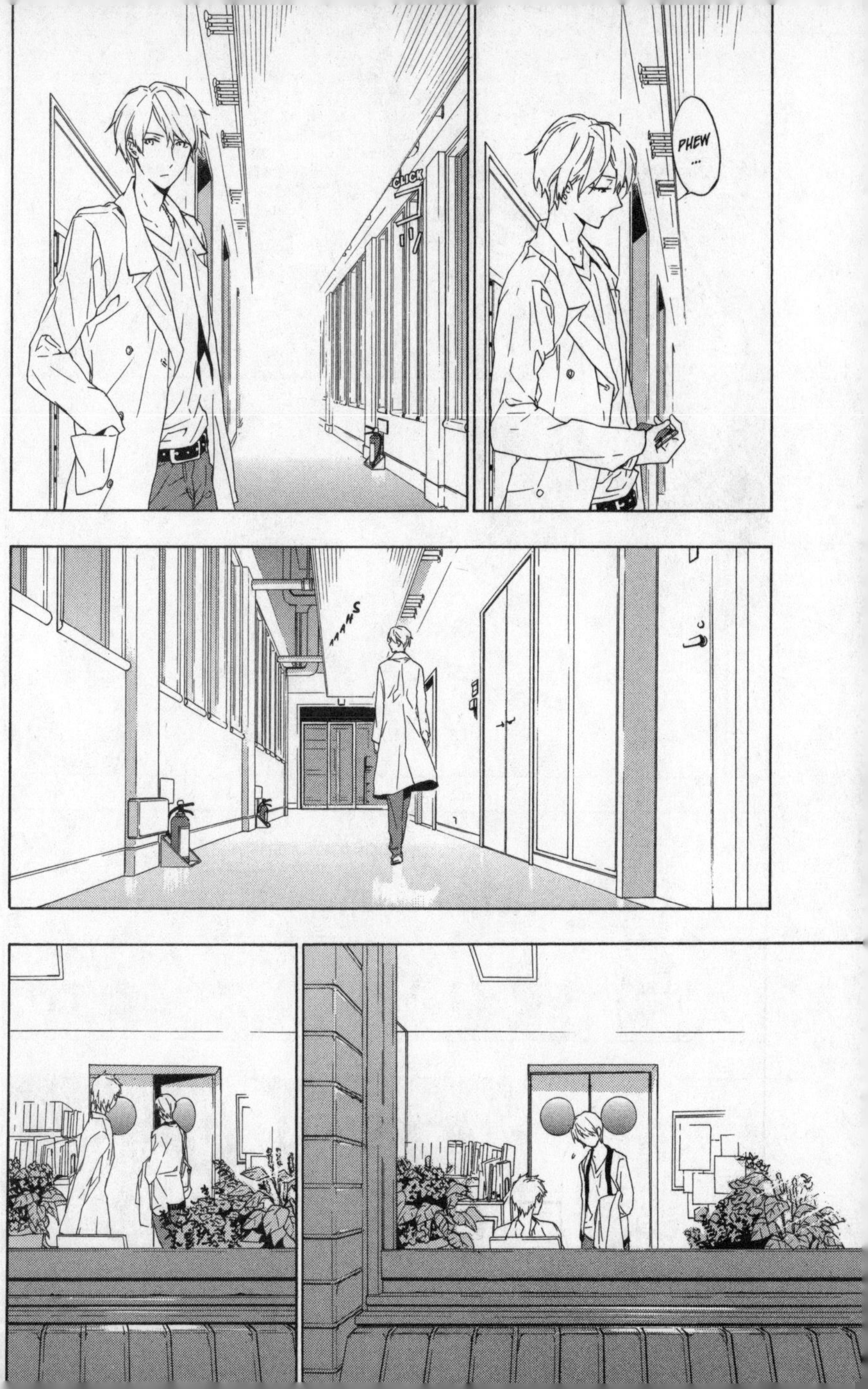
PHEW ...
CLICK
SHAAA

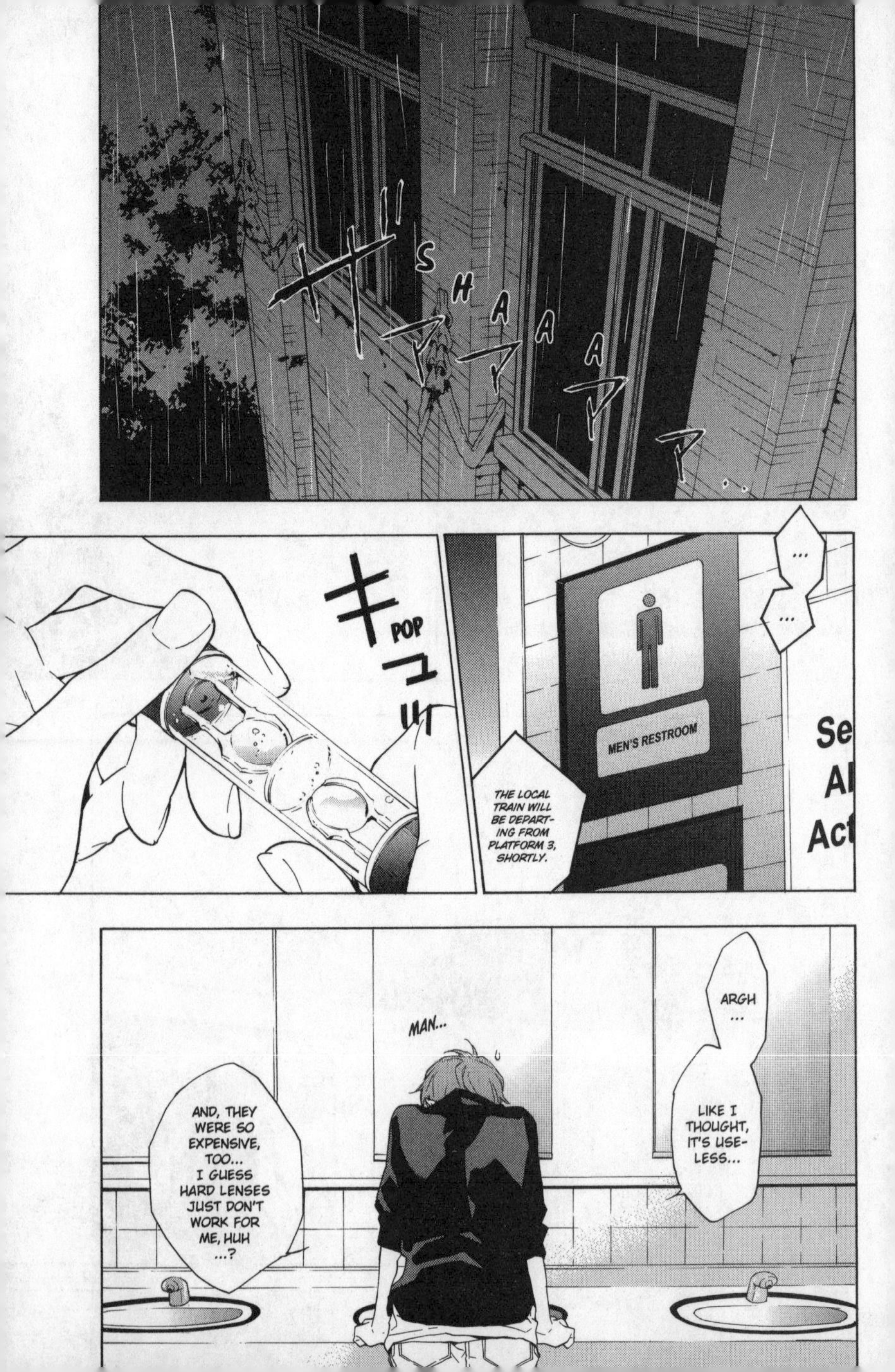

ザーアアア
SHAAAA..
...
...
MEN'S RESTROOM
THE LOCAL TRAIN WILL BE DEPARTING FROM PLATFORM 3, SHORTLY.
キュッ
POP
ARGH...
LIKE I THOUGHT, IT'S USELESS...
MAN...
AND, THEY WERE SO EXPENSIVE, TOO... I GUESS HARD LENSES JUST DON'T WORK FOR ME, HUH...?

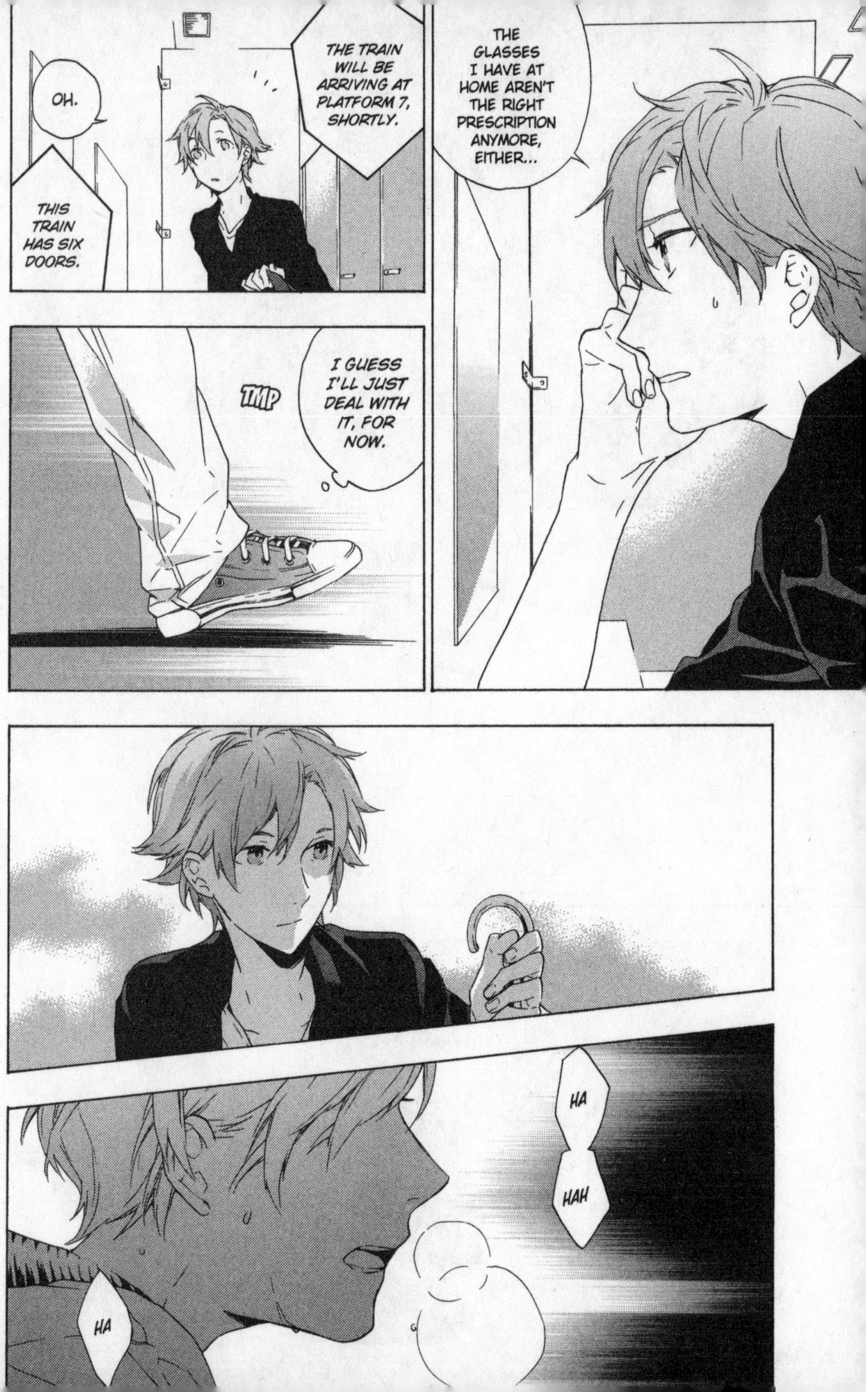
THE GLASSES I HAVE AT HOME AREN'T THE RIGHT PRESCRIPTION ANYMORE, EITHER...
THE TRAIN WILL BE ARRIVING AT PLATFORM 7, SHORTLY.
OH.
THIS TRAIN HAS SIX DOORS.
I GUESS I'LL JUST DEAL WITH IT, FOR NOW.
TMP
HA
HAH
HA

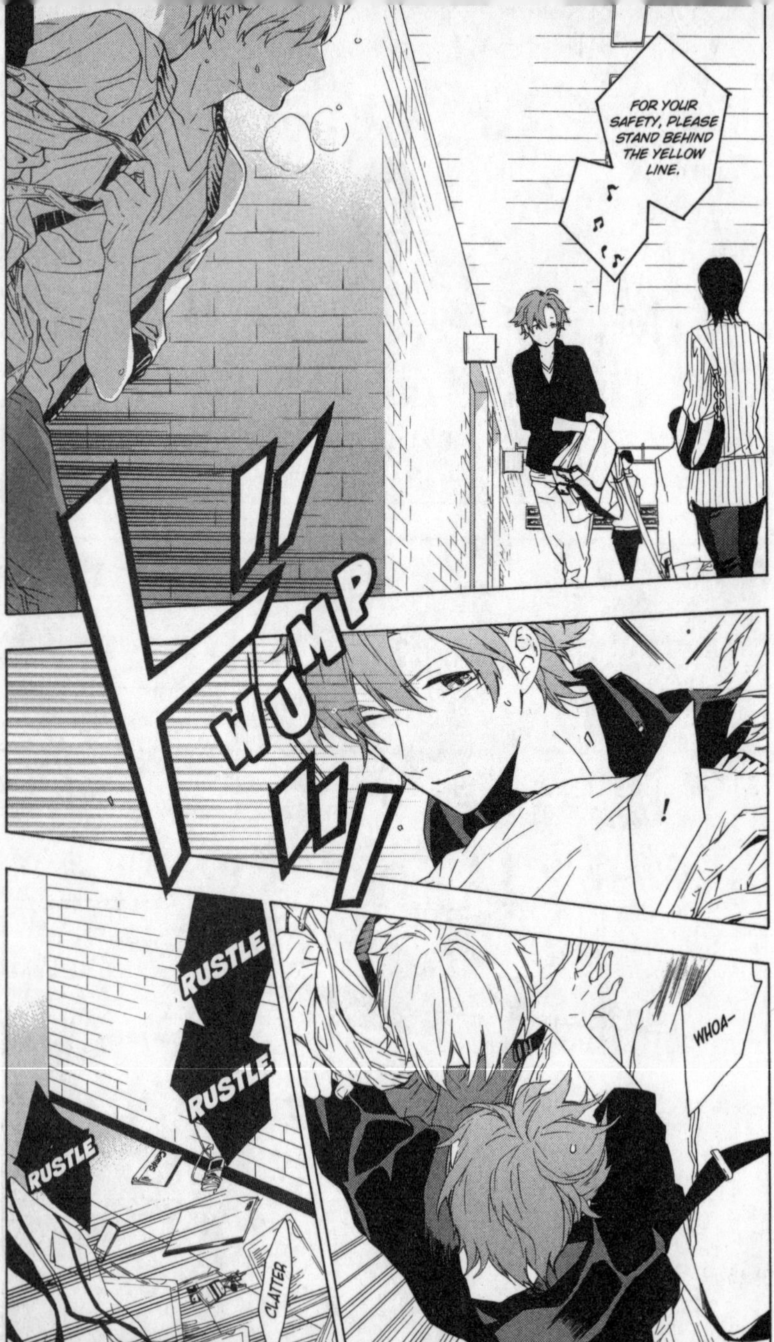
FOR YOUR SAFETY, PLEASE STAND BEHIND THE YELLOW LINE.
♪ ♪ ♪
WUMP
!
WHOA-
CLATTER
RUSTLE
RUSTLE
RUSTLE

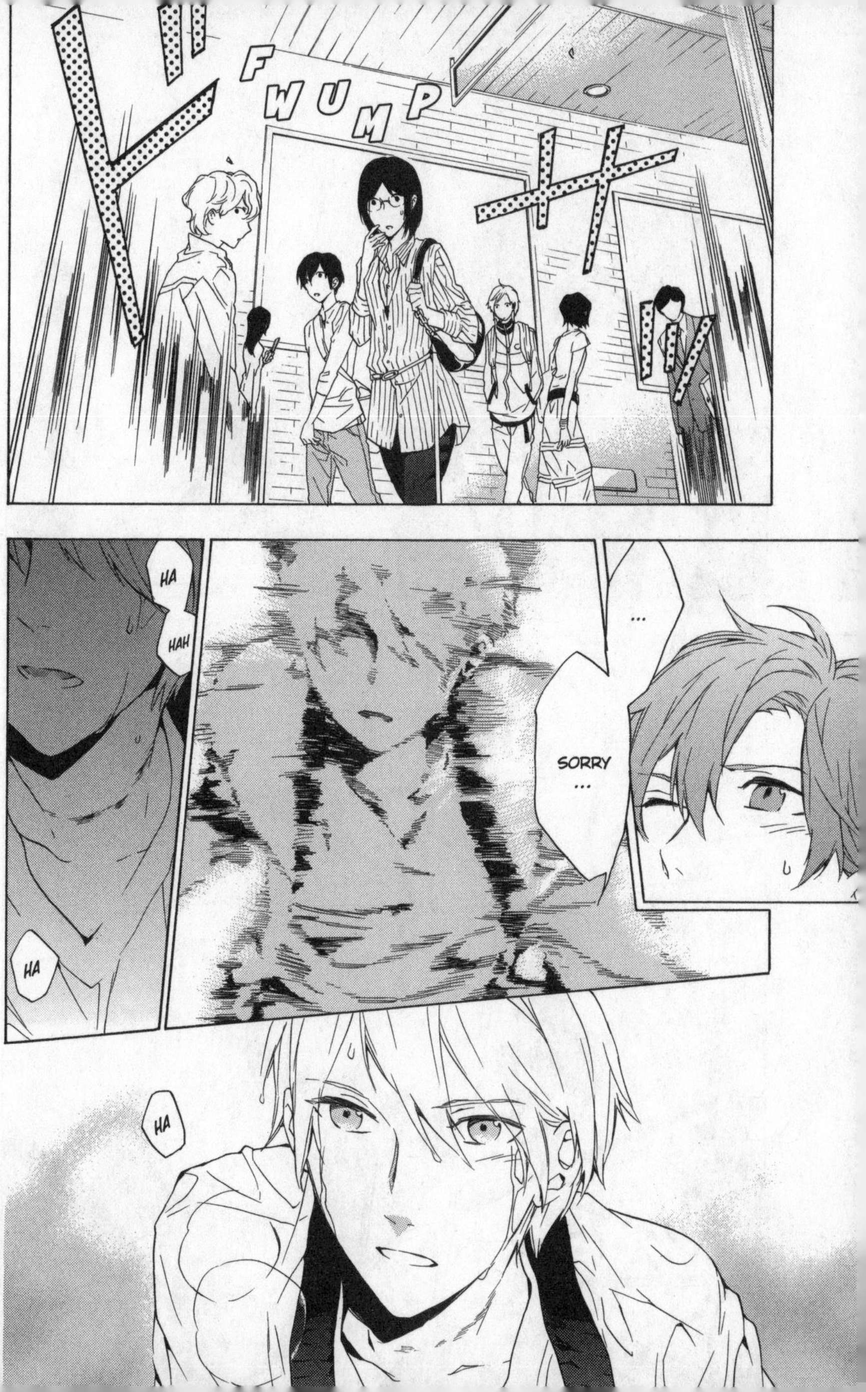
FWUMP
...
SORRY ...
HA
HAH
HA
HA

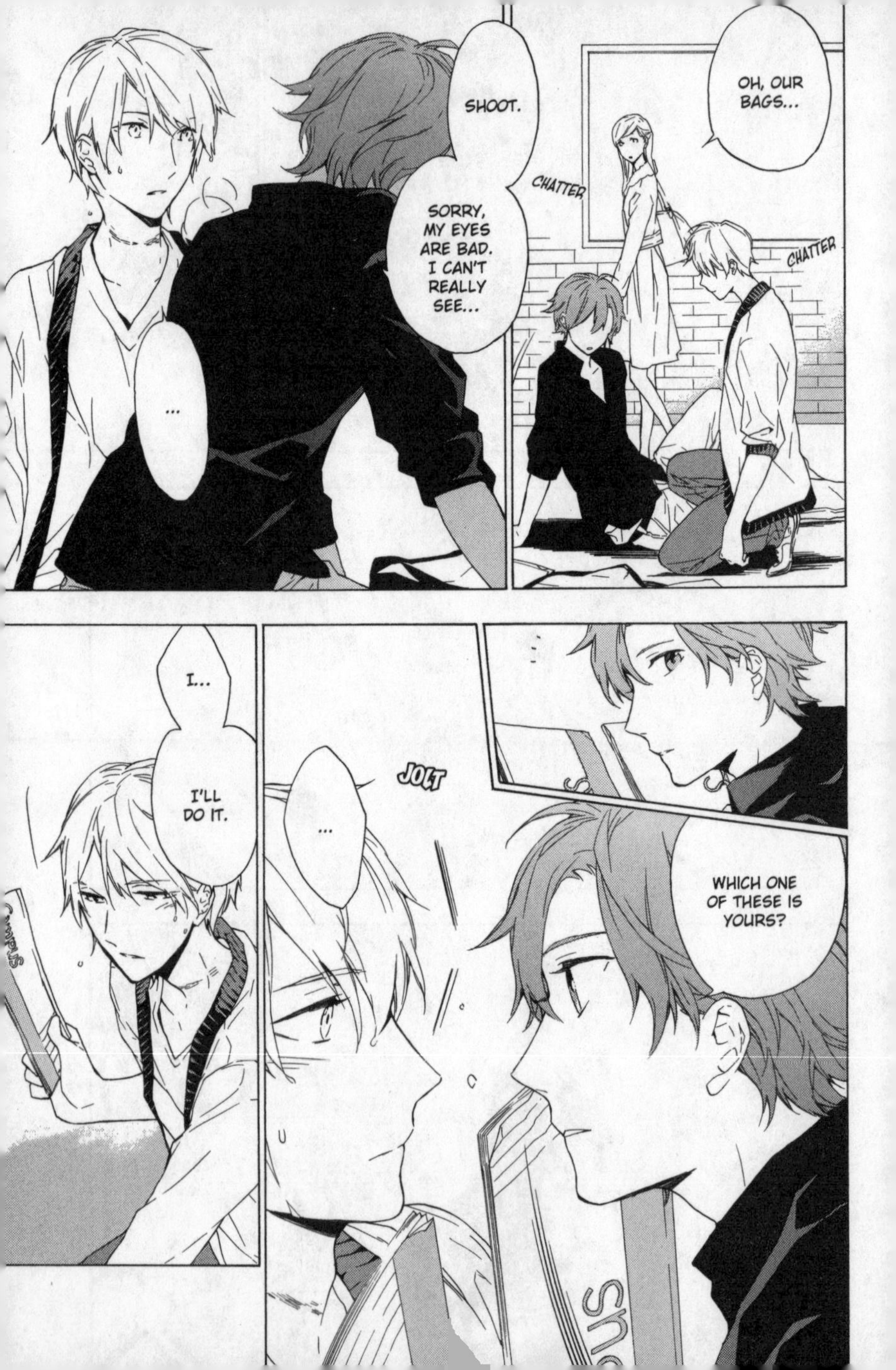
OH, OUR BAGS...
CHATTER
CHATTER
SHOOT.
SORRY, MY EYES ARE BAD. I CAN'T REALLY SEE...
...
...
WHICH ONE OF THESE IS YOURS?
JOLT
...
I...
I'LL DO IT.

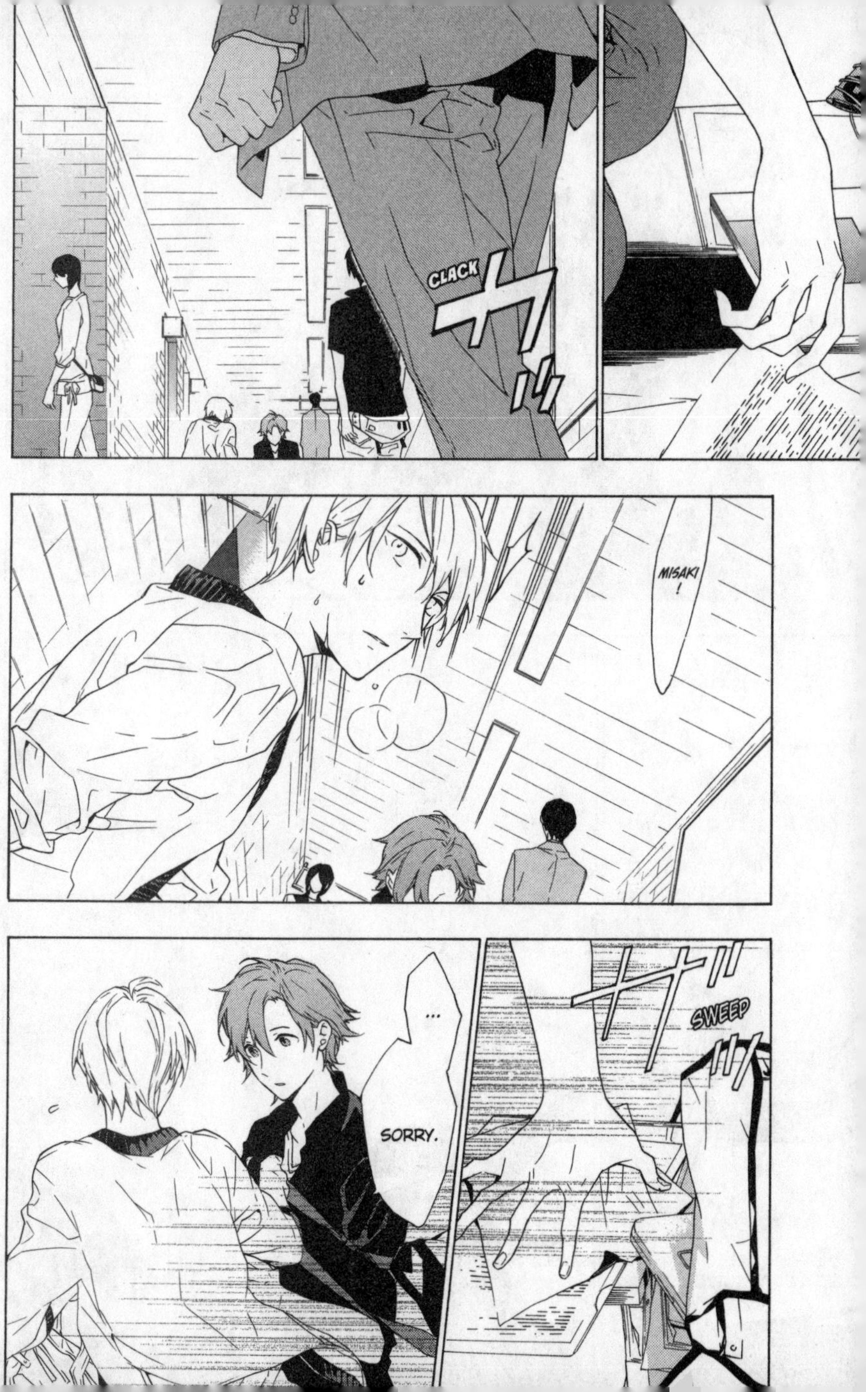
CLACK
MISAKI!
SWEEP
...
SORRY.

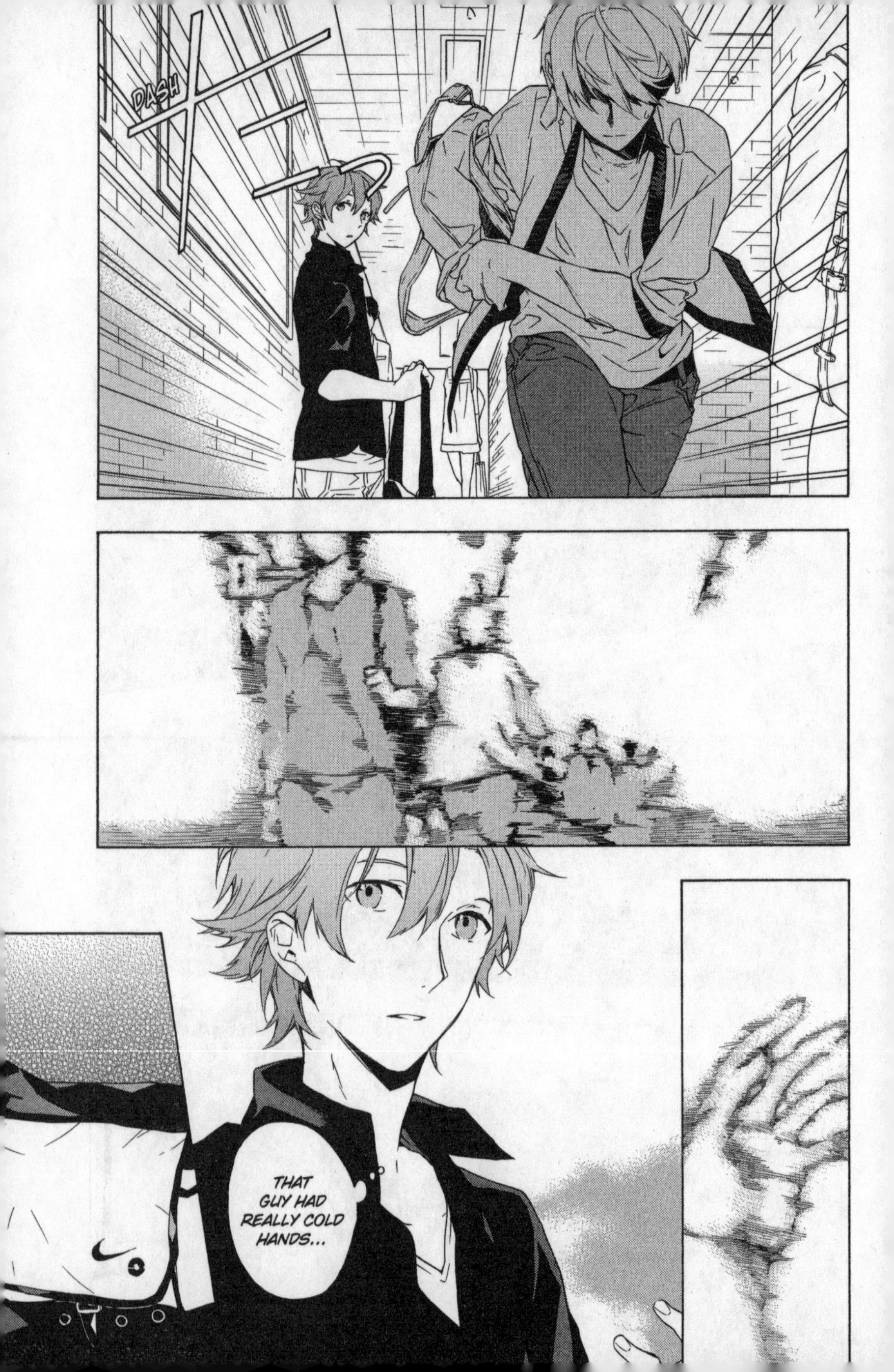
DASH
THAT GUY HAD REALLY COLD HANDS...

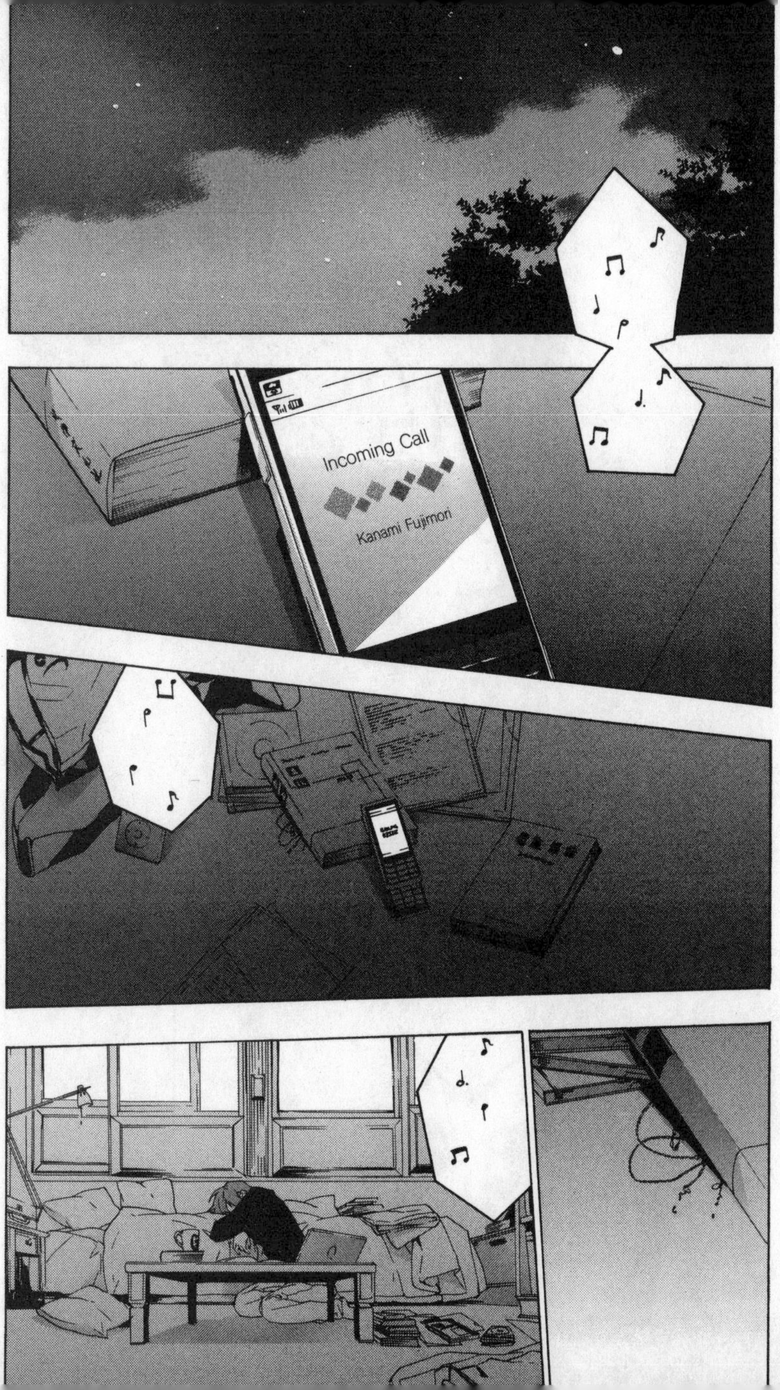
Incoming Call
Kanami Fujimori

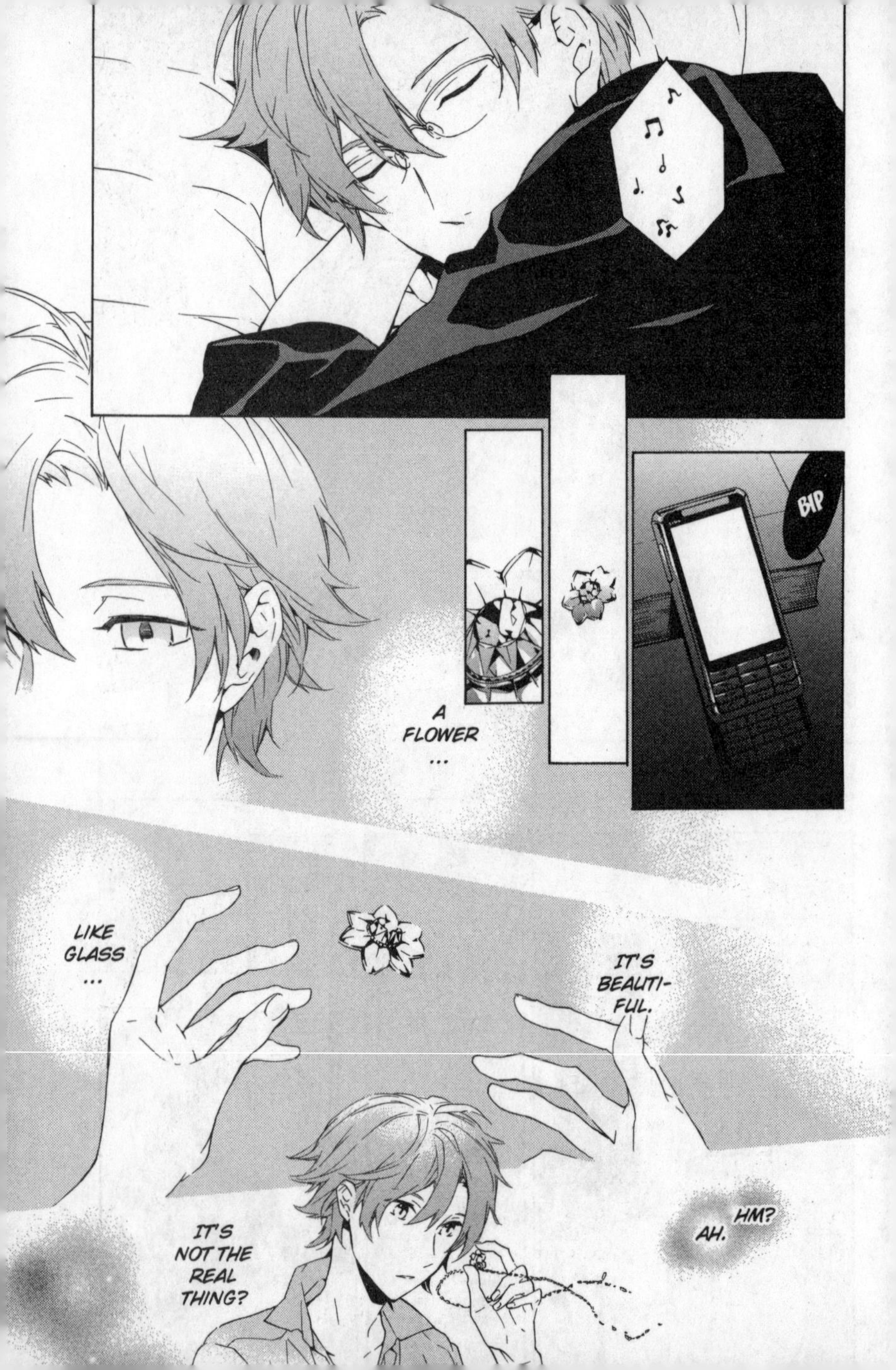
BIP
A FLOWER ...
IT'S BEAUTI-FUL.
LIKE GLASS ...
HM?
AH.
IT'S NOT THE REAL THING?

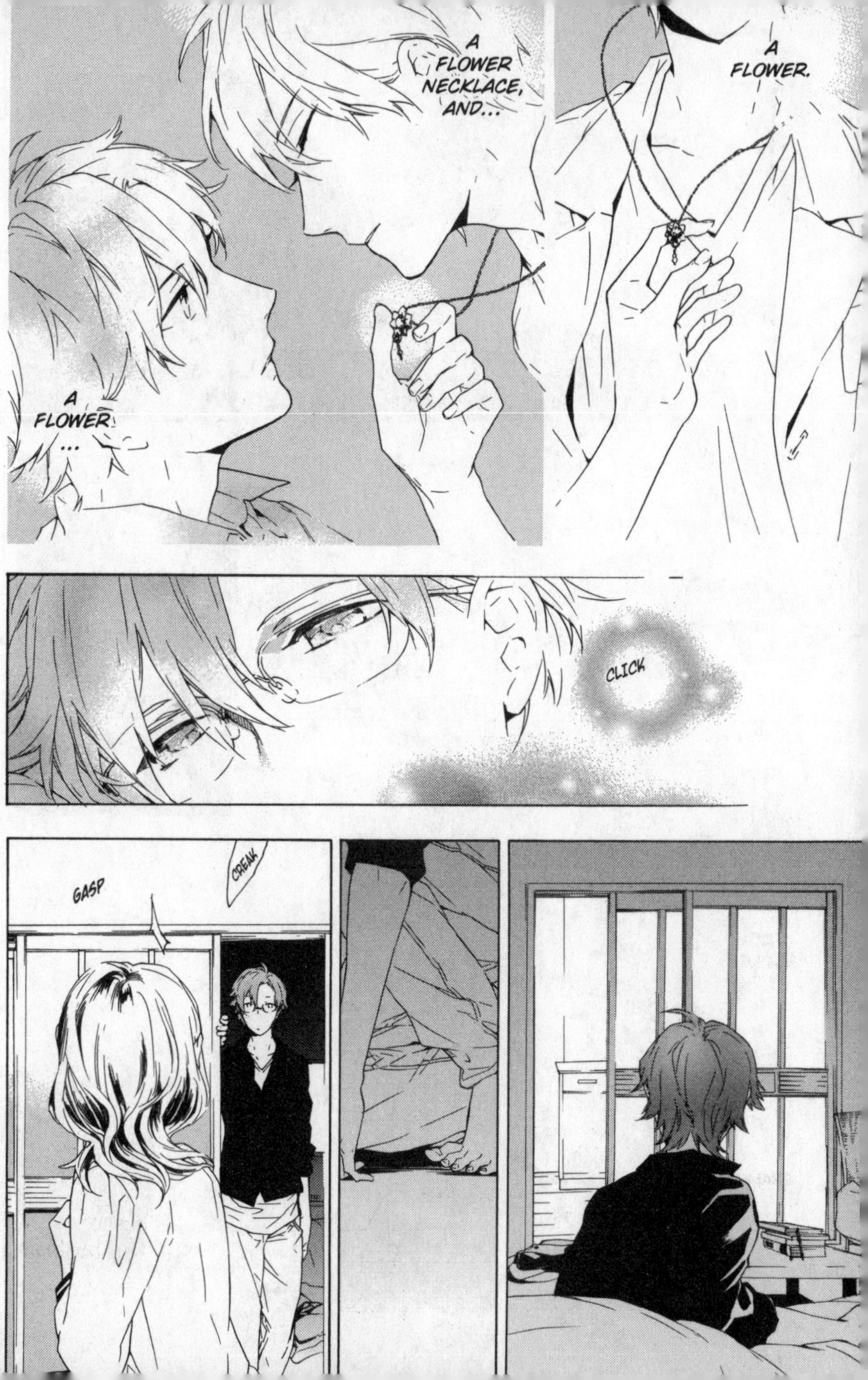
A FLOWER.
A FLOWER NECKLACE, AND...
A FLOWER...
CLICK
CREAK
GASP

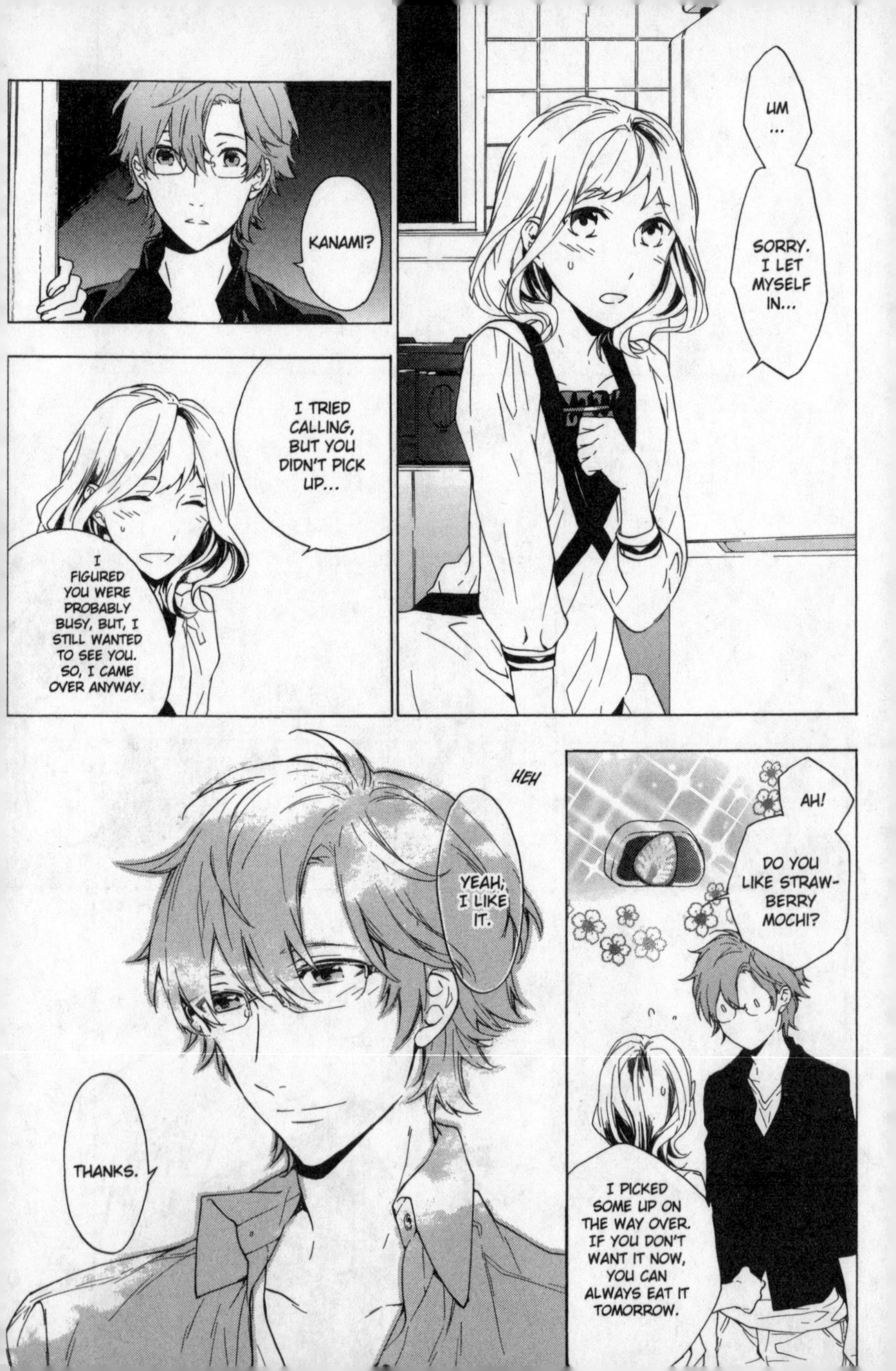
UM ...
SORRY. I LET MYSELF IN...
KANAMI?
I TRIED CALLING, BUT YOU DIDN'T PICK UP...
I FIGURED YOU WERE PROBABLY BUSY, BUT, I STILL WANTED TO SEE YOU. SO, I CAME OVER ANYWAY.
AH!
DO YOU LIKE STRAW-BERRY MOCHI?
I PICKED SOME UP ON THE WAY OVER. IF YOU DON'T WANT IT NOW, YOU CAN ALWAYS EAT IT TOMORROW.
HEH
YEAH, I LIKE IT.
THANKS.

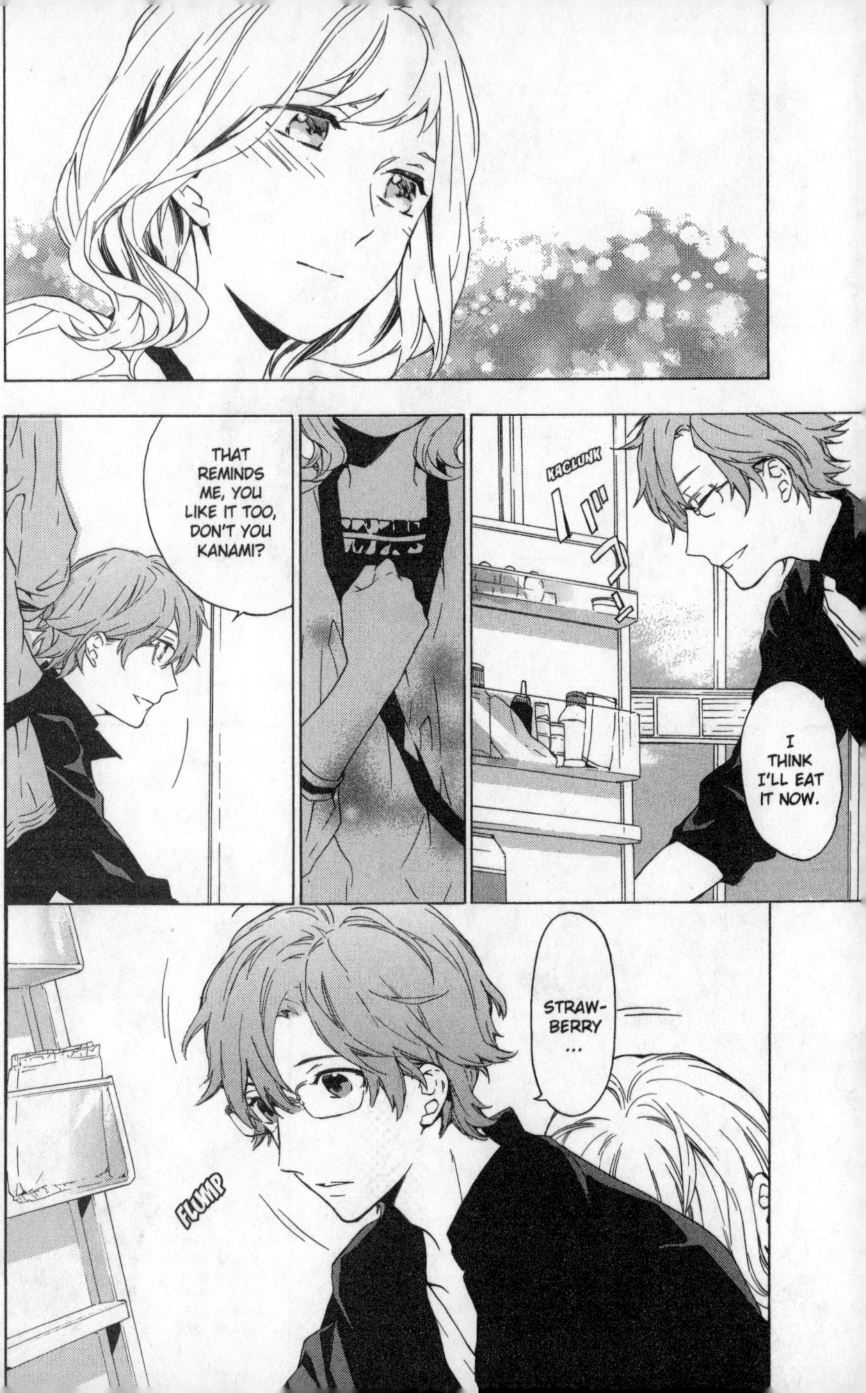
KAGLUNK
I THINK I'LL EAT IT NOW.
THAT REMINDS ME, YOU LIKE IT TOO, DON'T YOU KANAMI?
STRAW-BERRY ...
FLUMP

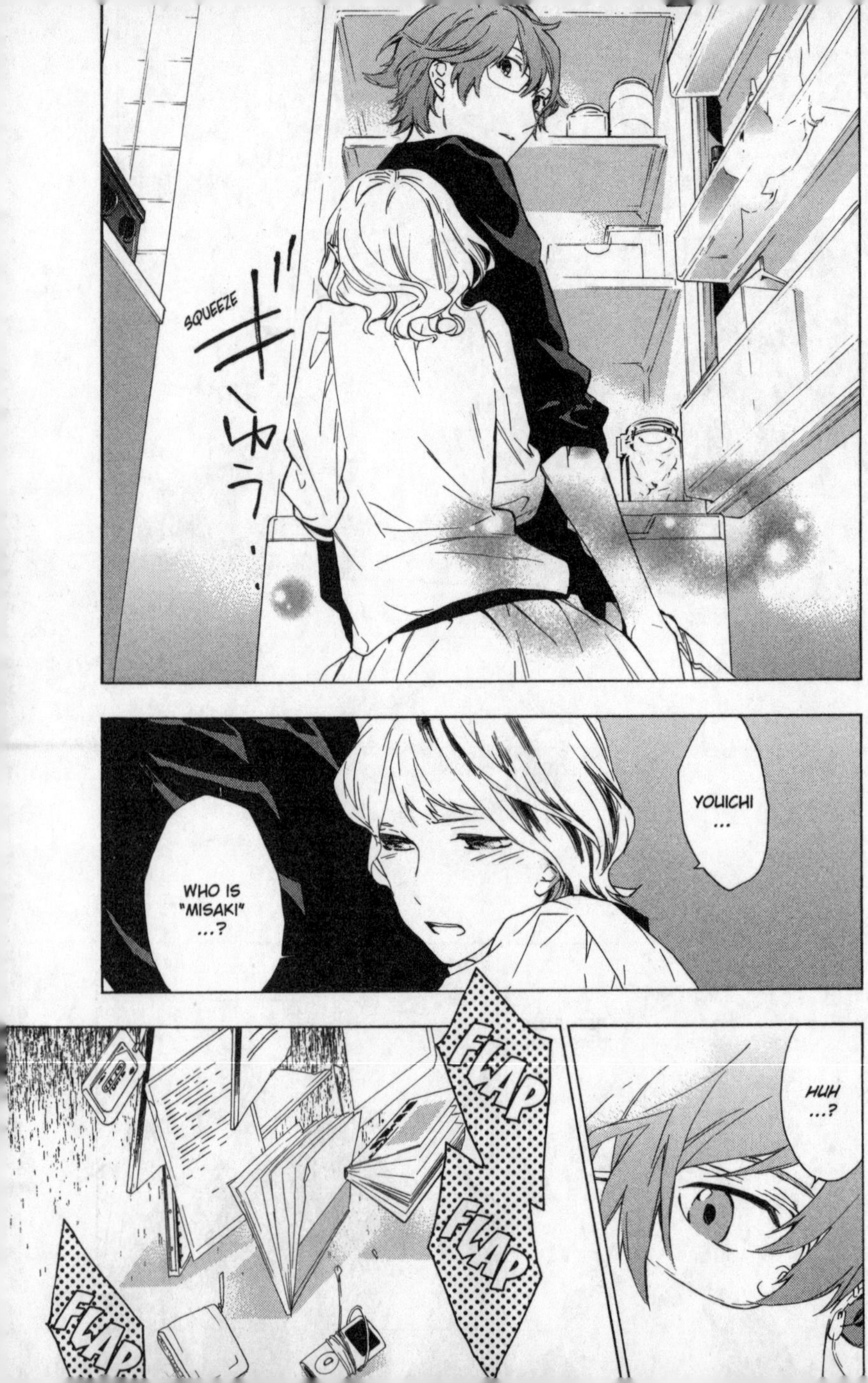
SQUEEZE
ギゅう…
YOUICHI ...
WHO IS "MISAKI" ...?
HUH ...?
FLAP
FLAP
FLAP

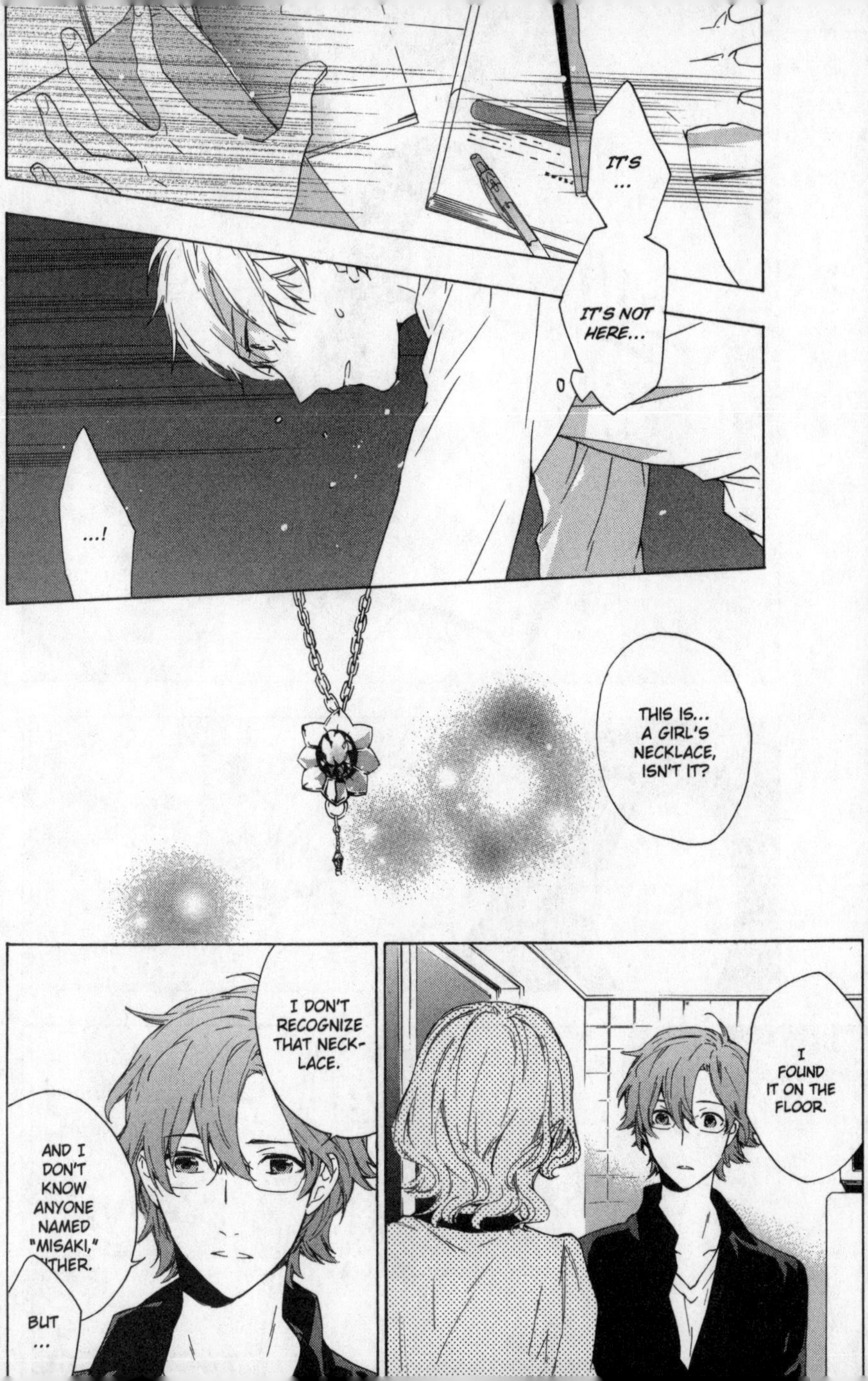
IT'S ...
IT'S NOT HERE...
...!
THIS IS... A GIRL'S NECKLACE, ISN'T IT?
I FOUND IT ON THE FLOOR.
I DON'T RECOGNIZE THAT NECK-LACE.
AND I DON'T KNOW ANYONE NAMED "MISAKI," ITHER.
BUT ...

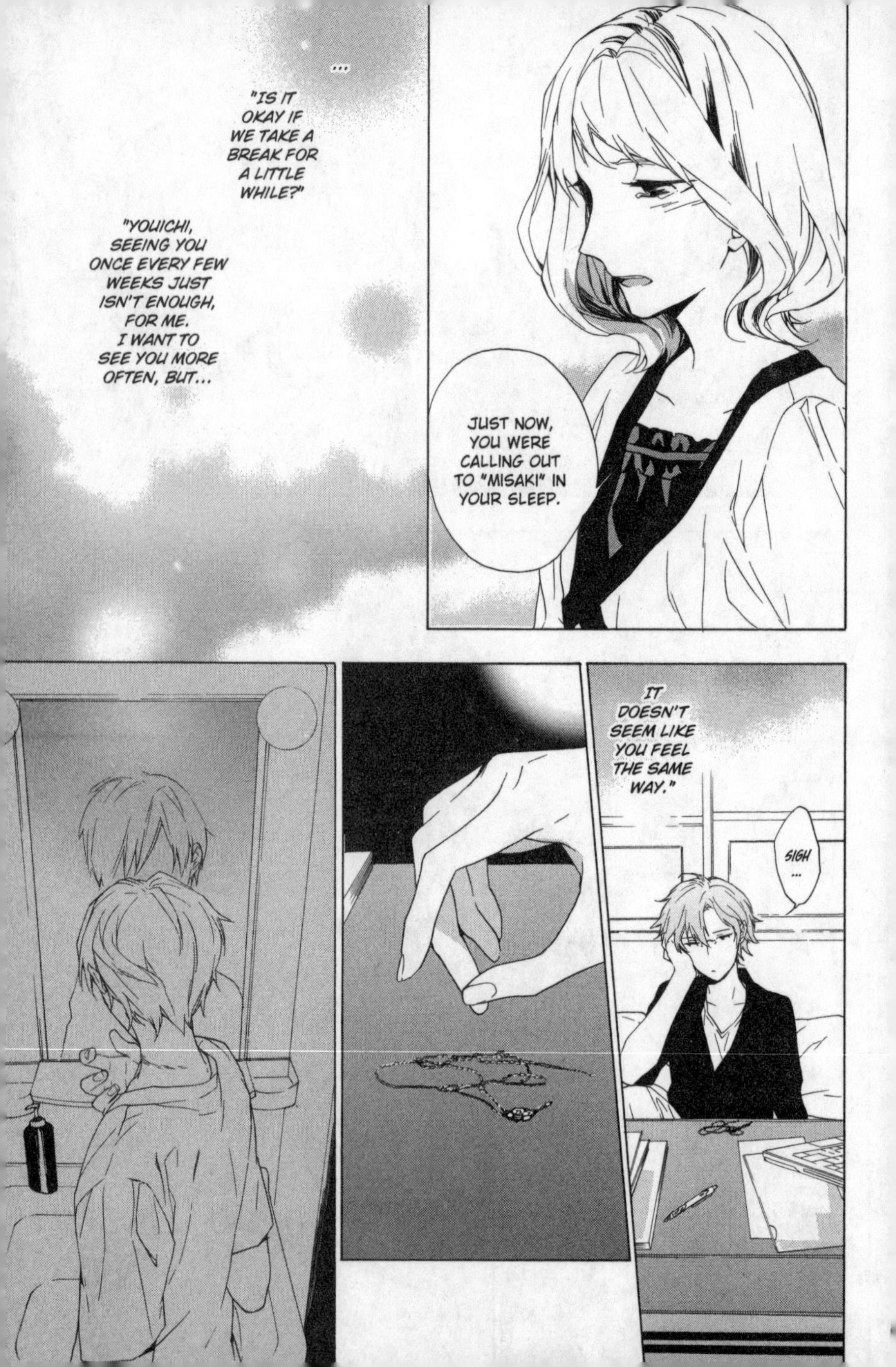
JUST NOW, YOU WERE CALLING OUT TO "MISAKI" IN YOUR SLEEP.
...
"IS IT OKAY IF WE TAKE A BREAK FOR A LITTLE WHILE?"
"YOUICHI, SEEING YOU ONCE EVERY FEW WEEKS JUST ISN'T ENOUGH, FOR ME. I WANT TO SEE YOU MORE OFTEN, BUT...
IT DOESN'T SEEM LIKE YOU FEEL THE SAME WAY."
SIGH ...

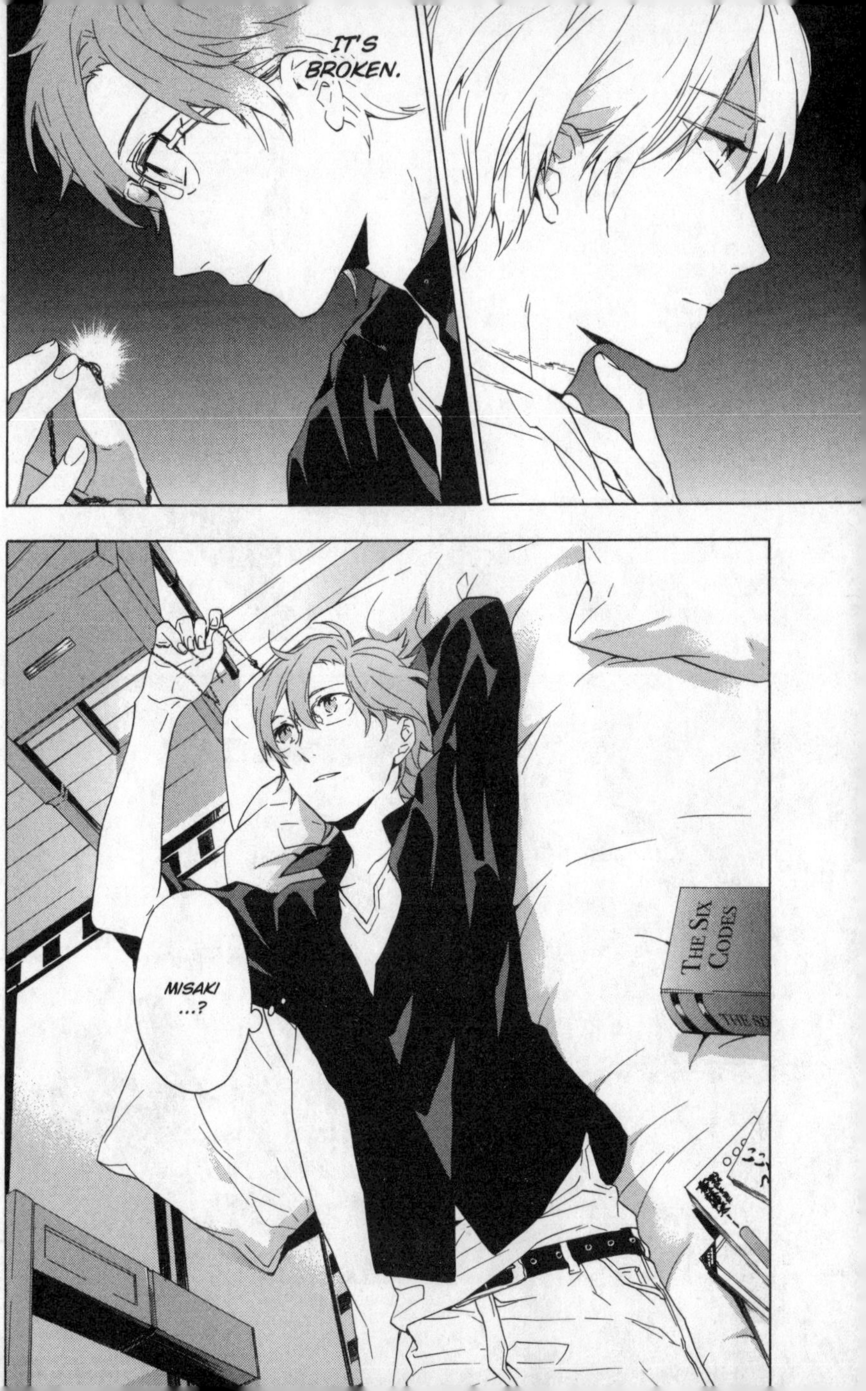
IT'S BROKEN.
MISAKI ...?
THE SIX CODES

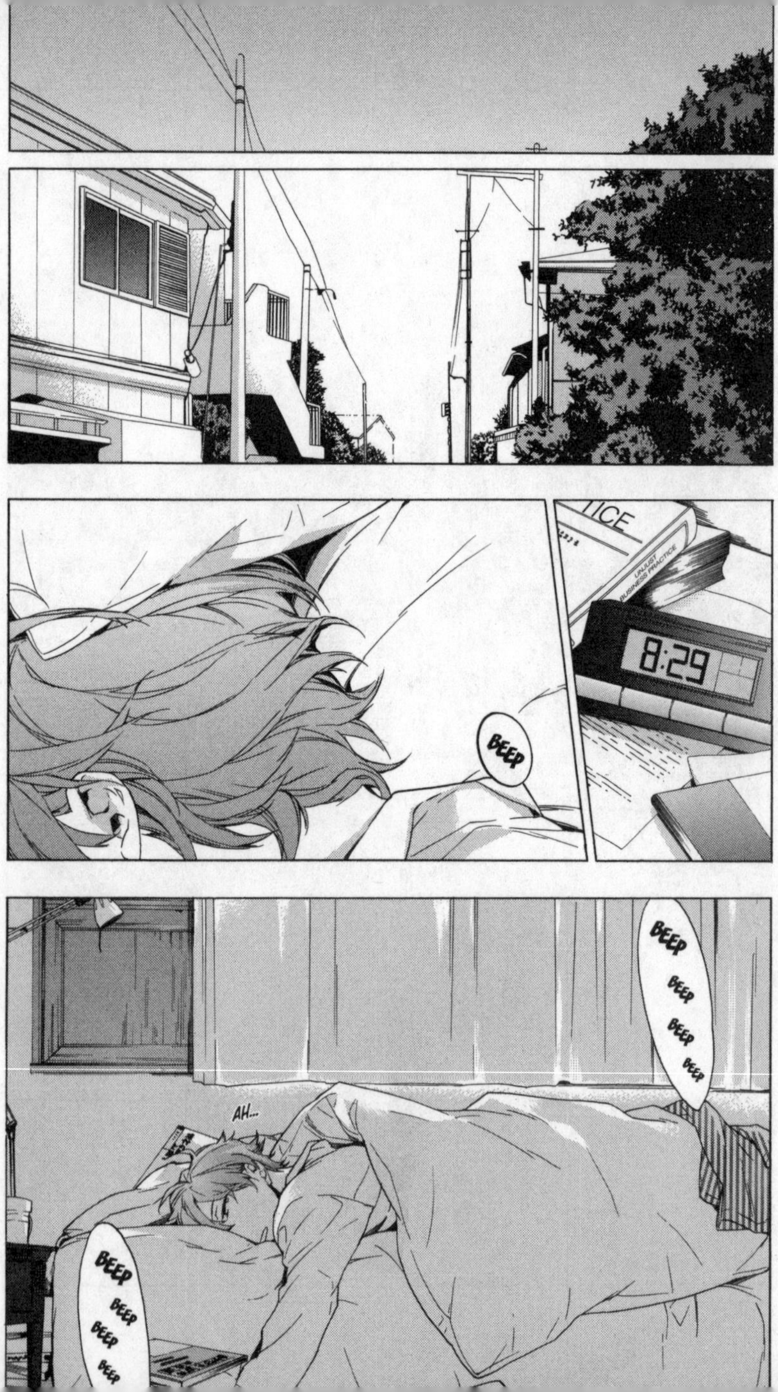
TICE
UNJUST BUSINESS PRACTICE
8:29
BEEP
BEEP BEEP BEEP BEEP
AH...
BEEP BEEP BEEP BEEP

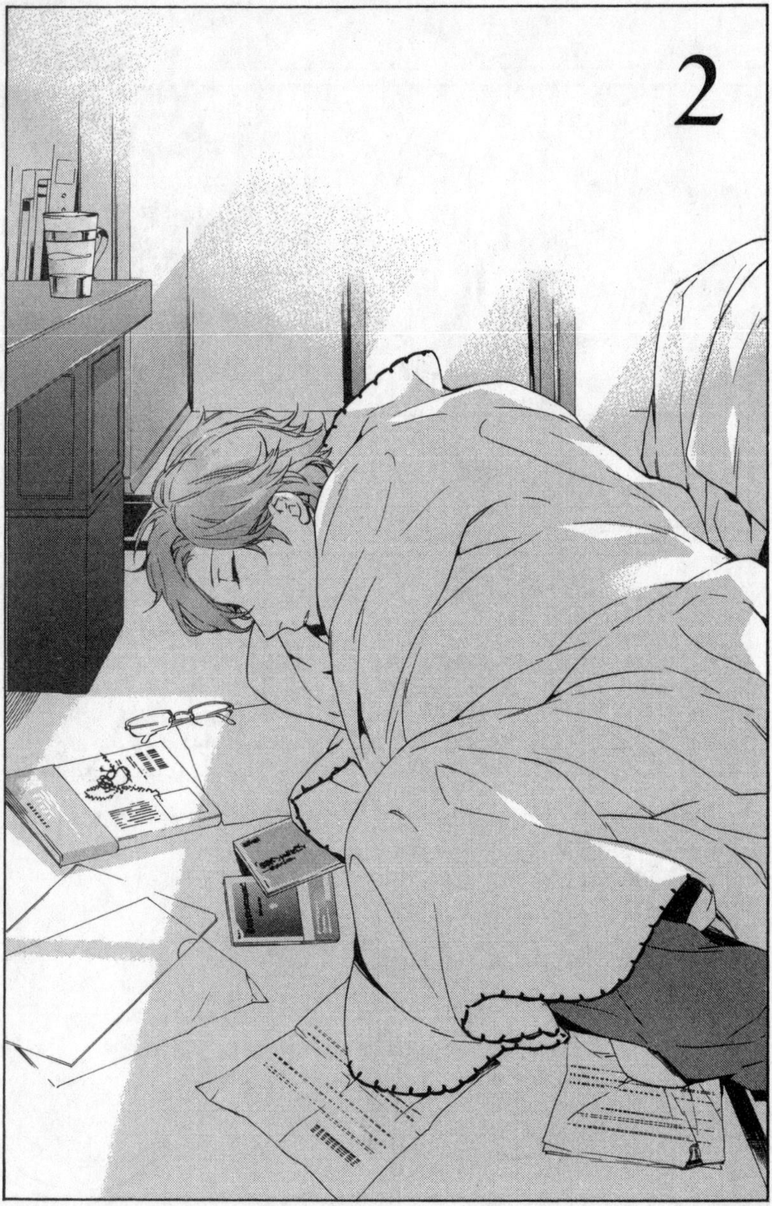
2

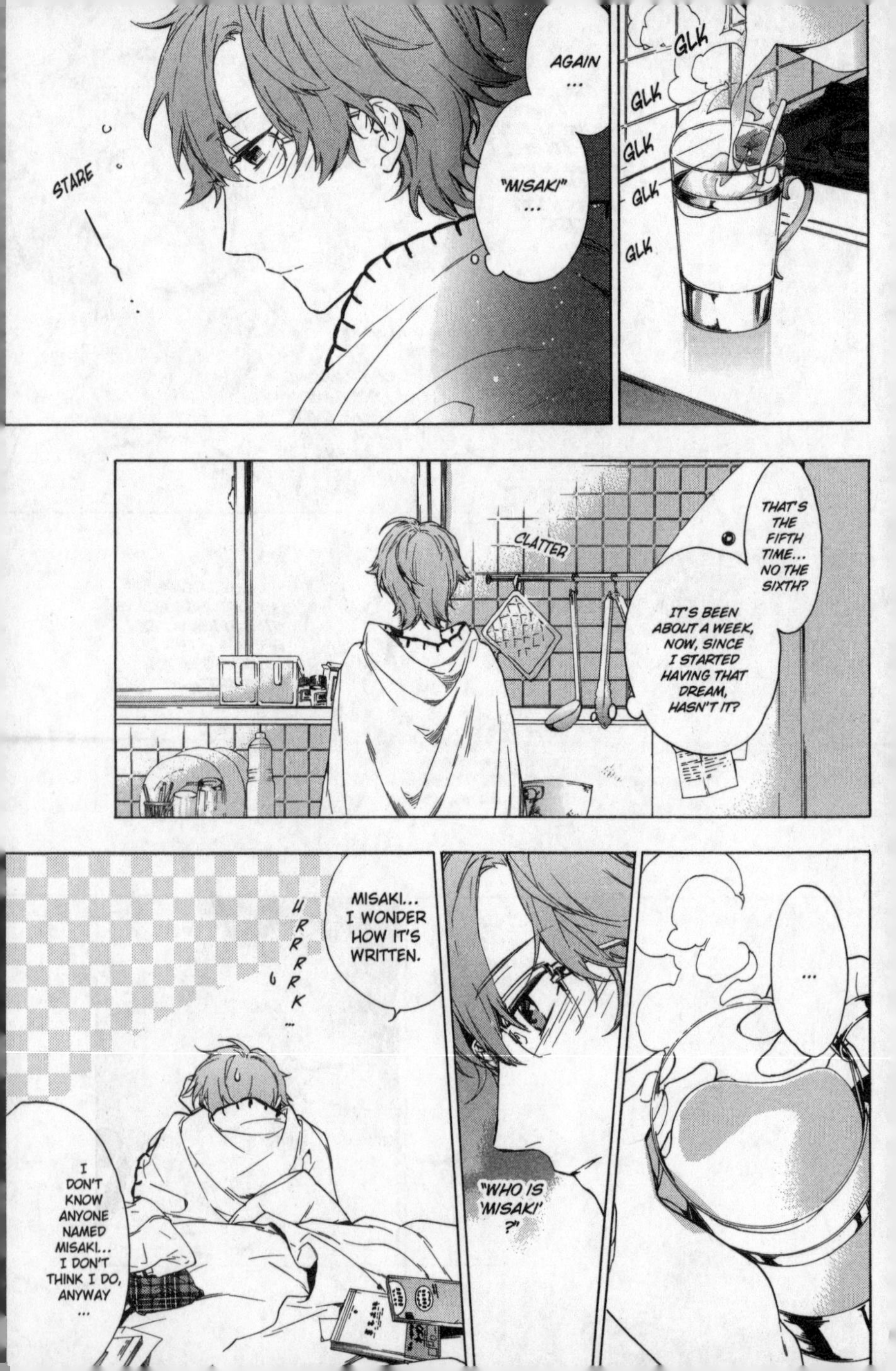
GLK
GLK
GLK
GLK
GLK
AGAIN ...
"MISAKI" ...
STARE
CLATTER
THAT'S THE FIFTH TIME... NO THE SIXTH?
IT'S BEEN ABOUT A WEEK, NOW, SINCE I STARTED HAVING THAT DREAM, HASN'T IT?
...
"WHO IS 'MISAKI' ?"
MISAKI... I WONDER HOW IT'S WRITTEN.
URRRRK ...
I DON'T KNOW ANYONE NAMED MISAKI... I DON'T THINK I DO, ANYWAY ...

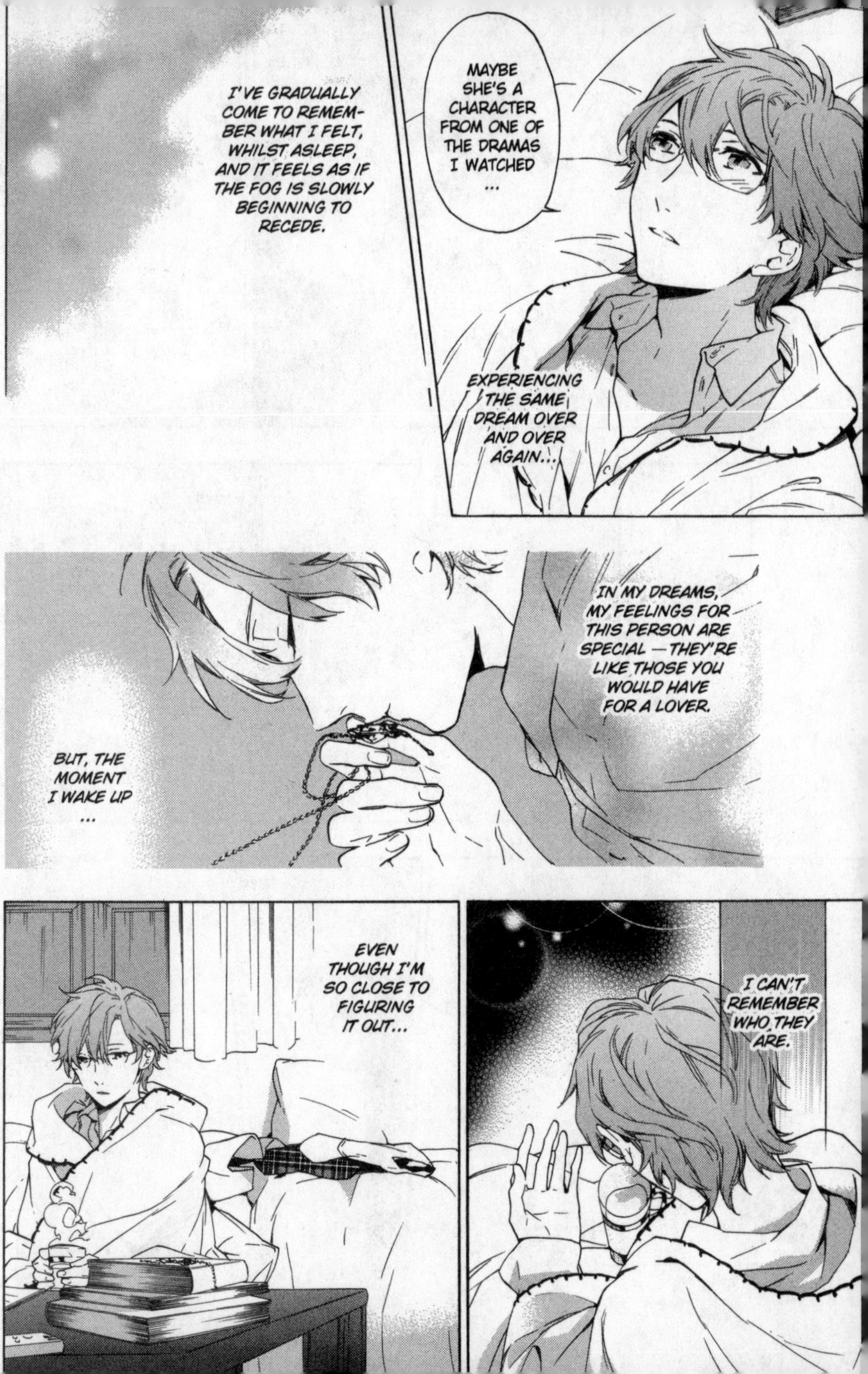
MAYBE SHE'S A CHARACTER FROM ONE OF THE DRAMAS I WATCHED ...
EXPERIENCING THE SAME DREAM OVER AND OVER AGAIN...
I'VE GRADUALLY COME TO REMEMBER WHAT I FELT, WHILST ASLEEP, AND IT FEELS AS IF THE FOG IS SLOWLY BEGINNING TO RECEDE.
IN MY DREAMS, MY FEELINGS FOR THIS PERSON ARE SPECIAL — THEY'RE LIKE THOSE YOU WOULD HAVE FOR A LOVER.
BUT, THE MOMENT I WAKE UP ...
I CAN'T REMEMBER WHO THEY ARE.
EVEN THOUGH I'M SO CLOSE TO FIGURING IT OUT...

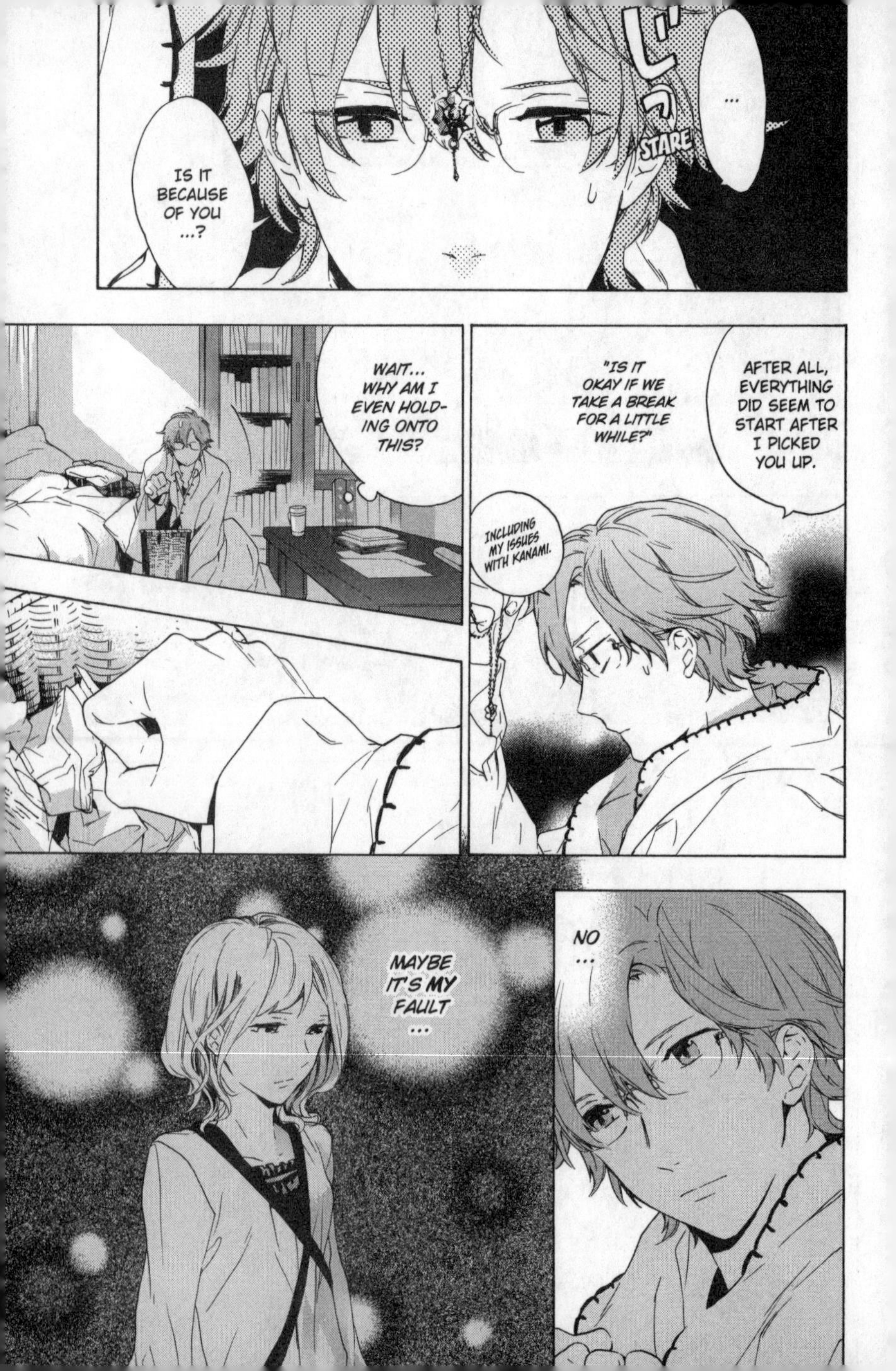
...
STARE
IS IT BECAUSE OF YOU ...?
AFTER ALL, EVERYTHING DID SEEM TO START AFTER I PICKED YOU UP.
"IS IT OKAY IF WE TAKE A BREAK FOR A LITTLE WHILE?"
INCLUDING MY ISSUES WITH KANAMI.
WAIT... WHY AM I EVEN HOLD-ING ONTO THIS?
NO ...
MAYBE IT'S MY FAULT ...

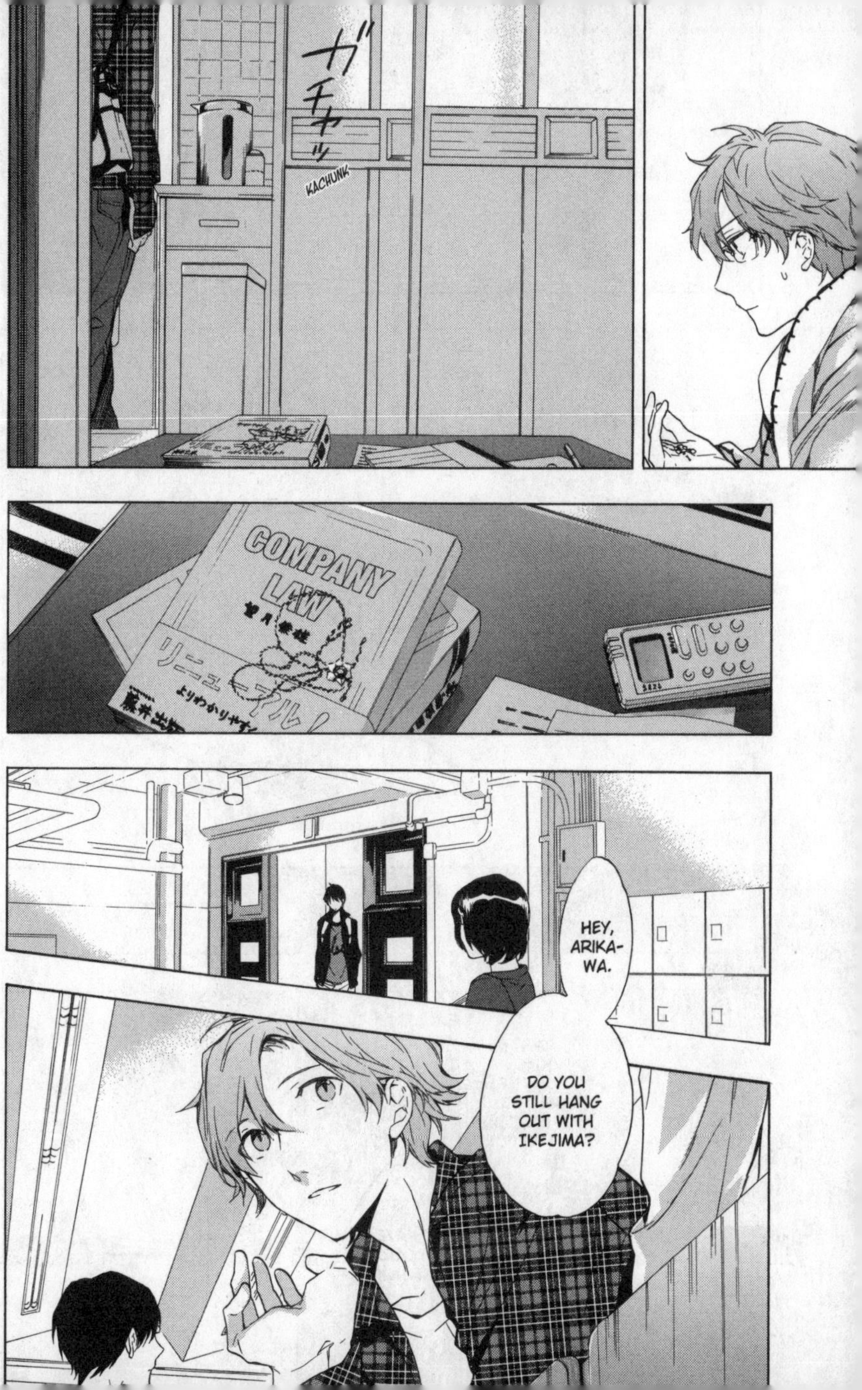
ガチャッ
KACHUNK
COMPANY LAW
HEY, ARIKAWA.
DO YOU STILL HANG OUT WITH IKEJIMA?

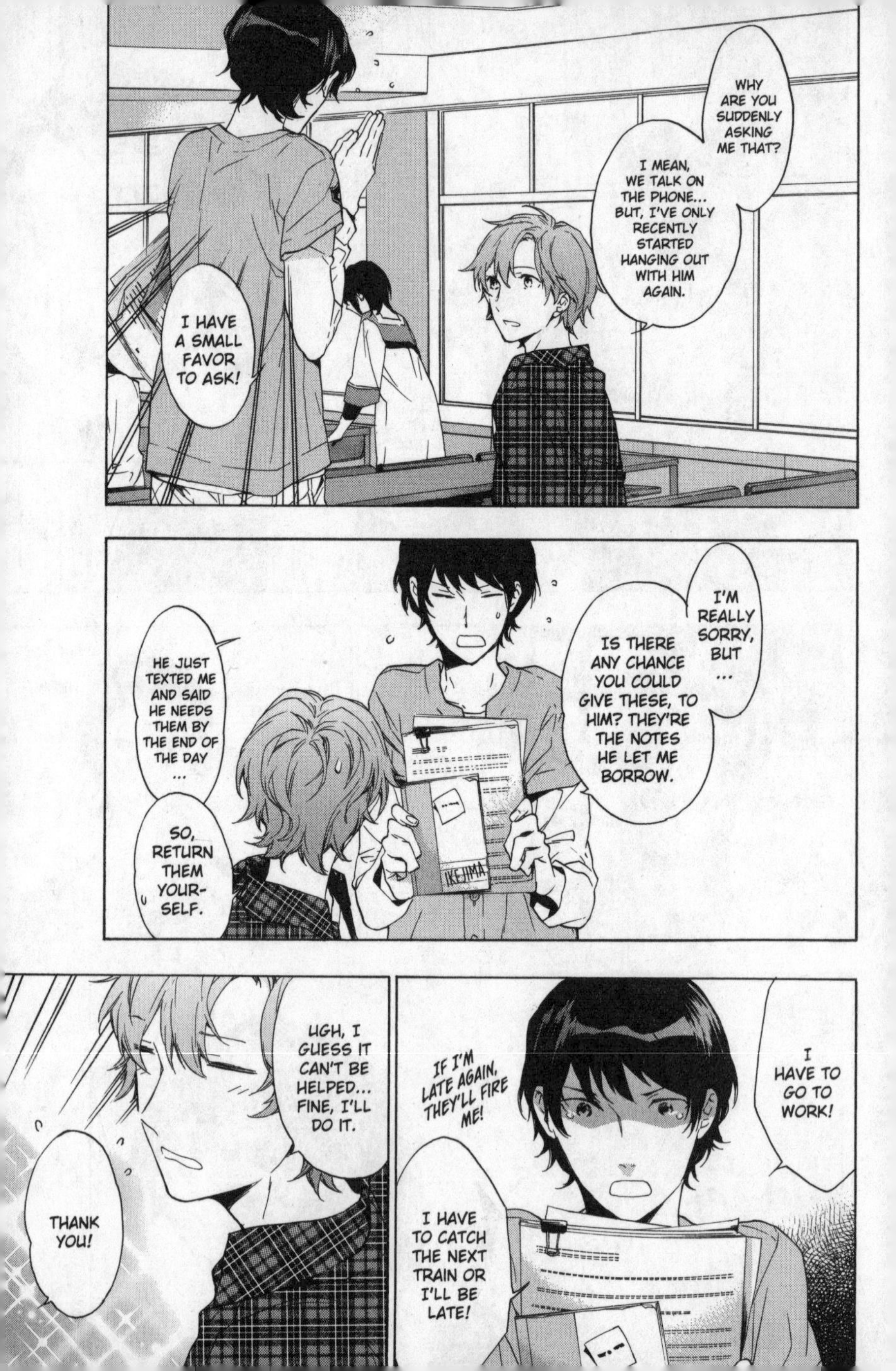
WHY ARE YOU SUDDENLY ASKING ME THAT?
I MEAN, WE TALK ON THE PHONE... BUT, I'VE ONLY RECENTLY STARTED HANGING OUT WITH HIM AGAIN.
I HAVE A SMALL FAVOR TO ASK!
I'M REALLY SORRY, BUT ...
IS THERE ANY CHANCE YOU COULD GIVE THESE, TO HIM? THEY'RE THE NOTES HE LET ME BORROW.
IKEJIMA
HE JUST TEXTED ME AND SAID HE NEEDS THEM BY THE END OF THE DAY ...
SO, RETURN THEM YOUR-SELF.
I HAVE TO GO TO WORK!
IF I'M LATE AGAIN, THEY'LL FIRE ME!
I HAVE TO CATCH THE NEXT TRAIN OR I'LL BE LATE!
UGH, I GUESS IT CAN'T BE HELPED... FINE, I'LL DO IT.
THANK YOU!

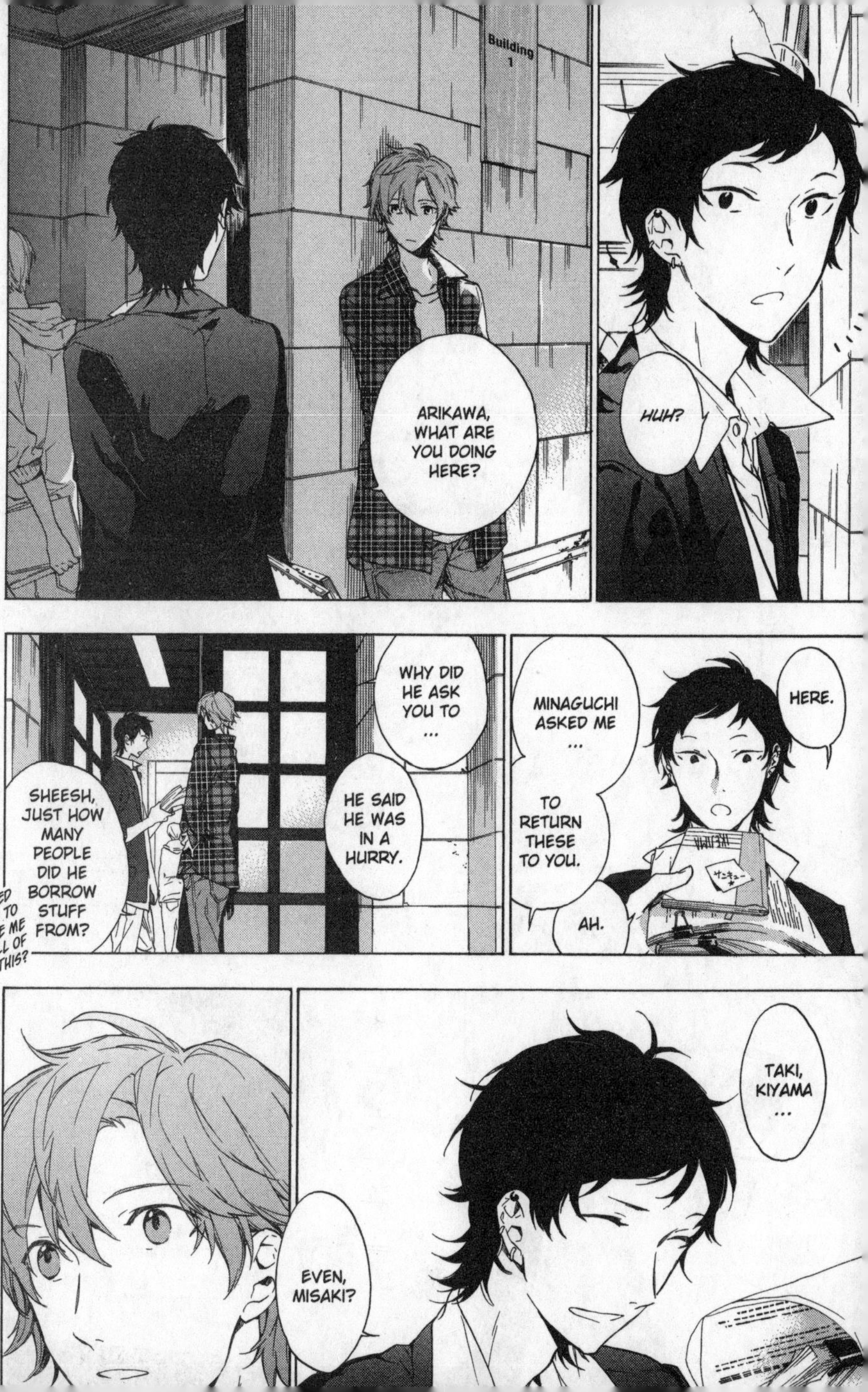
HUH?
Building 1
ARIKAWA, WHAT ARE YOU DOING HERE?
HERE.
MINAGUCHI ASKED ME ...
TO RETURN THESE TO YOU.
AH.
WHY DID HE ASK YOU TO ...
HE SAID HE WAS IN A HURRY.
SHEESH, JUST HOW MANY PEOPLE DID HE BORROW STUFF FROM?
HE ASKED YOU TO GIVE ME ALL OF THIS?
TAKI, KIYAMA ...
EVEN, MISAKI?

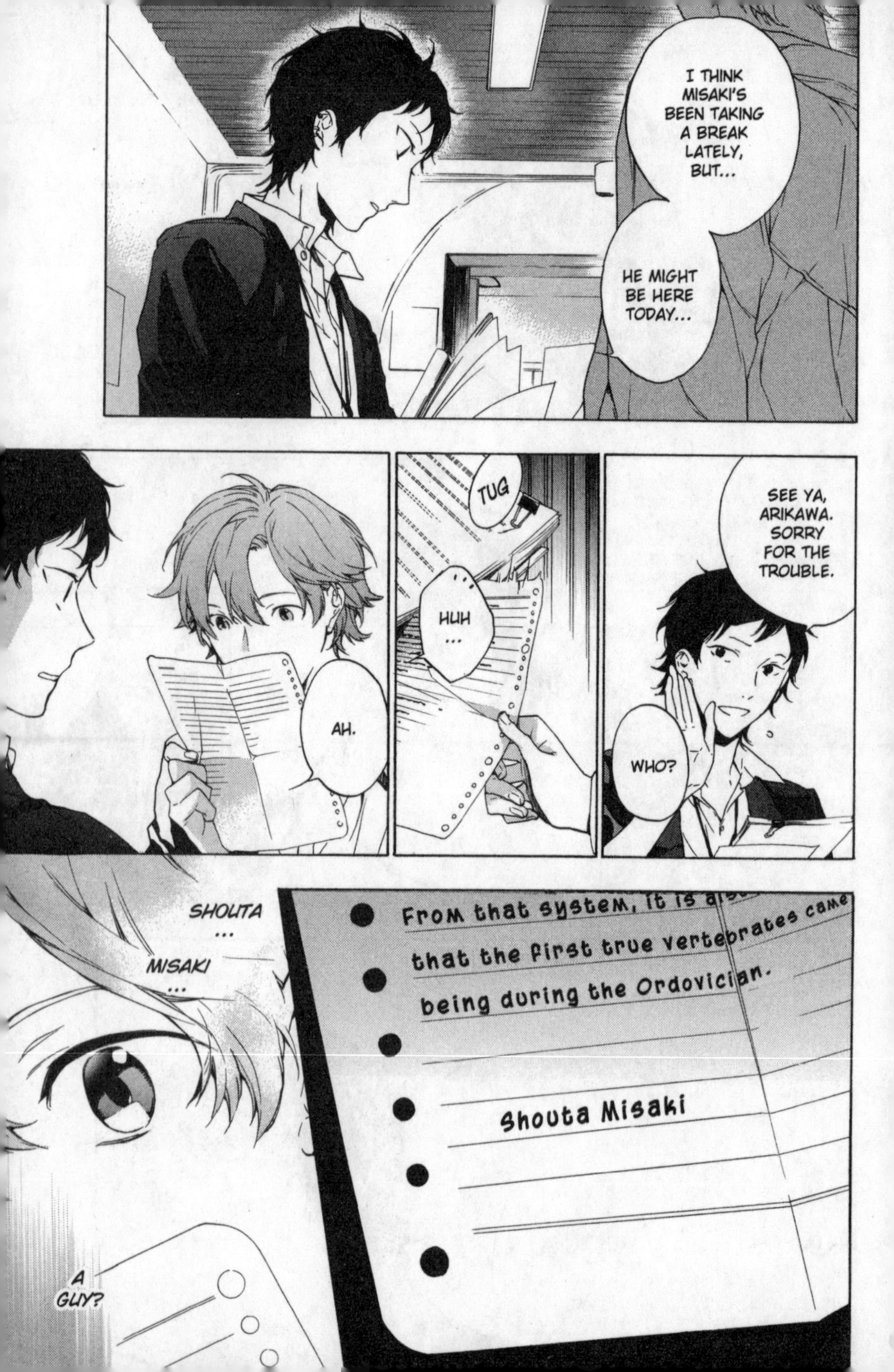
I THINK MISAKI'S BEEN TAKING A BREAK LATELY, BUT...
HE MIGHT BE HERE TODAY...
SEE YA, ARIKAWA. SORRY FOR THE TROUBLE.
WHO?
TUG
HUH ...
AH.
From that system, it is als
that the first true vertebrates came
being during the Ordovician.
Shouta Misaki
SHOUTA ...
MISAKI ...
A GUY?

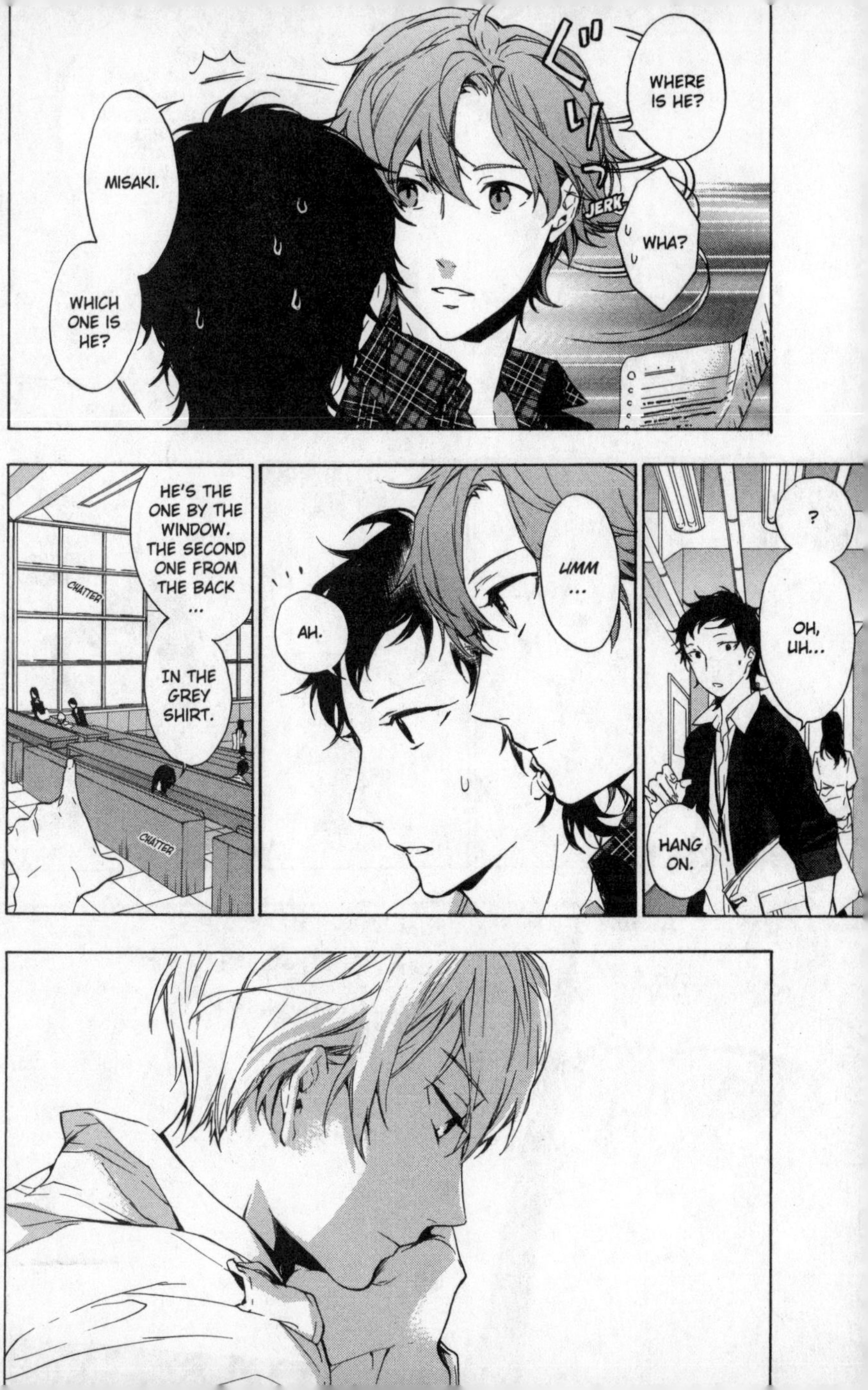
WHERE IS HE?
JERK
WHA?
MISAKI.
WHICH ONE IS HE?
?
OH, UH...
HANG ON.
UMM ...
AH.
HE'S THE ONE BY THE WINDOW. THE SECOND ONE FROM THE BACK ...
IN THE GREY SHIRT.
CHATTER
CHATTER

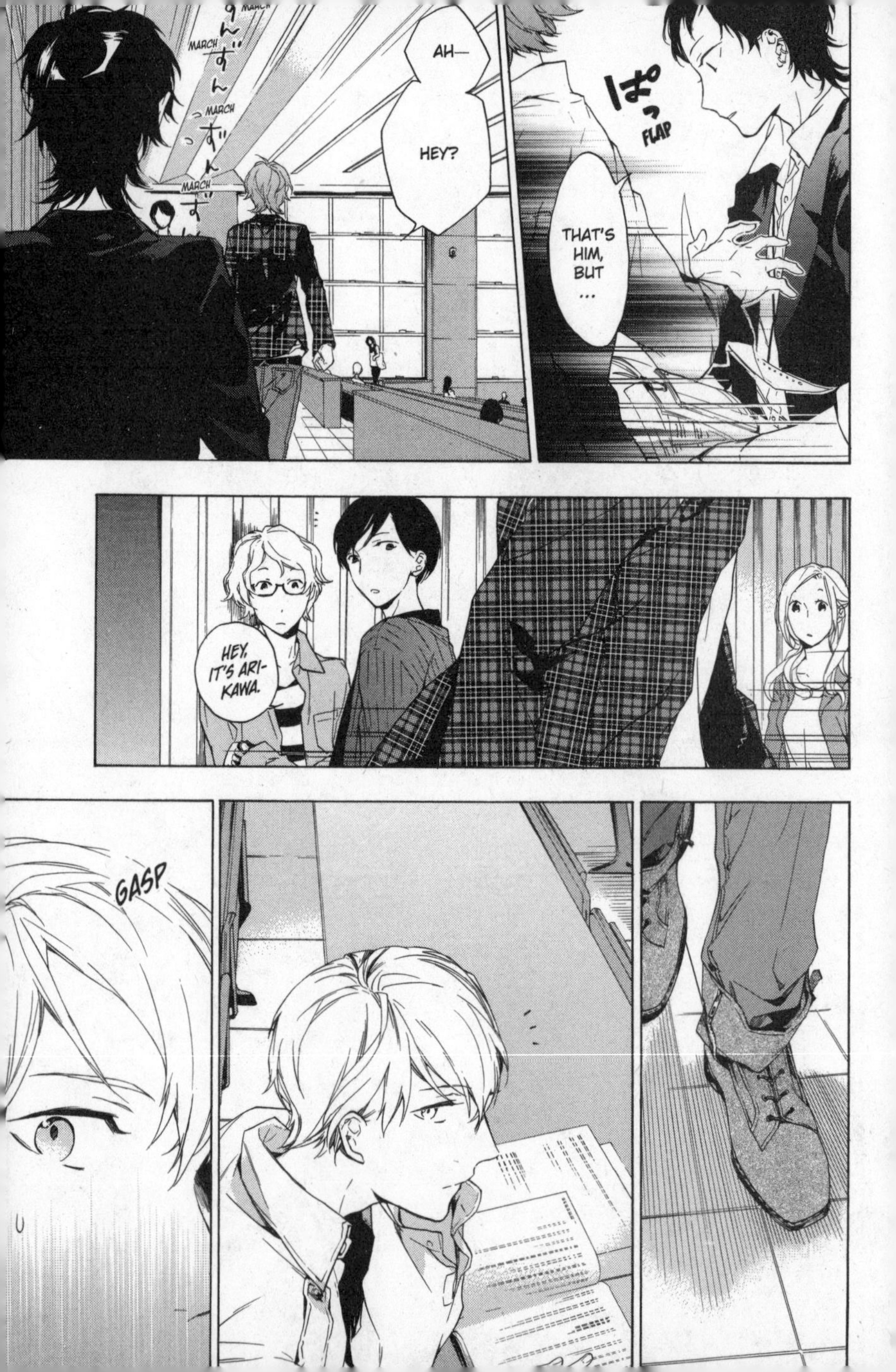
ぱっ
FLAP
THAT'S HIM, BUT ...
AH—
HEY?
MARCH
MARCH
MARCH
MARCH
HEY, IT'S ARI-KAWA.
GASP

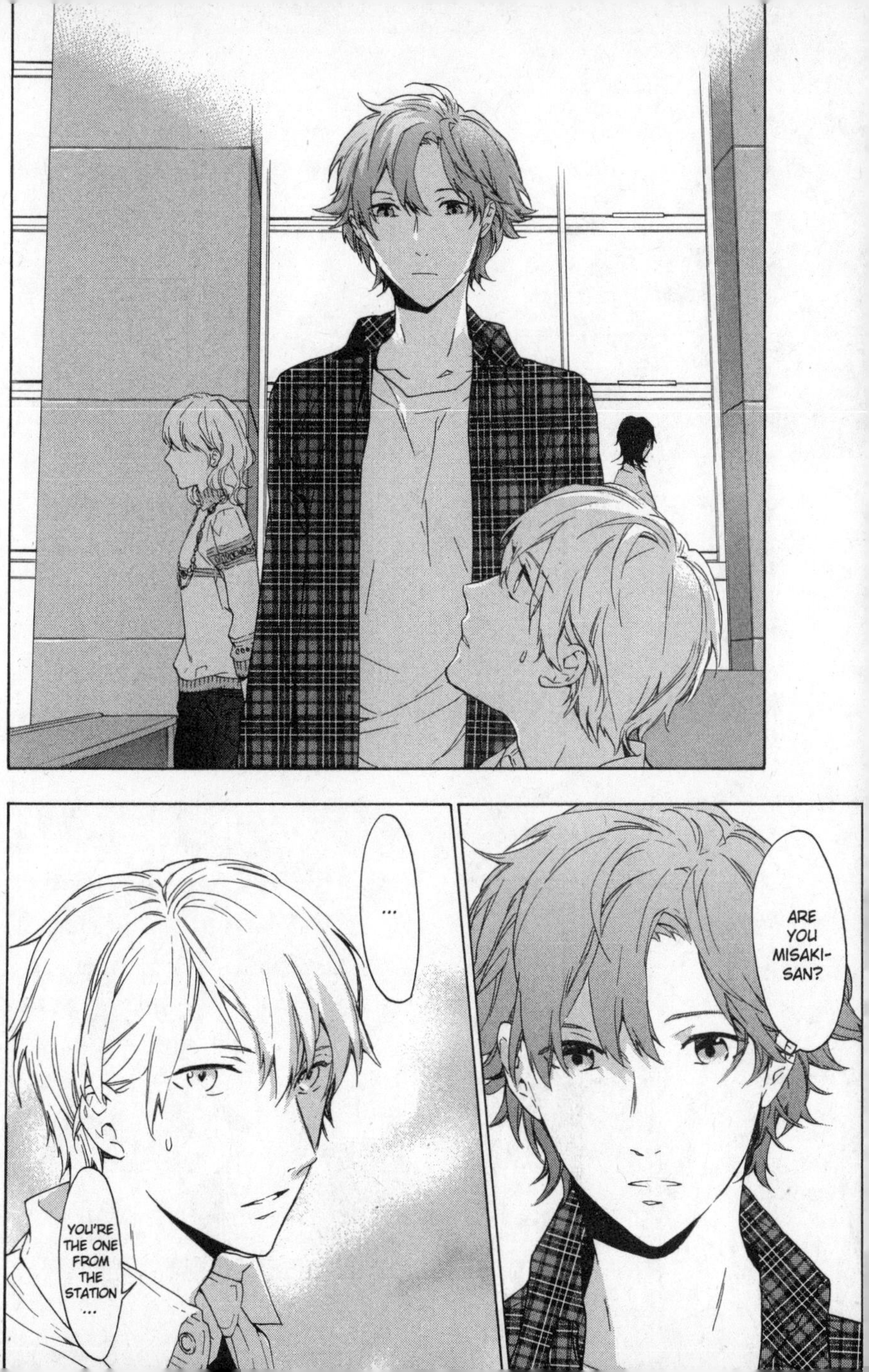
ARE YOU MISAKI-SAN?
...
YOU'RE THE ONE FROM THE STATION ...

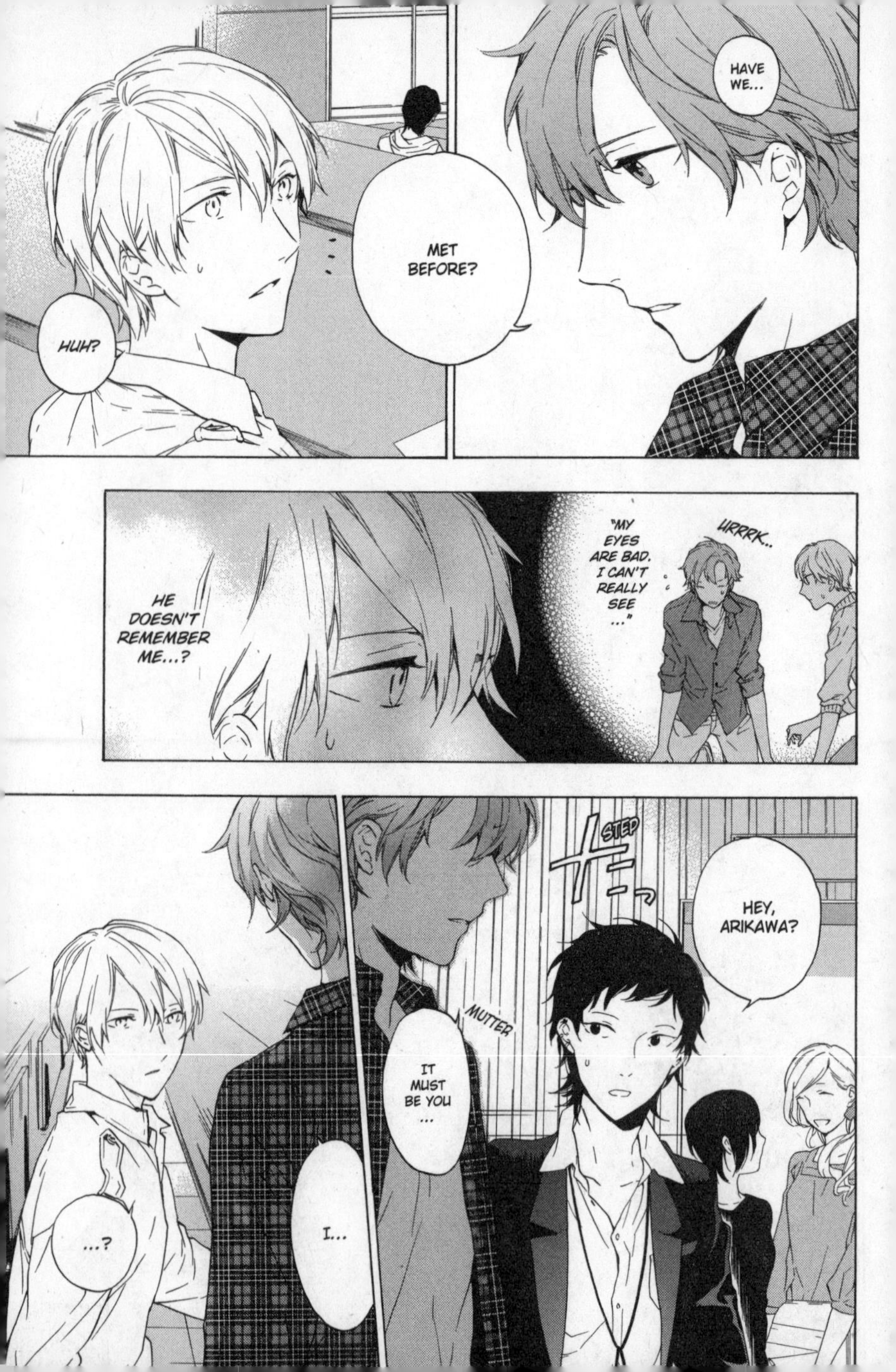
HAVE WE...
MET BEFORE?
HUH?
URRRK..
"MY EYES ARE BAD. I CAN'T REALLY SEE ..."
HE DOESN'T REMEMBER ME...?
STEP
HEY, ARIKAWA?
MUTTER
IT MUST BE YOU ...
I...
...?

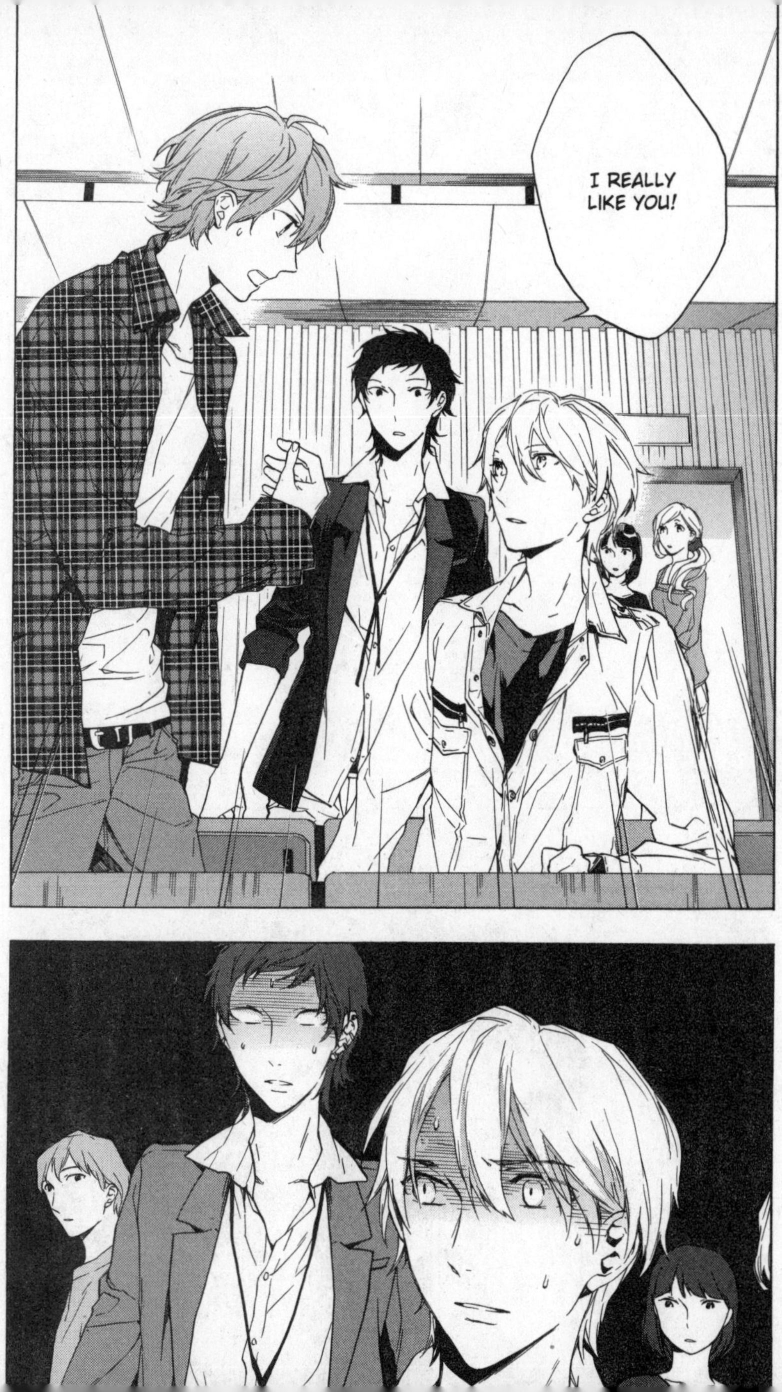
I REALLY LIKE YOU!

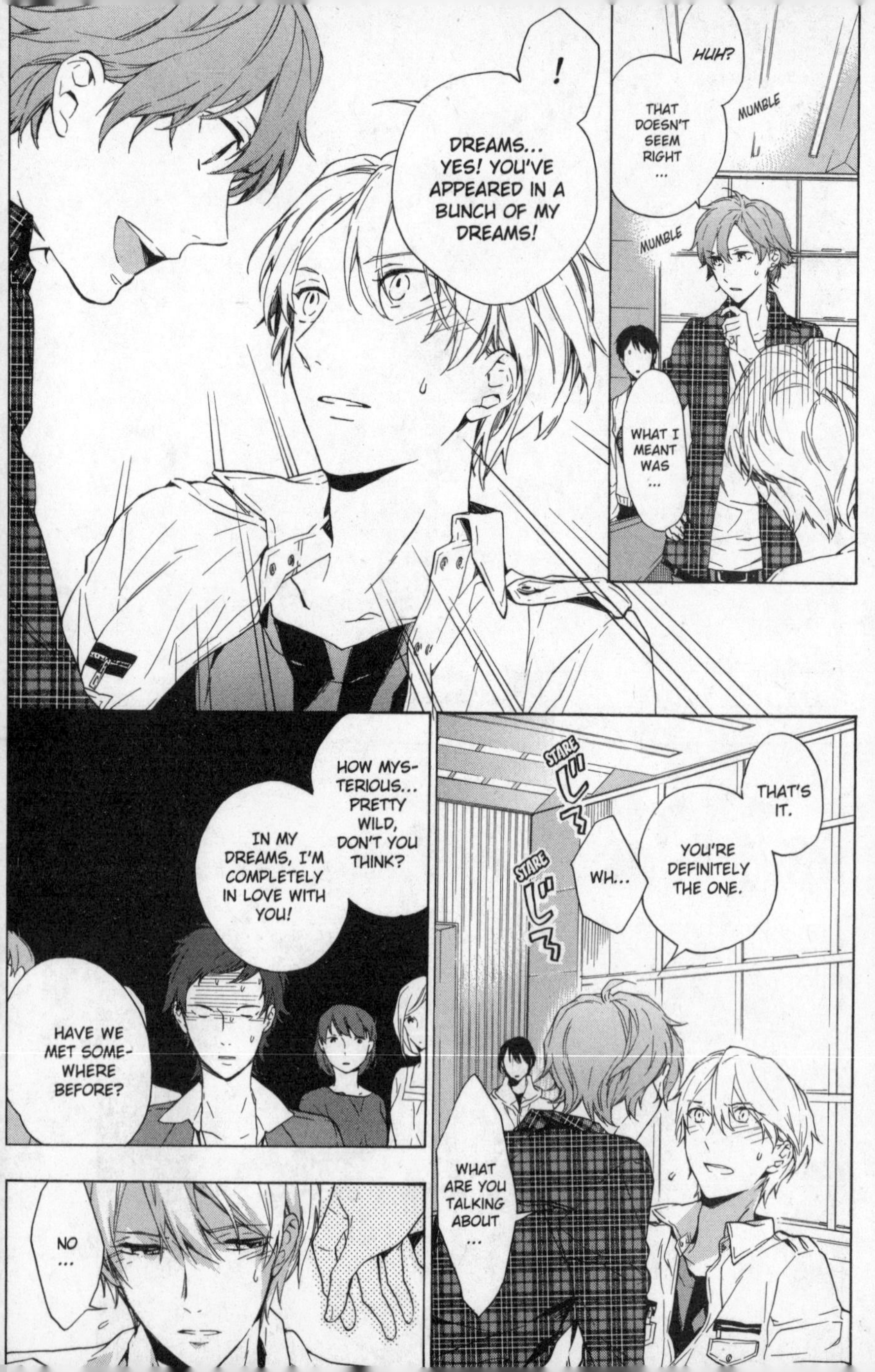
HUH?
THAT DOESN'T SEEM RIGHT ...
MUMBLE
MUMBLE
WHAT I MEANT WAS ...
!
DREAMS... YES! YOU'VE APPEARED IN A BUNCH OF MY DREAMS!
STARE
STARE
THAT'S IT.
YOU'RE DEFINITELY THE ONE.
WH...
WHAT ARE YOU TALKING ABOUT ...
HOW MYS-TERIOUS... PRETTY WILD, DON'T YOU THINK?
IN MY DREAMS, I'M COMPLETELY IN LOVE WITH YOU!
HAVE WE MET SOME-WHERE BEFORE?
NO ...

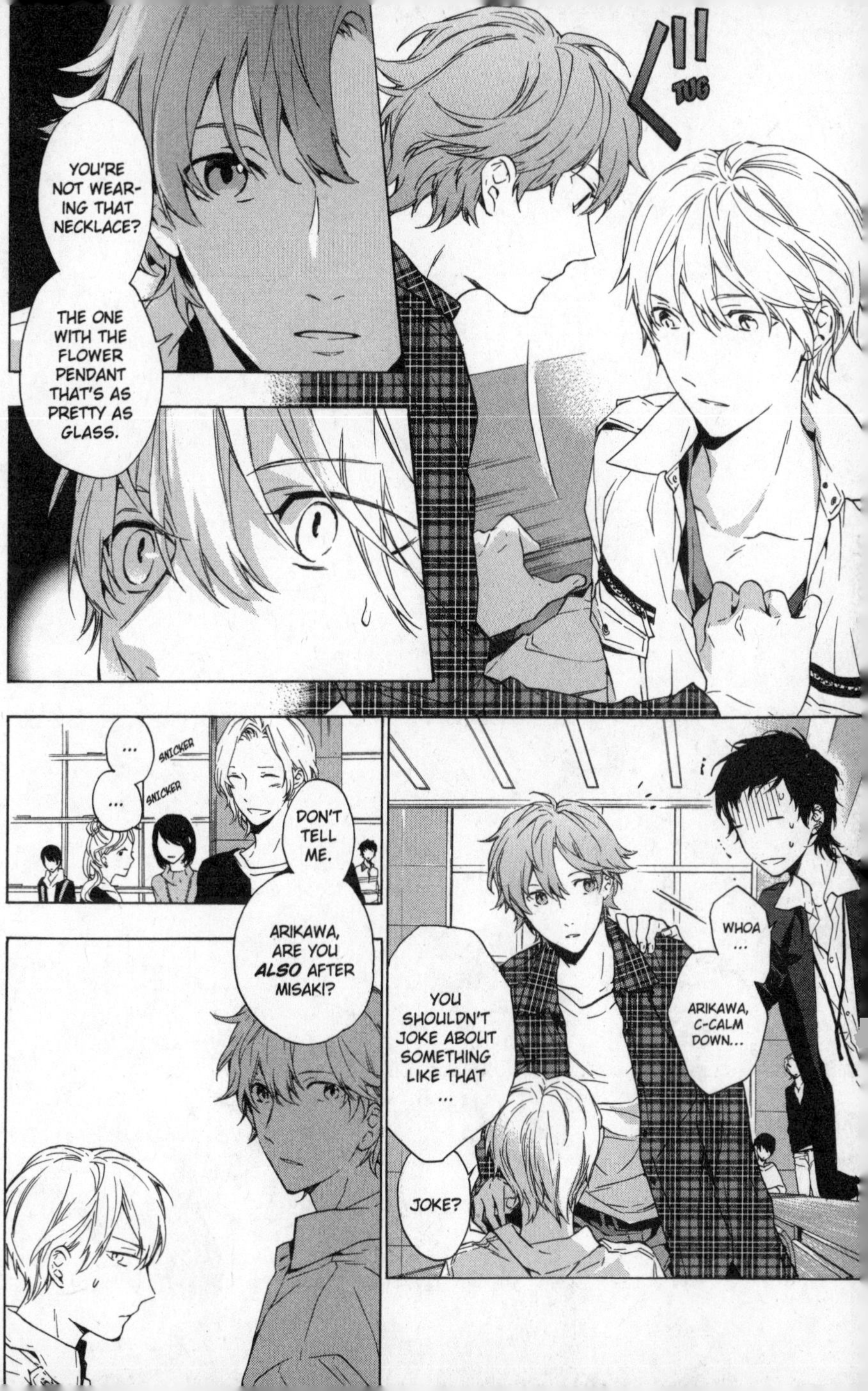
TUG
YOU'RE NOT WEARING THAT NECKLACE?
THE ONE WITH THE FLOWER PENDANT THAT'S AS PRETTY AS GLASS.
WHOA ...
ARIKAWA, C-CALM DOWN...
YOU SHOULDN'T JOKE ABOUT SOMETHING LIKE THAT ...
JOKE?
...
...
SNICKER
SNICKER
DON'T TELL ME.
ARIKAWA, ARE YOU *ALSO* AFTER MISAKI?

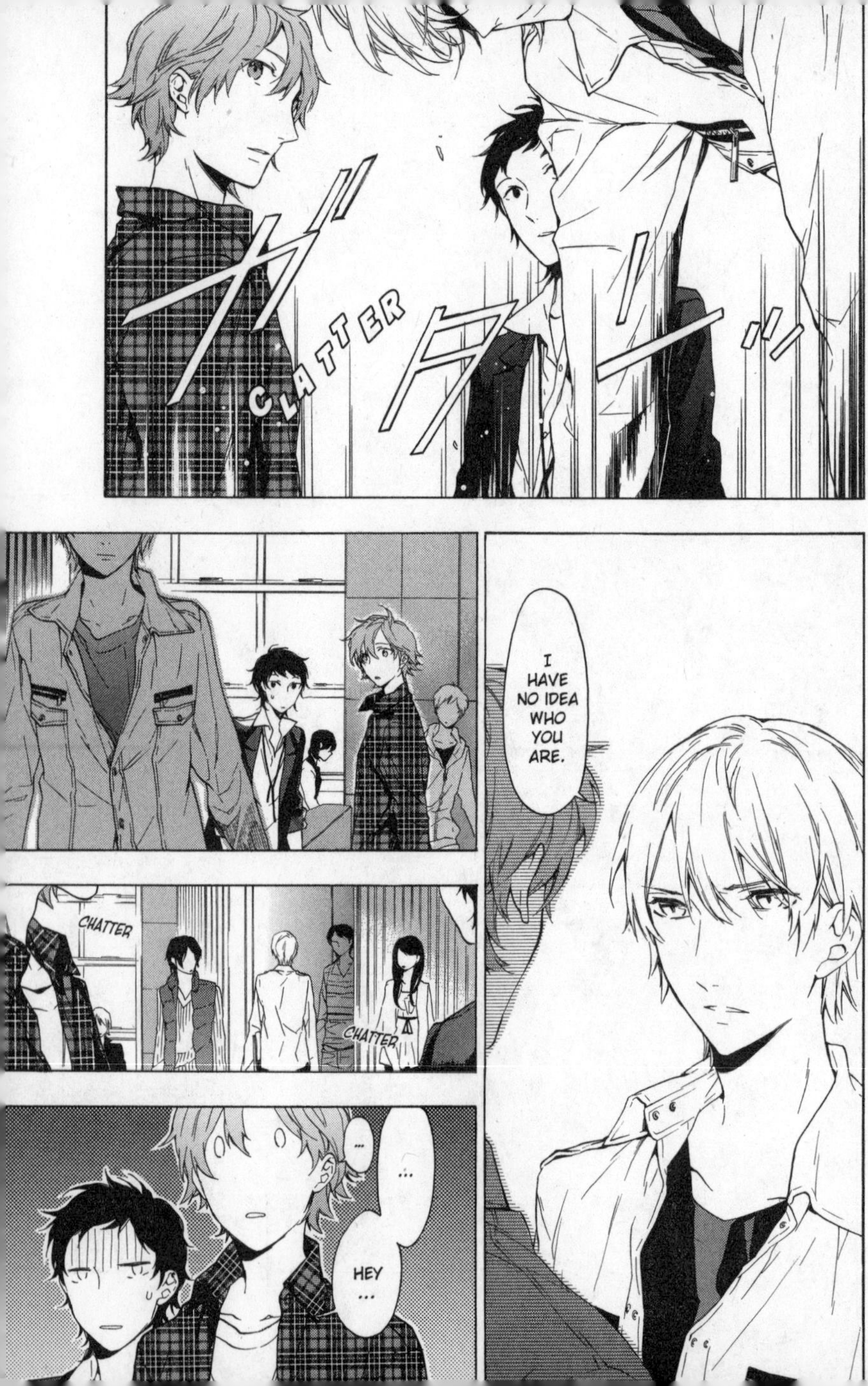
CLATTER
I HAVE NO IDEA WHO YOU ARE.
CHATTER
CHATTER
...
...
HEY ...

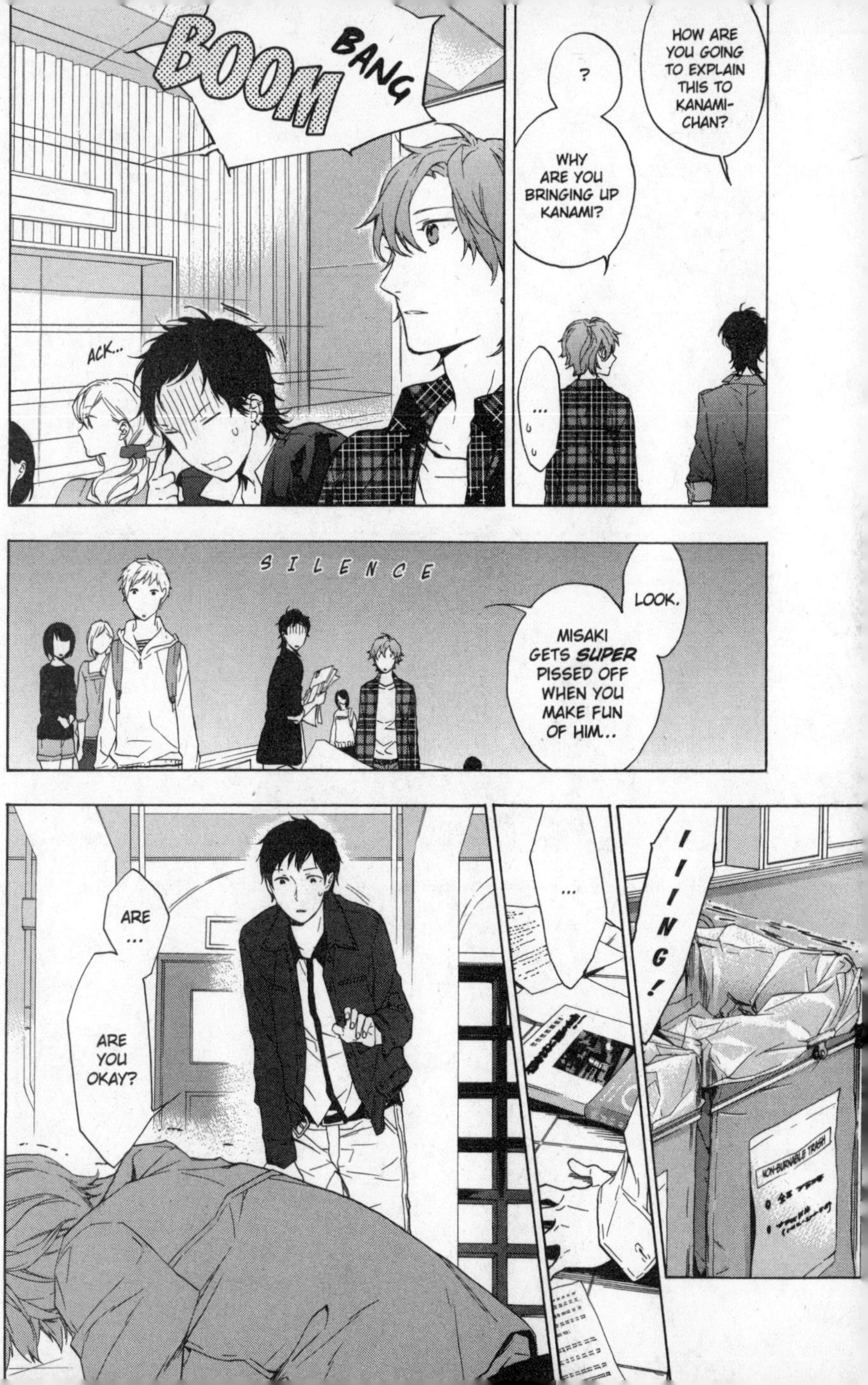
HOW ARE YOU GOING TO EXPLAIN THIS TO KANAMI-CHAN?
?
WHY ARE YOU BRINGING UP KANAMI?
...
BOOM
BANG
ACK...
SILENCE
LOOK.
MISAKI GETS SUPER PISSED OFF WHEN YOU MAKE FUN OF HIM...
IIIING!
NON-BURNABLE TRASH
...
ARE ...
ARE YOU OKAY?

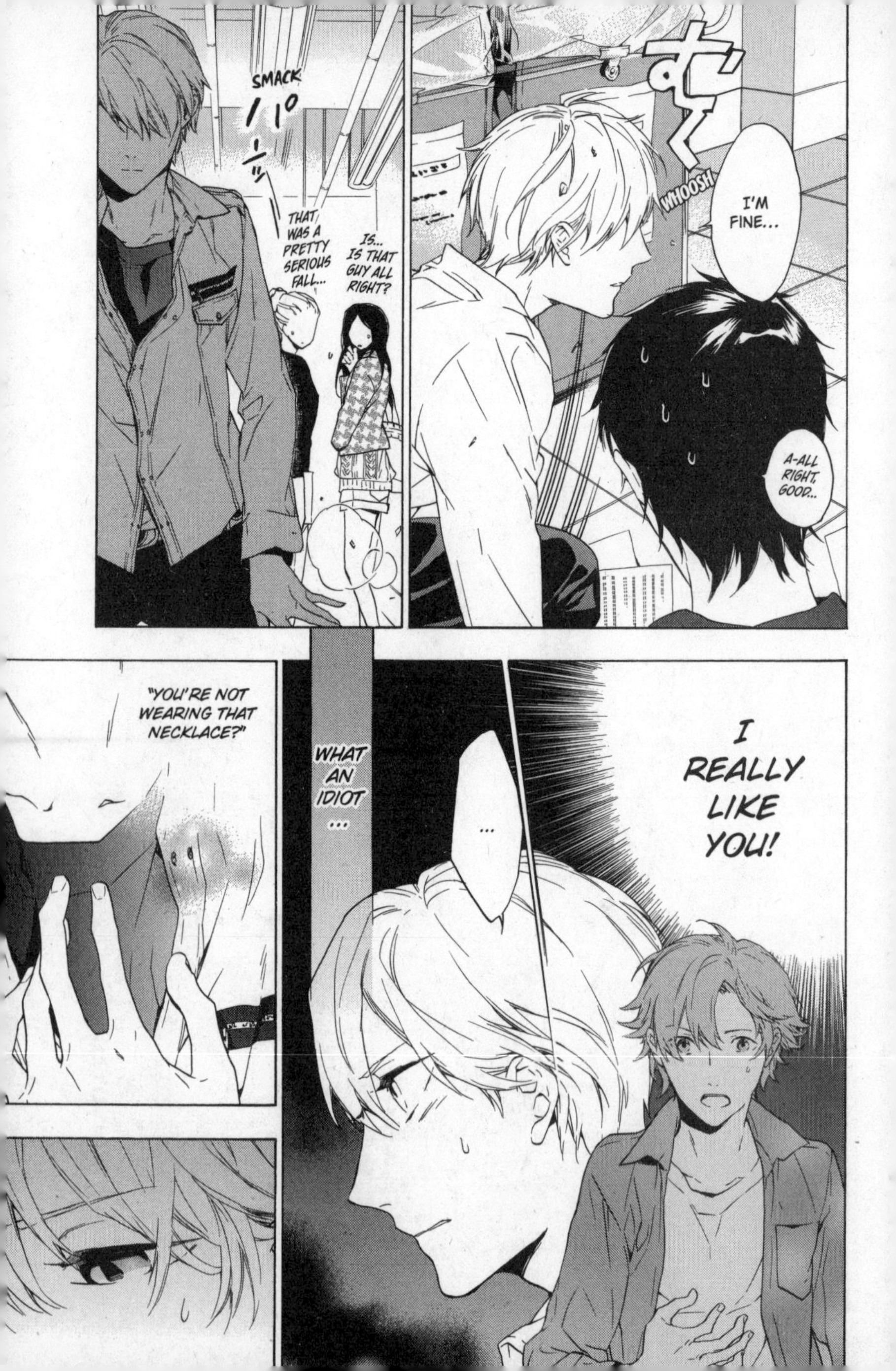
むく
I'M FINE...
WHOOSH
A-ALL RIGHT, GOOD...
SMACK
IS... IS THAT GUY ALL RIGHT?
THAT WAS A PRETTY SERIOUS FALL...
I REALLY LIKE YOU!
...
WHAT AN IDIOT ...
"YOU'RE NOT WEARING THAT NECKLACE?"

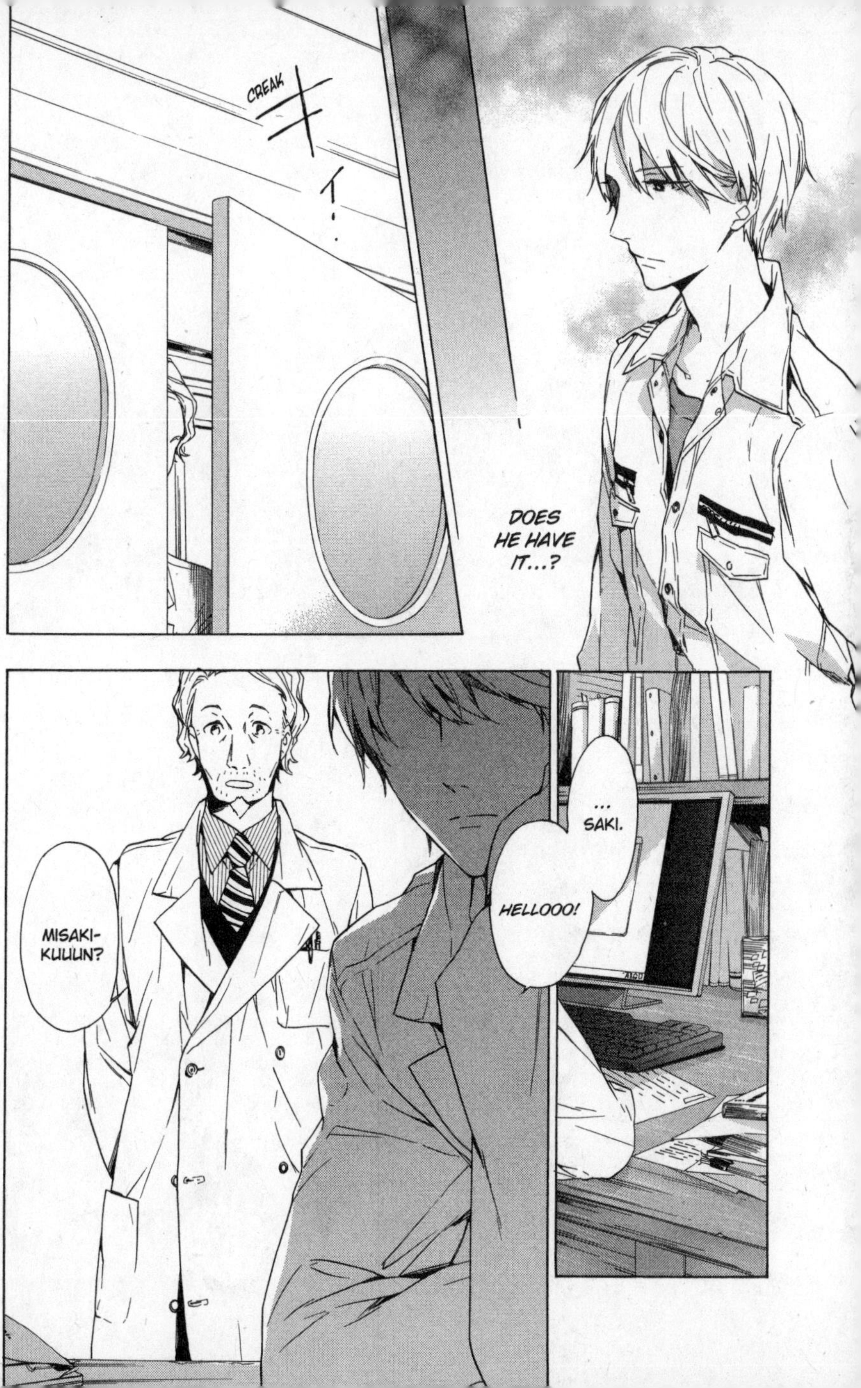
DOES HE HAVE IT...?
CREAK
... SAKI.
HELLOOO!
MISAKI-KUUUN?

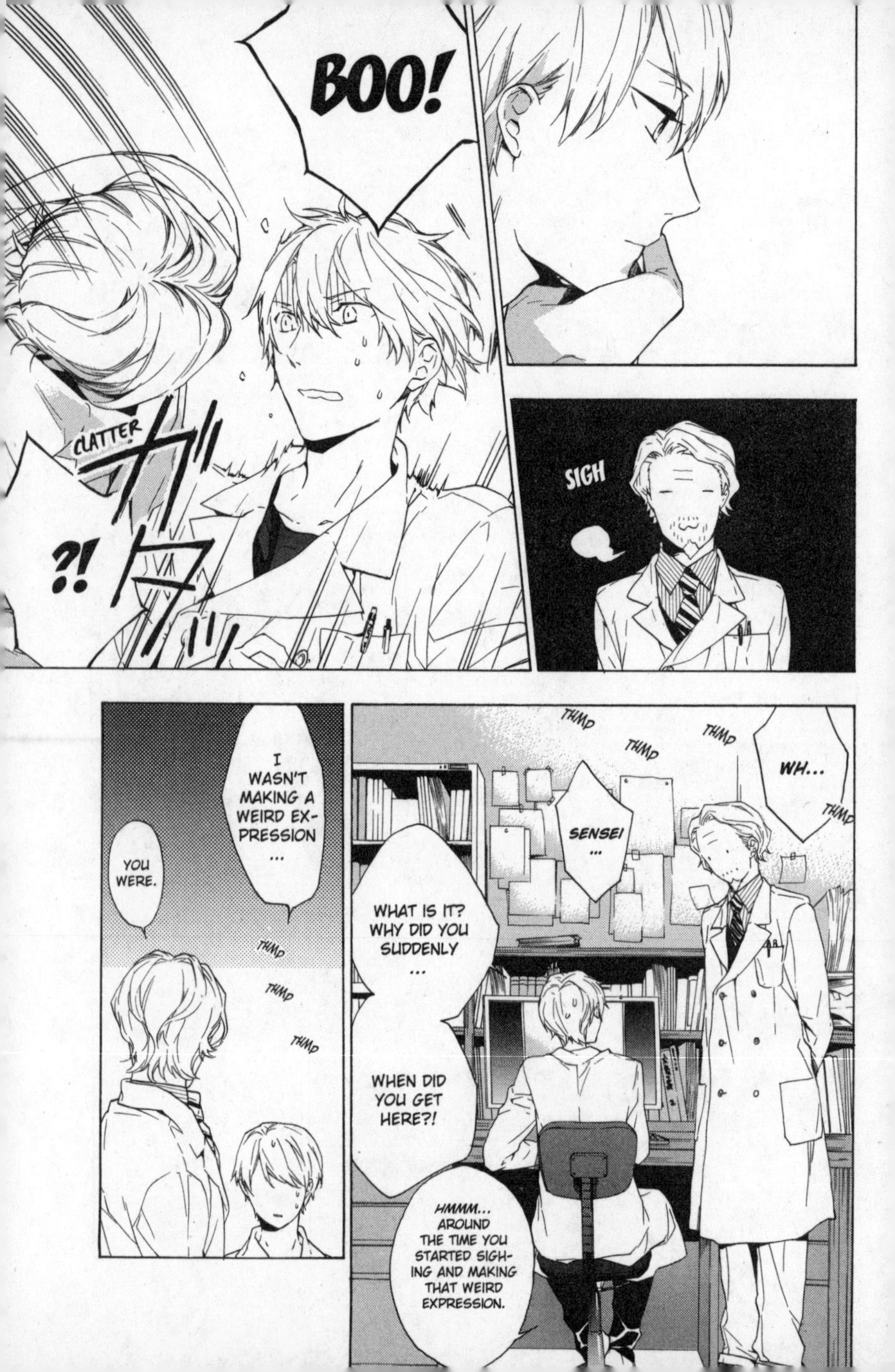
SIGH
BOO!
CLATTER
?!
THMP
THMP
THMP
WH...
THMP
SENSEI...
WHAT IS IT? WHY DID YOU SUDDENLY...
WHEN DID YOU GET HERE?!
HMMM... AROUND THE TIME YOU STARTED SIGHING AND MAKING THAT WEIRD EXPRESSION.
I WASN'T MAKING A WEIRD EXPRESSION...
YOU WERE.
THMP
THMP
THMP

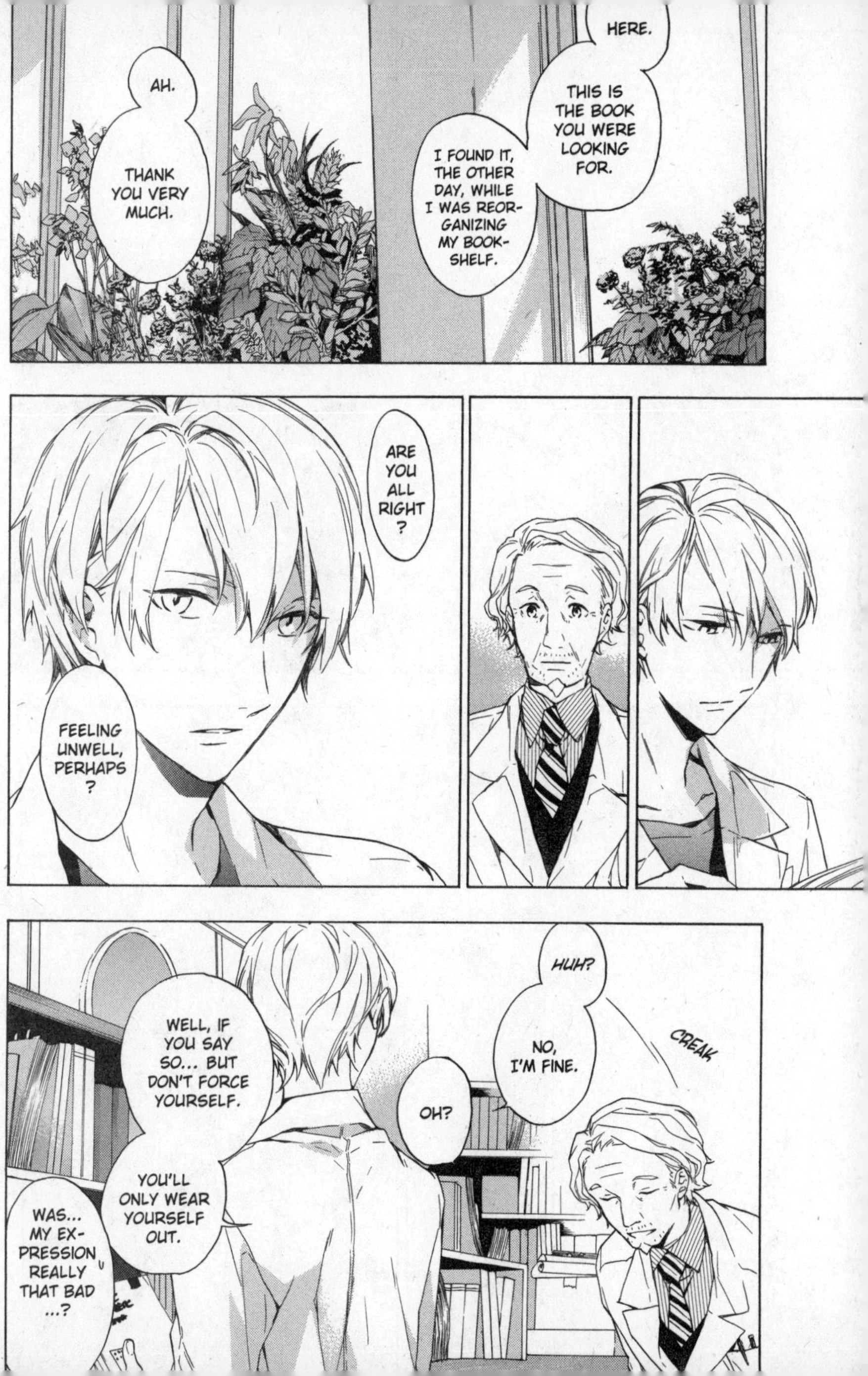
HERE.
THIS IS THE BOOK YOU WERE LOOKING FOR.
I FOUND IT, THE OTHER DAY, WHILE I WAS REORGANIZING MY BOOKSHELF.
AH.
THANK YOU VERY MUCH.
ARE YOU ALL RIGHT?
FEELING UNWELL, PERHAPS?
HUH?
CREAK
NO, I'M FINE.
OH?
WELL, IF YOU SAY SO... BUT DON'T FORCE YOURSELF.
YOU'LL ONLY WEAR YOURSELF OUT.
WAS... MY EXPRESSION REALLY THAT BAD...?

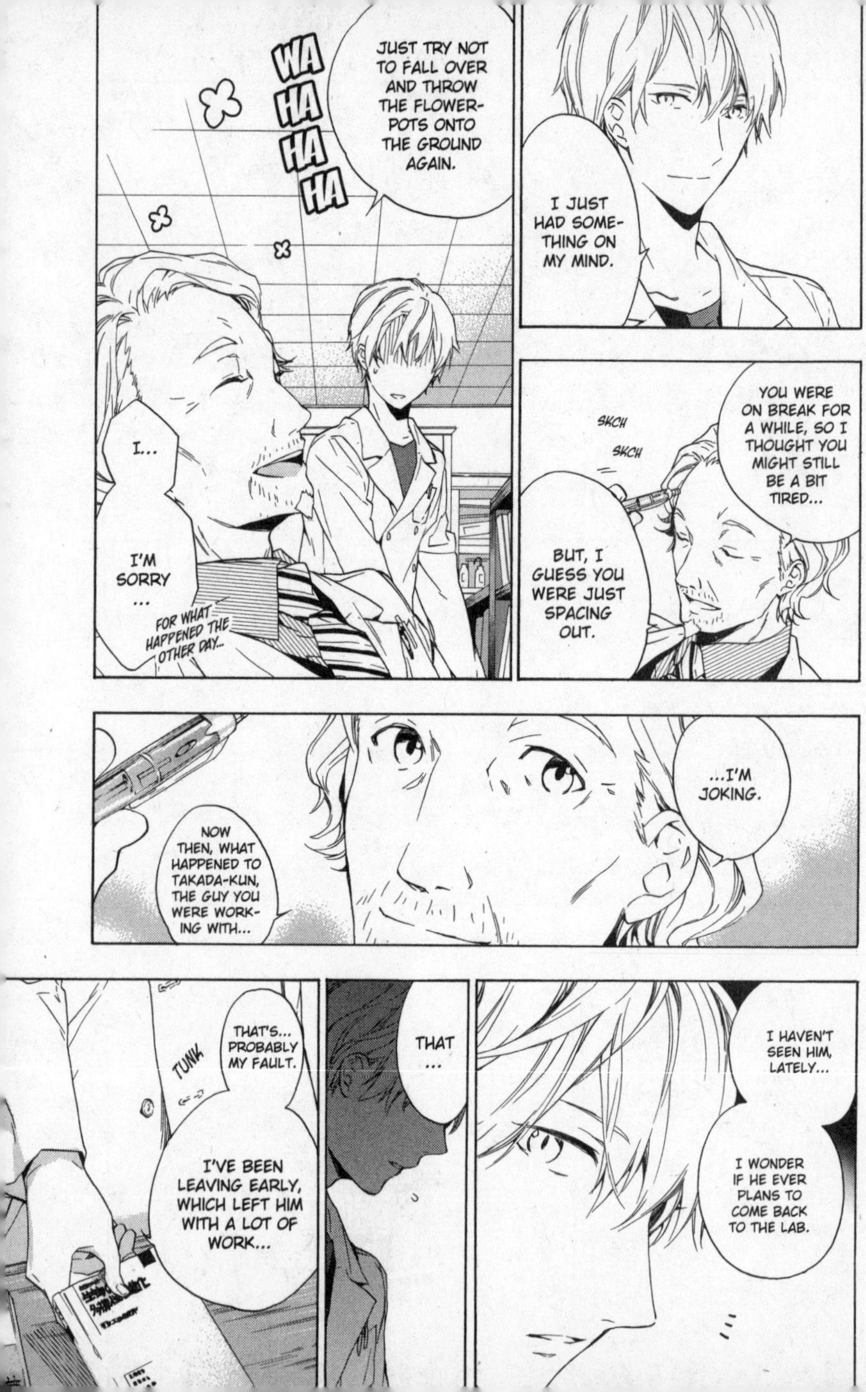
I JUST HAD SOMETHING ON MY MIND.
YOU WERE ON BREAK FOR A WHILE, SO I THOUGHT YOU MIGHT STILL BE A BIT TIRED...
SKCH
SKCH
BUT, I GUESS YOU WERE JUST SPACING OUT.
JUST TRY NOT TO FALL OVER AND THROW THE FLOWER-POTS ONTO THE GROUND AGAIN.
WA HA HA HA
I...
I'M SORRY ...
FOR WHAT HAPPENED THE OTHER DAY...
...I'M JOKING.
NOW THEN, WHAT HAPPENED TO TAKADA-KUN, THE GUY YOU WERE WORKING WITH...
I HAVEN'T SEEN HIM, LATELY...
I WONDER IF HE EVER PLANS TO COME BACK TO THE LAB.
THAT ...
THAT'S... PROBABLY MY FAULT.
TUNK
I'VE BEEN LEAVING EARLY, WHICH LEFT HIM WITH A LOT OF WORK...

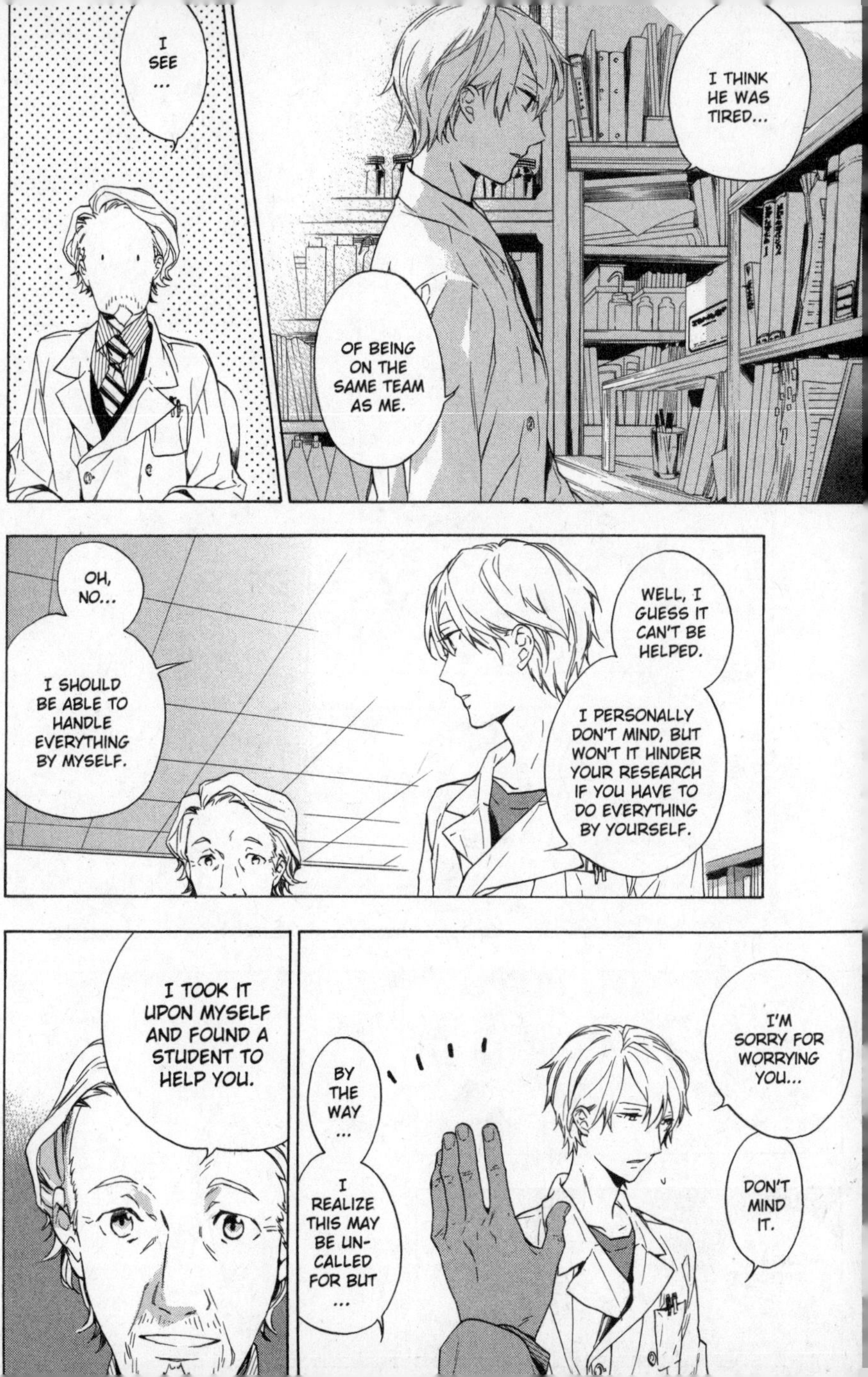
I THINK HE WAS TIRED...
OF BEING ON THE SAME TEAM AS ME.
I SEE ...
WELL, I GUESS IT CAN'T BE HELPED.
I PERSONALLY DON'T MIND, BUT WON'T IT HINDER YOUR RESEARCH IF YOU HAVE TO DO EVERYTHING BY YOURSELF.
OH, NO...
I SHOULD BE ABLE TO HANDLE EVERYTHING BY MYSELF.
I'M SORRY FOR WORRYING YOU...
DON'T MIND IT.
BY THE WAY ...
I REALIZE THIS MAY BE UN-CALLED FOR BUT ...
I TOOK IT UPON MYSELF AND FOUND A STUDENT TO HELP YOU.

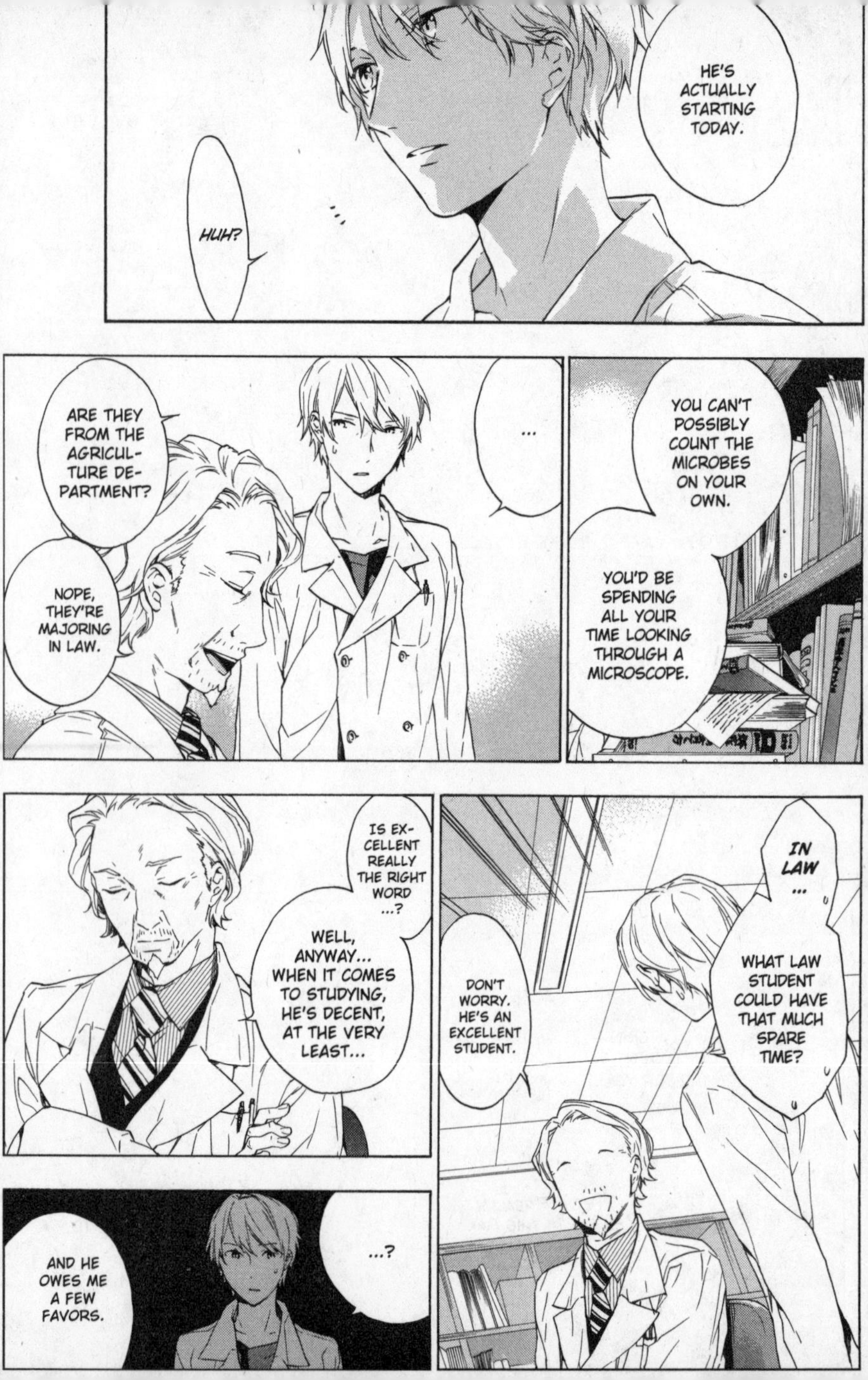

HE'S ACTUALLY STARTING TODAY.
HUH?
YOU CAN'T POSSIBLY COUNT THE MICROBES ON YOUR OWN.
YOU'D BE SPENDING ALL YOUR TIME LOOKING THROUGH A MICROSCOPE.
...
ARE THEY FROM THE AGRICUL-TURE DE-PARTMENT?
NOPE, THEY'RE MAJORING IN LAW.
IN LAW ...
WHAT LAW STUDENT COULD HAVE THAT MUCH SPARE TIME?
DON'T WORRY. HE'S AN EXCELLENT STUDENT.
IS EX-CELLENT REALLY THE RIGHT WORD ...?
WELL, ANYWAY... WHEN IT COMES TO STUDYING, HE'S DECENT, AT THE VERY LEAST...
...?
AND HE OWES ME A FEW FAVORS.

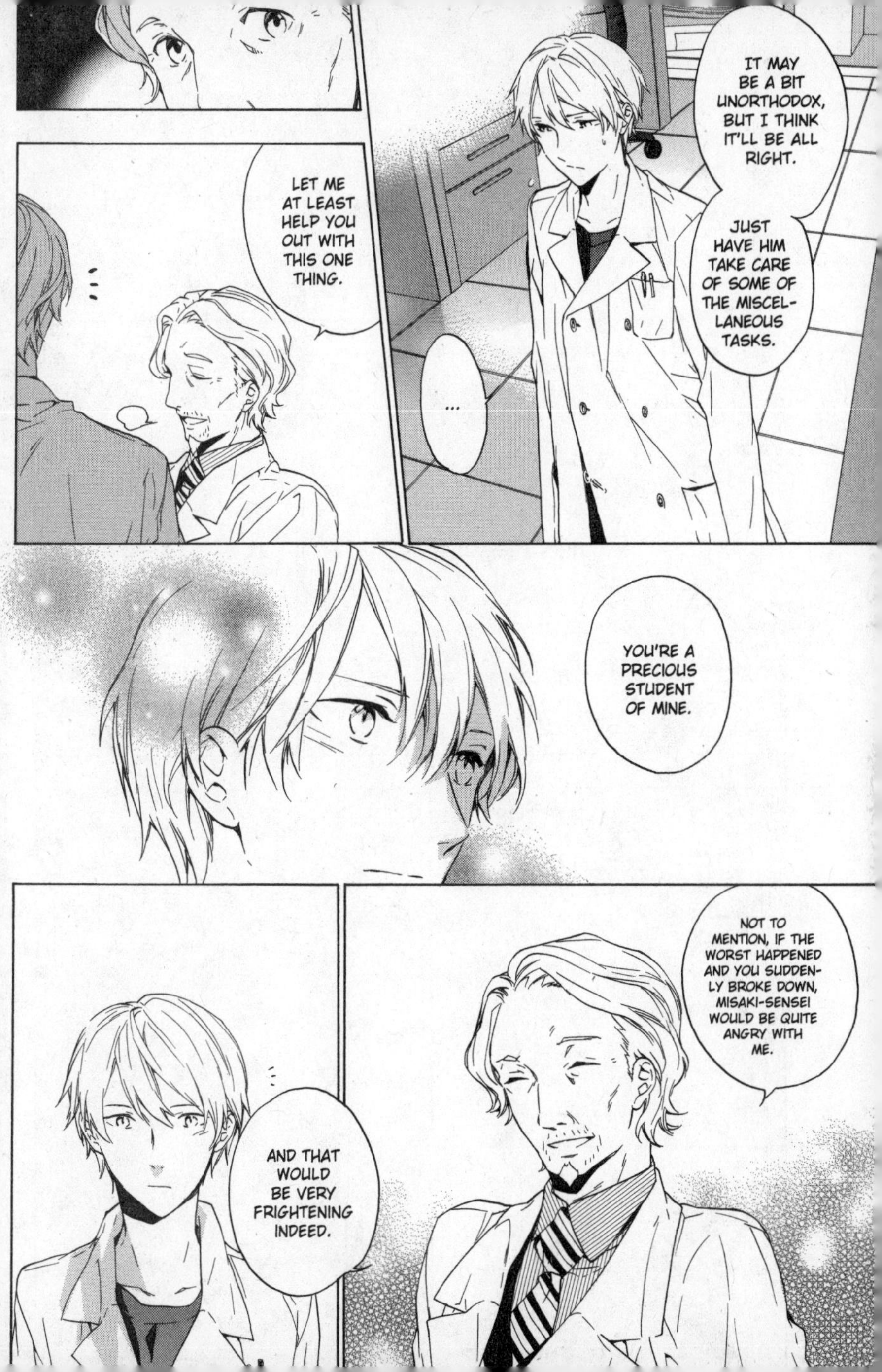
IT MAY BE A BIT UNORTHODOX, BUT I THINK IT'LL BE ALL RIGHT.
JUST HAVE HIM TAKE CARE OF SOME OF THE MISCEL-LANEOUS TASKS.
...
LET ME AT LEAST HELP YOU OUT WITH THIS ONE THING.
...
YOU'RE A PRECIOUS STUDENT OF MINE.
NOT TO MENTION, IF THE WORST HAPPENED AND YOU SUDDEN-LY BROKE DOWN, MISAKI-SENSEI WOULD BE QUITE ANGRY WITH ME.
...
AND THAT WOULD BE VERY FRIGHTENING INDEED.

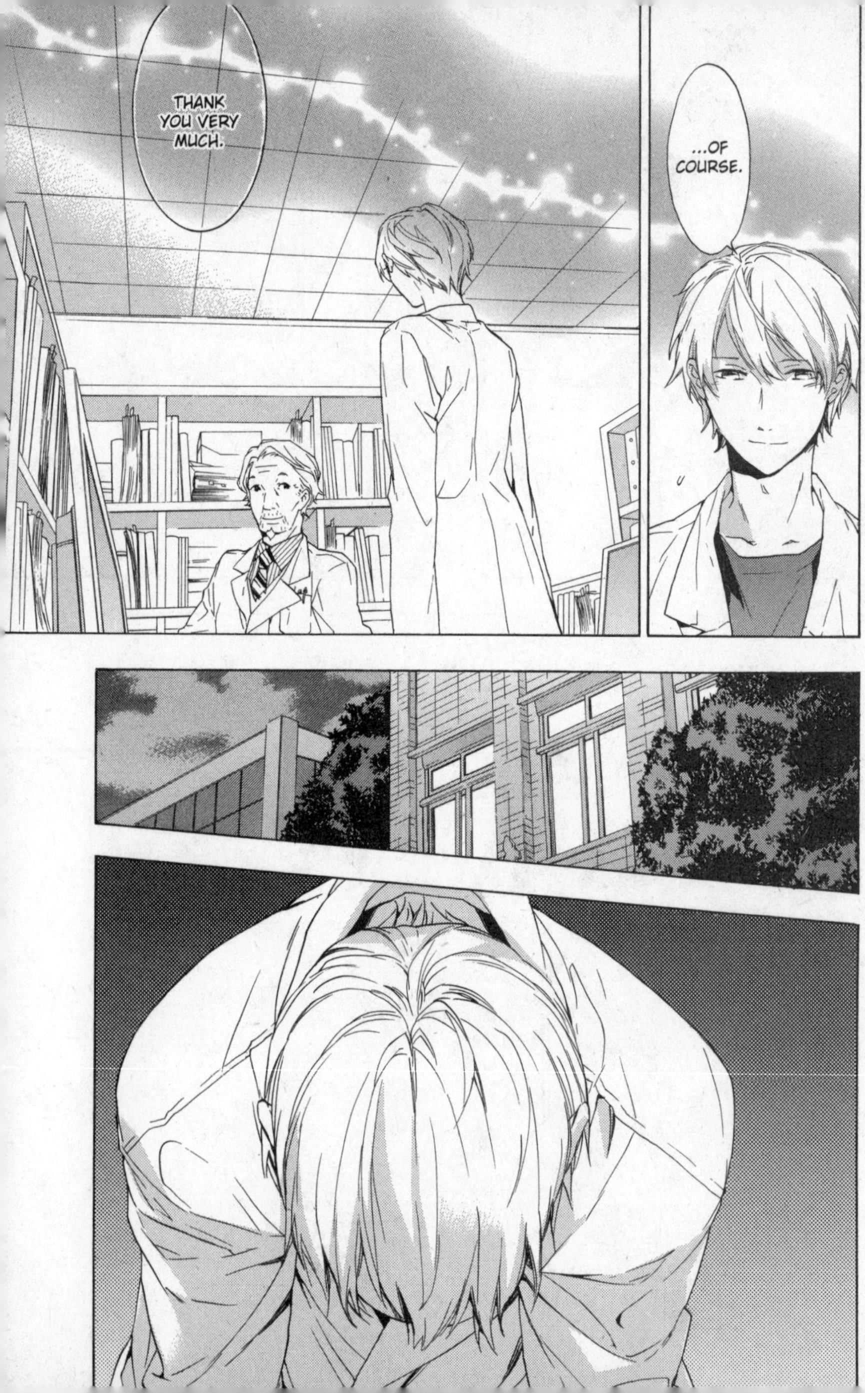
...OF COURSE.
THANK YOU VERY MUCH.

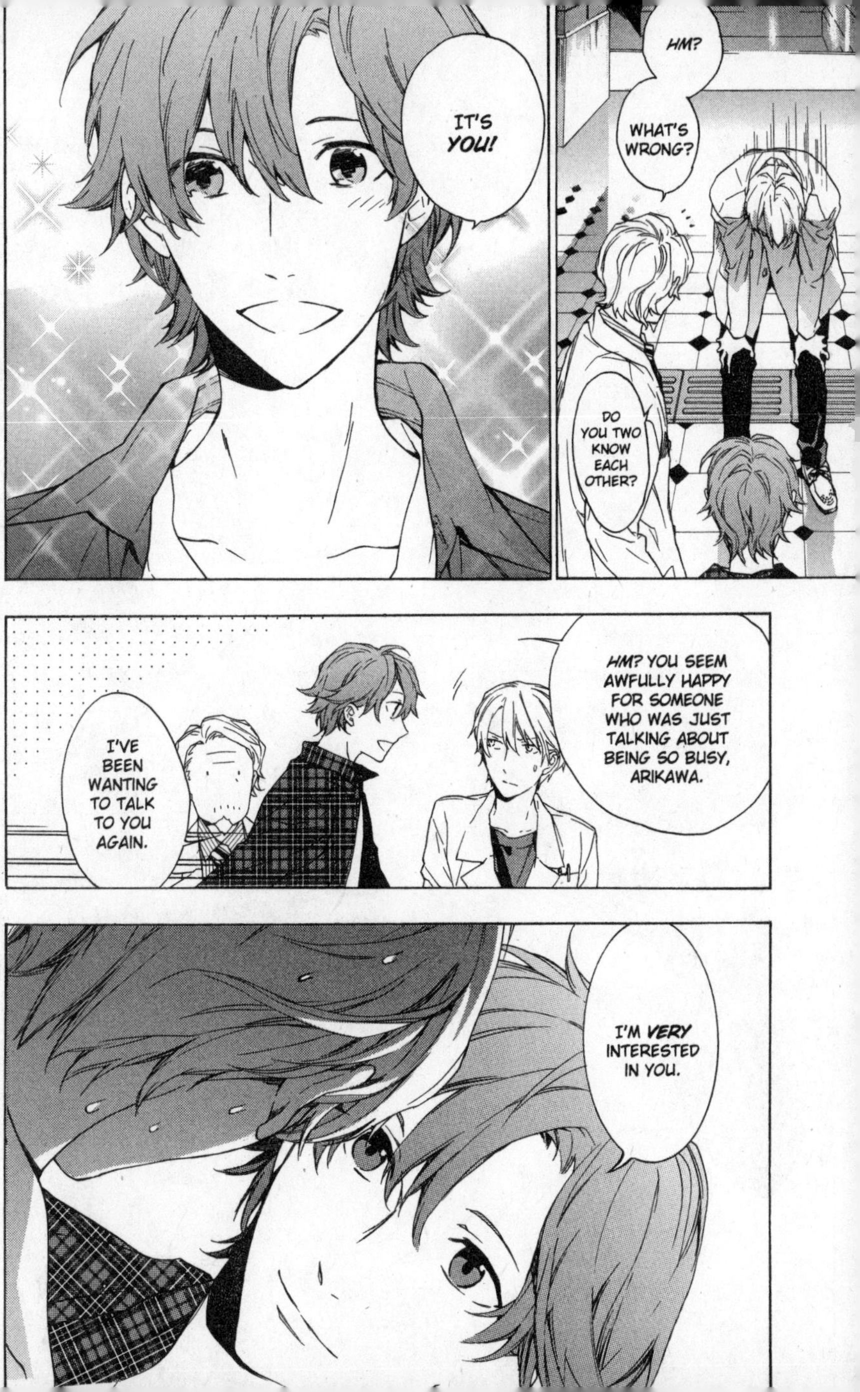

HM?
WHAT'S WRONG?
DO YOU TWO KNOW EACH OTHER?
IT'S *YOU!*
HM? YOU SEEM AWFULLY HAPPY FOR SOMEONE WHO WAS JUST TALKING ABOUT BEING SO BUSY, ARIKAWA.
I'VE BEEN WANTING TO TALK TO YOU AGAIN.
I'M *VERY* INTERESTED IN YOU.

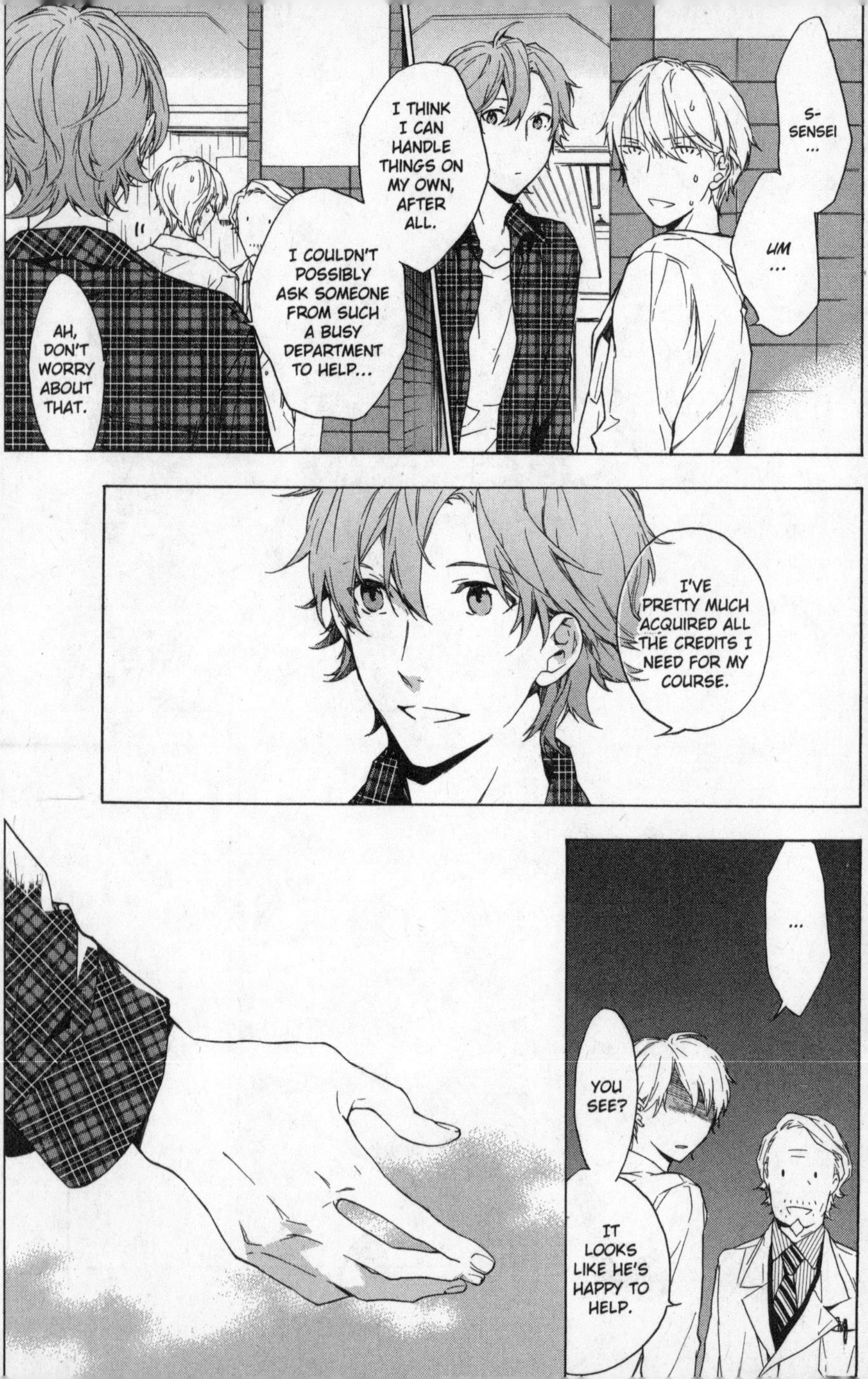
S-SENSEI ...
UM ...
I THINK I CAN HANDLE THINGS ON MY OWN, AFTER ALL.
I COULDN'T POSSIBLY ASK SOMEONE FROM SUCH A BUSY DEPARTMENT TO HELP...
AH, DON'T WORRY ABOUT THAT.
I'VE PRETTY MUCH ACQUIRED ALL THE CREDITS I NEED FOR MY COURSE.
...
YOU SEE?
IT LOOKS LIKE HE'S HAPPY TO HELP.

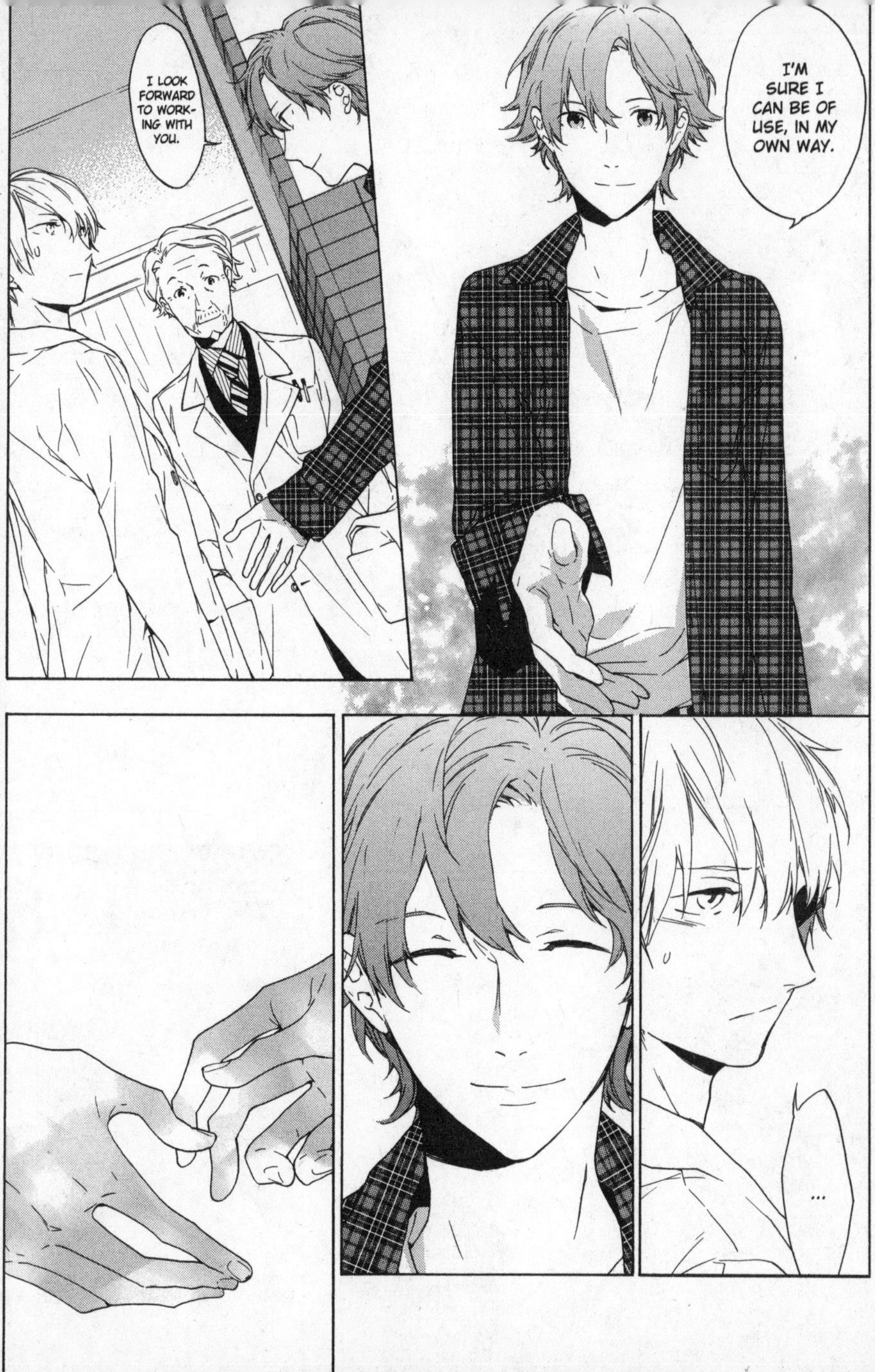
I'M SURE I CAN BE OF USE, IN MY OWN WAY.
I LOOK FORWARD TO WORKING WITH YOU.
...

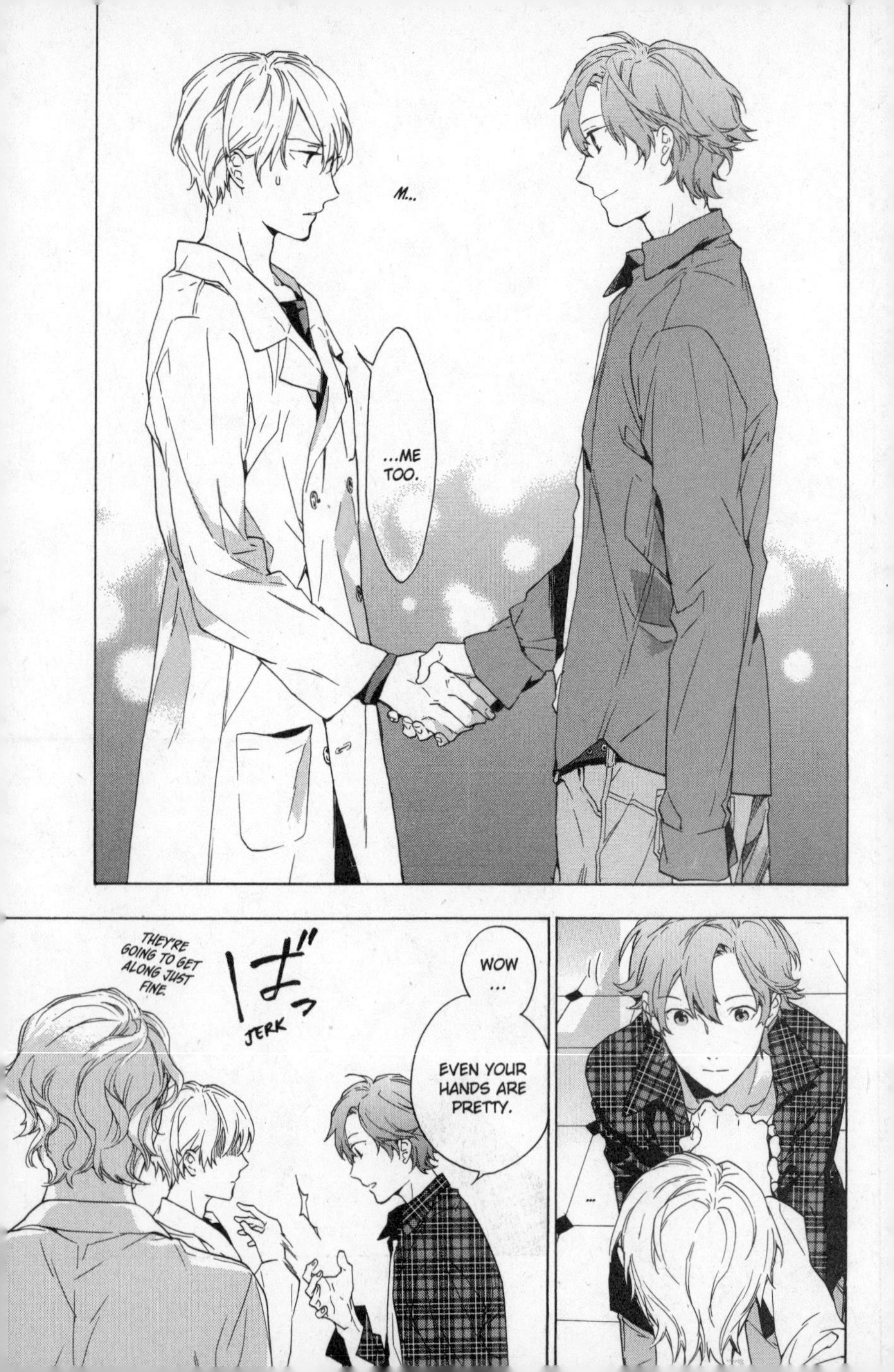
M...
...ME TOO.
...
WOW ...
EVEN YOUR HANDS ARE PRETTY.
ばっ
JERK
THEY'RE GOING TO GET ALONG JUST FINE.

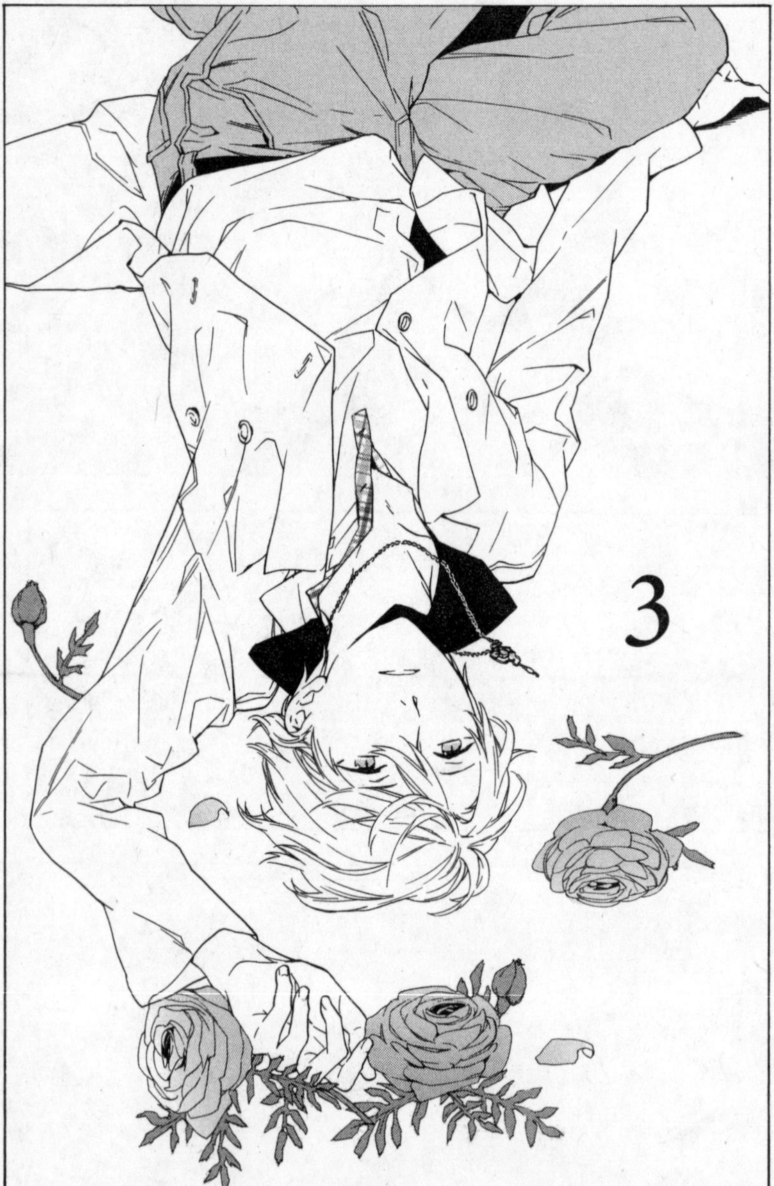
3

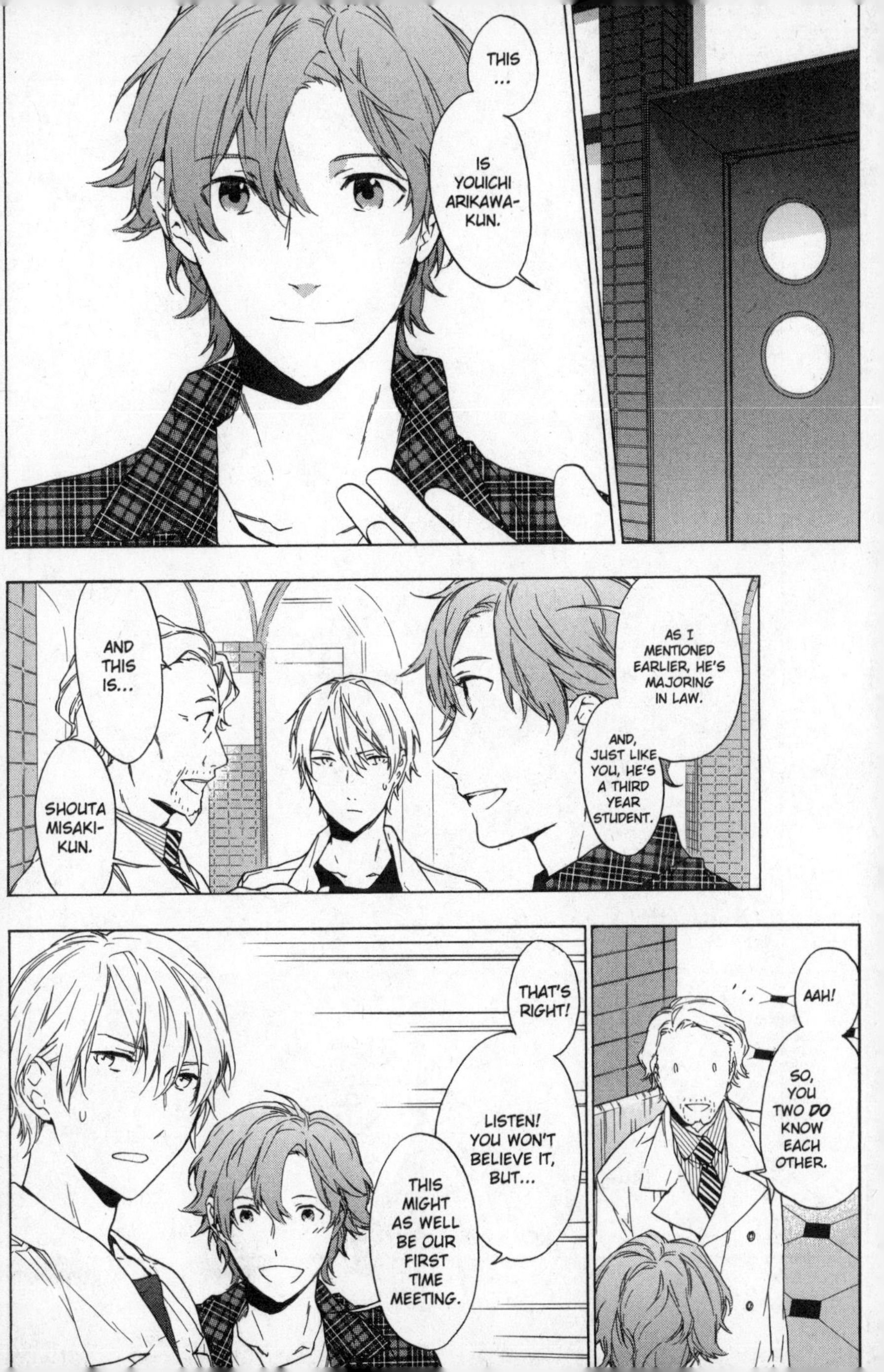
THIS ...
IS YOUICHI ARIKAWA-KUN.
AS I MENTIONED EARLIER, HE'S MAJORING IN LAW.
AND, JUST LIKE YOU, HE'S A THIRD YEAR STUDENT.
AND THIS IS...
SHOUTA MISAKI-KUN.
AAH!
SO, YOU TWO *DO* KNOW EACH OTHER.
THAT'S RIGHT!
LISTEN! YOU WON'T BELIEVE IT, BUT...
THIS MIGHT AS WELL BE OUR FIRST TIME MEETING.

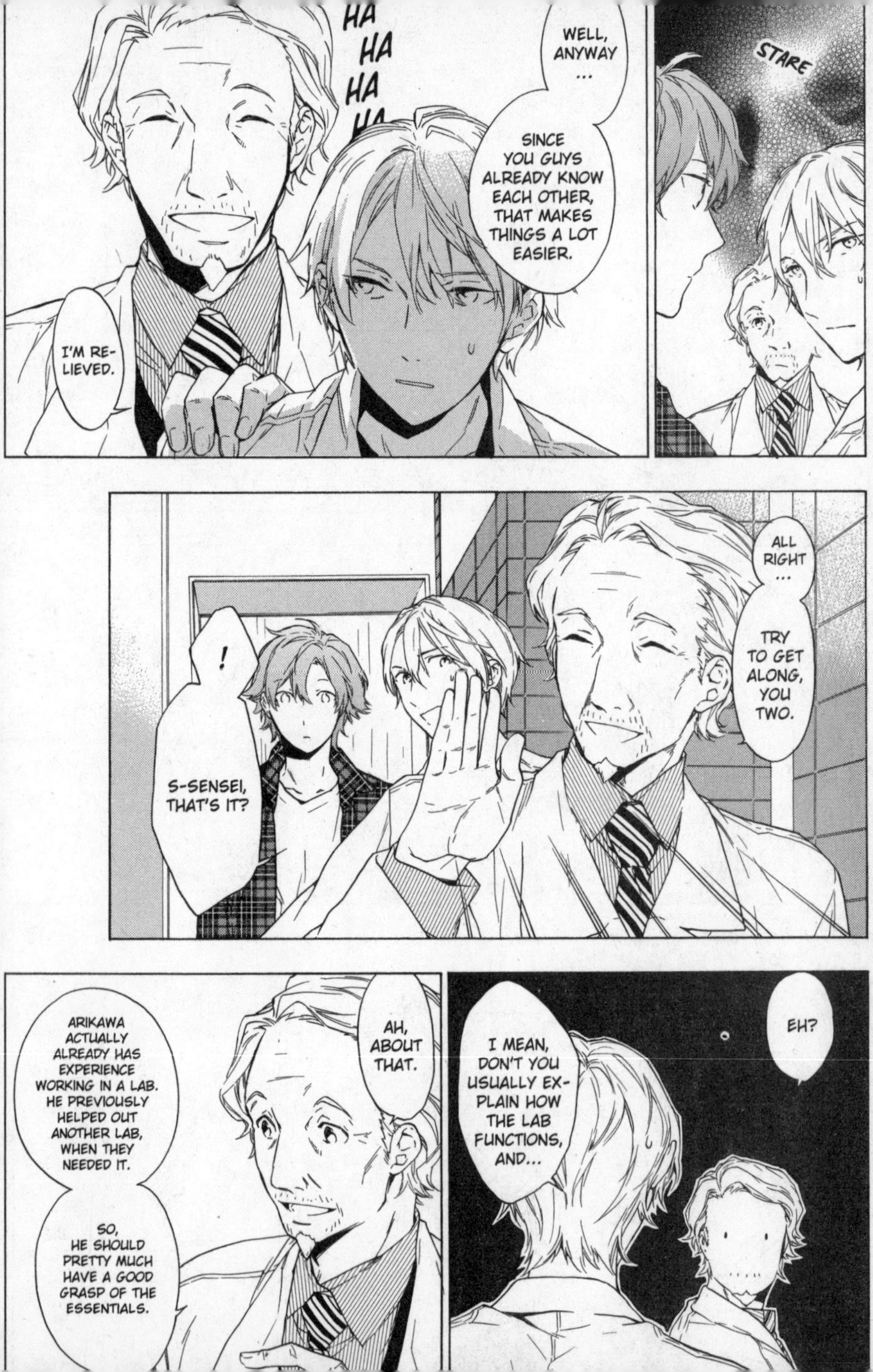
STARE
WELL, ANYWAY ...
SINCE YOU GUYS ALREADY KNOW EACH OTHER, THAT MAKES THINGS A LOT EASIER.
HA HA HA HA
I'M RE-LIEVED.
ALL RIGHT ...
TRY TO GET ALONG, YOU TWO.
!
S-SENSEI, THAT'S IT?
EH?
I MEAN, DON'T YOU USUALLY EX-PLAIN HOW THE LAB FUNCTIONS, AND...
AH, ABOUT THAT.
ARIKAWA ACTUALLY ALREADY HAS EXPERIENCE WORKING IN A LAB. HE PREVIOUSLY HELPED OUT ANOTHER LAB, WHEN THEY NEEDED IT.
SO, HE SHOULD PRETTY MUCH HAVE A GOOD GRASP OF THE ESSENTIALS.

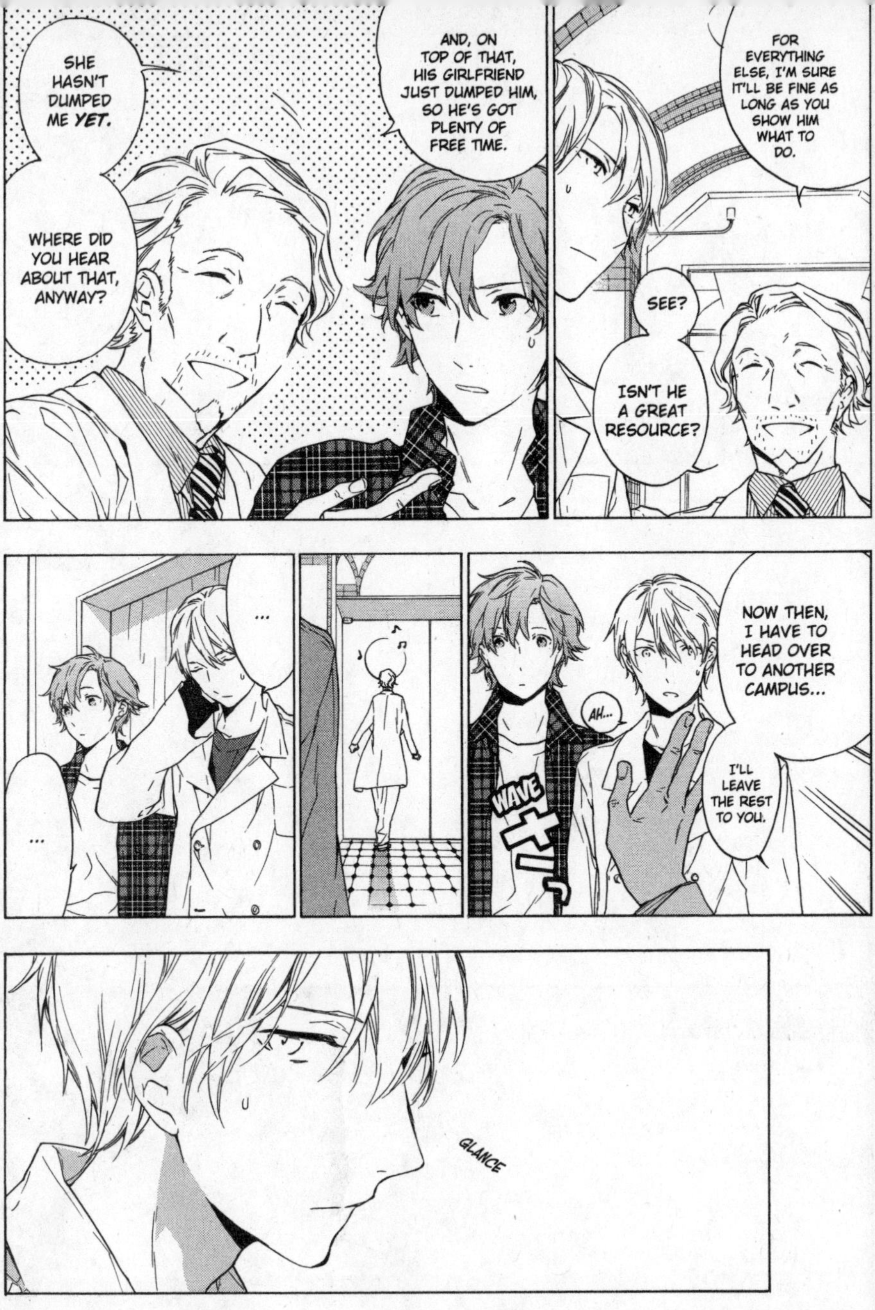
FOR EVERYTHING ELSE, I'M SURE IT'LL BE FINE AS LONG AS YOU SHOW HIM WHAT TO DO.
SEE?
ISN'T HE A GREAT RESOURCE?
AND, ON TOP OF THAT, HIS GIRLFRIEND JUST DUMPED HIM, SO HE'S GOT PLENTY OF FREE TIME.
SHE HASN'T DUMPED ME *YET*.
WHERE DID YOU HEAR ABOUT THAT, ANYWAY?
NOW THEN, I HAVE TO HEAD OVER TO ANOTHER CAMPUS...
AH...
I'LL LEAVE THE REST TO YOU.
WAVE
...
...
GLANCE

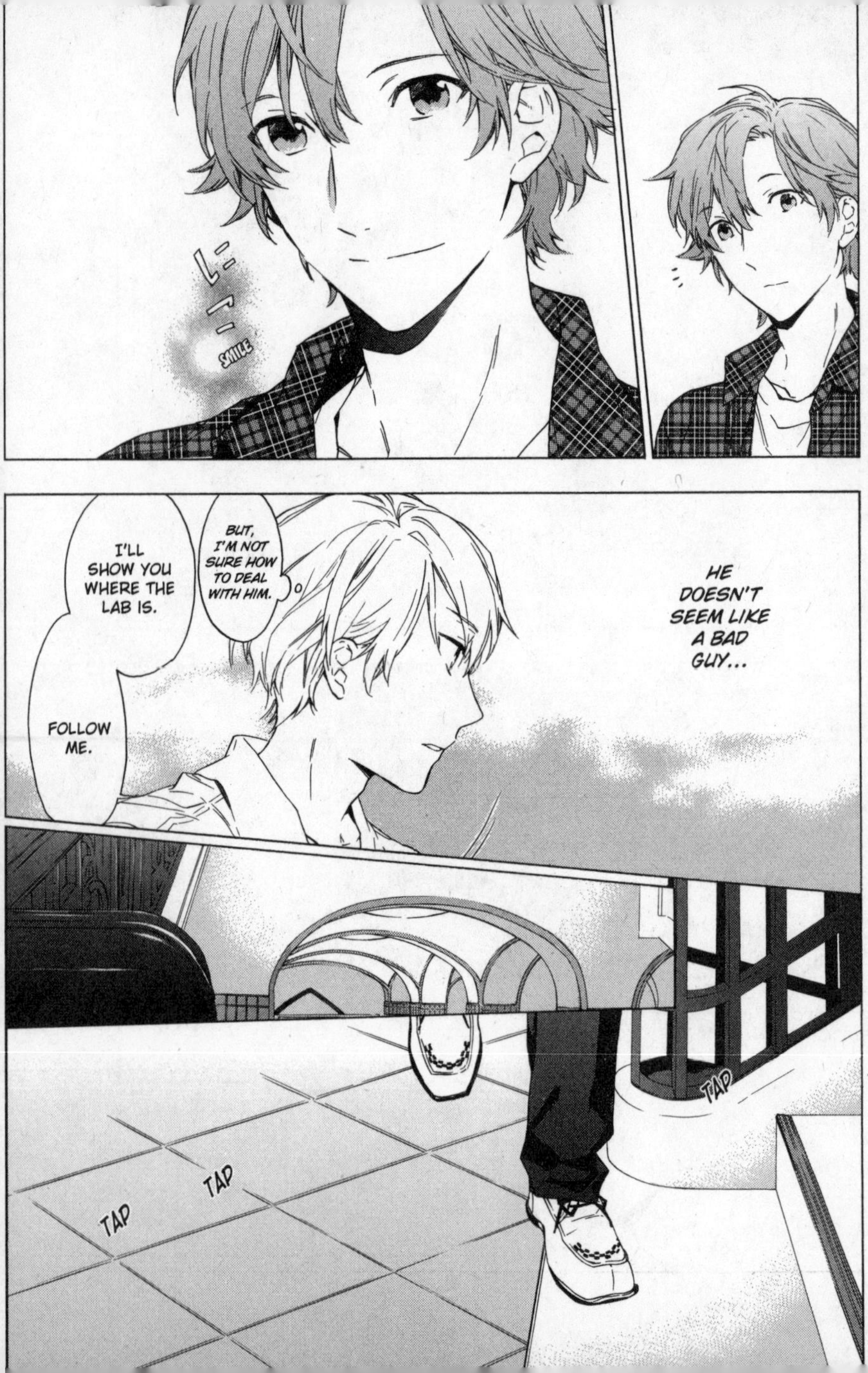
SMILE
HE DOESN'T SEEM LIKE A BAD GUY...
BUT, I'M NOT SURE HOW TO DEAL WITH HIM.
I'LL SHOW YOU WHERE THE LAB IS.
FOLLOW ME.
TAP
TAP
TAP

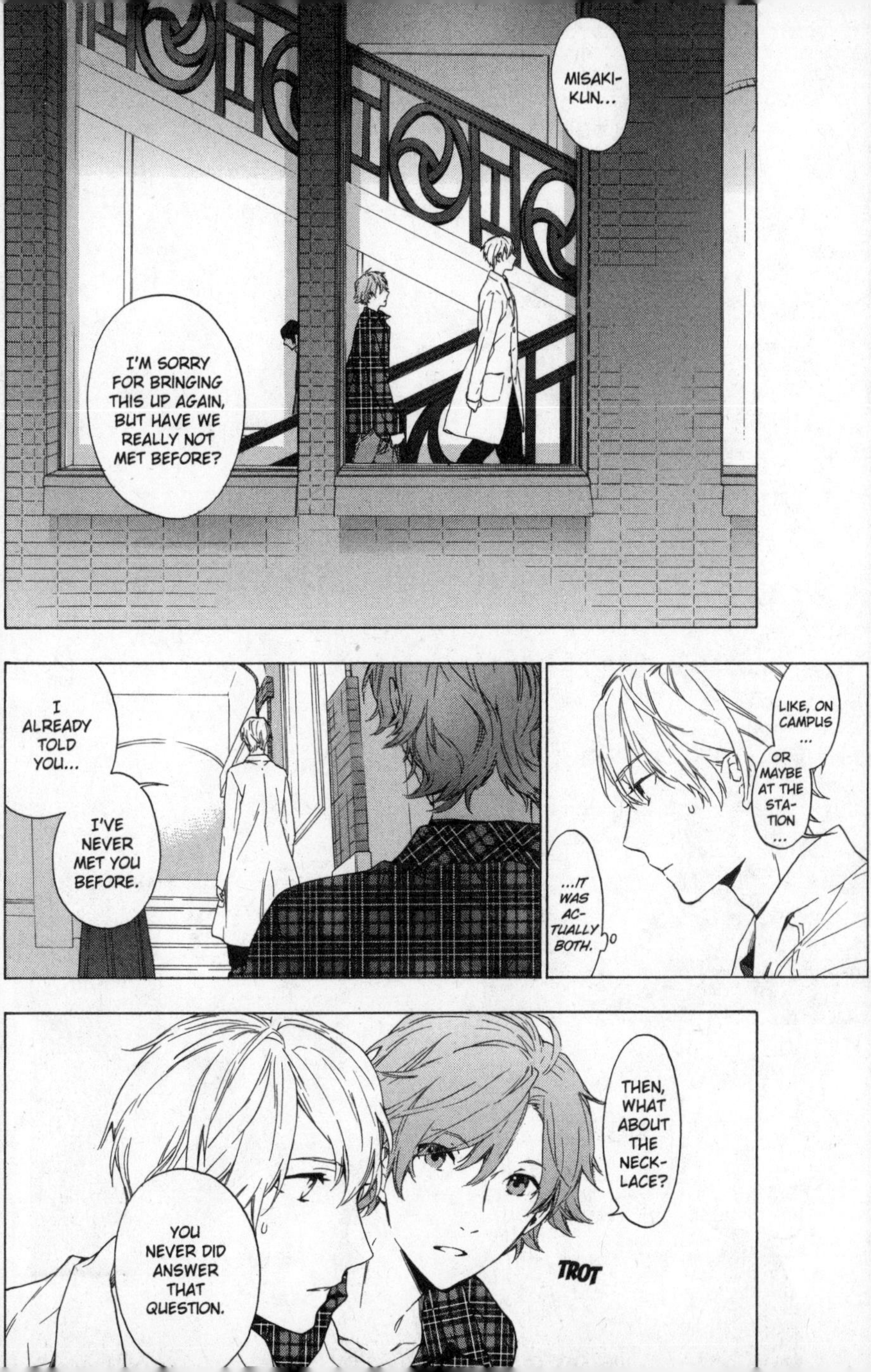
MISAKI-KUN...
I'M SORRY FOR BRINGING THIS UP AGAIN, BUT HAVE WE REALLY NOT MET BEFORE?
LIKE, ON CAMPUS...
OR MAYBE AT THE STATION...
...IT WAS ACTUALLY BOTH.
I ALREADY TOLD YOU...
I'VE NEVER MET YOU BEFORE.
THEN, WHAT ABOUT THE NECKLACE?
TROT
YOU NEVER DID ANSWER THAT QUESTION.

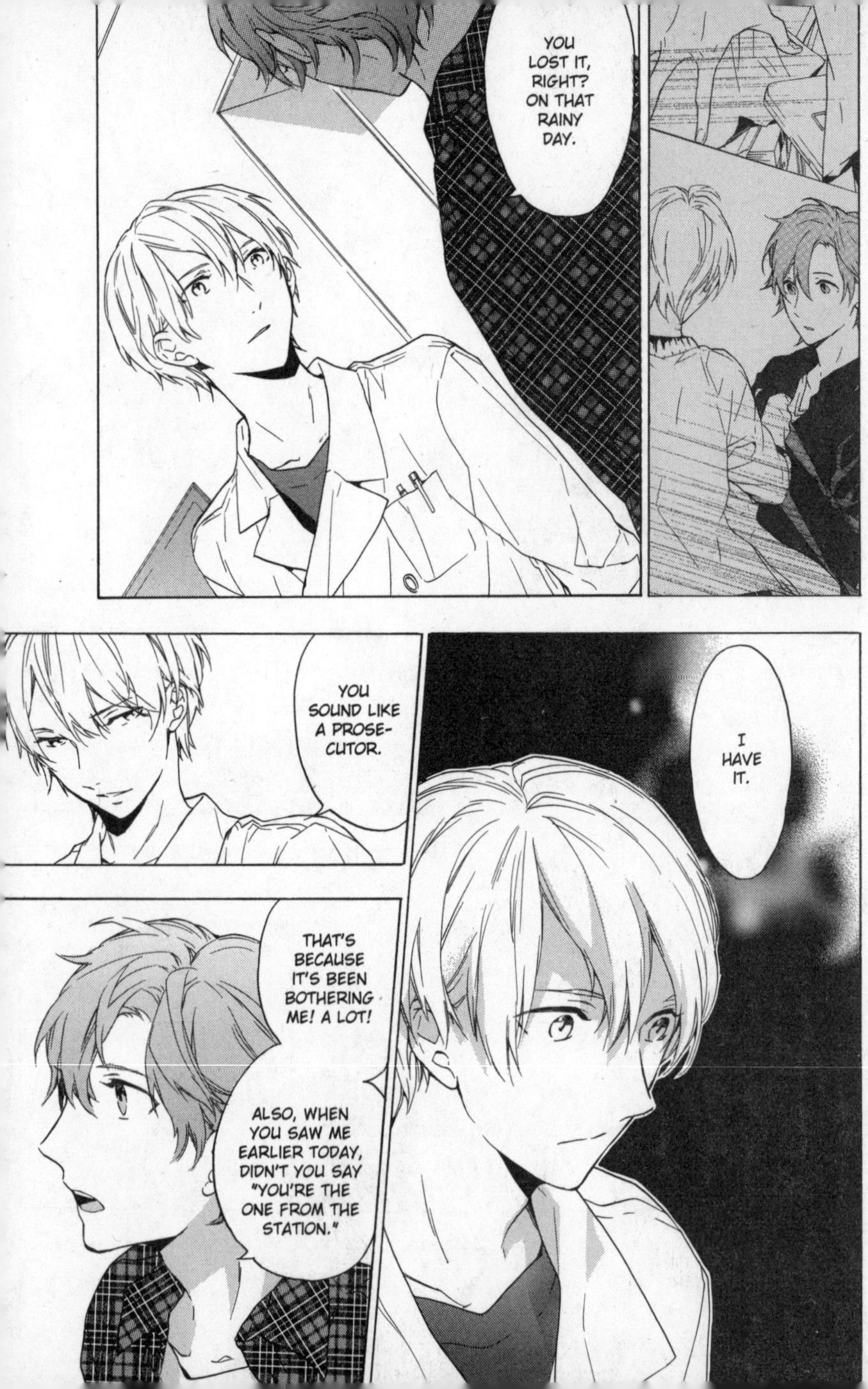
YOU LOST IT, RIGHT? ON THAT RAINY DAY.
I HAVE IT.
YOU SOUND LIKE A PROSE-CUTOR.
THAT'S BECAUSE IT'S BEEN BOTHERING ME! A LOT!
ALSO, WHEN YOU SAW ME EARLIER TODAY, DIDN'T YOU SAY "YOU'RE THE ONE FROM THE STATION."

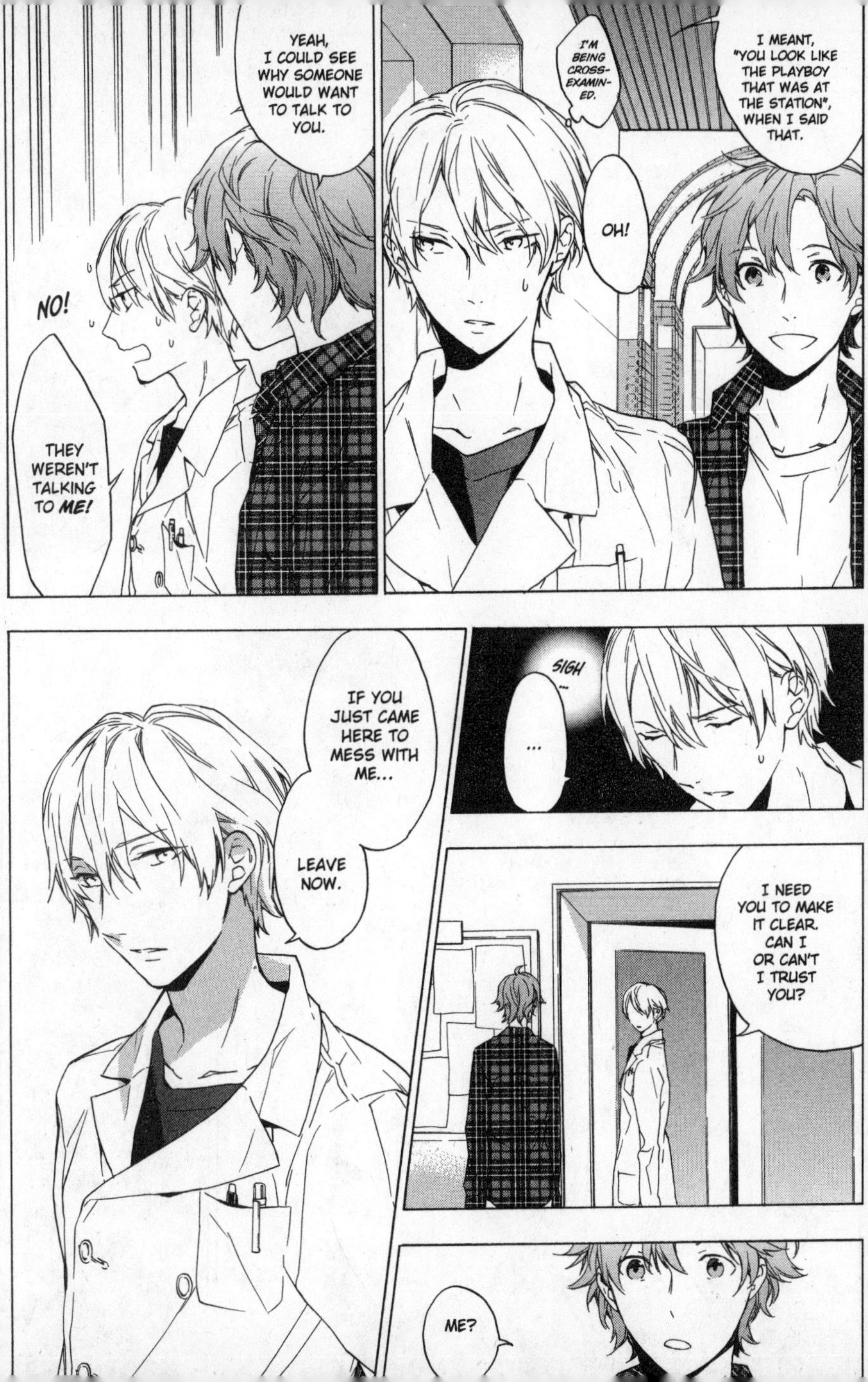
I MEANT, "YOU LOOK LIKE THE PLAYBOY THAT WAS AT THE STATION", WHEN I SAID THAT.
I'M BEING CROSS-EXAMINED.
OH!
YEAH, I COULD SEE WHY SOMEONE WOULD WANT TO TALK TO YOU.
NO!
THEY WEREN'T TALKING TO ME!
SIGH...
...
I NEED YOU TO MAKE IT CLEAR. CAN I OR CAN'T I TRUST YOU?
ME?
IF YOU JUST CAME HERE TO MESS WITH ME...
LEAVE NOW.

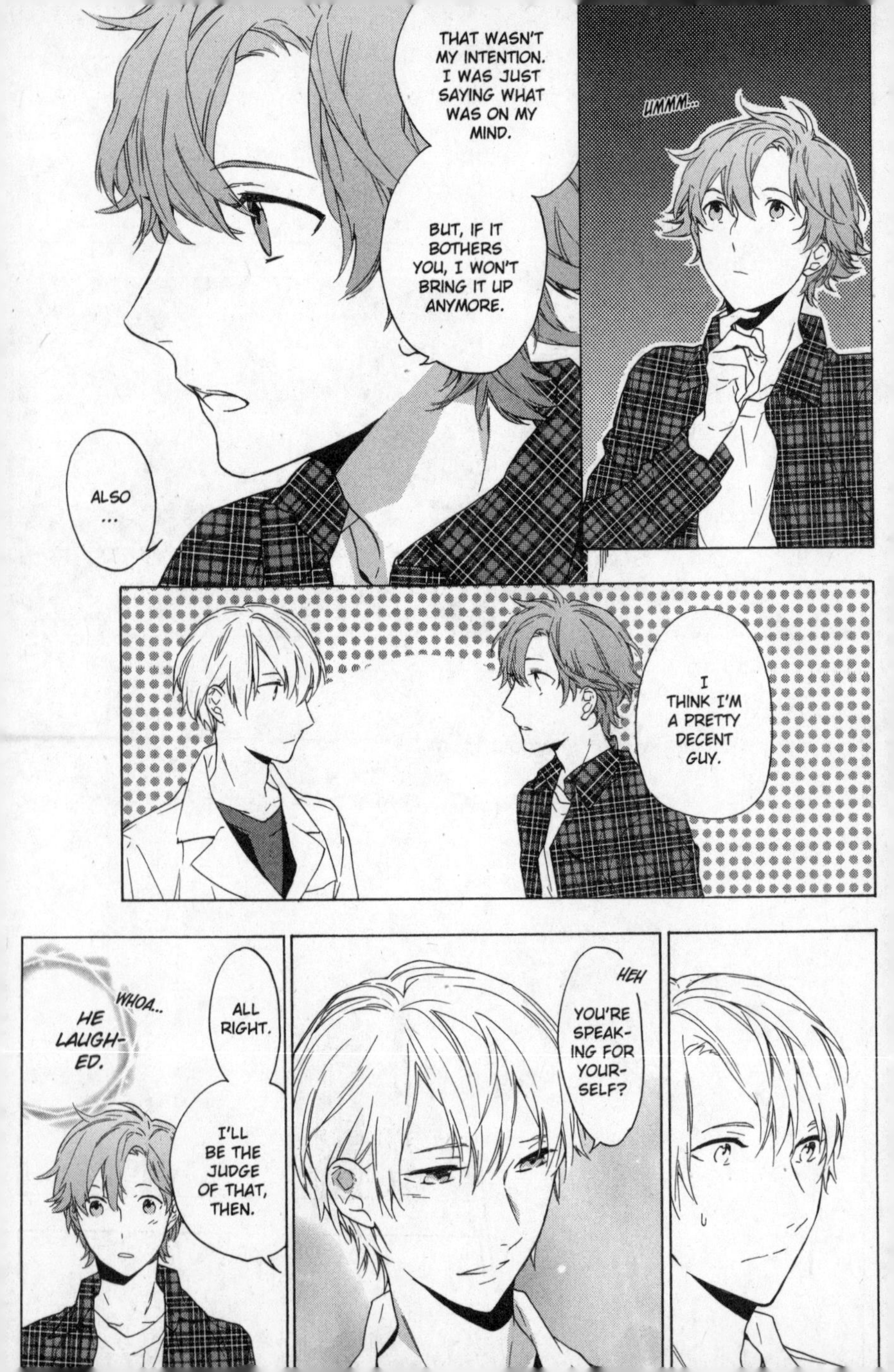
UMMM...
THAT WASN'T MY INTENTION. I WAS JUST SAYING WHAT WAS ON MY MIND.
BUT, IF IT BOTHERS YOU, I WON'T BRING IT UP ANYMORE.
ALSO ...
I THINK I'M A PRETTY DECENT GUY.
HEH
YOU'RE SPEAK-ING FOR YOUR-SELF?
ALL RIGHT.
I'LL BE THE JUDGE OF THAT, THEN.
WHOA...
HE LAUGH-ED.

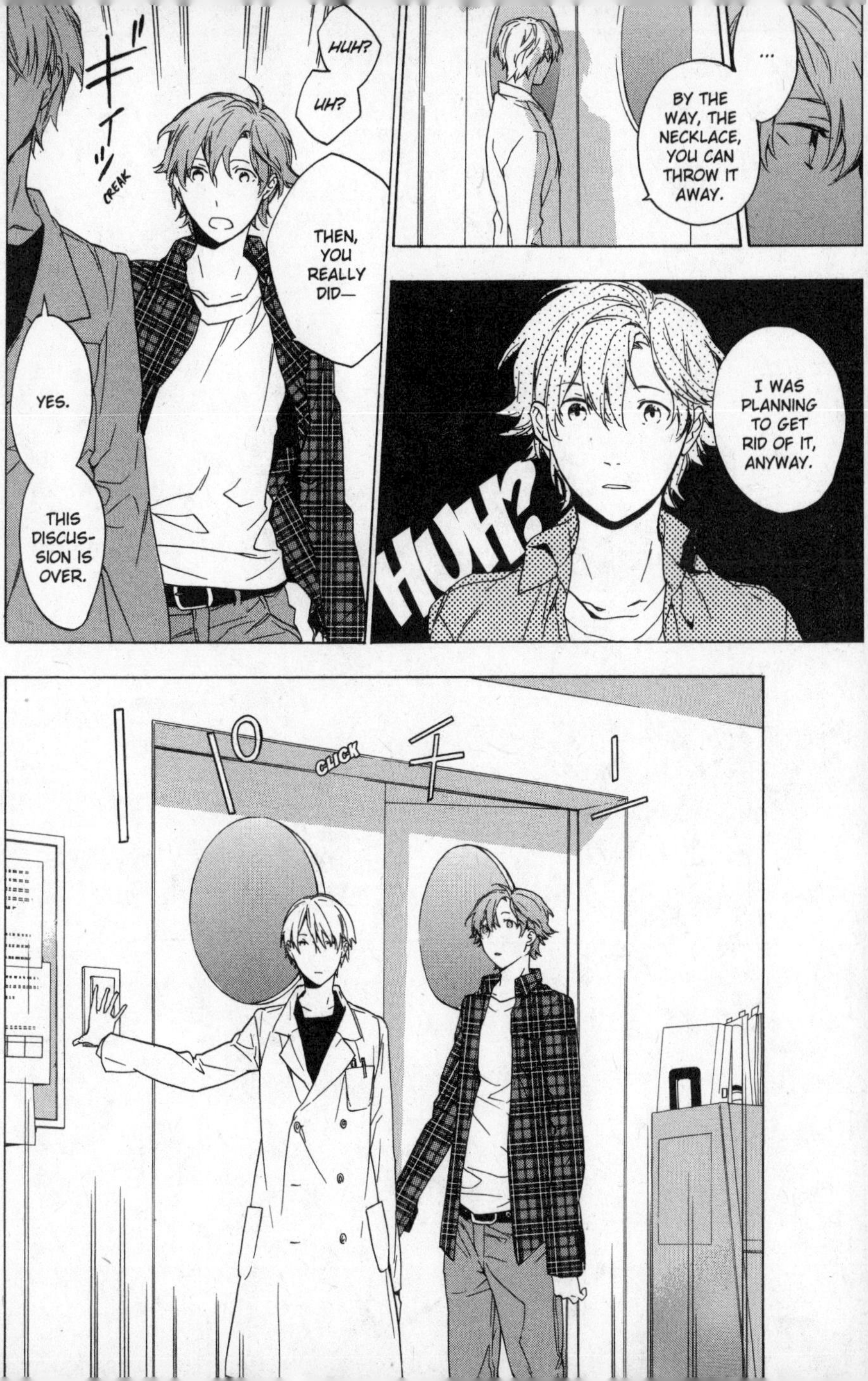
...
BY THE WAY, THE NECKLACE, YOU CAN THROW IT AWAY.
I WAS PLANNING TO GET RID OF IT, ANYWAY.
HUH?
CREAK
HUH?
UH?
THEN, YOU REALLY DID—
YES.
THIS DISCUSSION IS OVER.
CLICK

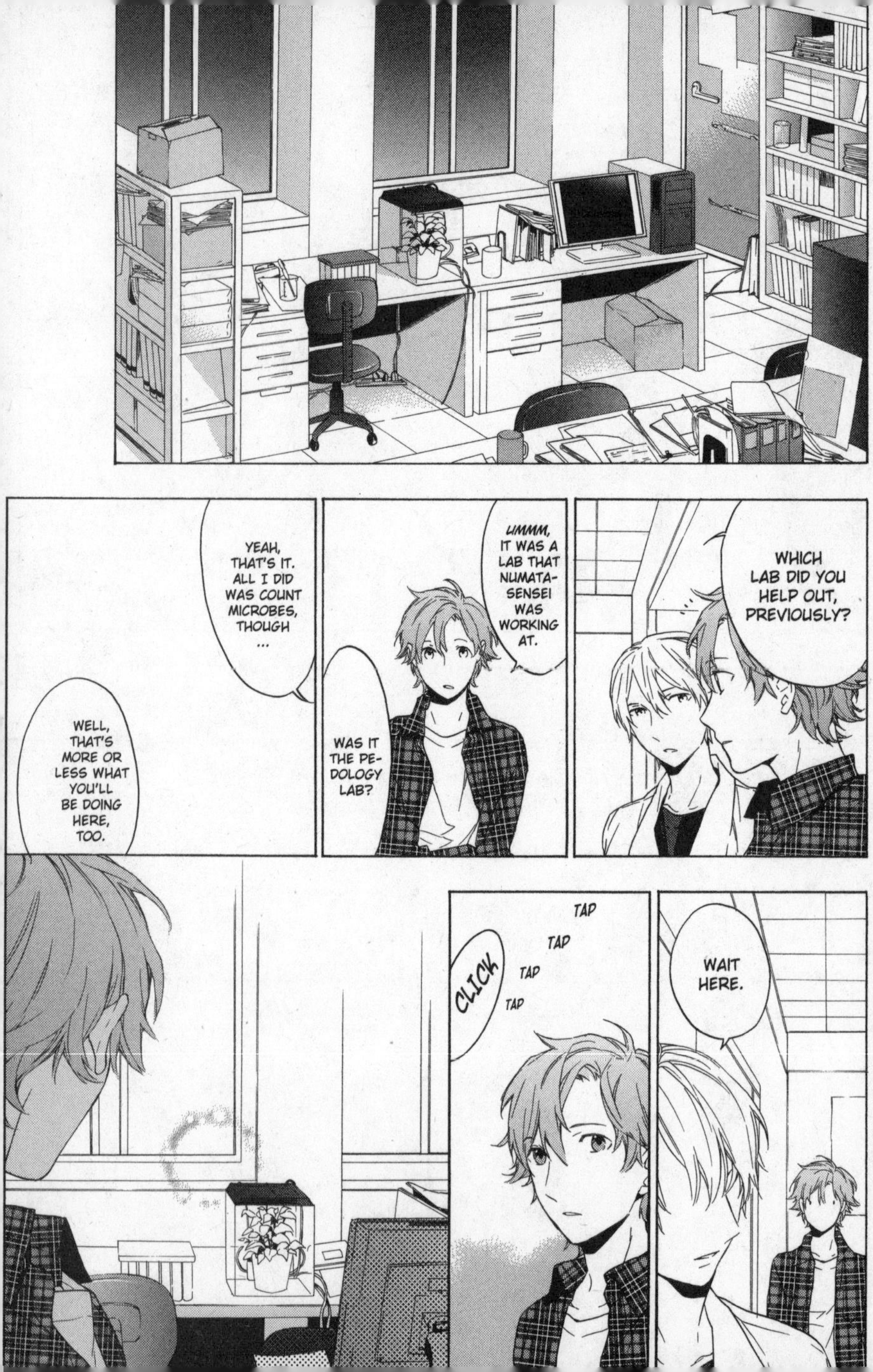
WHICH LAB DID YOU HELP OUT, PREVIOUSLY?
UMMM, IT WAS A LAB THAT NUMATA-SENSEI WAS WORKING AT.
WAS IT THE PE-DOLOGY LAB?
YEAH, THAT'S IT. ALL I DID WAS COUNT MICROBES, THOUGH ...
WELL, THAT'S MORE OR LESS WHAT YOU'LL BE DOING HERE, TOO.
WAIT HERE.
TAP
TAP
TAP
TAP
CLICK

PEDOLOGY - THE STUDY OF SOIL SCIENCE.

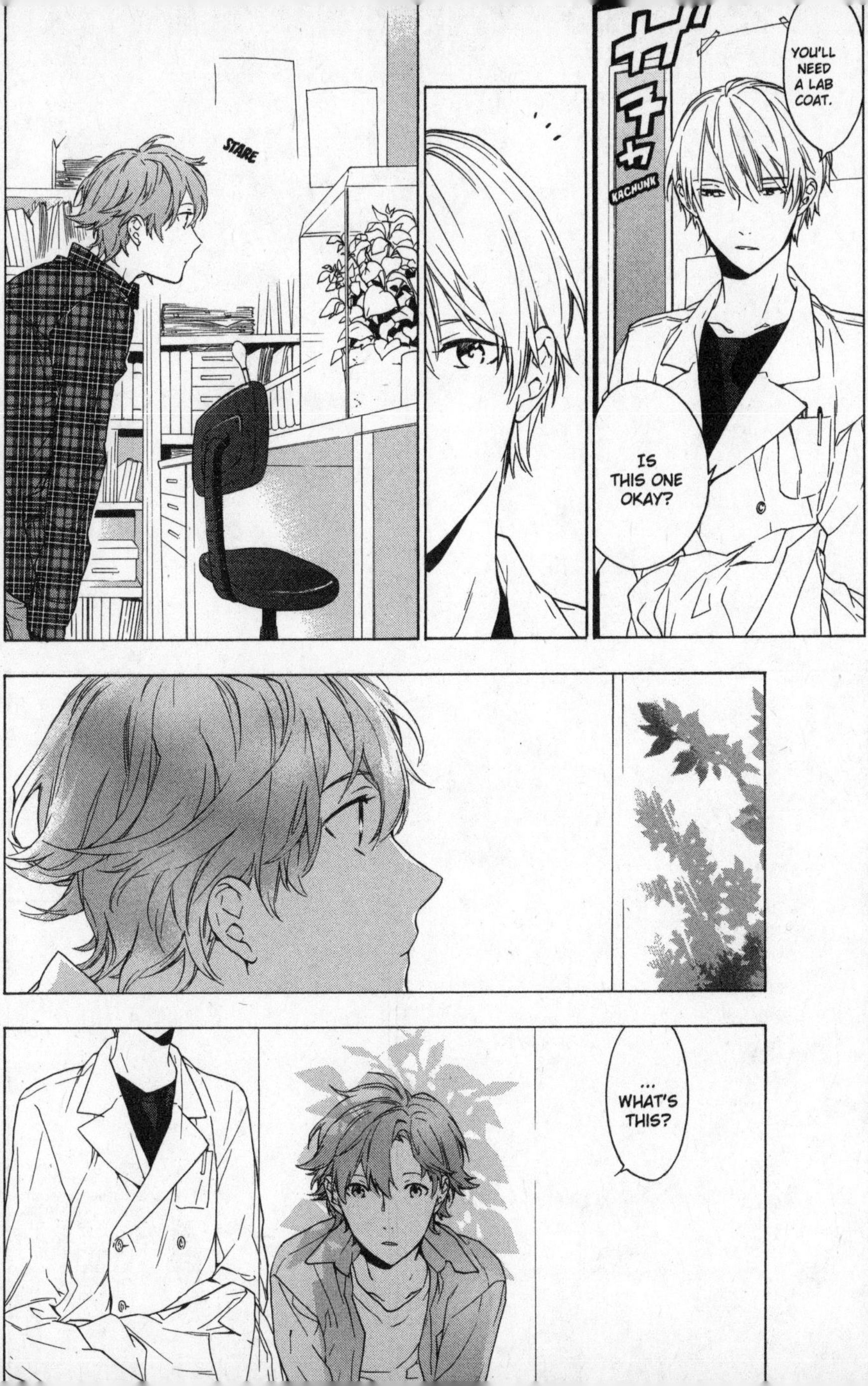
YOU'LL NEED A LAB COAT.
KACHUNK
IS THIS ONE OKAY?
...
STARE
... WHAT'S THIS?

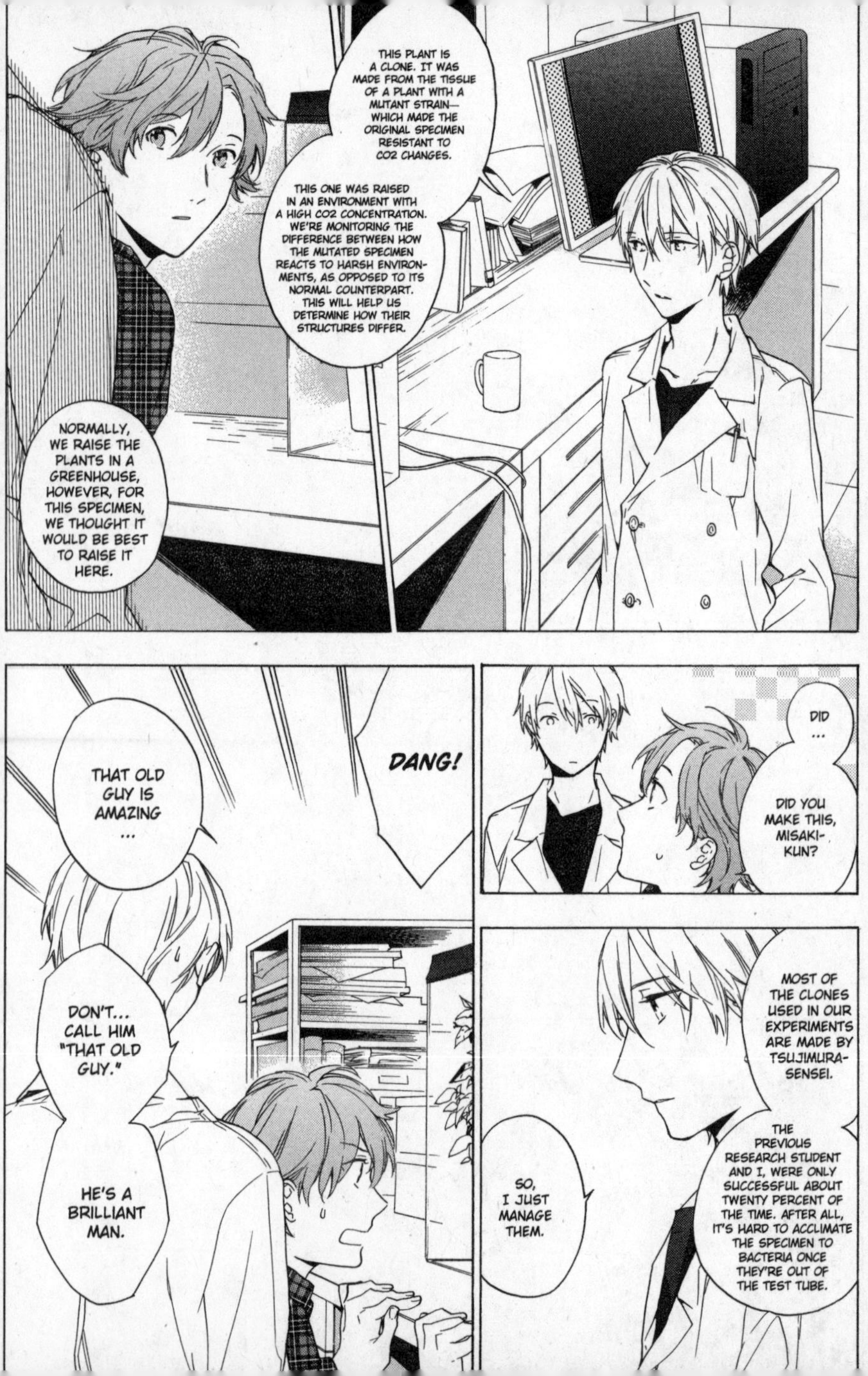
THIS PLANT IS A CLONE. IT WAS MADE FROM THE TISSUE OF A PLANT WITH A MUTANT STRAIN— WHICH MADE THE ORIGINAL SPECIMEN RESISTANT TO CO2 CHANGES.
THIS ONE WAS RAISED IN AN ENVIRONMENT WITH A HIGH CO2 CONCENTRATION. WE'RE MONITORING THE DIFFERENCE BETWEEN HOW THE MUTATED SPECIMEN REACTS TO HARSH ENVIRONMENTS, AS OPPOSED TO ITS NORMAL COUNTERPART. THIS WILL HELP US DETERMINE HOW THEIR STRUCTURES DIFFER.
NORMALLY, WE RAISE THE PLANTS IN A GREENHOUSE, HOWEVER, FOR THIS SPECIMEN, WE THOUGHT IT WOULD BE BEST TO RAISE IT HERE.
DID ...
DID YOU MAKE THIS, MISAKI-KUN?
MOST OF THE CLONES USED IN OUR EXPERIMENTS ARE MADE BY TSUJIMURA-SENSEI.
THE PREVIOUS RESEARCH STUDENT AND I, WERE ONLY SUCCESSFUL ABOUT TWENTY PERCENT OF THE TIME. AFTER ALL, IT'S HARD TO ACCLIMATE THE SPECIMEN TO BACTERIA ONCE THEY'RE OUT OF THE TEST TUBE.
SO, I JUST MANAGE THEM.
DANG!
THAT OLD GUY IS AMAZING ...
DON'T... CALL HIM "THAT OLD GUY."
HE'S A BRILLIANT MAN.

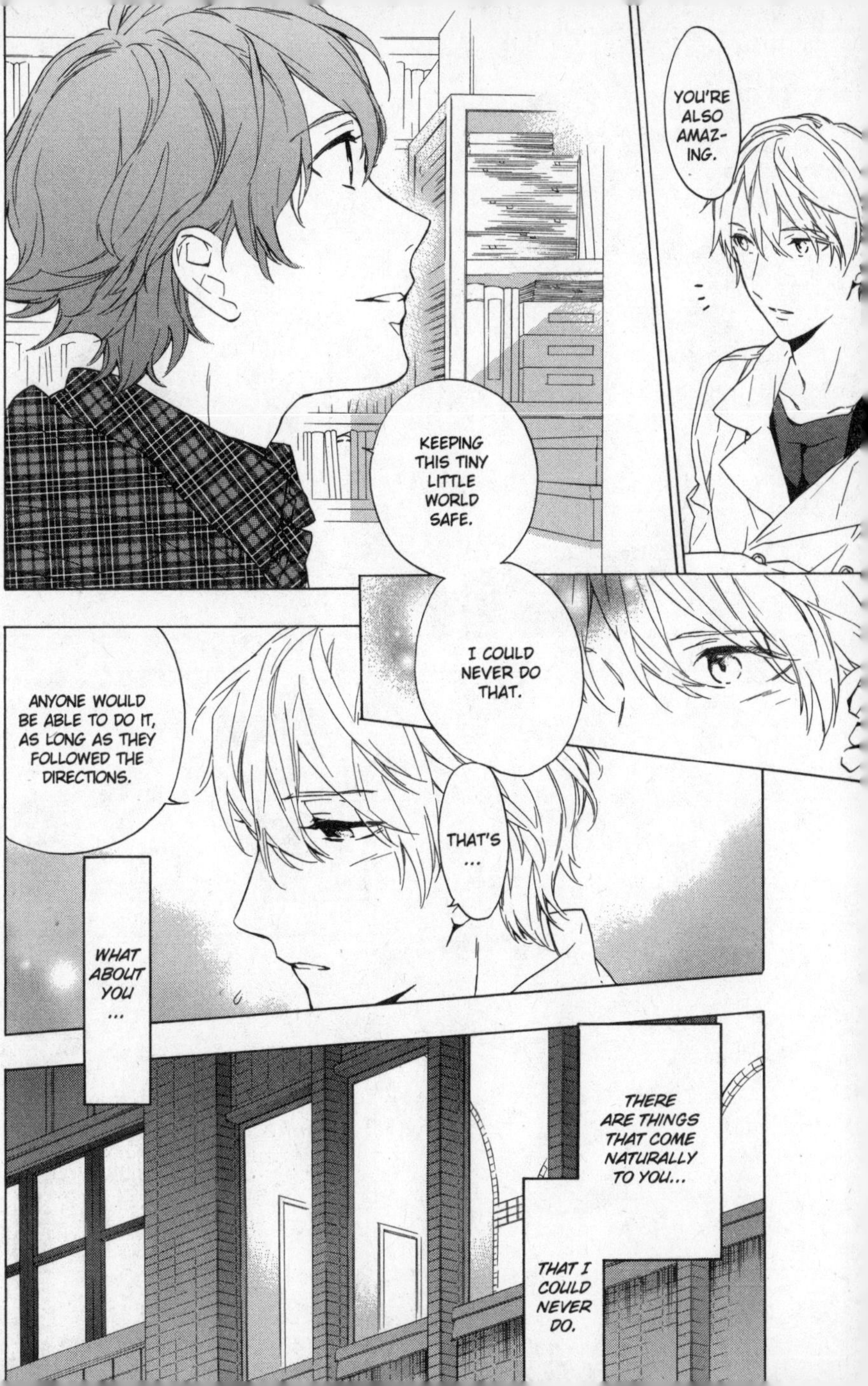
YOU'RE ALSO AMAZ-ING.
KEEPING THIS TINY LITTLE WORLD SAFE.
I COULD NEVER DO THAT.
THAT'S ...
ANYONE WOULD BE ABLE TO DO IT, AS LONG AS THEY FOLLOWED THE DIRECTIONS.
WHAT ABOUT YOU ...
THERE ARE THINGS THAT COME NATURALLY TO YOU...
THAT I COULD NEVER DO.

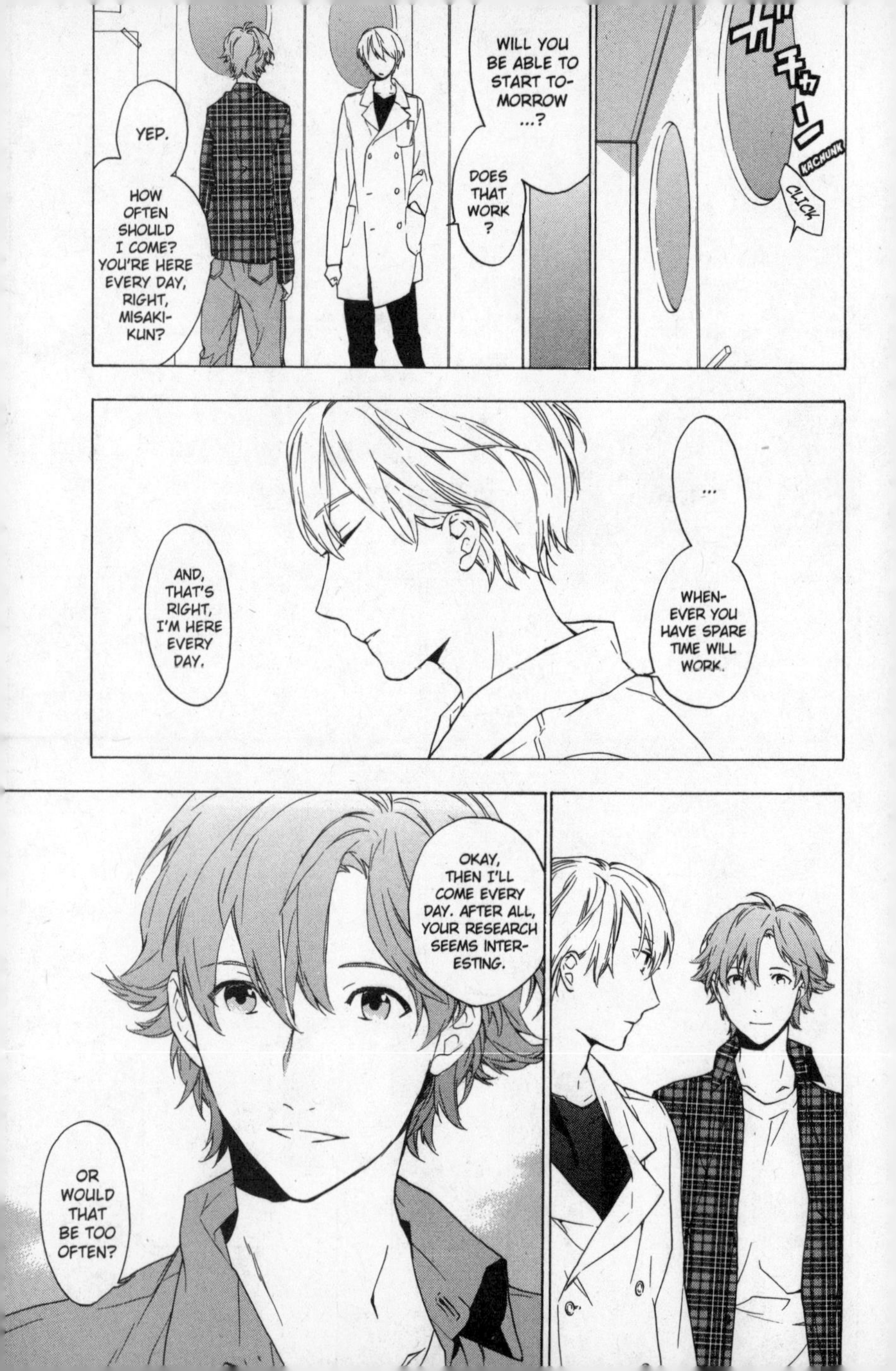
KACHUNK
CLICK
WILL YOU BE ABLE TO START TO-MORROW ...?
DOES THAT WORK ?
YEP.
HOW OFTEN SHOULD I COME? YOU'RE HERE EVERY DAY, RIGHT, MISAKI-KUN?
...
WHEN-EVER YOU HAVE SPARE TIME WILL WORK.
AND, THAT'S RIGHT, I'M HERE EVERY DAY.
OKAY, THEN I'LL COME EVERY DAY. AFTER ALL, YOUR RESEARCH SEEMS INTER-ESTING.
OR WOULD THAT BE TOO OFTEN?

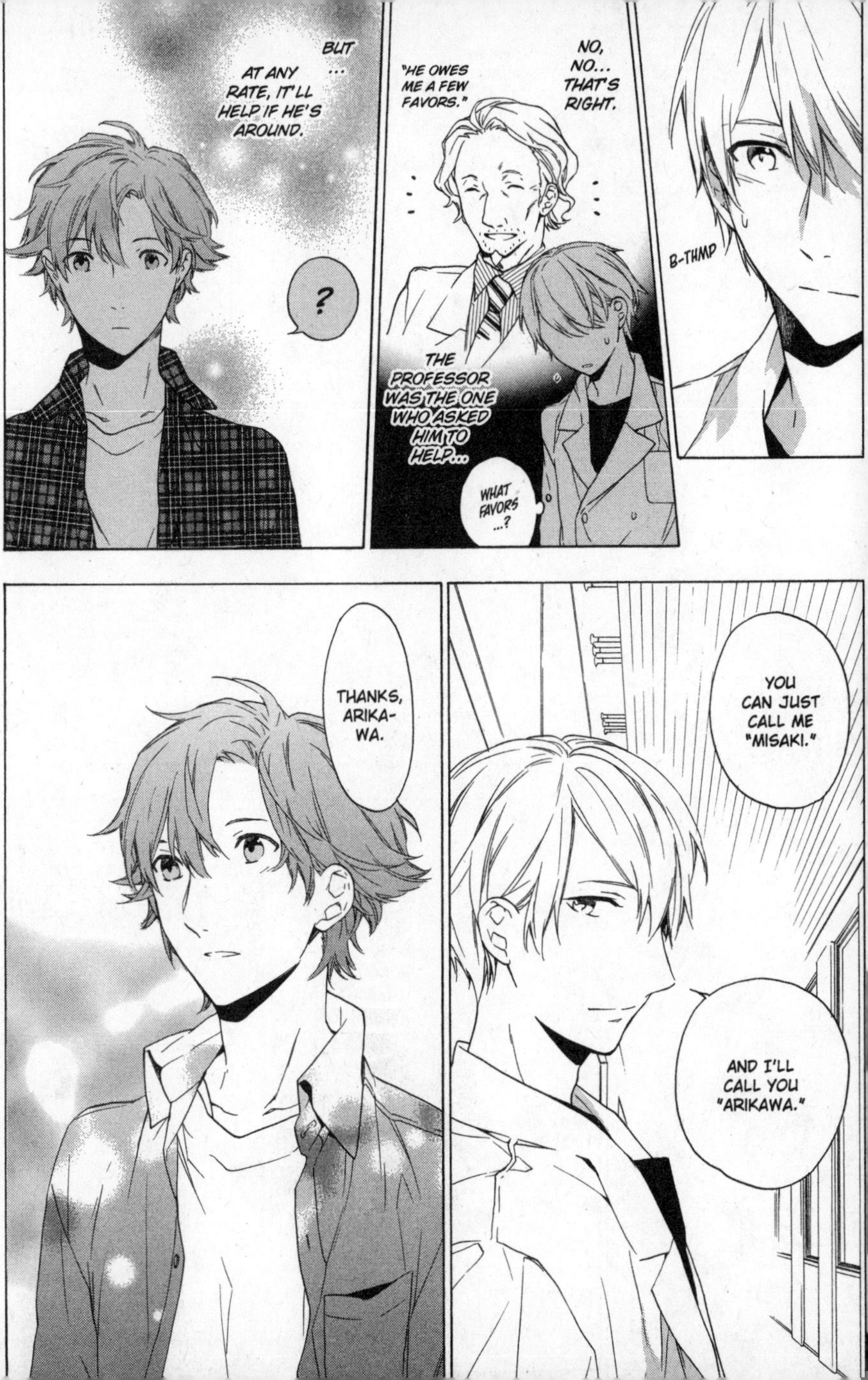
B-THMP
NO, NO... THAT'S RIGHT.
"HE OWES ME A FEW FAVORS."
THE PROFESSOR WAS THE ONE WHO ASKED HIM TO HELP...
WHAT FAVORS ...?
BUT ...
AT ANY RATE, IT'LL HELP IF HE'S AROUND.
?
YOU CAN JUST CALL ME "MISAKI."
AND I'LL CALL YOU "ARIKAWA."
THANKS, ARIKA-WA.

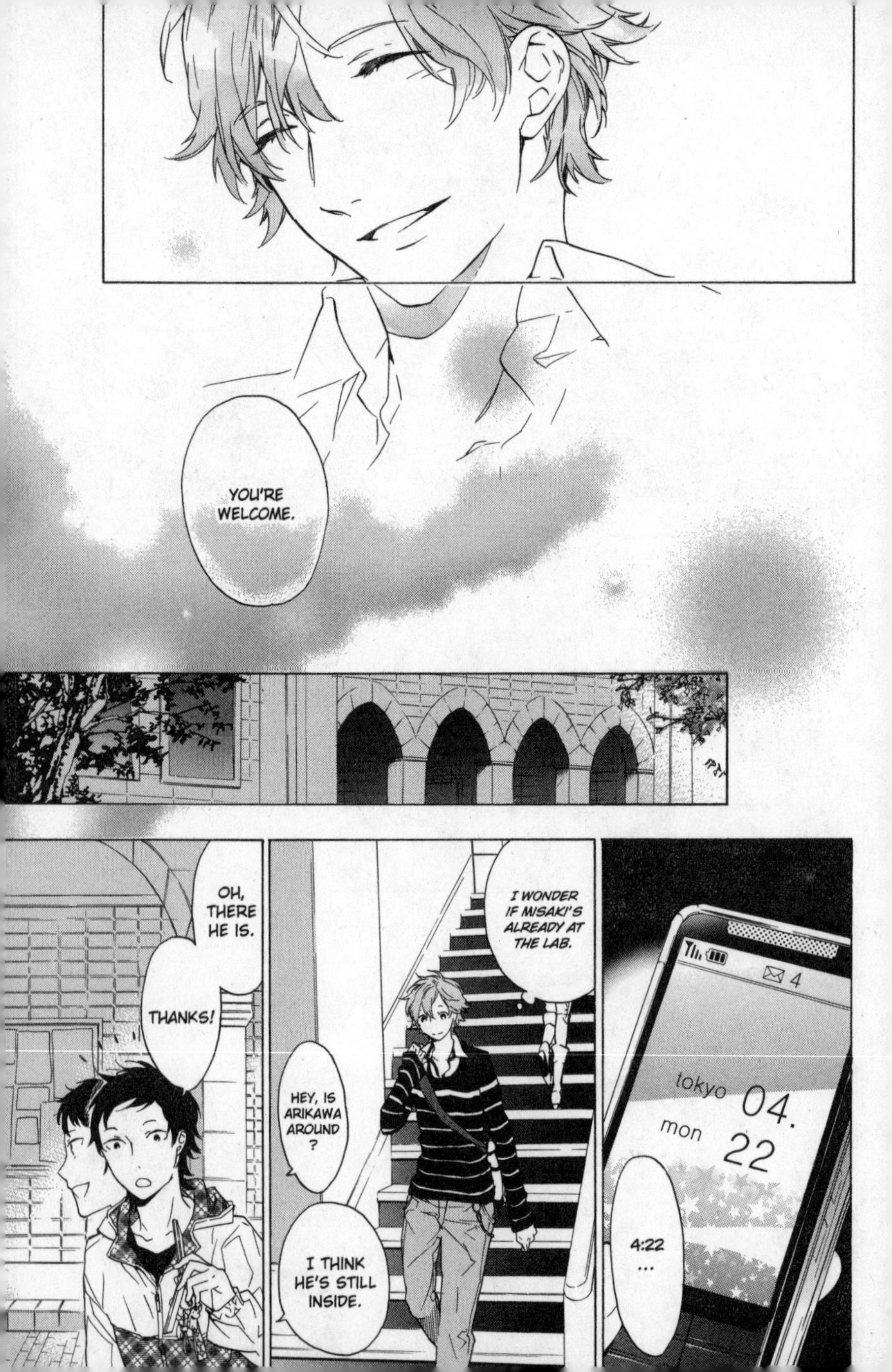
YOU'RE WELCOME.
4
tokyo 04.
mon 22
4:22 ...
I WONDER IF MISAKI'S ALREADY AT THE LAB.
HEY, IS ARIKAWA AROUND?
I THINK HE'S STILL INSIDE.
OH, THERE HE IS.
THANKS!

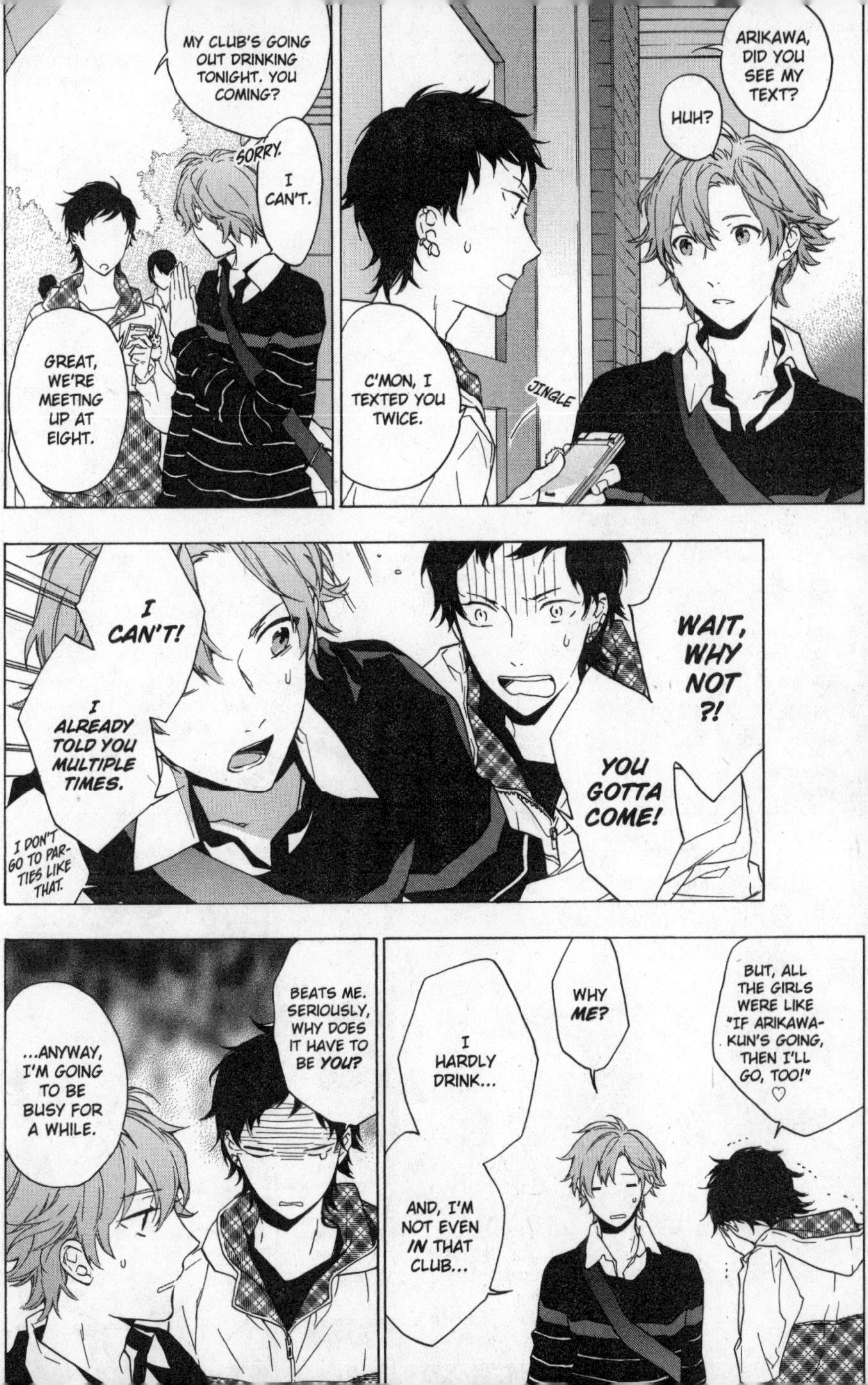
ARIKAWA, DID YOU SEE MY TEXT?
HUH?
JINGLE
C'MON, I TEXTED YOU TWICE.
MY CLUB'S GOING OUT DRINKING TONIGHT. YOU COMING?
SORRY.
I CAN'T.
GREAT, WE'RE MEETING UP AT EIGHT.
WAIT, WHY NOT ?!
YOU GOTTA COME!
I CAN'T!
I ALREADY TOLD YOU MULTIPLE TIMES.
I DON'T GO TO PARTIES LIKE THAT.
BUT, ALL THE GIRLS WERE LIKE "IF ARIKAWA-KUN'S GOING, THEN I'LL GO, TOO!" ♡
WHY *ME*?
I HARDLY DRINK...
AND, I'M NOT EVEN *IN* THAT CLUB...
BEATS ME. SERIOUSLY, WHY DOES IT HAVE TO BE *YOU*?
...ANYWAY, I'M GOING TO BE BUSY FOR A WHILE.

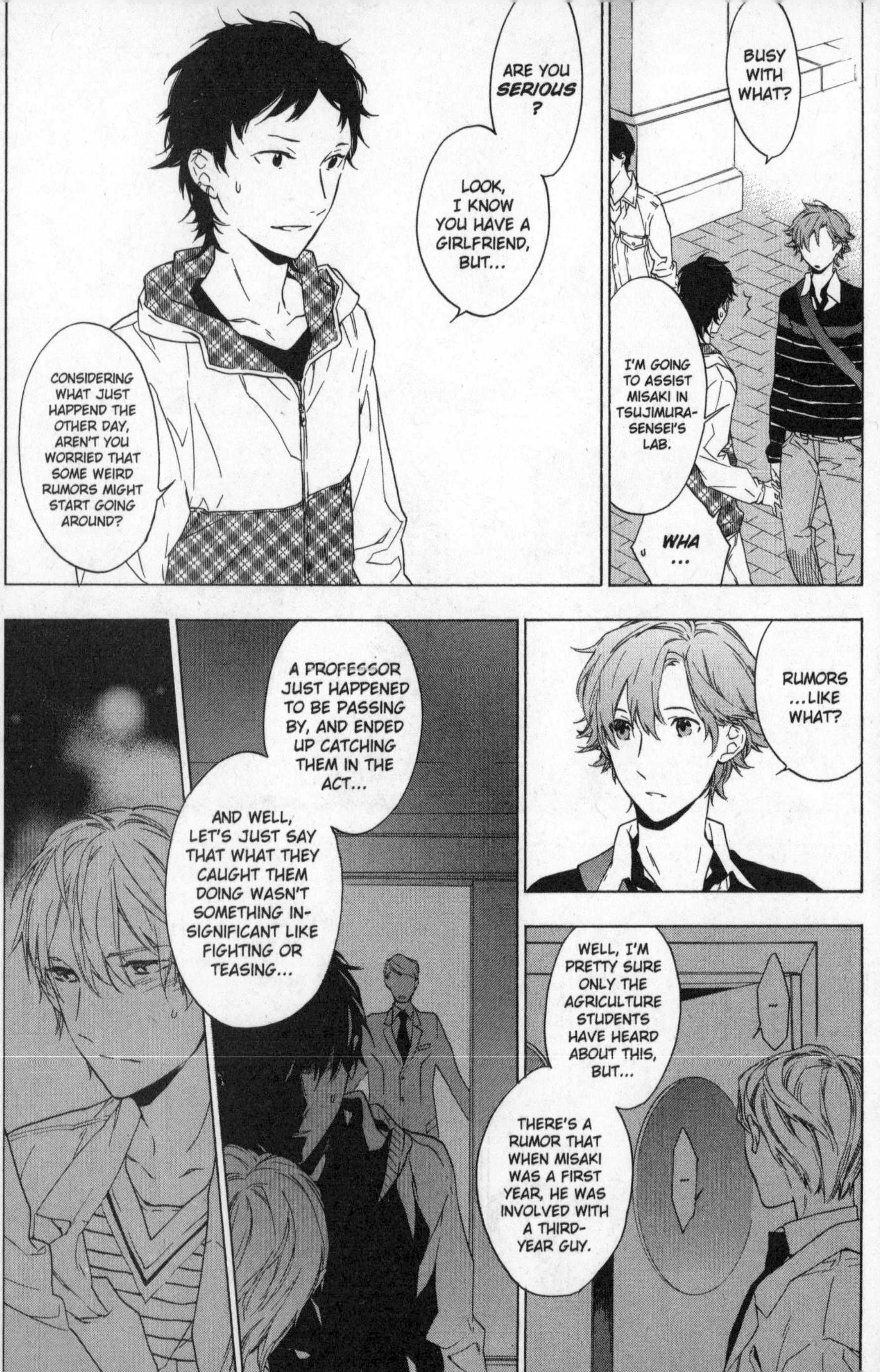
BUSY WITH WHAT?
I'M GOING TO ASSIST MISAKI IN TSUJIMURA-SENSEI'S LAB.
WHA...
ARE YOU *SERIOUS*?
LOOK, I KNOW YOU HAVE A GIRLFRIEND, BUT...
CONSIDERING WHAT JUST HAPPEND THE OTHER DAY, AREN'T YOU WORRIED THAT SOME WEIRD RUMORS MIGHT START GOING AROUND?
RUMORS ...LIKE WHAT?
WELL, I'M PRETTY SURE ONLY THE AGRICULTURE STUDENTS HAVE HEARD ABOUT THIS, BUT...
...
THERE'S A RUMOR THAT WHEN MISAKI WAS A FIRST YEAR, HE WAS INVOLVED WITH A THIRD-YEAR GUY.
...
A PROFESSOR JUST HAPPENED TO BE PASSING BY, AND ENDED UP CATCHING THEM IN THE ACT...
AND WELL, LET'S JUST SAY THAT WHAT THEY CAUGHT THEM DOING WASN'T SOMETHING IN-SIGNIFICANT LIKE FIGHTING OR TEASING...

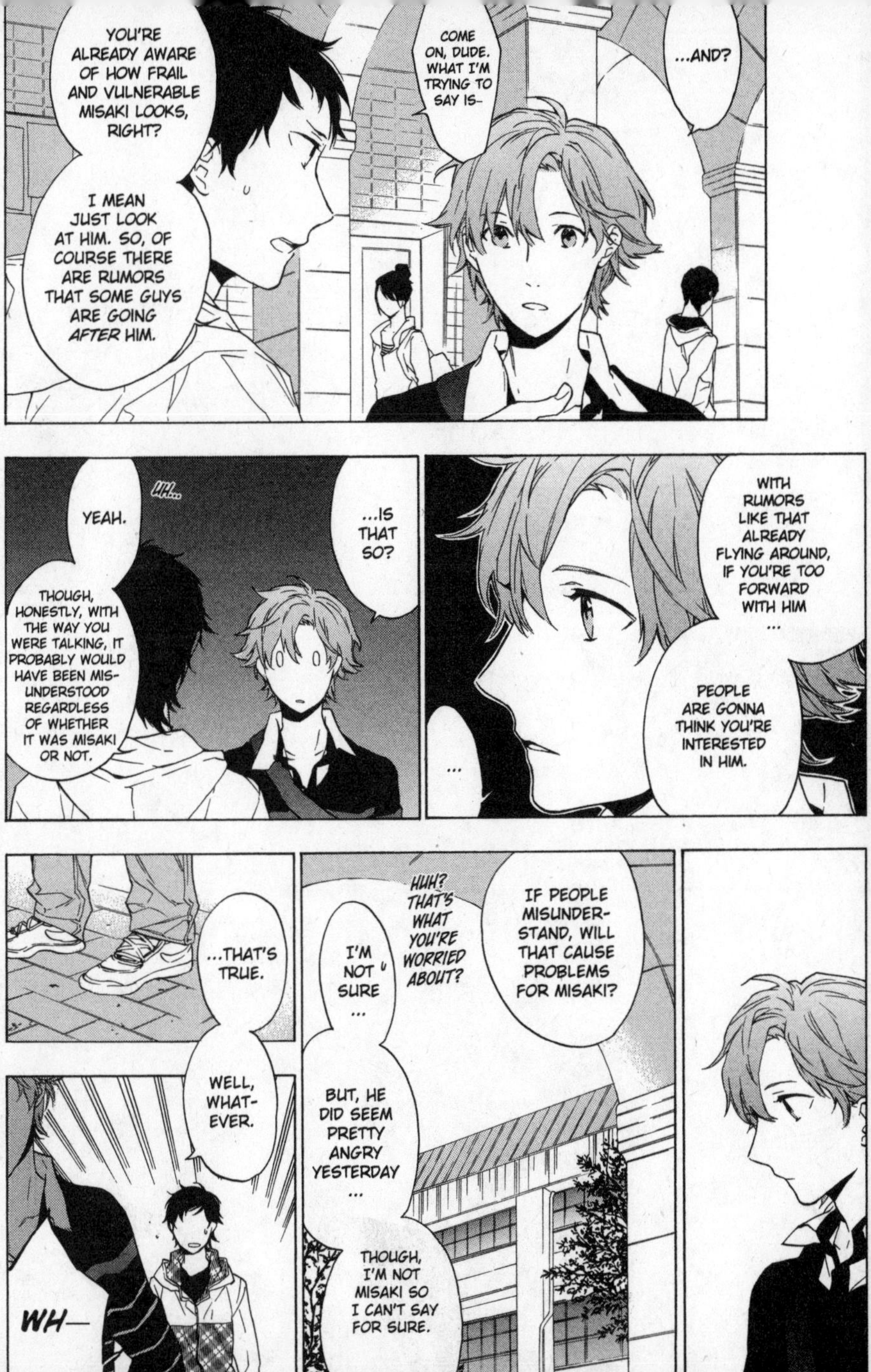
...AND?
COME ON, DUDE. WHAT I'M TRYING TO SAY IS-
YOU'RE ALREADY AWARE OF HOW FRAIL AND VULNERABLE MISAKI LOOKS, RIGHT?
I MEAN JUST LOOK AT HIM. SO, OF COURSE THERE ARE RUMORS THAT SOME GUYS ARE GOING *AFTER* HIM.
WITH RUMORS LIKE THAT ALREADY FLYING AROUND, IF YOU'RE TOO FORWARD WITH HIM ...
PEOPLE ARE GONNA THINK YOU'RE INTERESTED IN HIM.
...
...IS THAT SO?
UH...
YEAH.
THOUGH, HONESTLY, WITH THE WAY YOU WERE TALKING, IT PROBABLY WOULD HAVE BEEN MIS-UNDERSTOOD REGARDLESS OF WHETHER IT WAS MISAKI OR NOT.
IF PEOPLE MISUNDER-STAND, WILL THAT CAUSE PROBLEMS FOR MISAKI?
HUH? THAT'S WHAT YOU'RE WORRIED ABOUT?
I'M NOT SURE ...
BUT, HE DID SEEM PRETTY ANGRY YESTERDAY ...
THOUGH, I'M NOT MISAKI SO I CAN'T SAY FOR SURE.
...THAT'S TRUE.
WELL, WHAT-EVER.
WH—

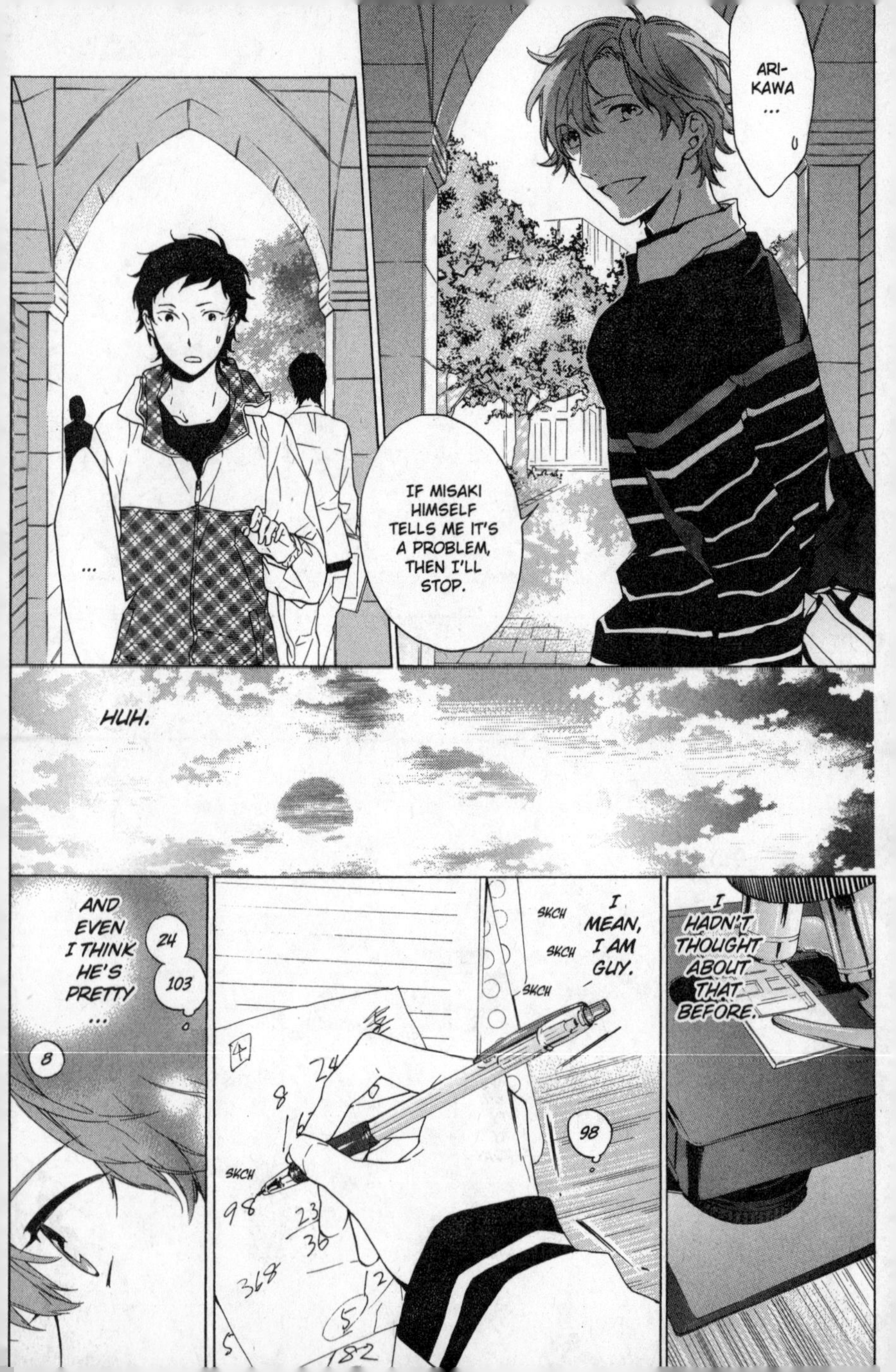
ARI-KAWA...
IF MISAKI HIMSELF TELLS ME IT'S A PROBLEM, THEN I'LL STOP.
...
HUH.
I HADN'T THOUGHT ABOUT THAT BEFORE.
I MEAN, I AM GUY.
SKCH
SKCH
SKCH
98
SKCH
AND EVEN I THINK HE'S PRETTY...
24
103
8

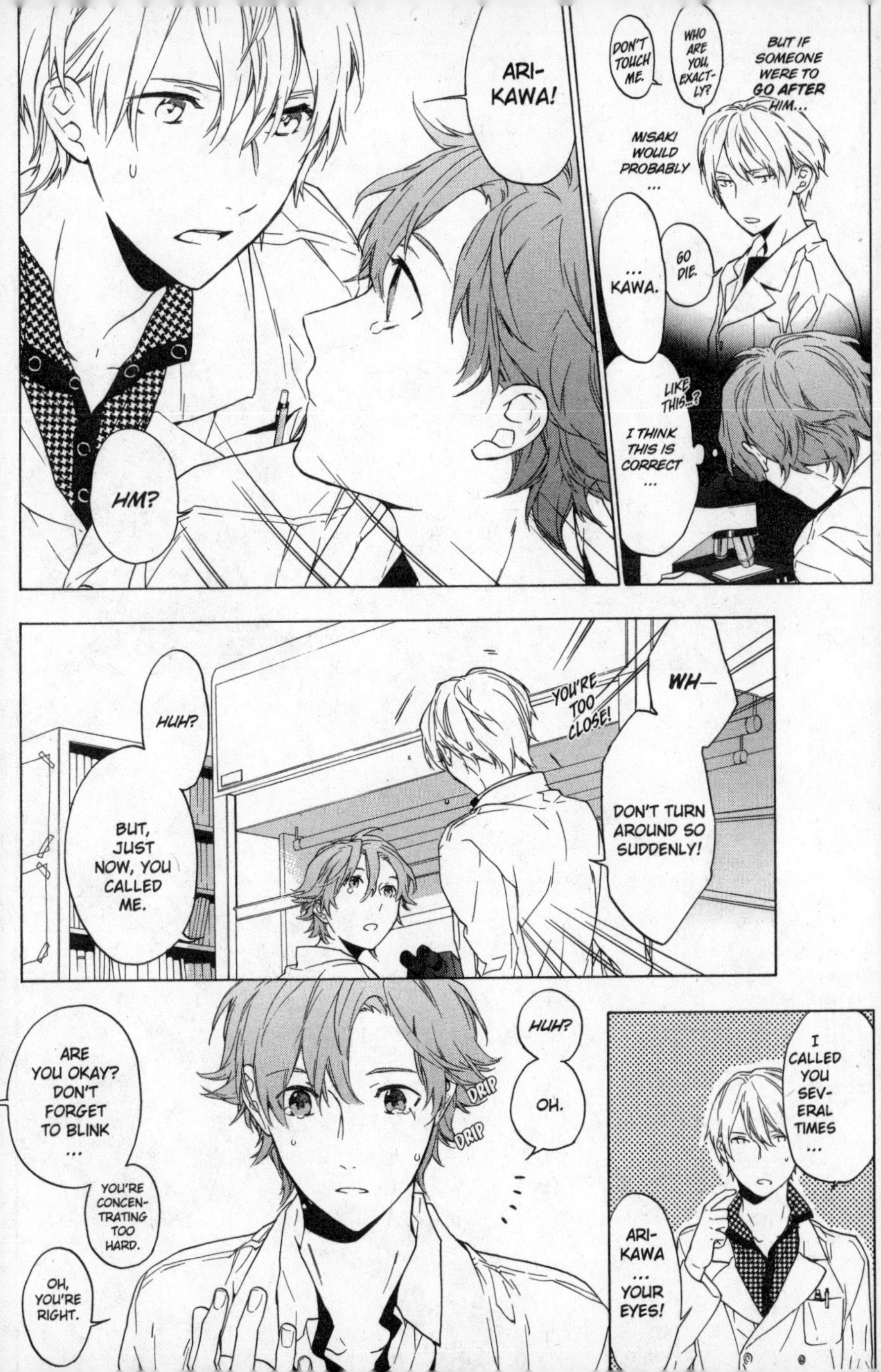
BUT IF SOMEONE WERE TO GO AFTER HIM...
WHO ARE YOU, EXACTLY?
DON'T TOUCH ME.
MISAKI WOULD PROBABLY ...
GO DIE.
... KAWA.
LIKE THIS...?
I THINK THIS IS CORRECT ...
ARI-KAWA!
HM?
WH—
YOU'RE TOO CLOSE!
DON'T TURN AROUND SO SUDDENLY!
HUH?
BUT, JUST NOW, YOU CALLED ME.
I CALLED YOU SEV-ERAL TIMES ...
ARI-KAWA ... YOUR EYES!
HUH?
OH.
DRIP
DRIP
...
ARE YOU OKAY? DON'T FORGET TO BLINK ...
YOU'RE CONCEN-TRATING TOO HARD.
OH, YOU'RE RIGHT.

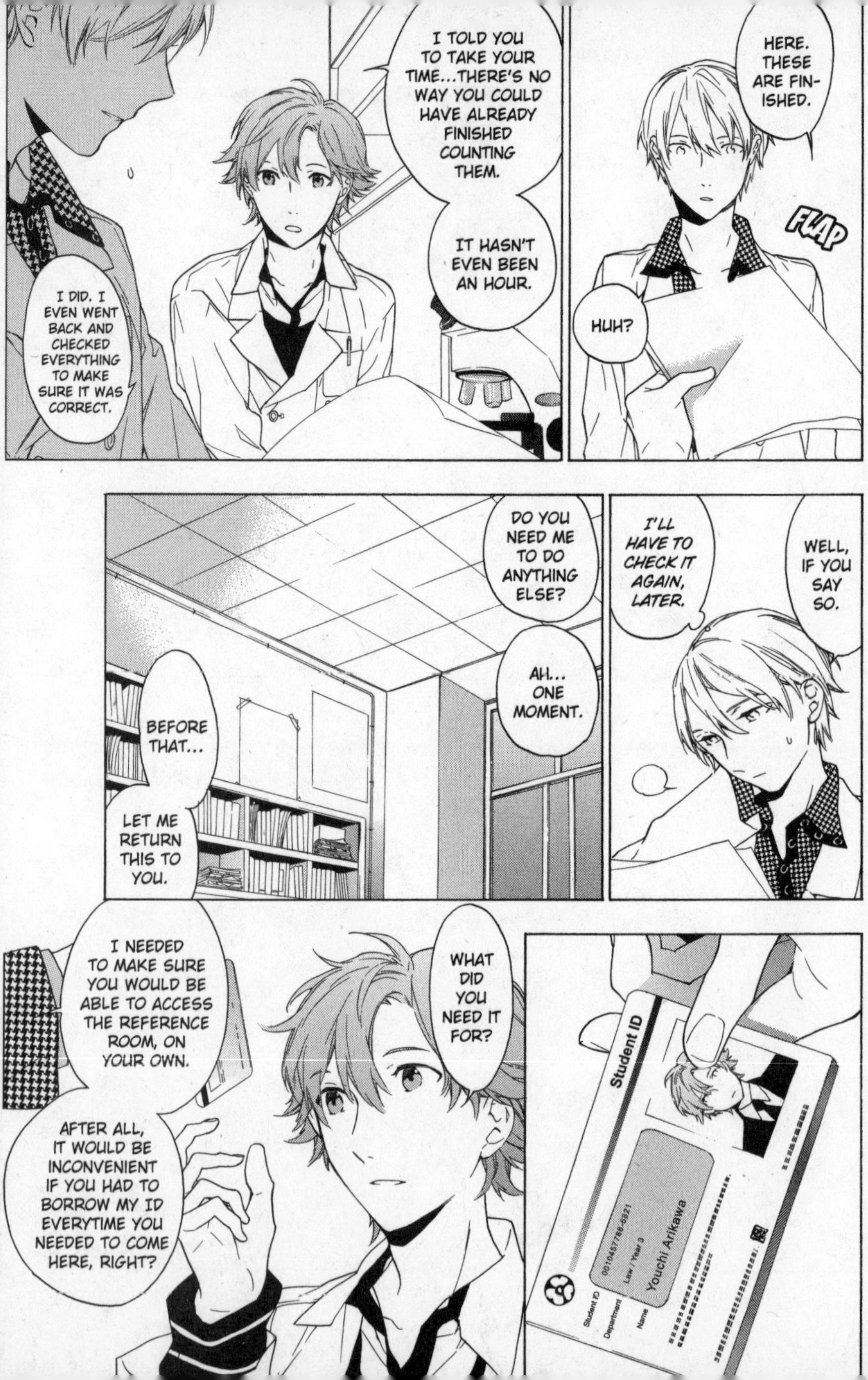
HERE. THESE ARE FIN-ISHED.
FLAP
HUH?
I TOLD YOU TO TAKE YOUR TIME...THERE'S NO WAY YOU COULD HAVE ALREADY FINISHED COUNTING THEM.
IT HASN'T EVEN BEEN AN HOUR.
I DID. I EVEN WENT BACK AND CHECKED EVERYTHING TO MAKE SURE IT WAS CORRECT.
WELL, IF YOU SAY SO.
I'LL HAVE TO CHECK IT AGAIN, LATER.
DO YOU NEED ME TO DO ANYTHING ELSE?
AH... ONE MOMENT.
BEFORE THAT...
LET ME RETURN THIS TO YOU.
Student ID
Student ID
Department Law / Year 3
Name Youchi Arikawa
WHAT DID YOU NEED IT FOR?
I NEEDED TO MAKE SURE YOU WOULD BE ABLE TO ACCESS THE REFERENCE ROOM, ON YOUR OWN.
AFTER ALL, IT WOULD BE INCONVENIENT IF YOU HAD TO BORROW MY ID EVERYTIME YOU NEEDED TO COME HERE, RIGHT?

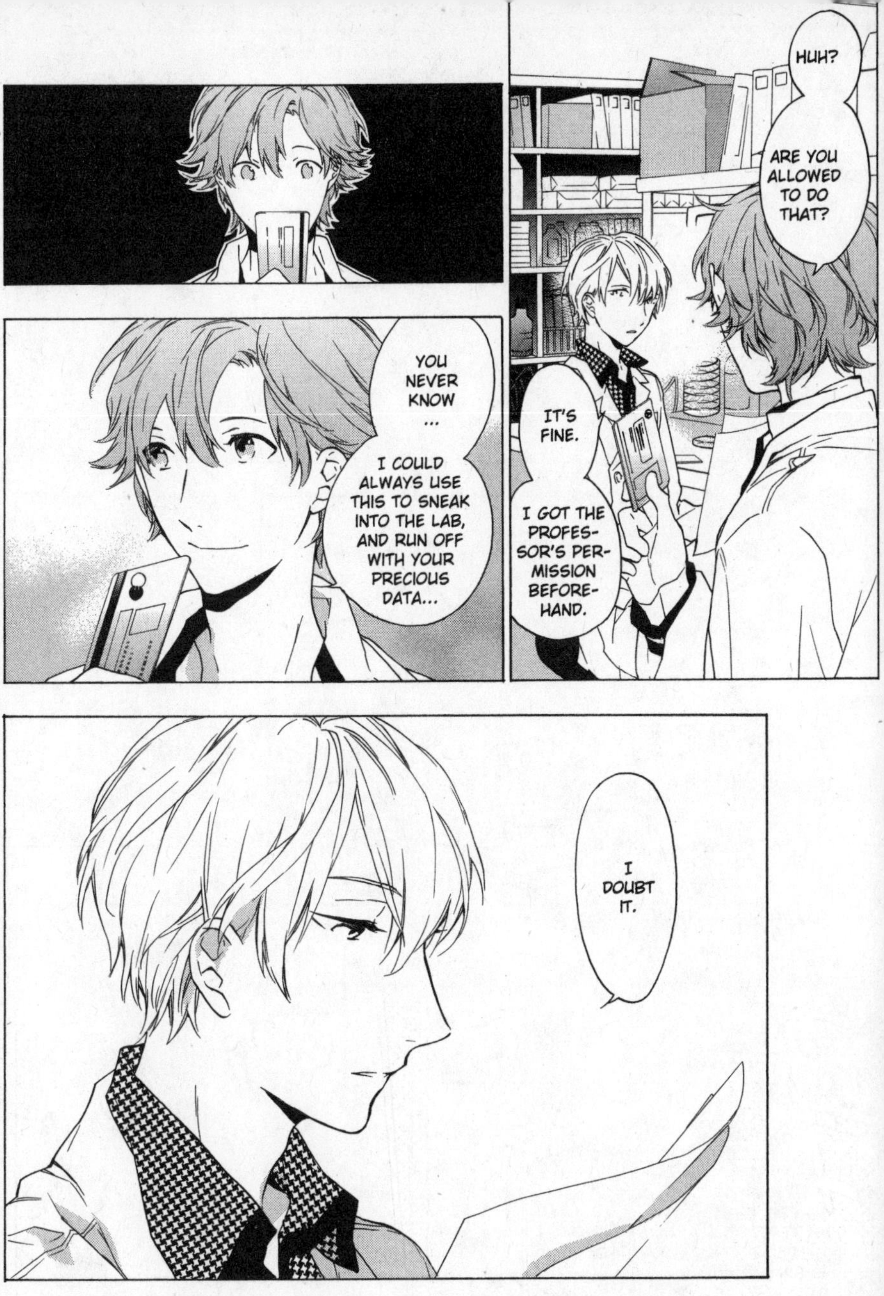
HUH?
ARE YOU ALLOWED TO DO THAT?
IT'S FINE.
I GOT THE PROFES-SOR'S PER-MISSION BEFORE-HAND.
YOU NEVER KNOW ...
I COULD ALWAYS USE THIS TO SNEAK INTO THE LAB, AND RUN OFF WITH YOUR PRECIOUS DATA...
I DOUBT IT.

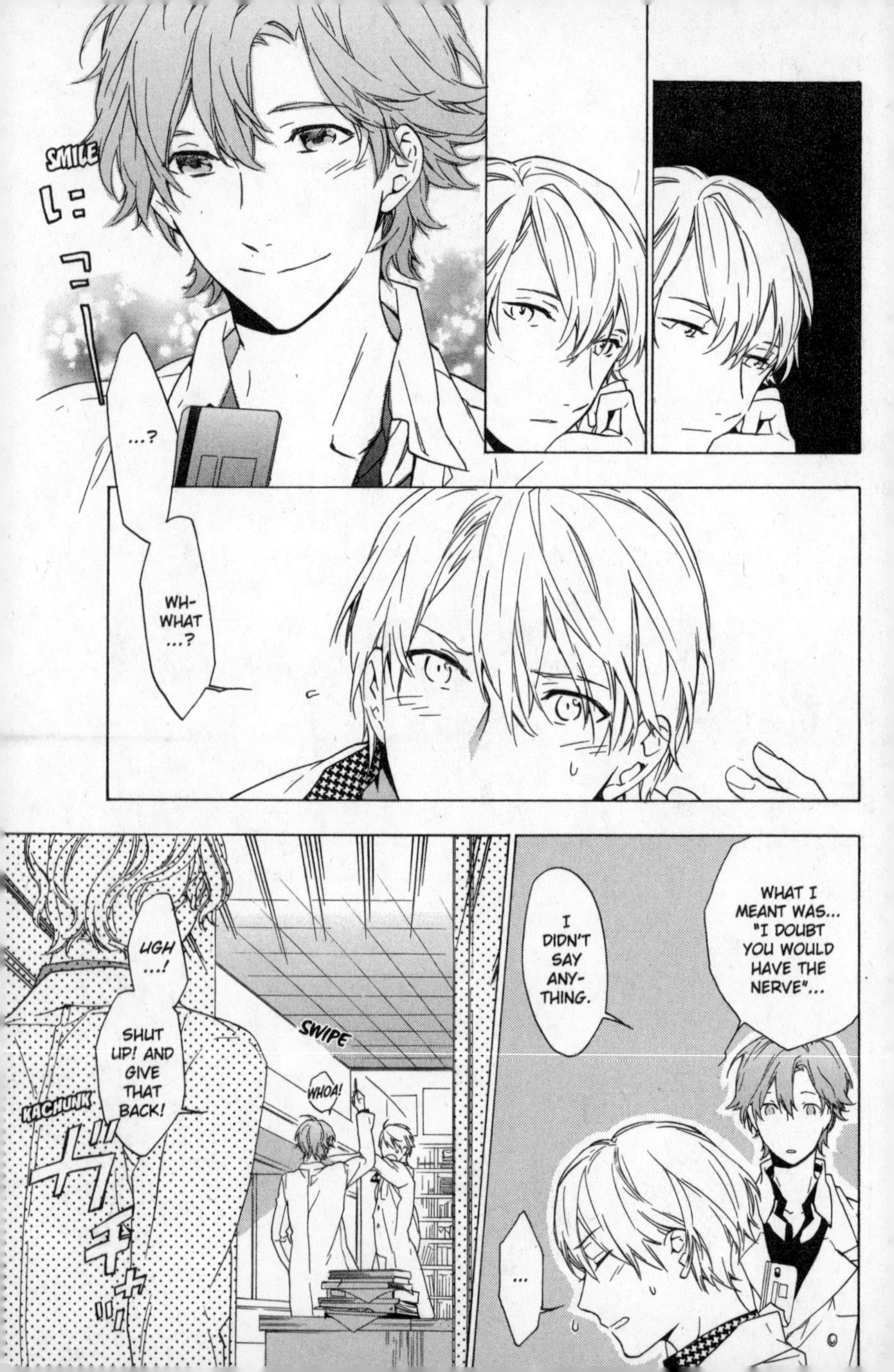
SMILE
...?
WH-WHAT ...?
WHAT I MEANT WAS... "I DOUBT YOU WOULD HAVE THE NERVE"...
I DIDN'T SAY ANY-THING.
...
UGH ...!
SHUT UP! AND GIVE THAT BACK!
SWIPE
WHOA!
KACHUNK

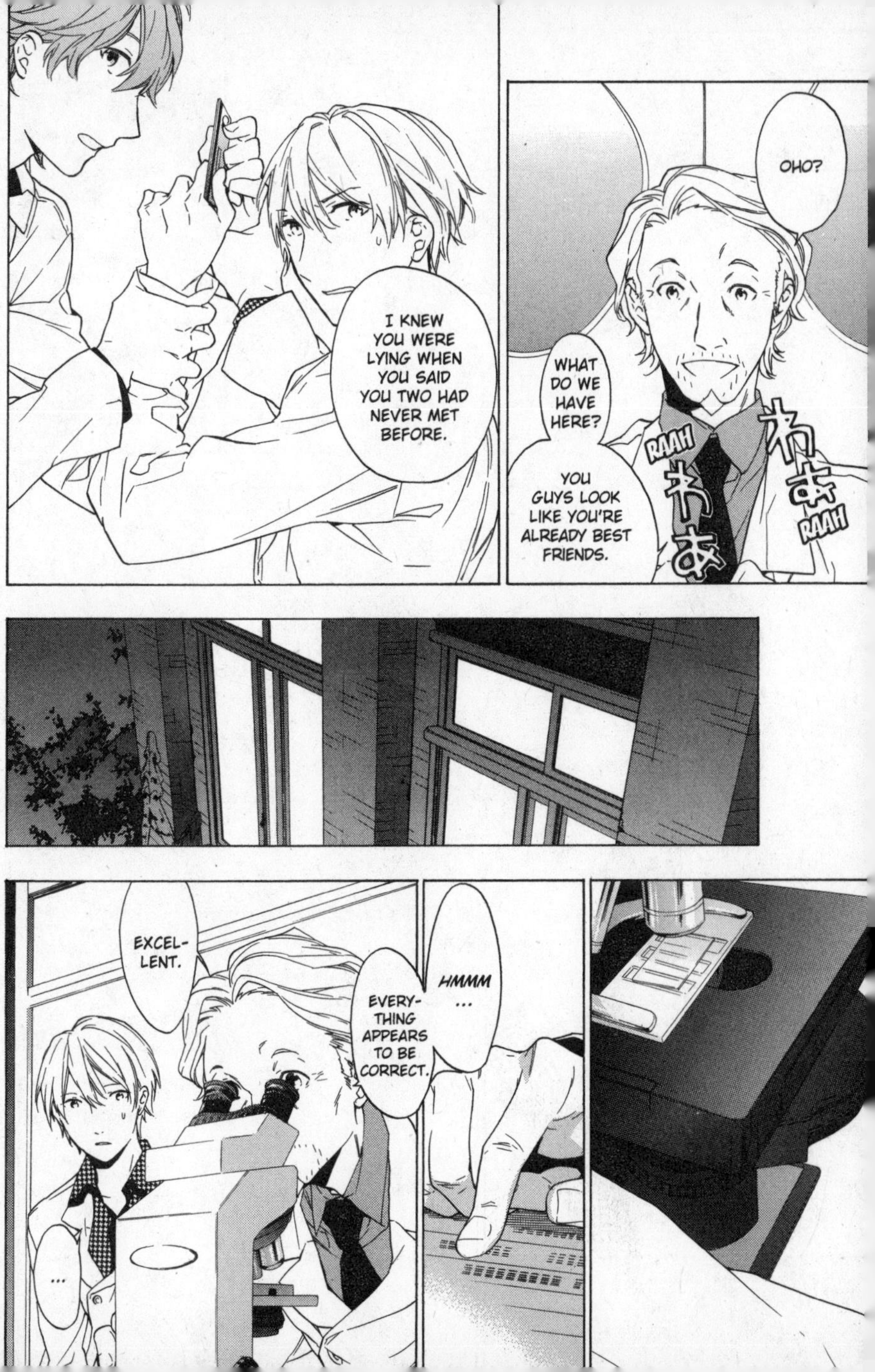
OHO?
WHAT DO WE HAVE HERE?
YOU GUYS LOOK LIKE YOU'RE ALREADY BEST FRIENDS.
わぁ RAAH
わぁ RAAH
I KNEW YOU WERE LYING WHEN YOU SAID YOU TWO HAD NEVER MET BEFORE.
HMMM...
EVERYTHING APPEARS TO BE CORRECT.
EXCEL-LENT.
...

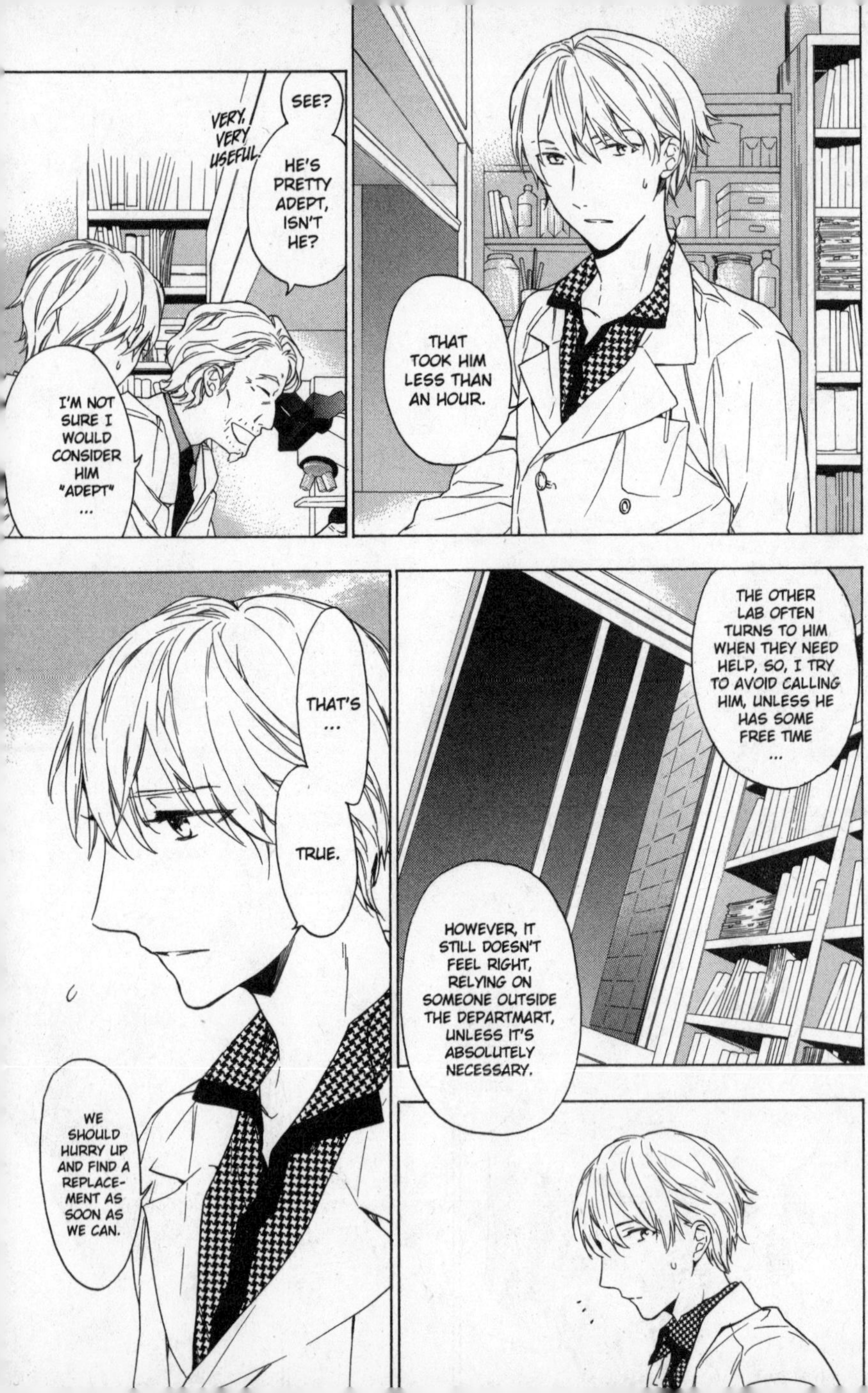
THAT TOOK HIM LESS THAN AN HOUR.
SEE?
HE'S PRETTY ADEPT, ISN'T HE?
VERY, VERY USEFUL.
I'M NOT SURE I WOULD CONSIDER HIM "ADEPT" ...
THE OTHER LAB OFTEN TURNS TO HIM WHEN THEY NEED HELP, SO, I TRY TO AVOID CALLING HIM, UNLESS HE HAS SOME FREE TIME ...
HOWEVER, IT STILL DOESN'T FEEL RIGHT, RELYING ON SOMEONE OUTSIDE THE DEPARTMART, UNLESS IT'S ABSOLUTELY NECESSARY.
THAT'S ...
TRUE.
WE SHOULD HURRY UP AND FIND A REPLACE-MENT AS SOON AS WE CAN.

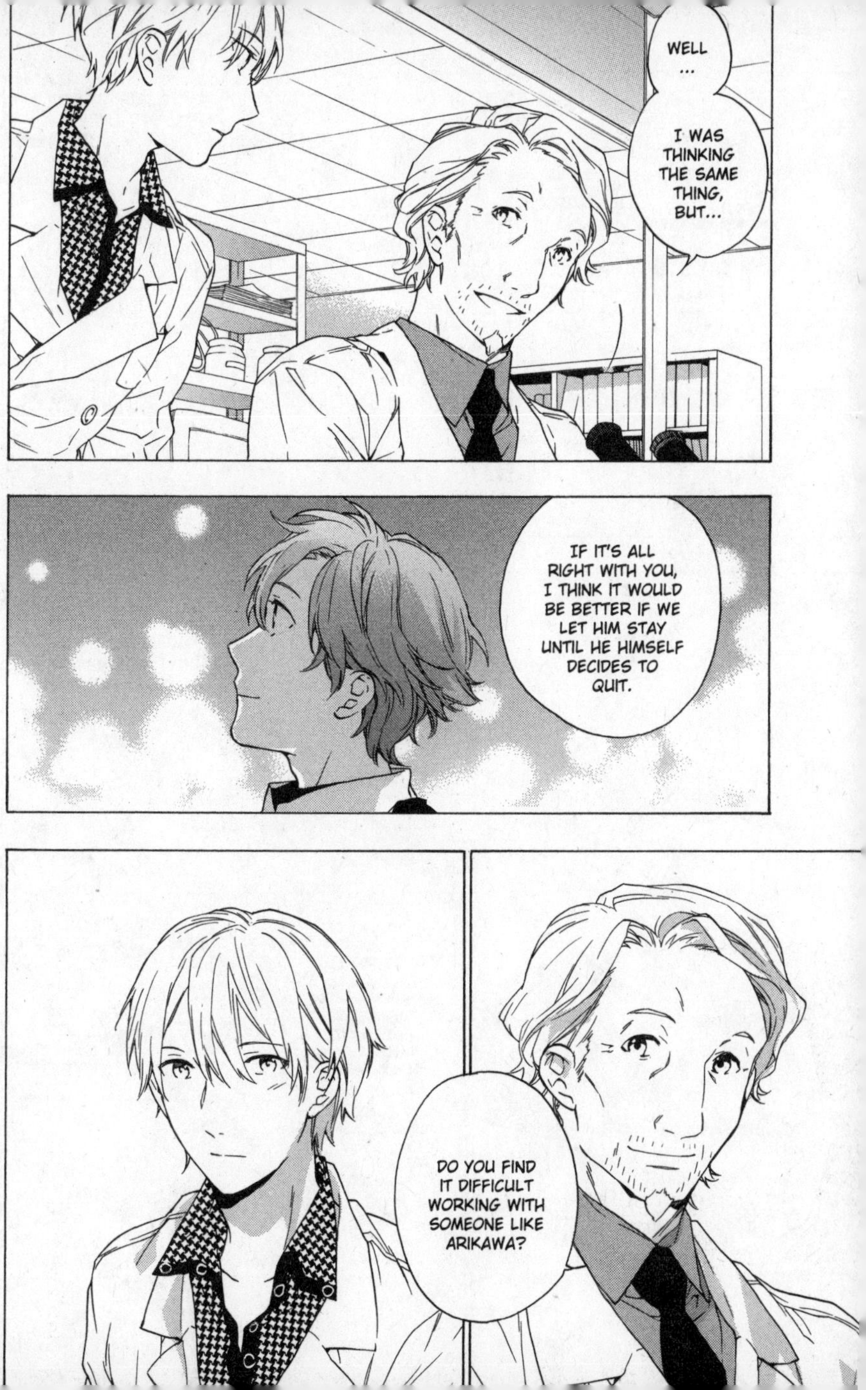
WELL ...
I WAS THINKING THE SAME THING, BUT...
IF IT'S ALL RIGHT WITH YOU, I THINK IT WOULD BE BETTER IF WE LET HIM STAY UNTIL HE HIMSELF DECIDES TO QUIT.
DO YOU FIND IT DIFFICULT WORKING WITH SOMEONE LIKE ARIKAWA?

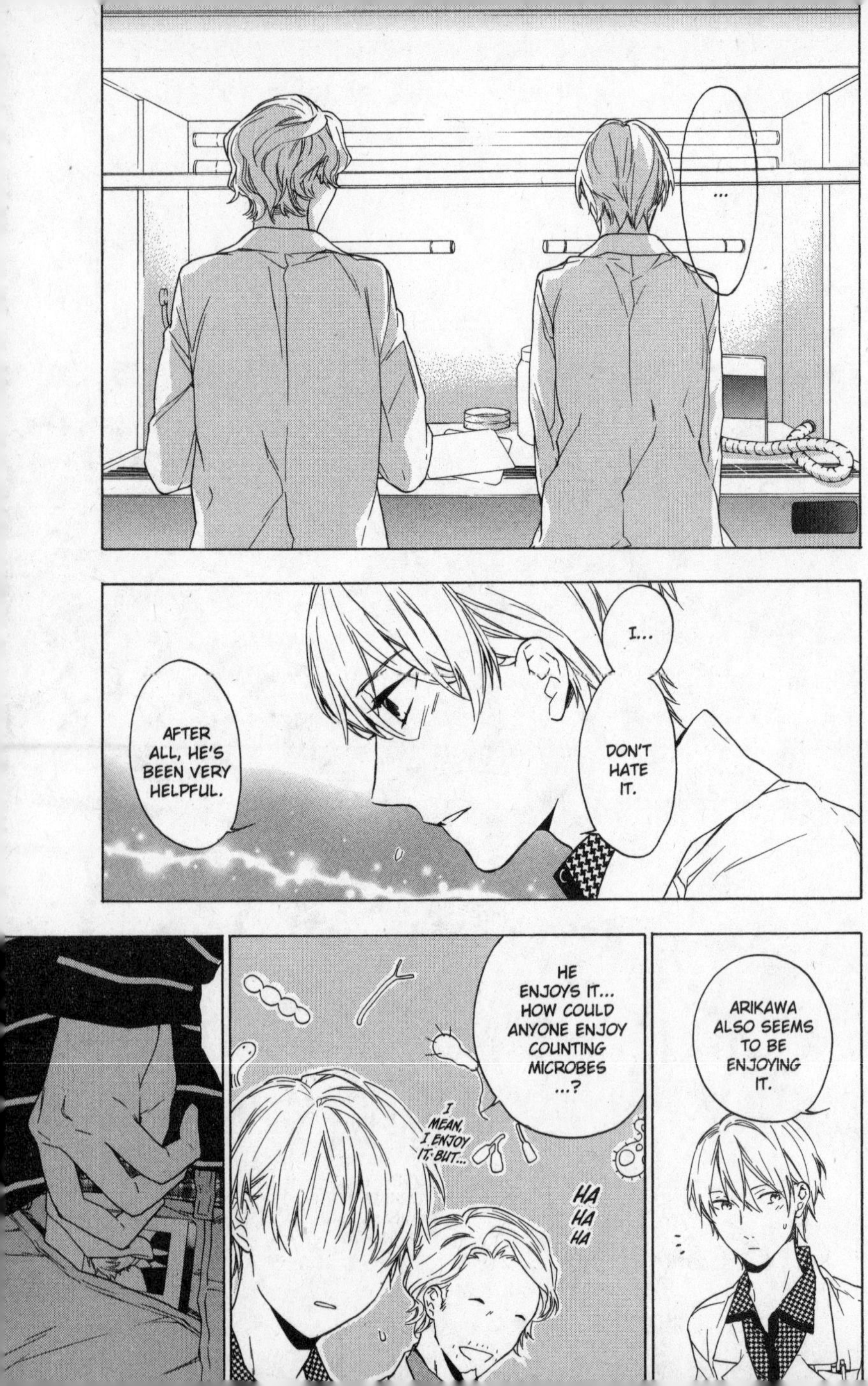
...
I...
DON'T HATE IT.
AFTER ALL, HE'S BEEN VERY HELPFUL.
ARIKAWA ALSO SEEMS TO BE ENJOYING IT.
HE ENJOYS IT... HOW COULD ANYONE ENJOY COUNTING MICROBES ...?
I MEAN, I ENJOY IT, BUT...
HA HA HA

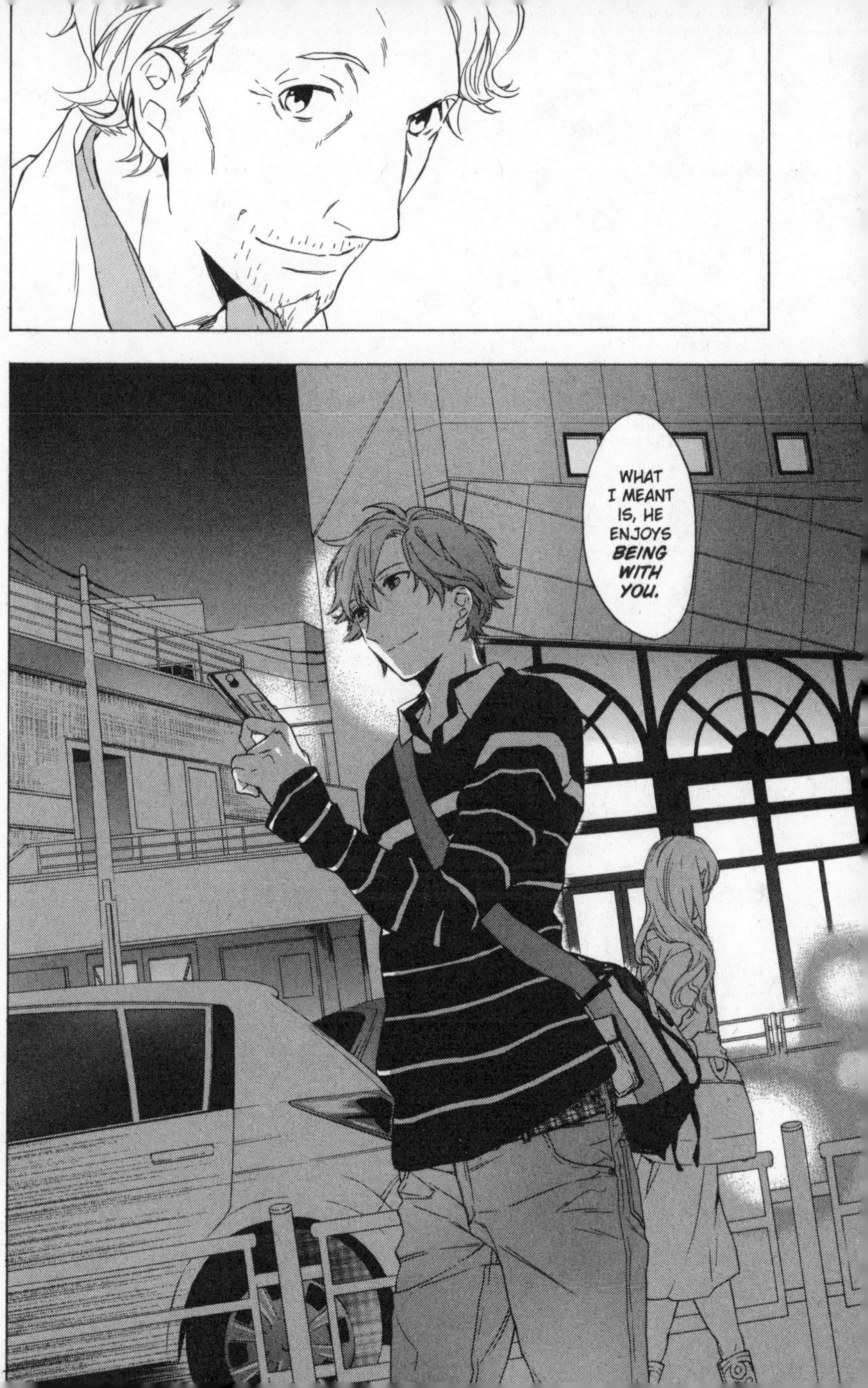
WHAT I MEANT IS, HE ENJOYS *BEING WITH YOU.*

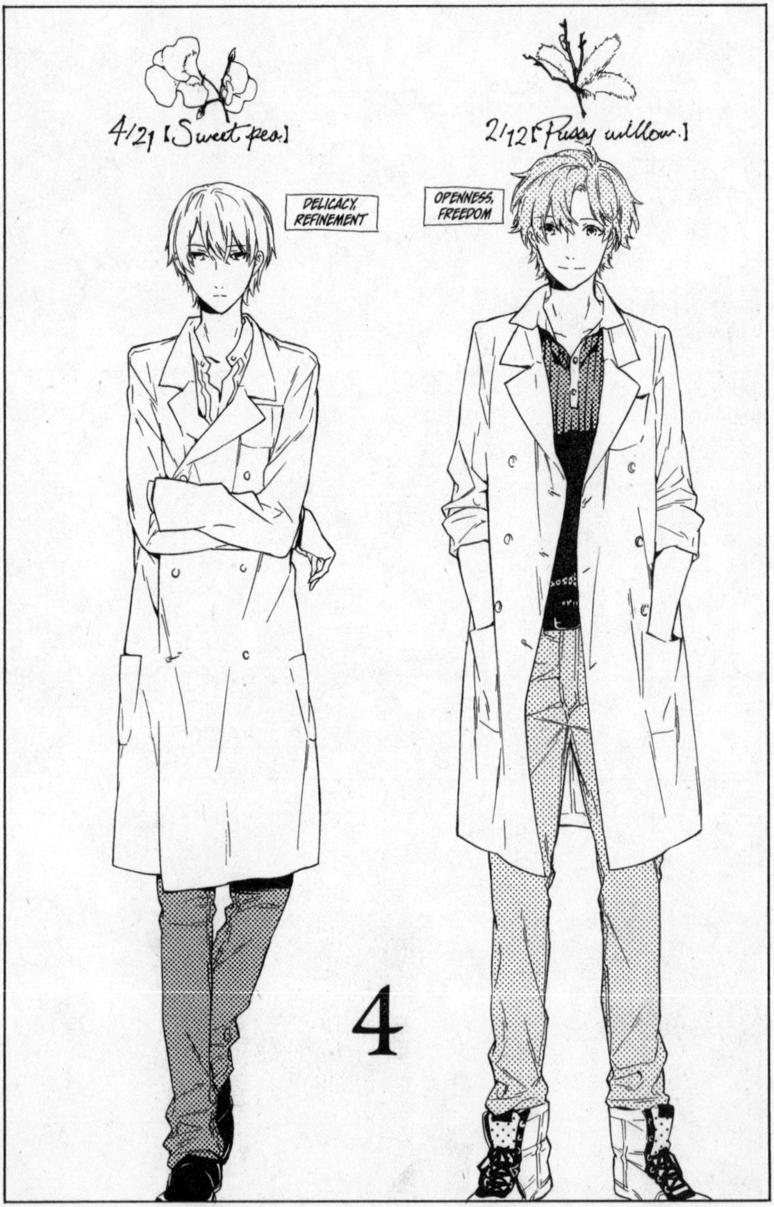
2/12 [Pussy willow.]
OPENNESS, FREEDOM
4/21 [Sweet pea.]
DELICACY, REFINEMENT
4

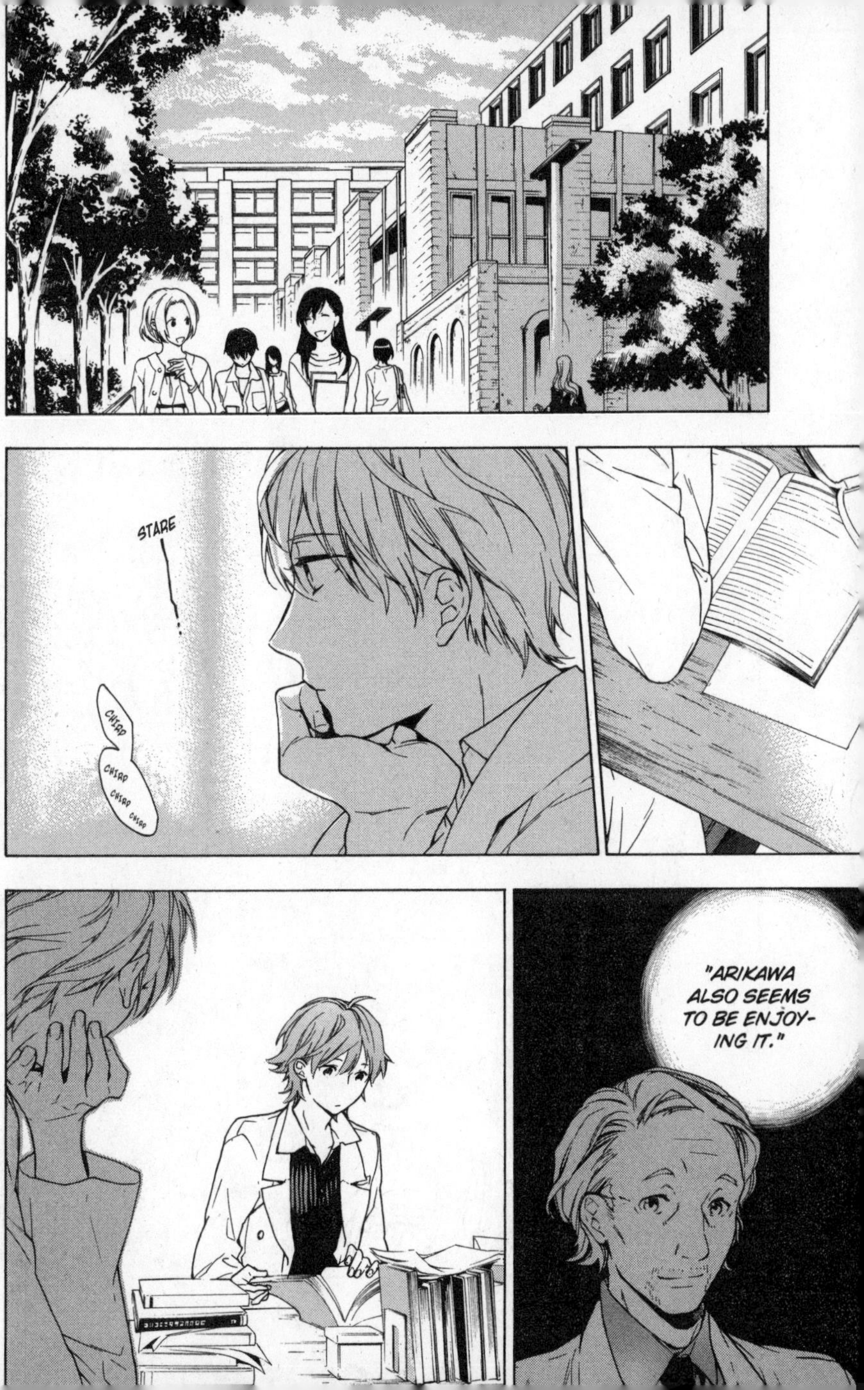
STARE
CHIRP
CHIRP
CHIRP
CHIRP
"ARIKAWA ALSO SEEMS TO BE ENJOY-ING IT."

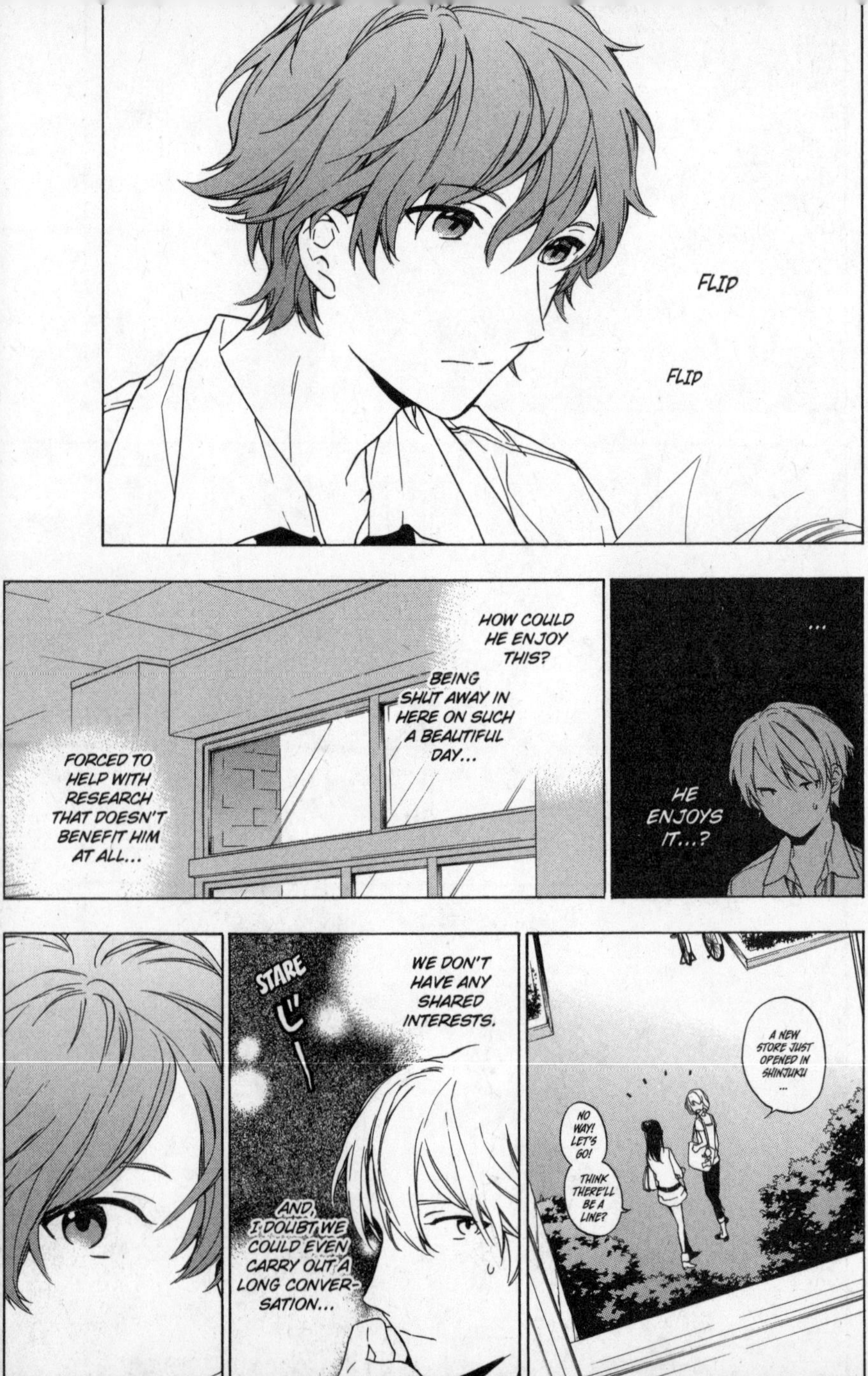
FLIP
FLIP
...
HE ENJOYS IT...?
HOW COULD HE ENJOY THIS?
BEING SHUT AWAY IN HERE ON SUCH A BEAUTIFUL DAY...
FORCED TO HELP WITH RESEARCH THAT DOESN'T BENEFIT HIM AT ALL...
A NEW STORE JUST OPENED IN SHINJUKU ...
NO WAY! LET'S GO!
THINK THERE'LL BE A LINE?
WE DON'T HAVE ANY SHARED INTERESTS.
STARE
じー
AND, I DOUBT WE COULD EVEN CARRY OUT A LONG CONVER-SATION...

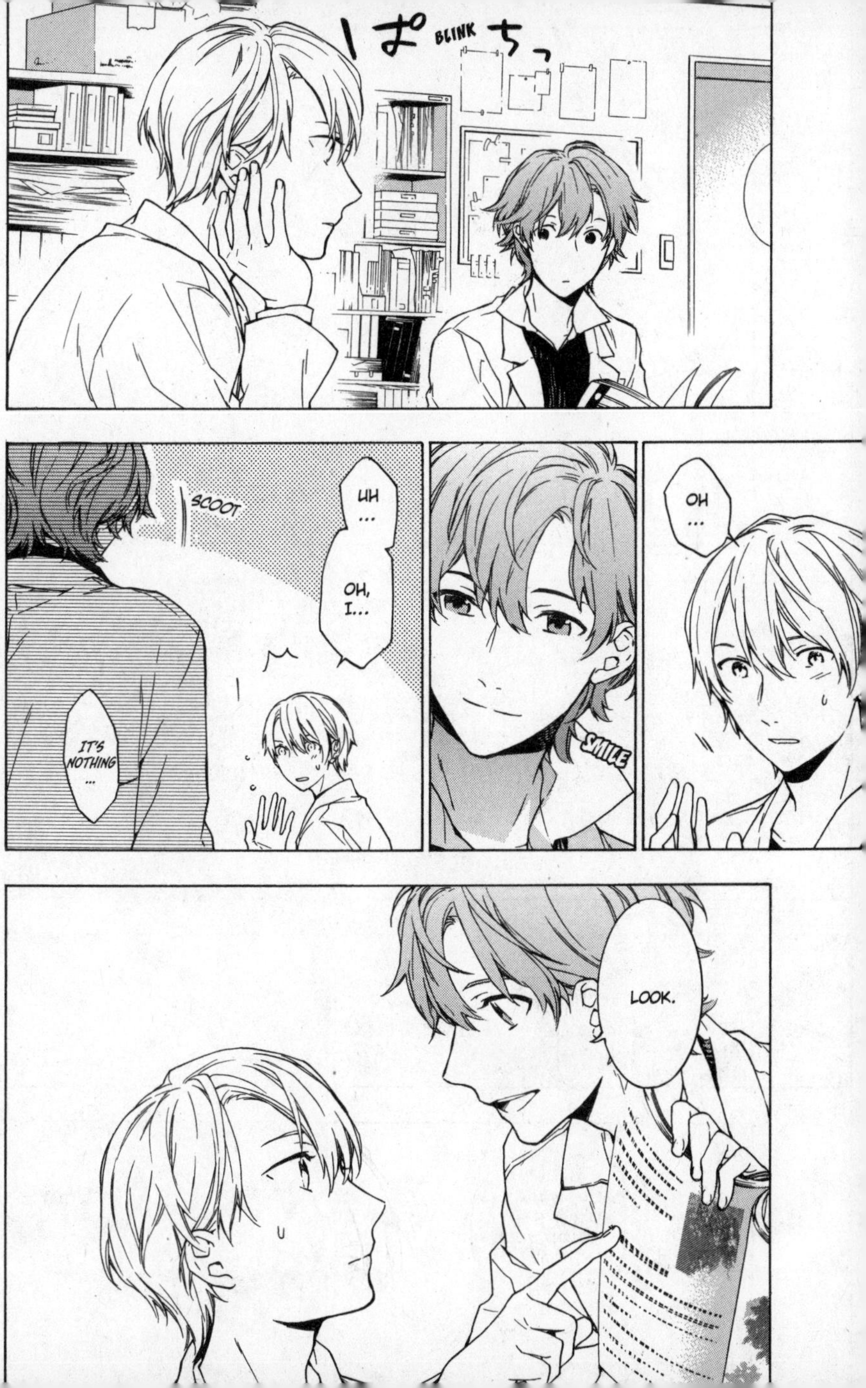
ぱちっ
BLINK
OH ...
SMILE
UH ...
OH, I...
SCOOT
IT'S NOTHING ...
LOOK.

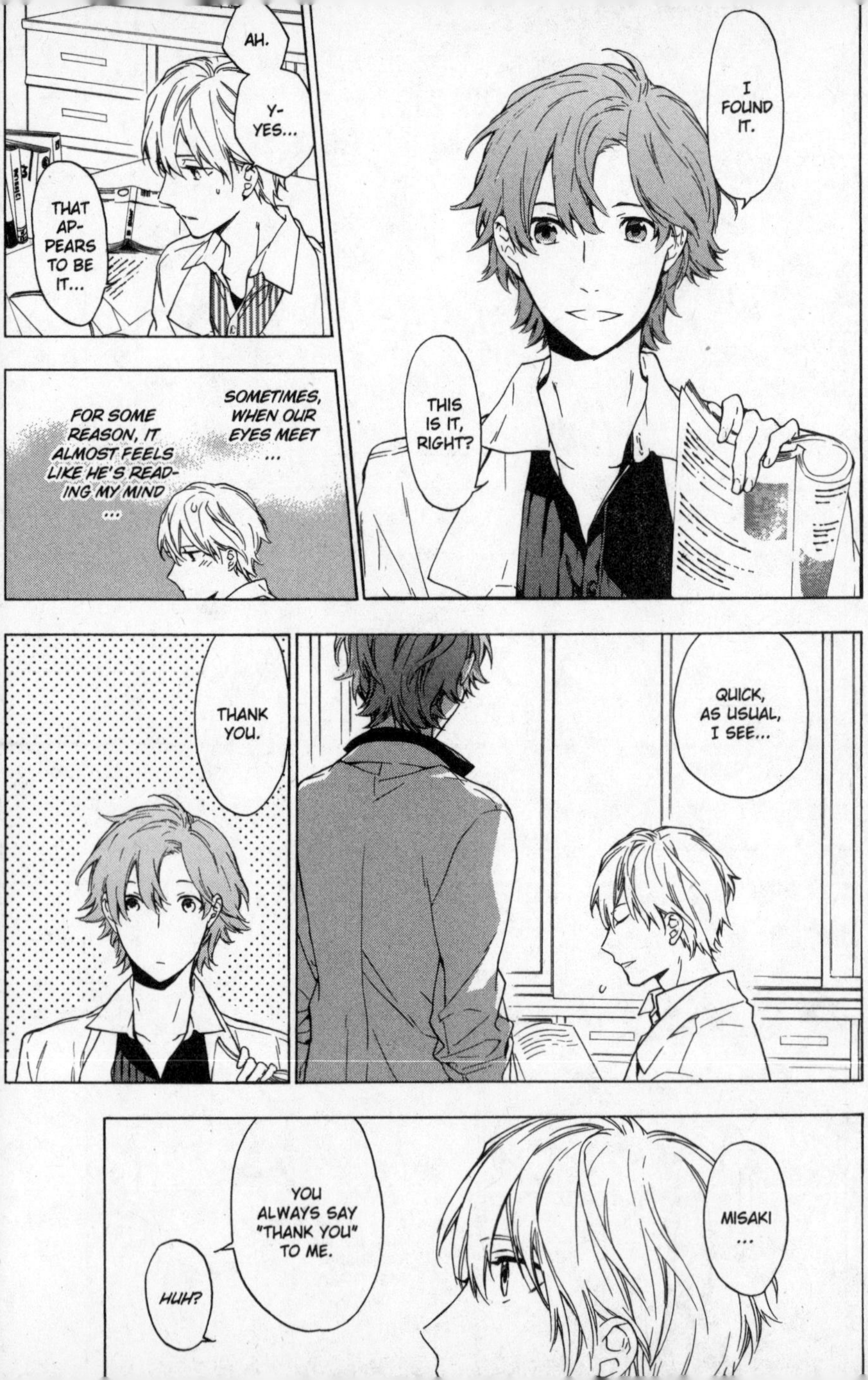
I FOUND IT.
THIS IS IT, RIGHT?
AH.
Y-YES...
THAT APPEARS TO BE IT...
SOMETIMES, WHEN OUR EYES MEET ...
FOR SOME REASON, IT ALMOST FEELS LIKE HE'S READING MY MIND ...
QUICK, AS USUAL, I SEE...
THANK YOU.
MISAKI ...
YOU ALWAYS SAY "THANK YOU" TO ME.
HUH?

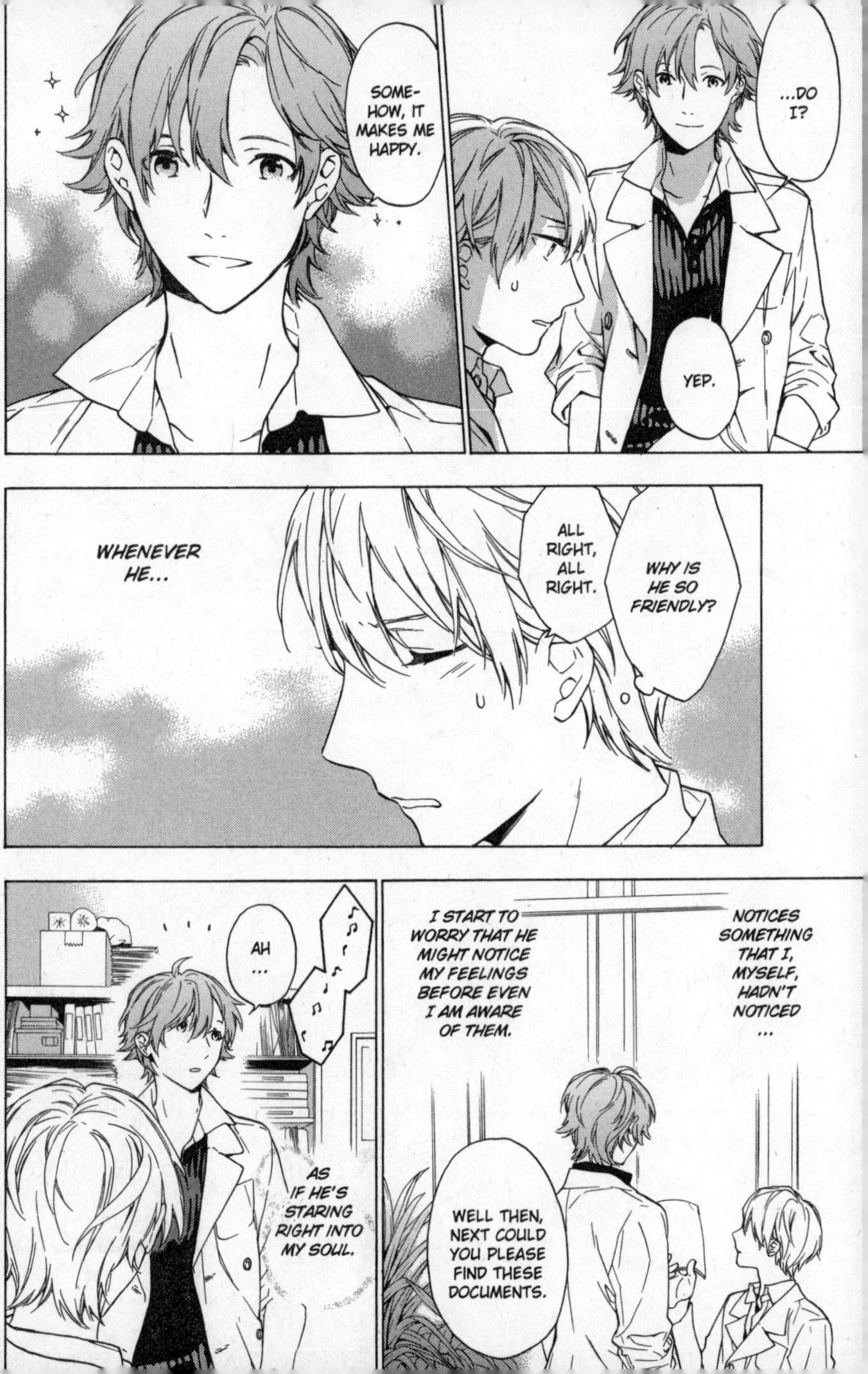
...DO I?
YEP.
SOME-HOW, IT MAKES ME HAPPY.
WHY IS HE SO FRIENDLY?
ALL RIGHT, ALL RIGHT.
WHENEVER HE...
NOTICES SOMETHING THAT I, MYSELF, HADN'T NOTICED ...
I START TO WORRY THAT HE MIGHT NOTICE MY FEELINGS BEFORE EVEN I AM AWARE OF THEM.
WELL THEN, NEXT COULD YOU PLEASE FIND THESE DOCUMENTS.
AH ...
AS IF HE'S STARING RIGHT INTO MY SOUL.

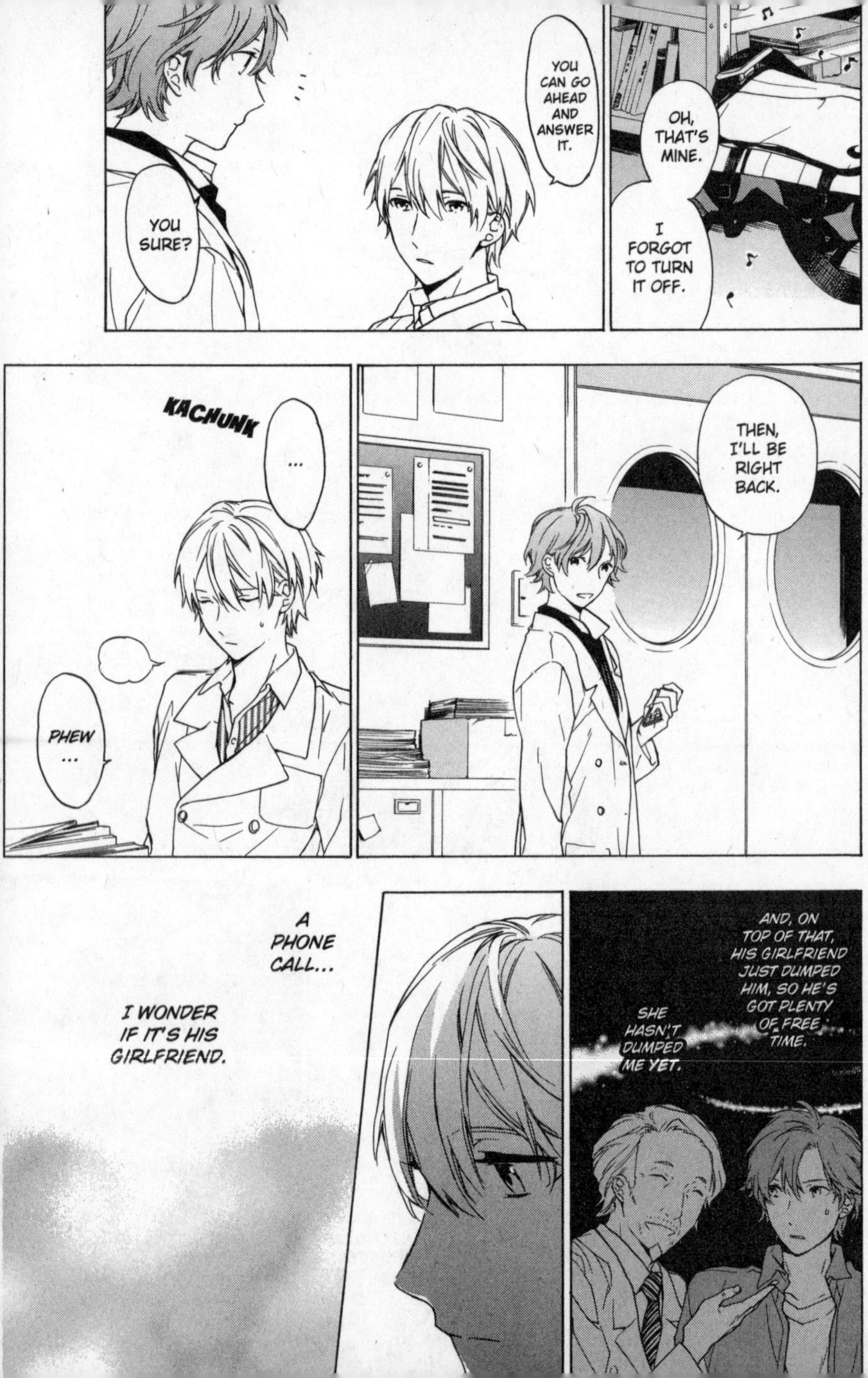
OH, THAT'S MINE.
I FORGOT TO TURN IT OFF.
YOU CAN GO AHEAD AND ANSWER IT.
YOU SURE?
THEN, I'LL BE RIGHT BACK.
KACHUNK
...
PHEW...
AND, ON TOP OF THAT, HIS GIRLFRIEND JUST DUMPED HIM, SO HE'S GOT PLENTY OF FREE TIME.
SHE HASN'T DUMPED ME YET.
A PHONE CALL...
I WONDER IF IT'S HIS GIRLFRIEND.

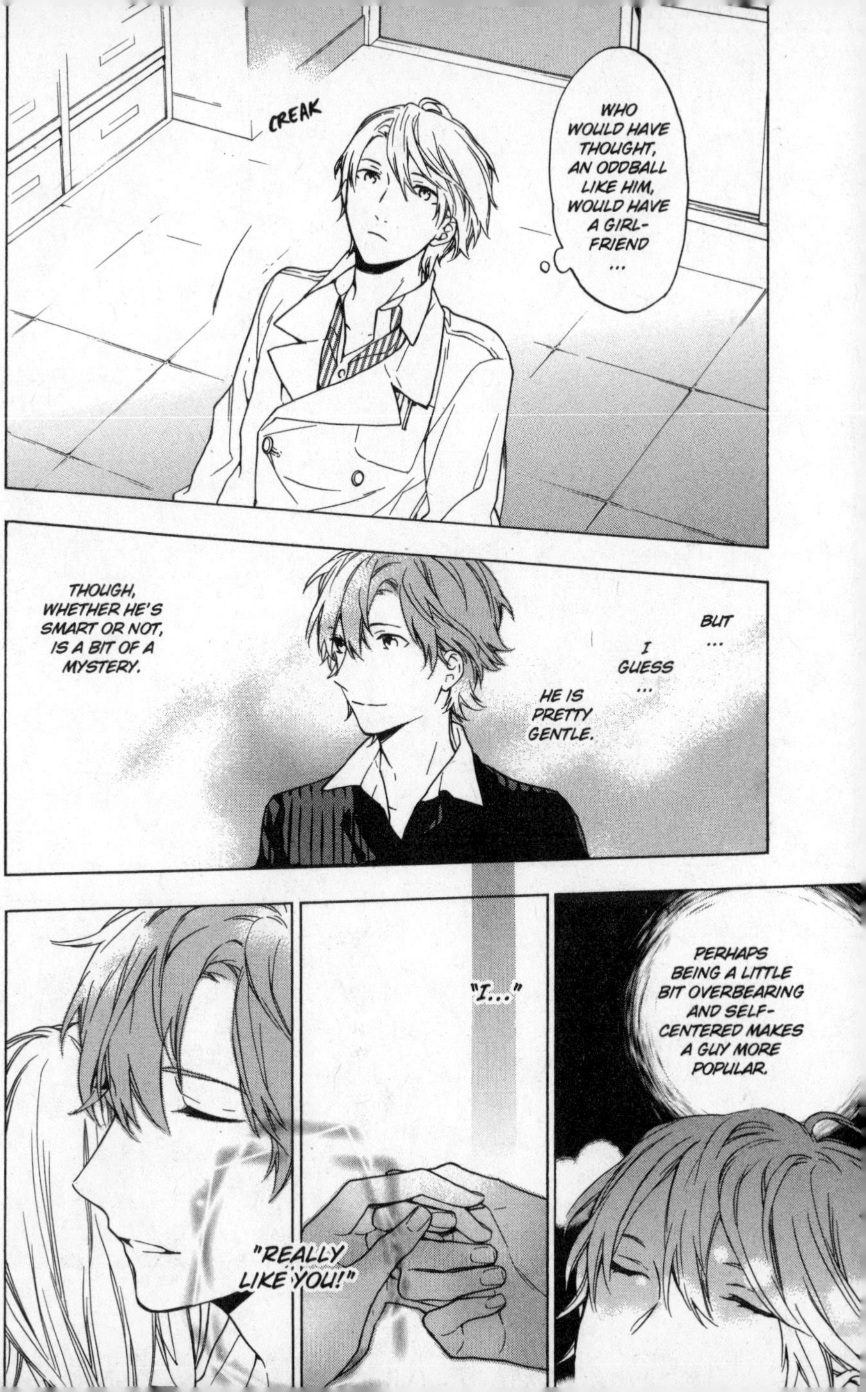
WHO WOULD HAVE THOUGHT, AN ODDBALL LIKE HIM, WOULD HAVE A GIRL-FRIEND ...
CREAK
BUT ...
I GUESS ...
HE IS PRETTY GENTLE.
THOUGH, WHETHER HE'S SMART OR NOT, IS A BIT OF A MYSTERY.
PERHAPS BEING A LITTLE BIT OVERBEARING AND SELF-CENTERED MAKES A GUY MORE POPULAR.
"I..."
"REALLY LIKE YOU!"

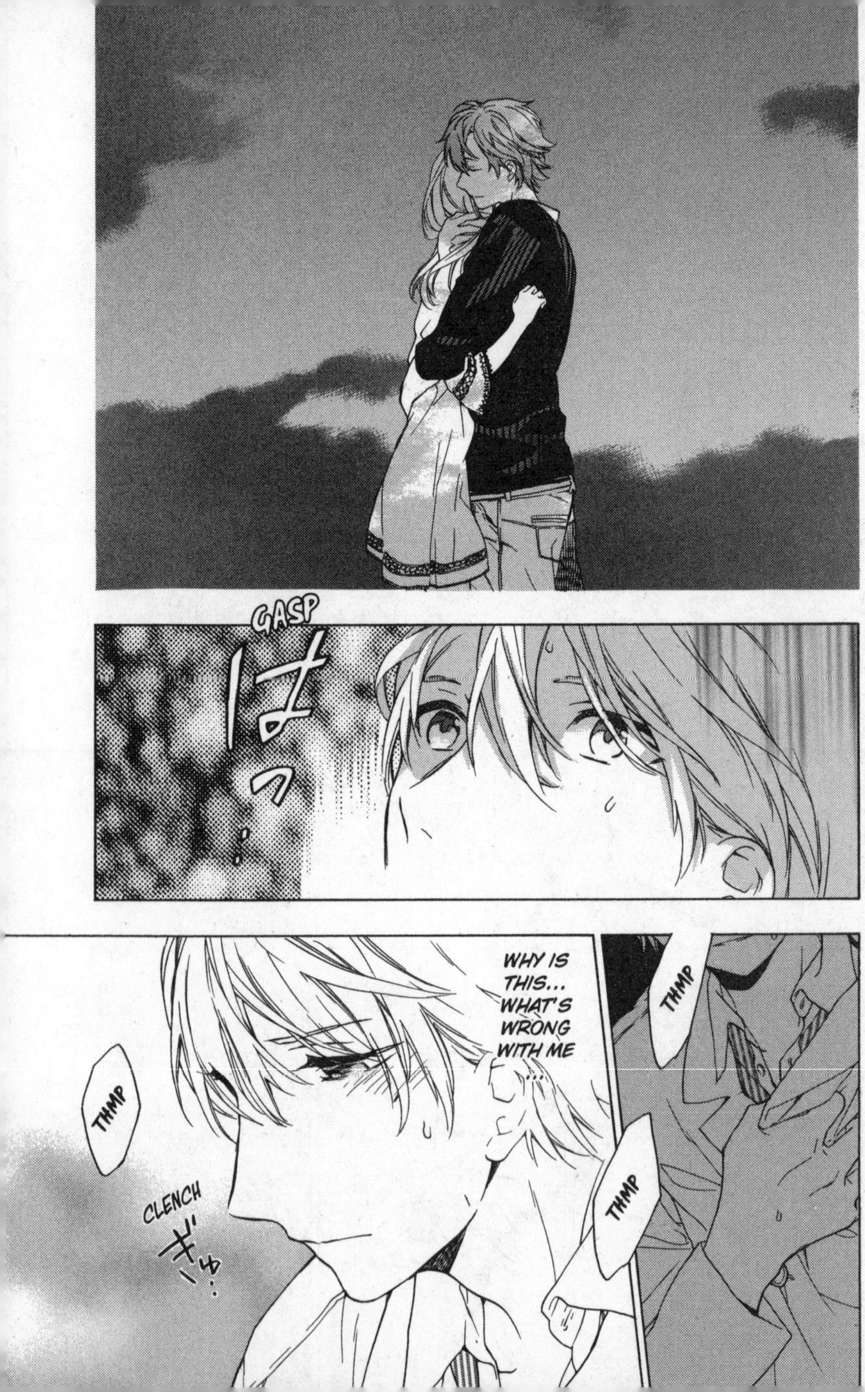
GASP
はっ…
THMP
WHY IS THIS… WHAT'S WRONG WITH ME…
THMP
THMP
CLENCH
ぎゅ…

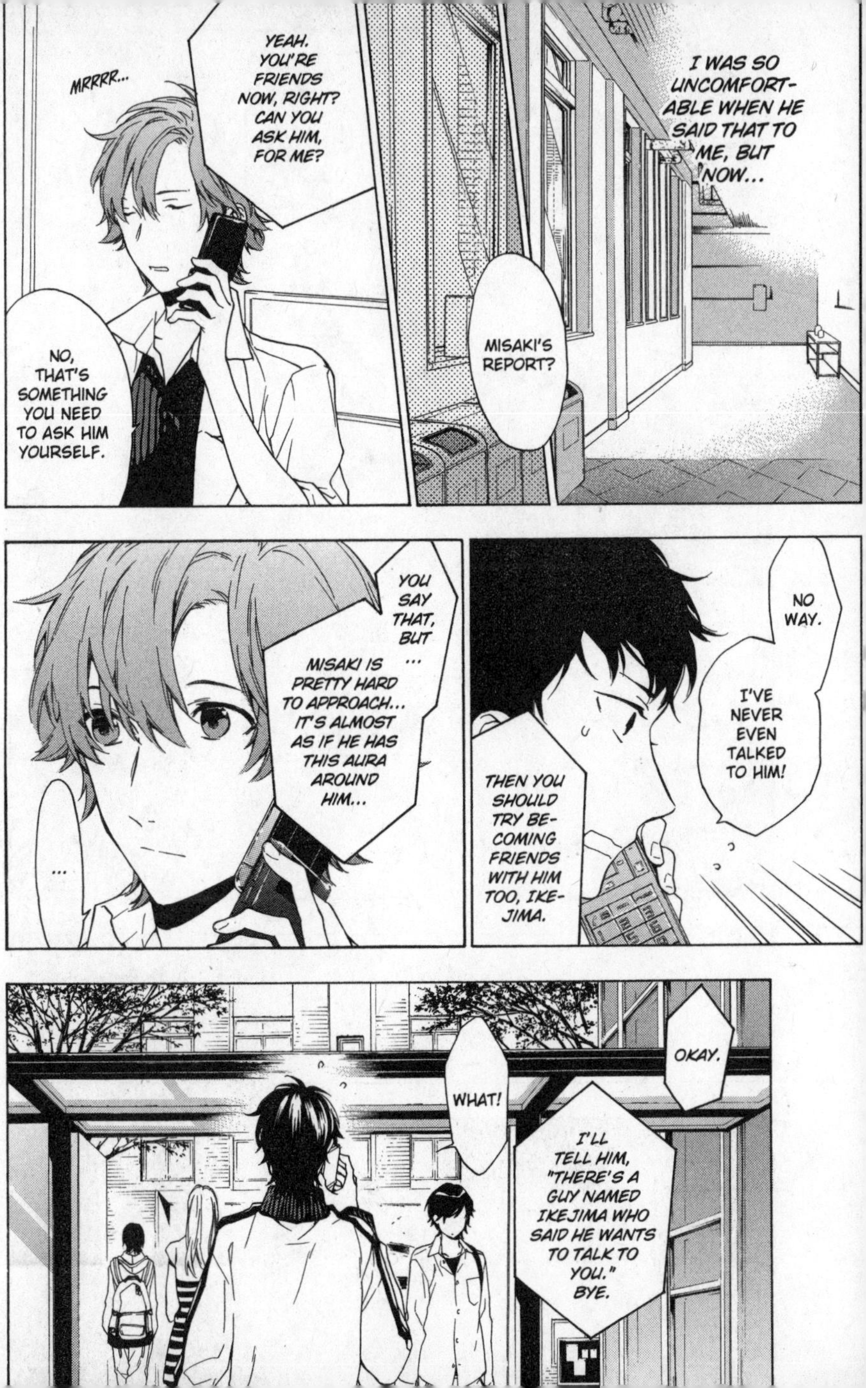
I WAS SO UNCOMFORTABLE WHEN HE SAID THAT TO ME, BUT NOW...
MISAKI'S REPORT?
YEAH. YOU'RE FRIENDS NOW, RIGHT? CAN YOU ASK HIM, FOR ME?
MRRRR...
NO, THAT'S SOMETHING YOU NEED TO ASK HIM YOURSELF.
NO WAY.
I'VE NEVER EVEN TALKED TO HIM!
THEN YOU SHOULD TRY BE-COMING FRIENDS WITH HIM TOO, IKE-JIMA.
YOU SAY THAT, BUT ...
MISAKI IS PRETTY HARD TO APPROACH... IT'S ALMOST AS IF HE HAS THIS AURA AROUND HIM...
...
OKAY.
WHAT!
I'LL TELL HIM, "THERE'S A GUY NAMED IKEJIMA WHO SAID HE WANTS TO TALK TO YOU." BYE.

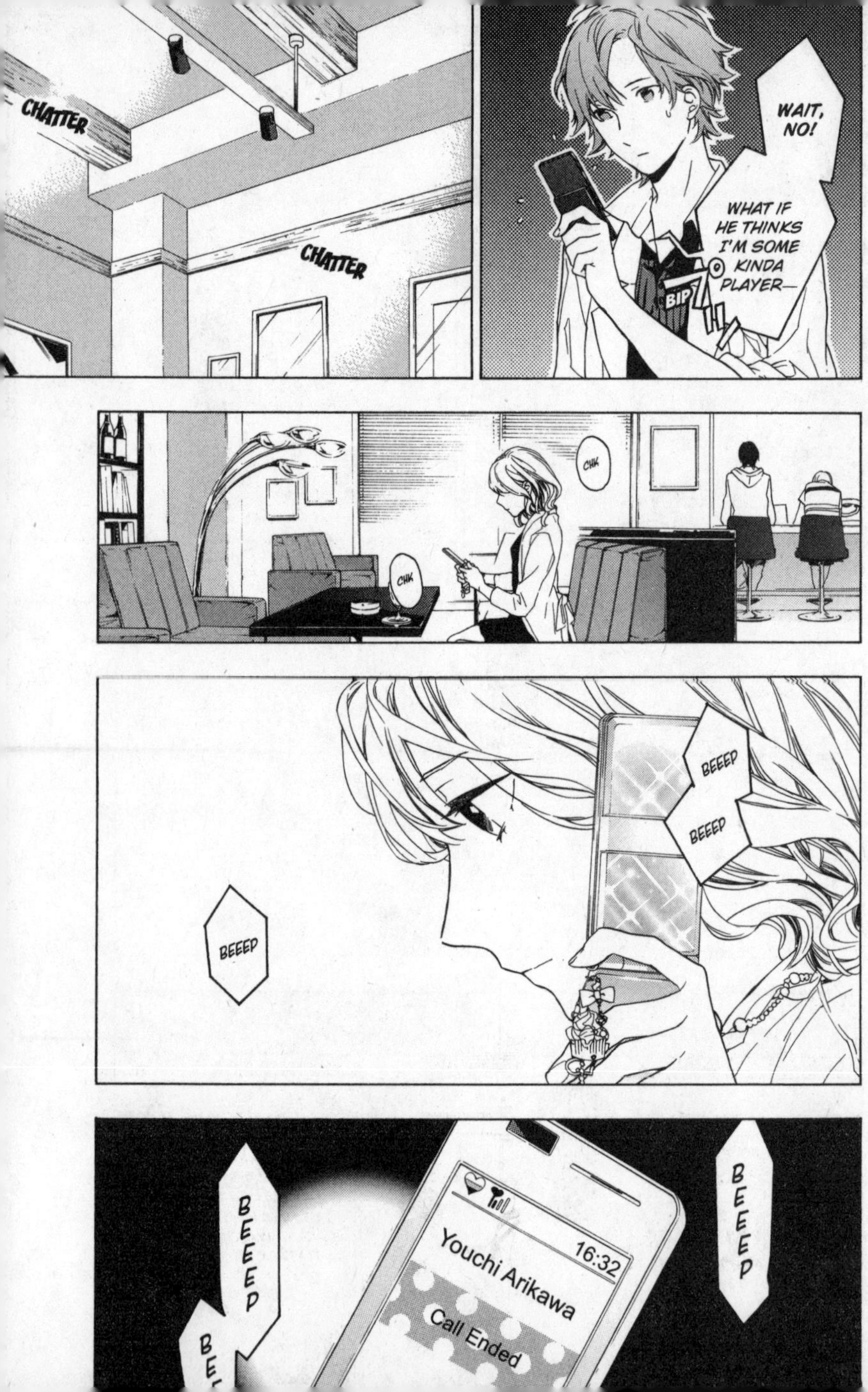
WAIT, NO!
WHAT IF HE THINKS I'M SOME KINDA PLAYER—
BIP
CHATTER
CHATTER
CHK
CHK
BEEEP
BEEEP
BEEEP
BEEEP
16:32
Youchi Arikawa
Call Ended
BEEEP

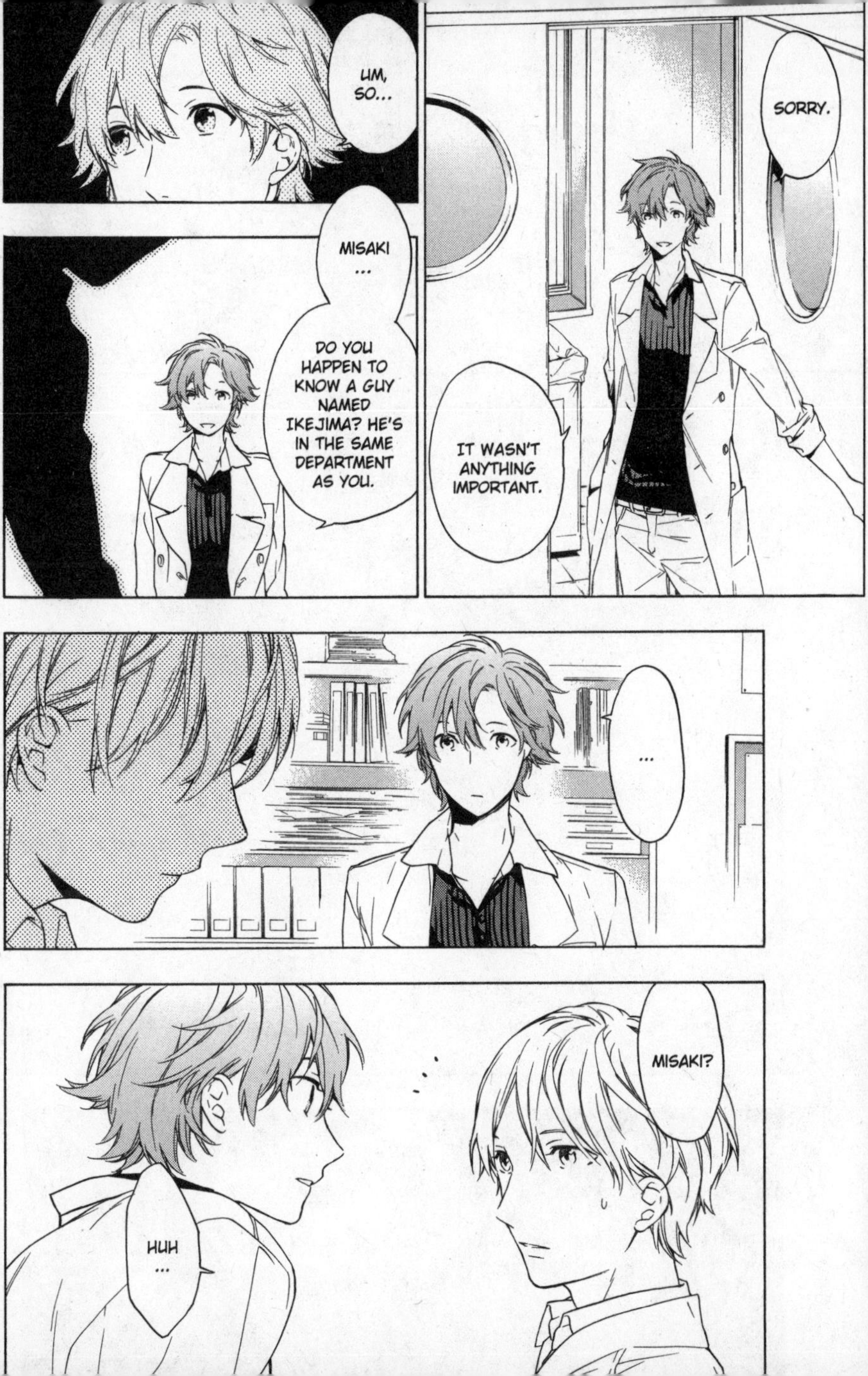
SORRY.
IT WASN'T ANYTHING IMPORTANT.
UM, SO...
MISAKI ...
DO YOU HAPPEN TO KNOW A GUY NAMED IKEJIMA? HE'S IN THE SAME DEPARTMENT AS YOU.
...
MISAKI?
HUH ...

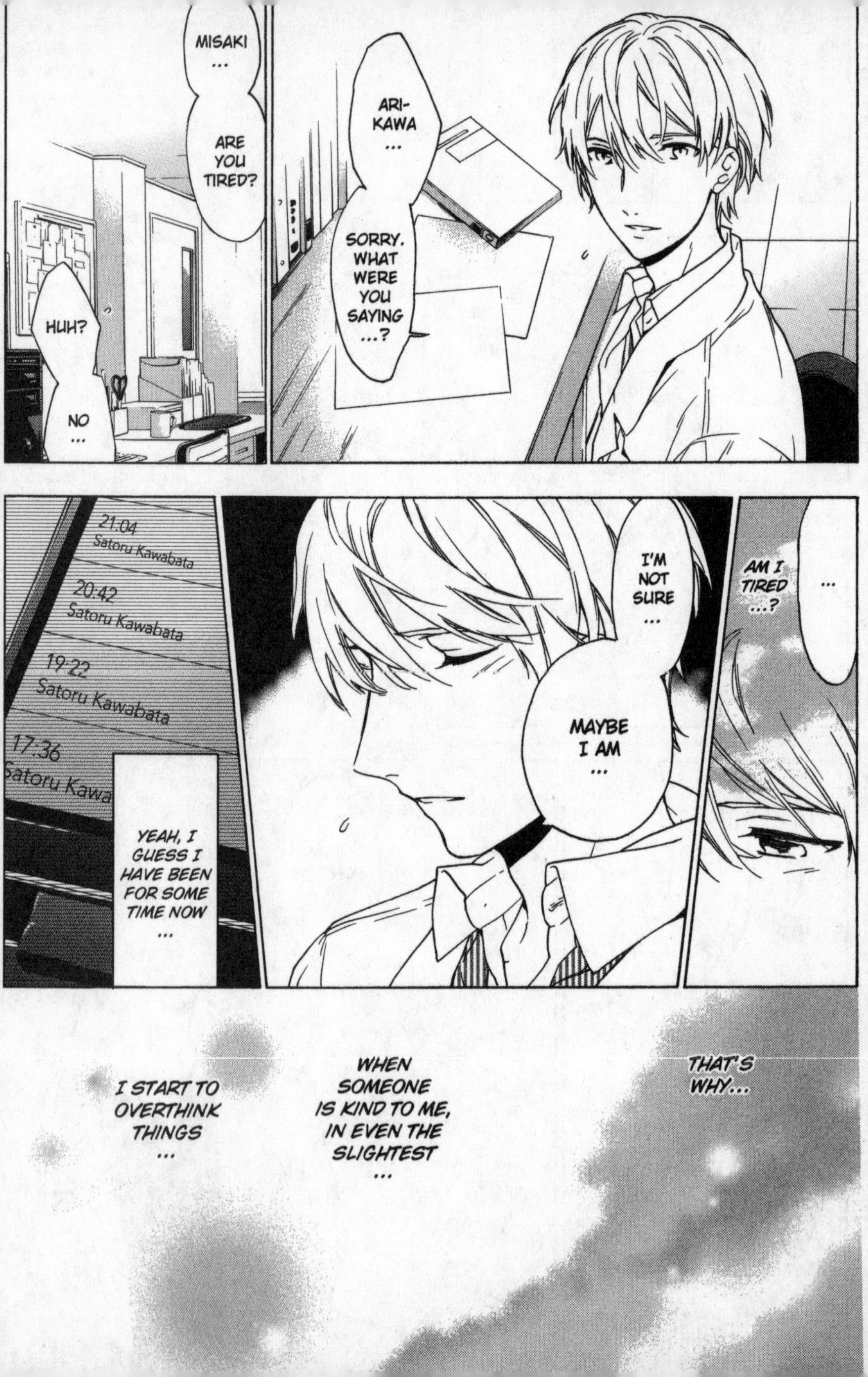
ARI-KAWA ...
SORRY. WHAT WERE YOU SAYING ...?
MISAKI ...
ARE YOU TIRED?
HUH?
NO ...
...
AM I TIRED ...?
I'M NOT SURE ...
MAYBE I AM ...
21:04
Satoru Kawabata
20:42
Satoru Kawabata
19:22
Satoru Kawabata
17:36
Satoru Kawa
YEAH, I GUESS I HAVE BEEN FOR SOME TIME NOW ...
THAT'S WHY...
WHEN SOMEONE IS KIND TO ME, IN EVEN THE SLIGHTEST ...
I START TO OVERTHINK THINGS ...

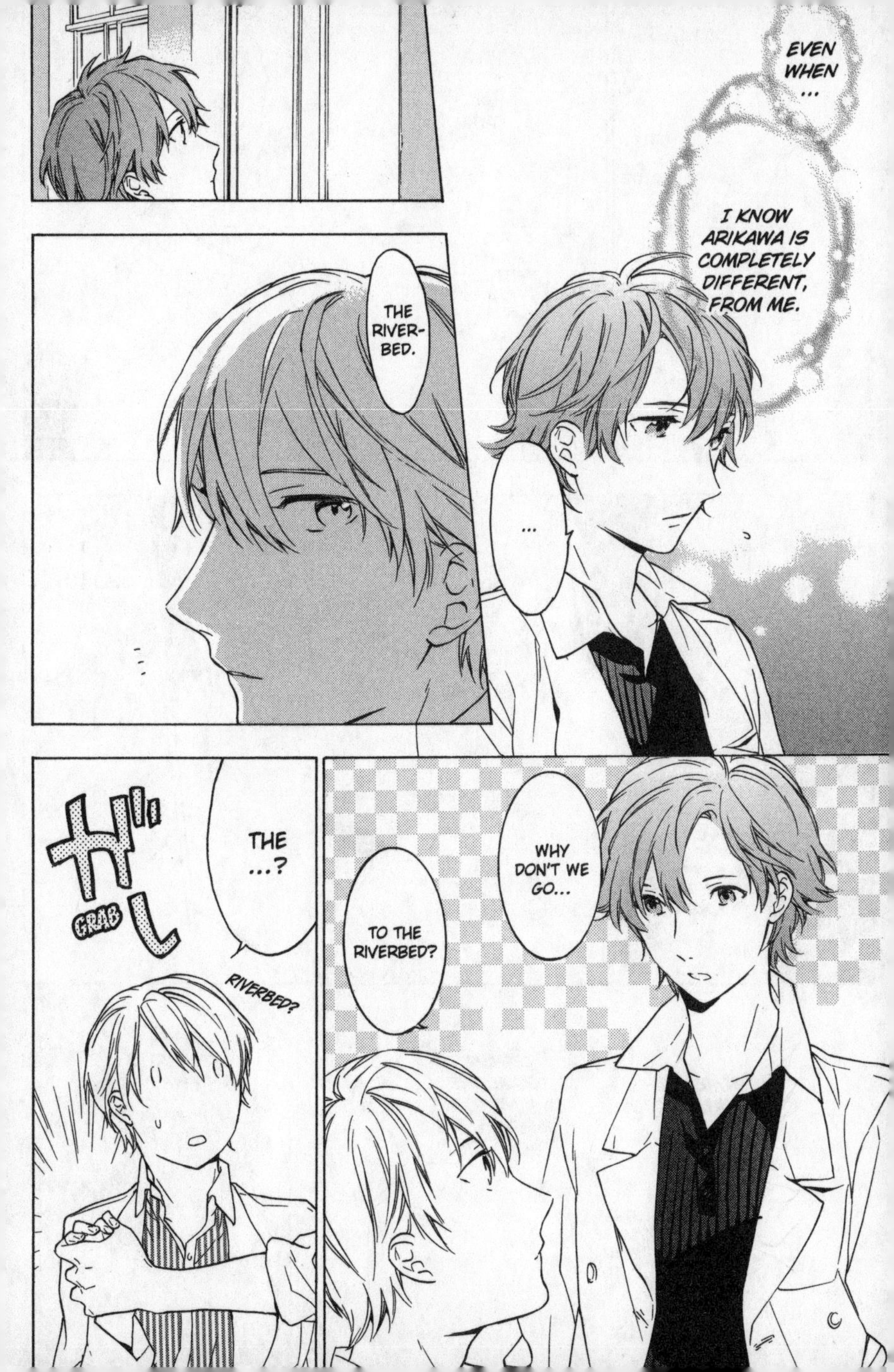
EVEN WHEN...
I KNOW ARIKAWA IS COMPLETELY DIFFERENT, FROM ME.
...
THE RIVER-BED.
WHY DON'T WE GO...
TO THE RIVERBED?
THE ...?
ガし
GRAB
RIVERBED?

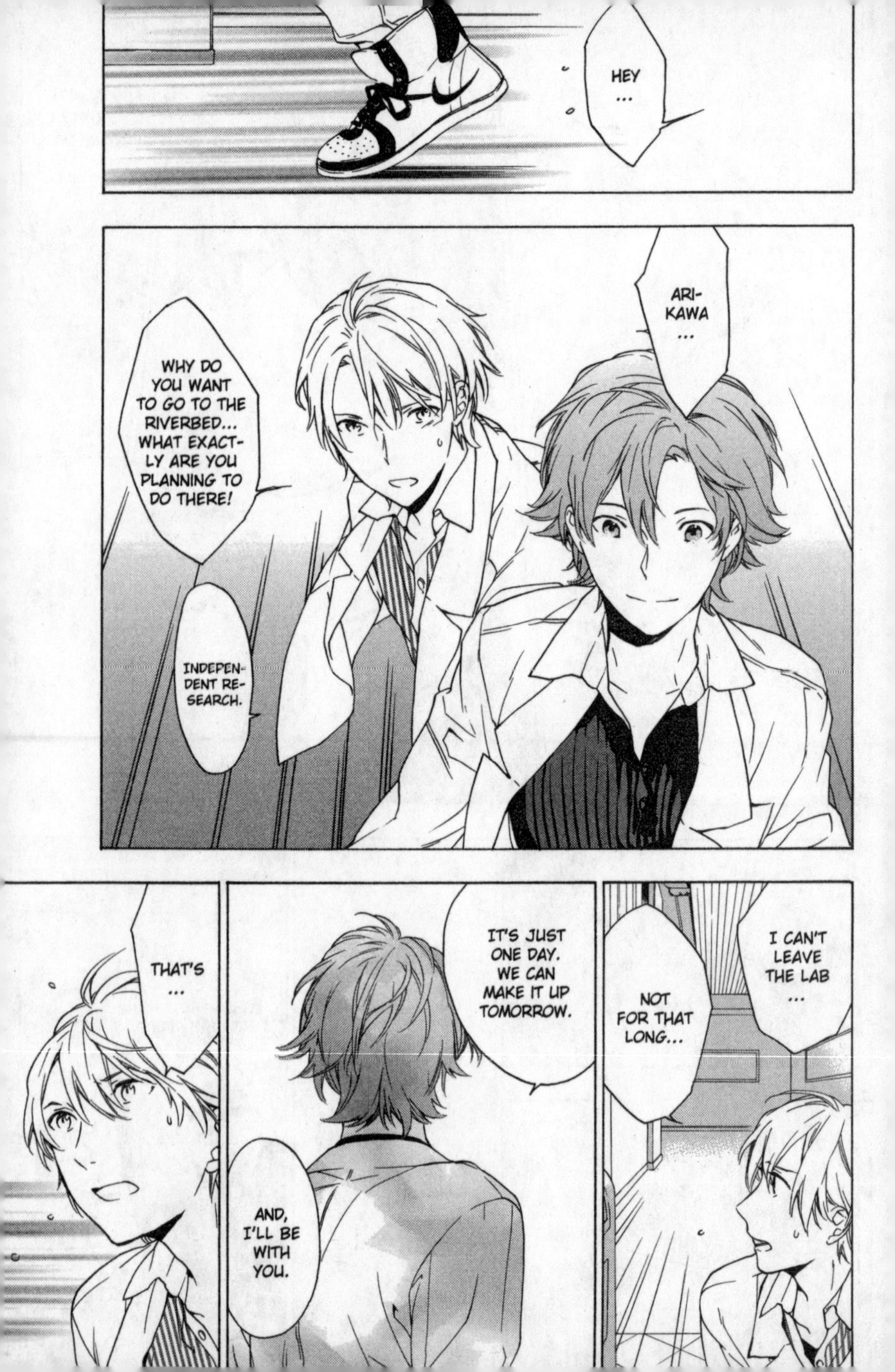
HEY ...
ARI-KAWA ...
WHY DO YOU WANT TO GO TO THE RIVERBED... WHAT EXACTLY ARE YOU PLANNING TO DO THERE!
INDEPENDENT RESEARCH.
I CAN'T LEAVE THE LAB ...
NOT FOR THAT LONG...
IT'S JUST ONE DAY. WE CAN MAKE IT UP TOMORROW.
AND, I'LL BE WITH YOU.
THAT'S ...

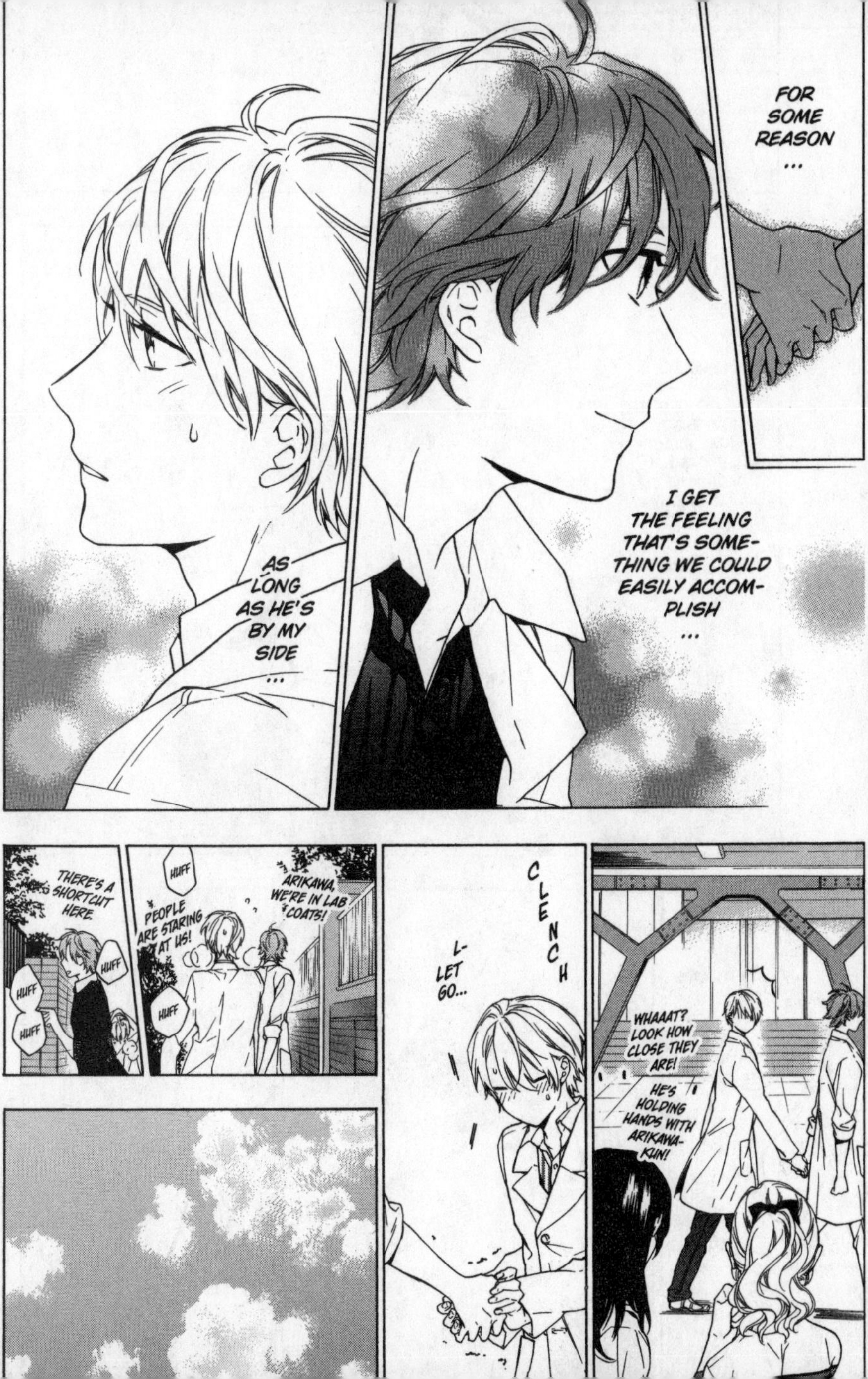

FOR SOME REASON...
I GET THE FEELING THAT'S SOME-THING WE COULD EASILY ACCOM-PLISH...
AS LONG AS HE'S BY MY SIDE...
WHAAAT? LOOK HOW CLOSE THEY ARE!
HE'S HOLDING HANDS WITH ARIKAWA-KUN!
CLENCH
L-LET GO...
HUFF
ARIKAWA, WE'RE IN LAB COATS!
PEOPLE ARE STARING AT US!
HUFF
THERE'S A SHORTCUT HERE.
HUFF
HUFF
HUFF

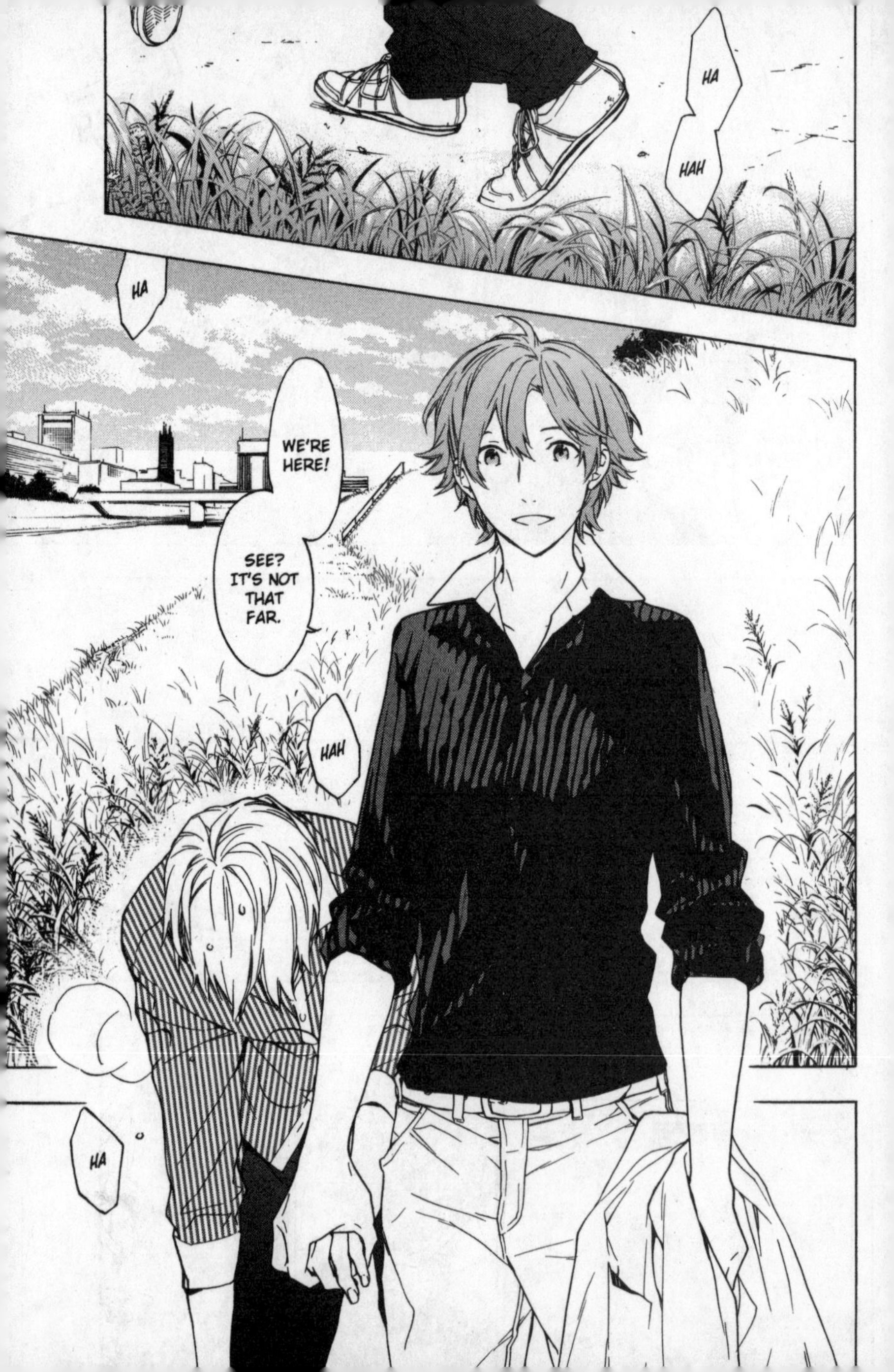
HA
HAH
HA
WE'RE HERE!
SEE? IT'S NOT THAT FAR.
HAH
HA

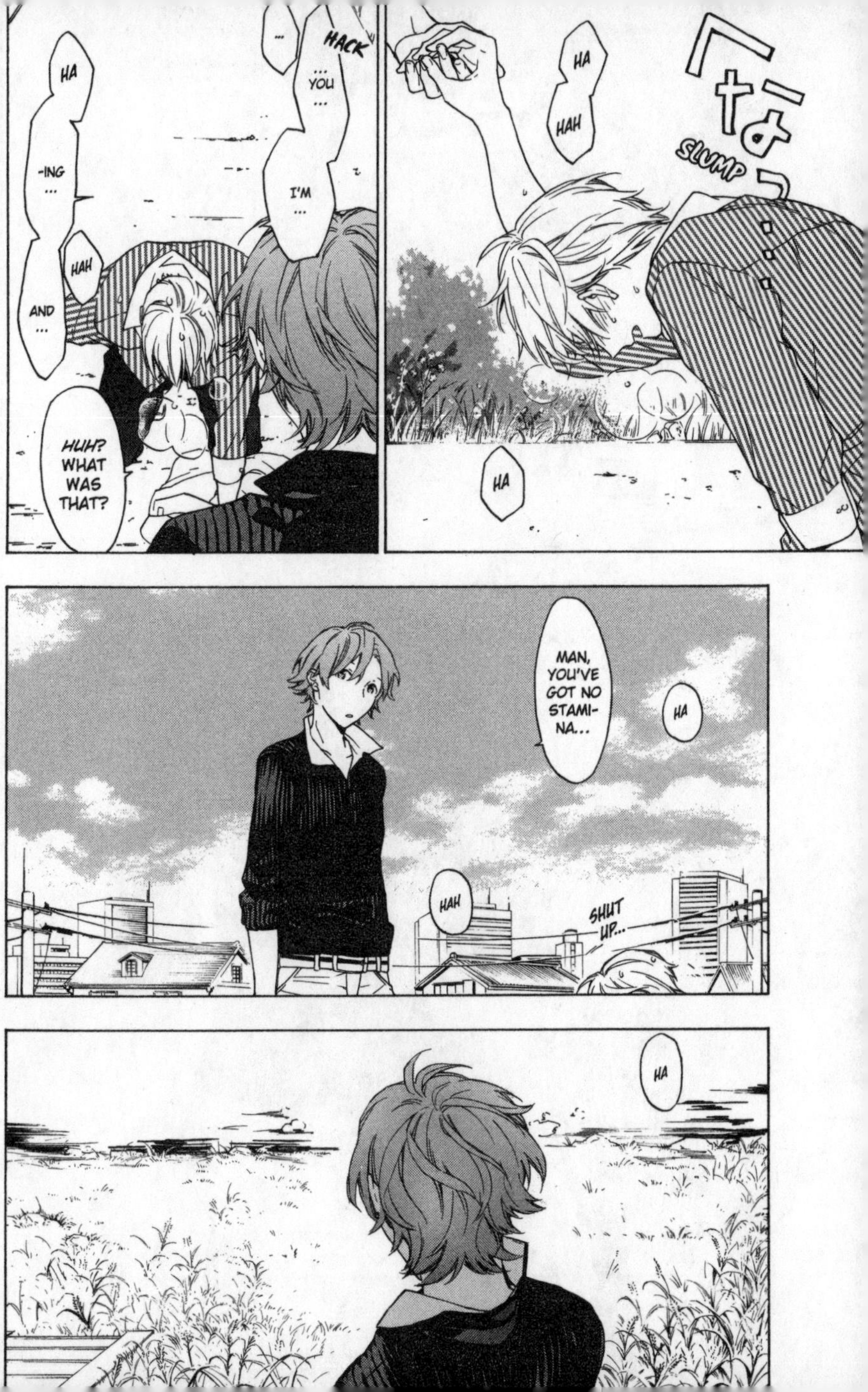
HA
HAH
へなっ
SLUMP
HA
...
HACK
... YOU ...
I'M ...
HA
-ING ...
HAH
AND ...
HUH? WHAT WAS THAT?
HA
MAN, YOU'VE GOT NO STAMI-NA...
SHUT UP...
HAH
HA

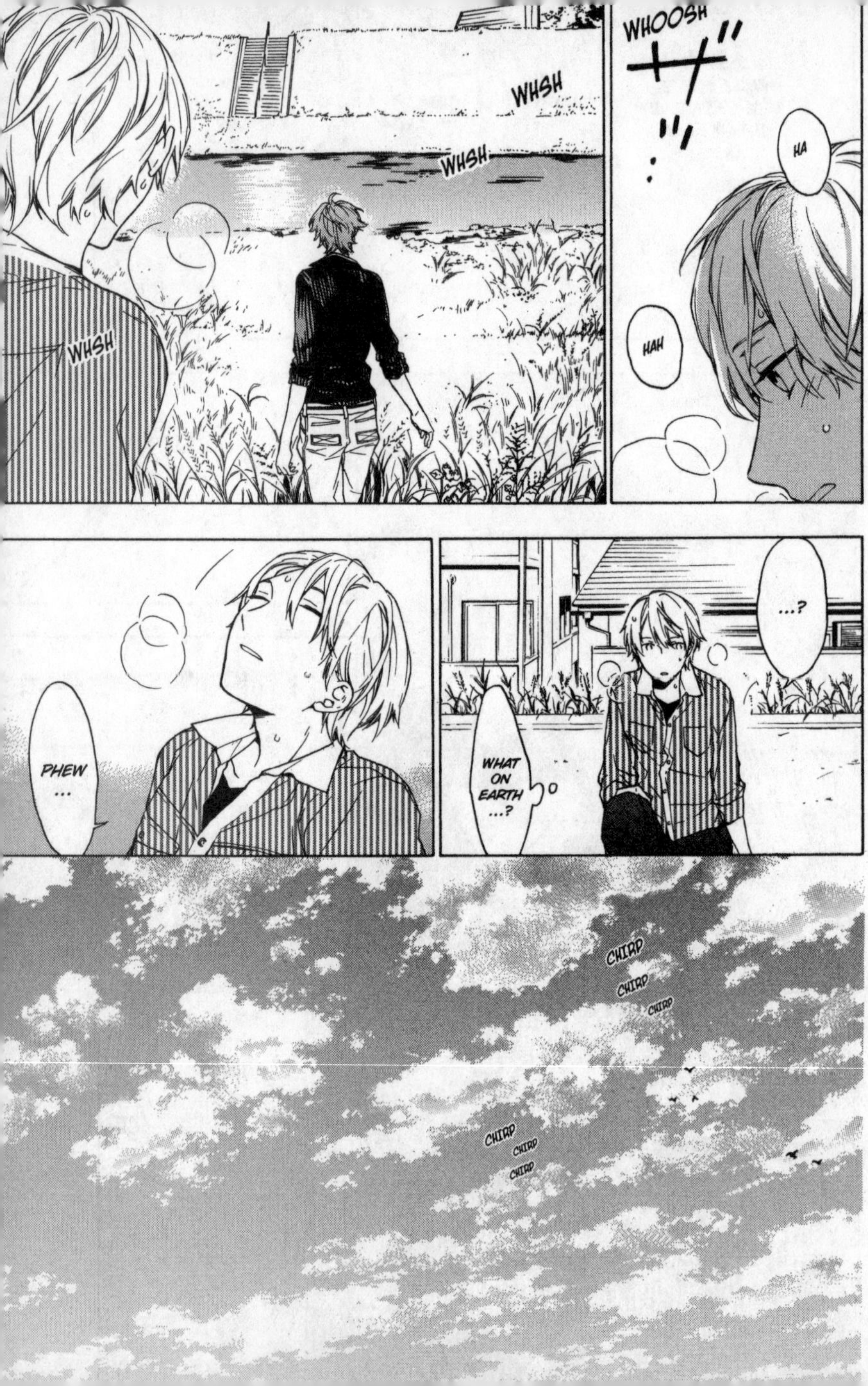
WHOOSH
HA
HAH
WHSH
WHSH
WHSH
...?
WHAT ON EARTH ...?
PHEW ...
CHIRP
CHIRP
CHIRP
CHIRP
CHIRP
CHIRP

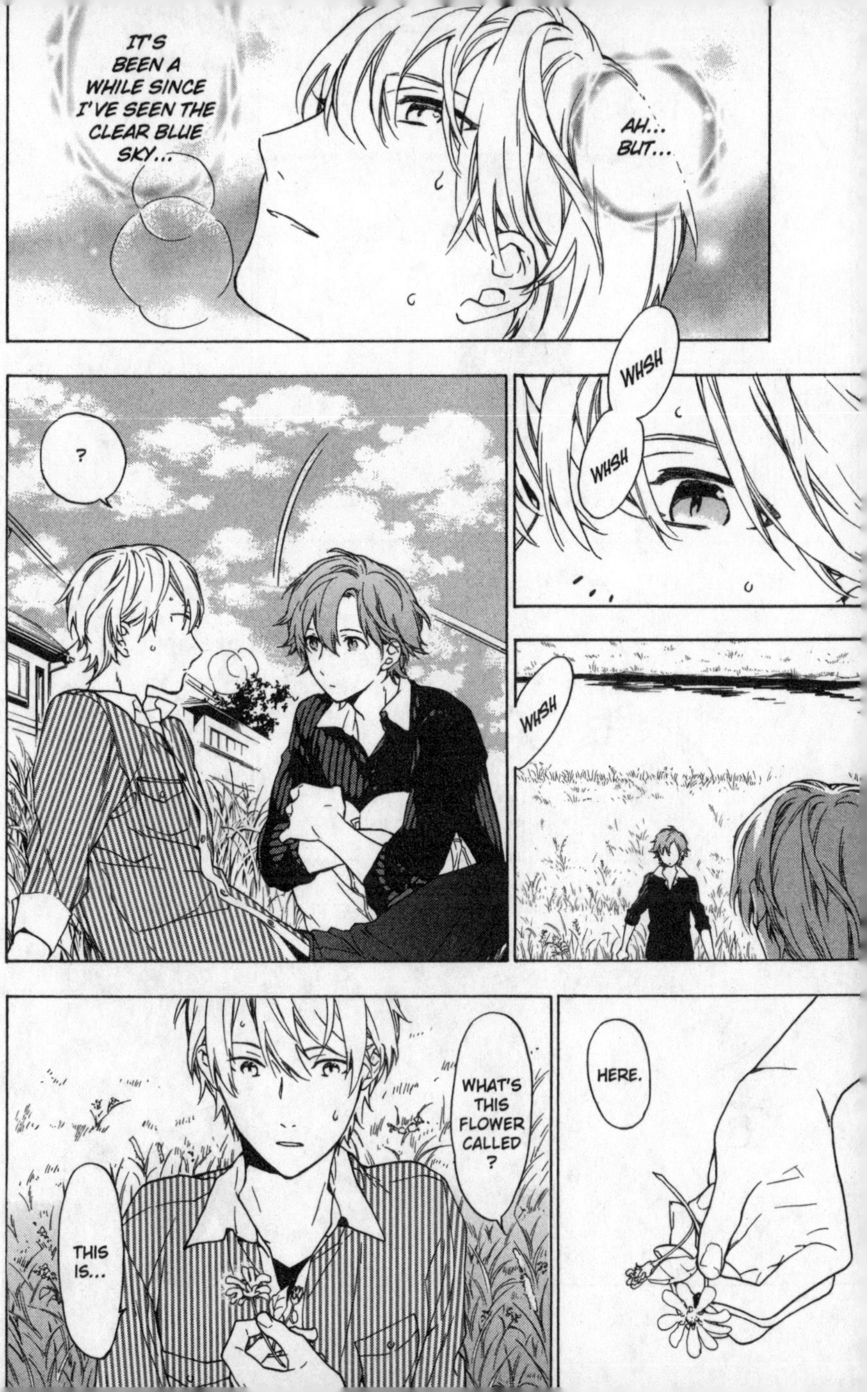
IT'S BEEN A WHILE SINCE I'VE SEEN THE CLEAR BLUE SKY...
AH... BUT...
WHSH
WHSH
...
WHSH
?
HERE.
WHAT'S THIS FLOWER CALLED?
THIS IS...

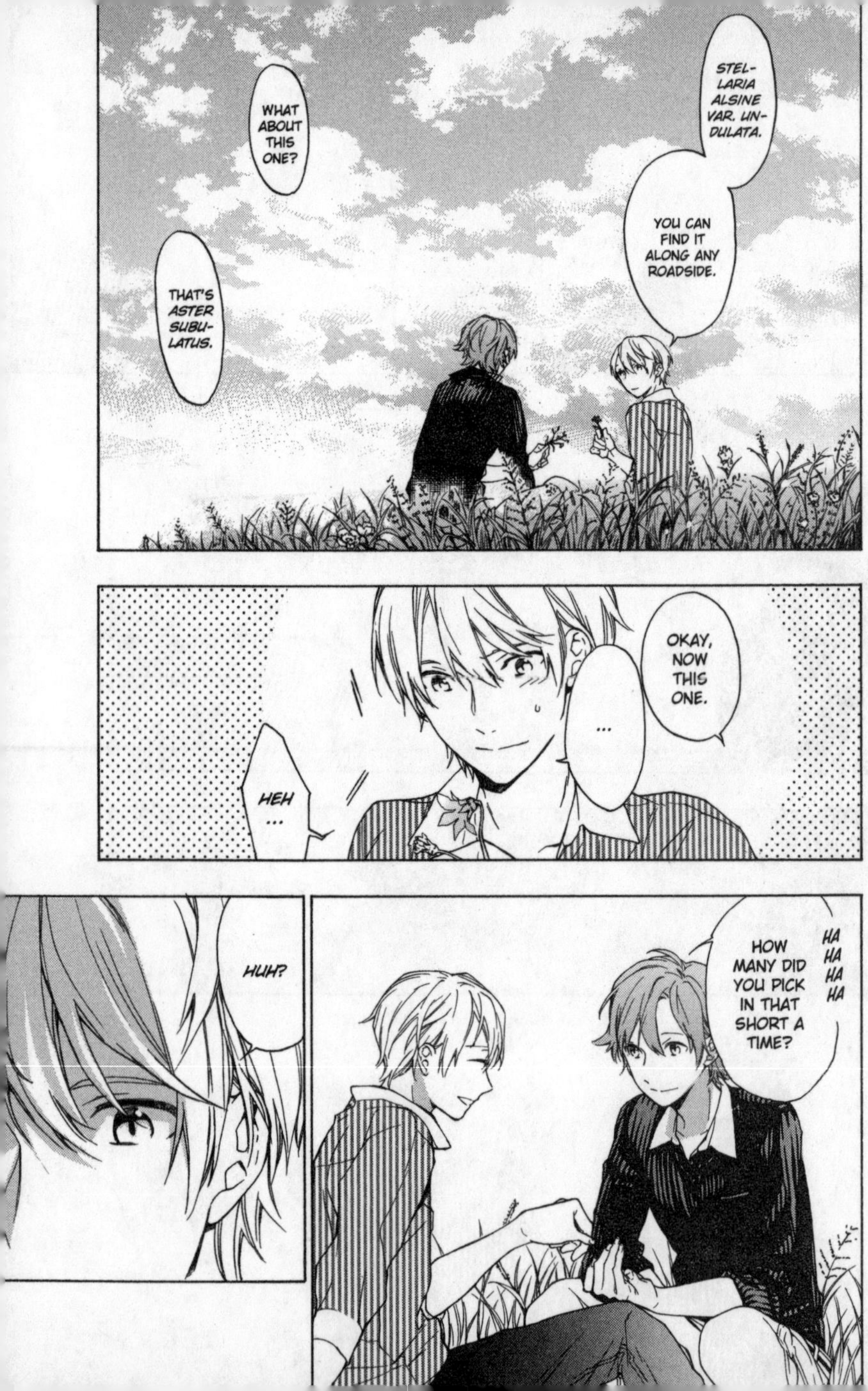
STEL-LARIA ALSINE VAR. UN-DULATA.
YOU CAN FIND IT ALONG ANY ROADSIDE.
WHAT ABOUT THIS ONE?
THAT'S ASTER SUBU-LATUS.
OKAY, NOW THIS ONE.
...
HEH ...
HA HA HA HA
HOW MANY DID YOU PICK IN THAT SHORT A TIME?
HUH?

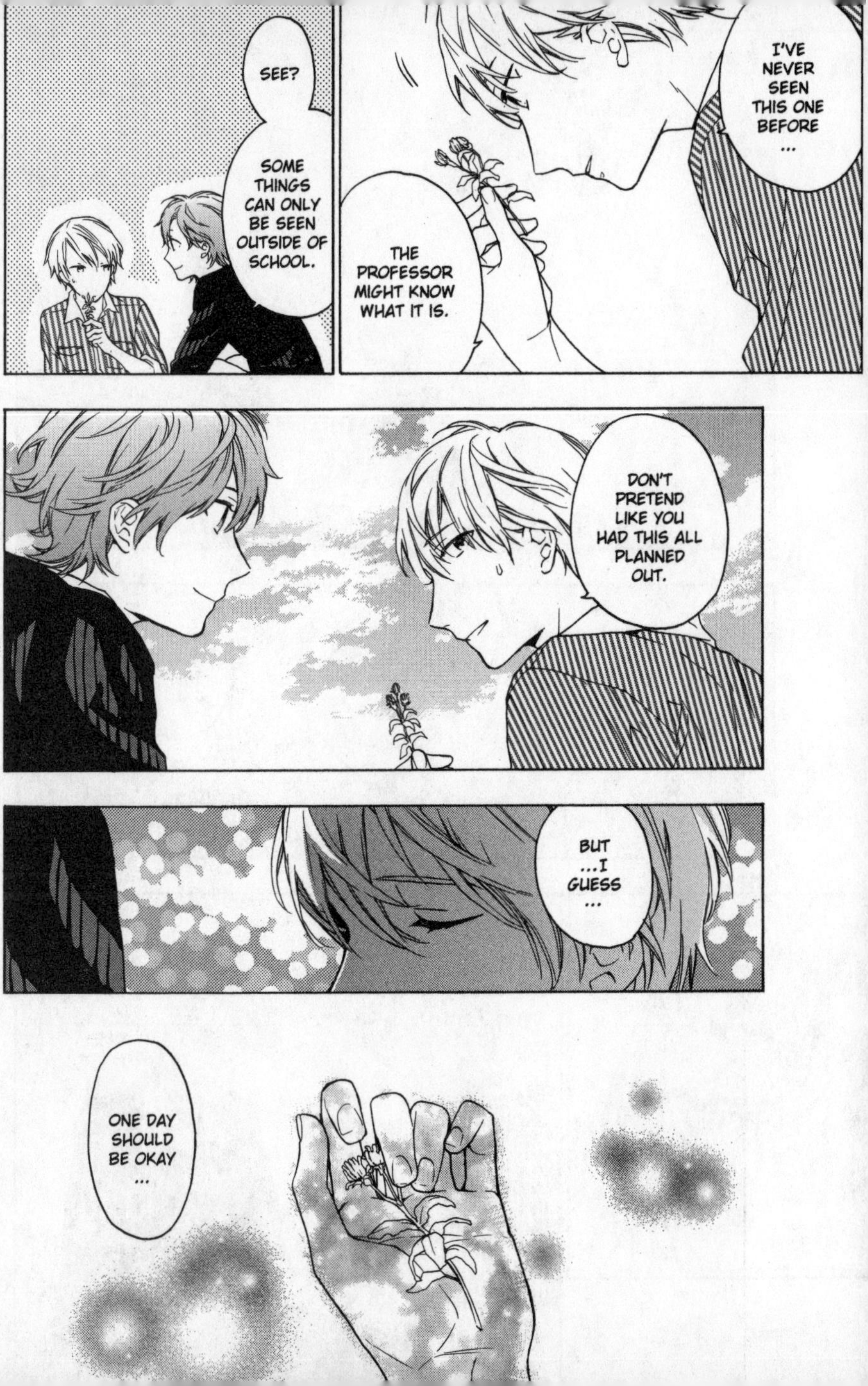
I'VE NEVER SEEN THIS ONE BEFORE ...
THE PROFESSOR MIGHT KNOW WHAT IT IS.
SEE?
SOME THINGS CAN ONLY BE SEEN OUTSIDE OF SCHOOL.
DON'T PRETEND LIKE YOU HAD THIS ALL PLANNED OUT.
BUT ...I GUESS ...
ONE DAY SHOULD BE OKAY ...

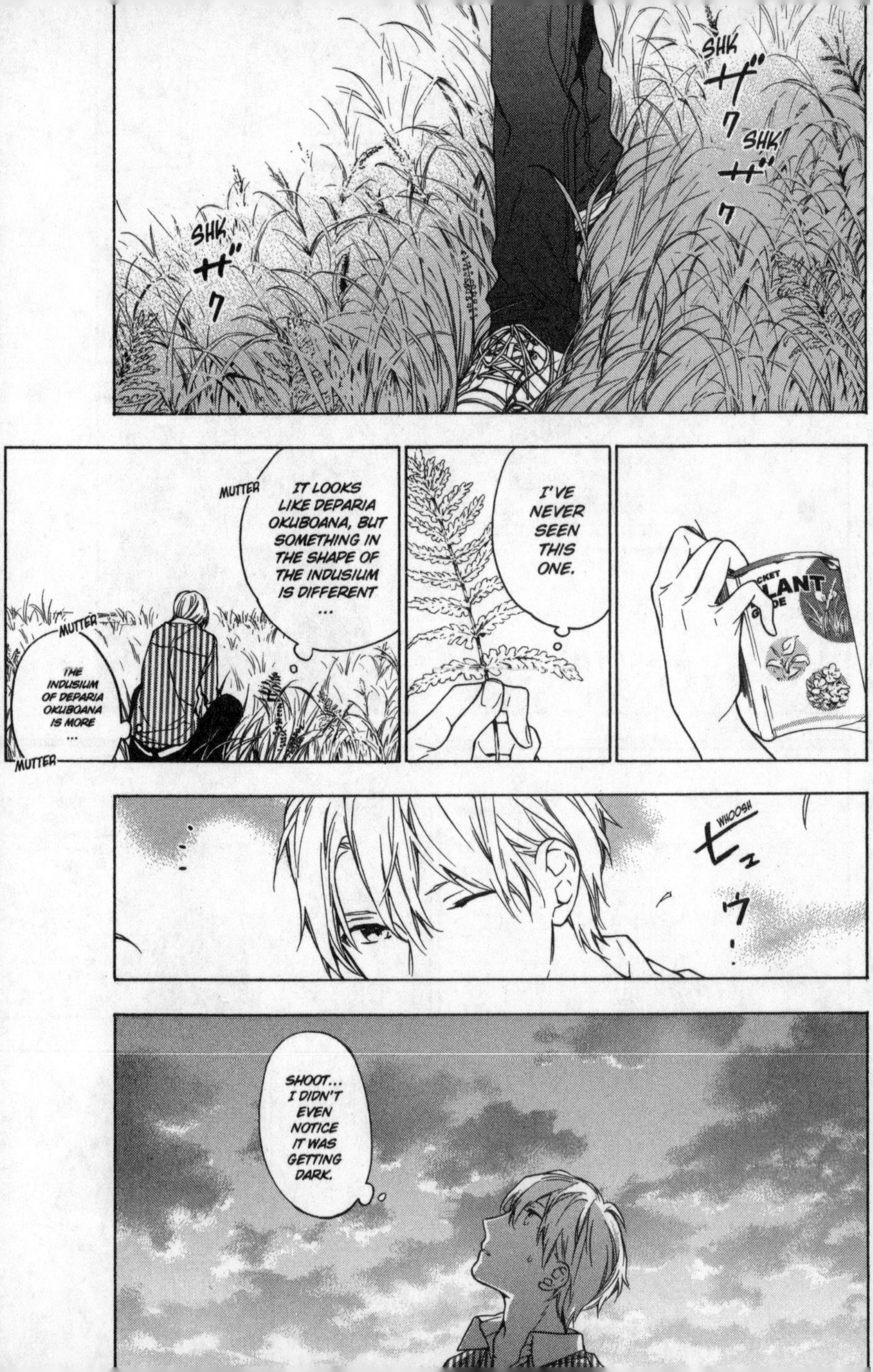
SHK
ザク
SHK
ザク
SHK
ザク
I'VE NEVER SEEN THIS ONE.
MUTTER
IT LOOKS LIKE DEPARIA OKUBOANA, BUT SOMETHING IN THE SHAPE OF THE INDUSIUM IS DIFFERENT ...
MUTTER
THE INDUSIUM OF DEPARIA OKUBOANA IS MORE ...
MUTTER
WHOOSH
ヒュウ
...
SHOOT... I DIDN'T EVEN NOTICE IT WAS GETTING DARK.

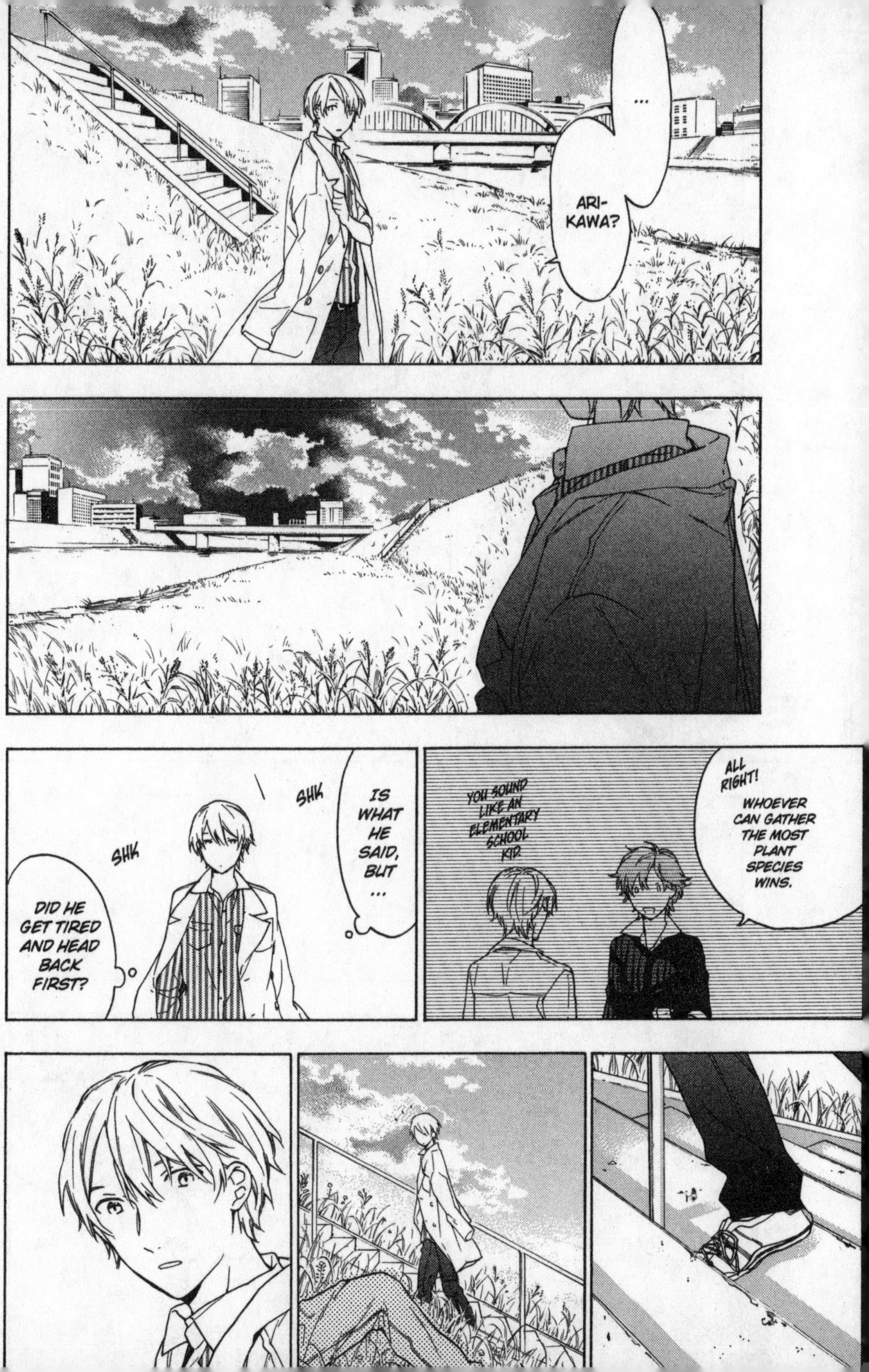
...
ARI-KAWA?
ALL RIGHT!
WHOEVER CAN GATHER THE MOST PLANT SPECIES WINS.
YOU SOUND LIKE AN ELEMENTARY SCHOOL KID.
SHK
IS WHAT HE SAID, BUT ...
SHK
DID HE GET TIRED AND HEAD BACK FIRST?

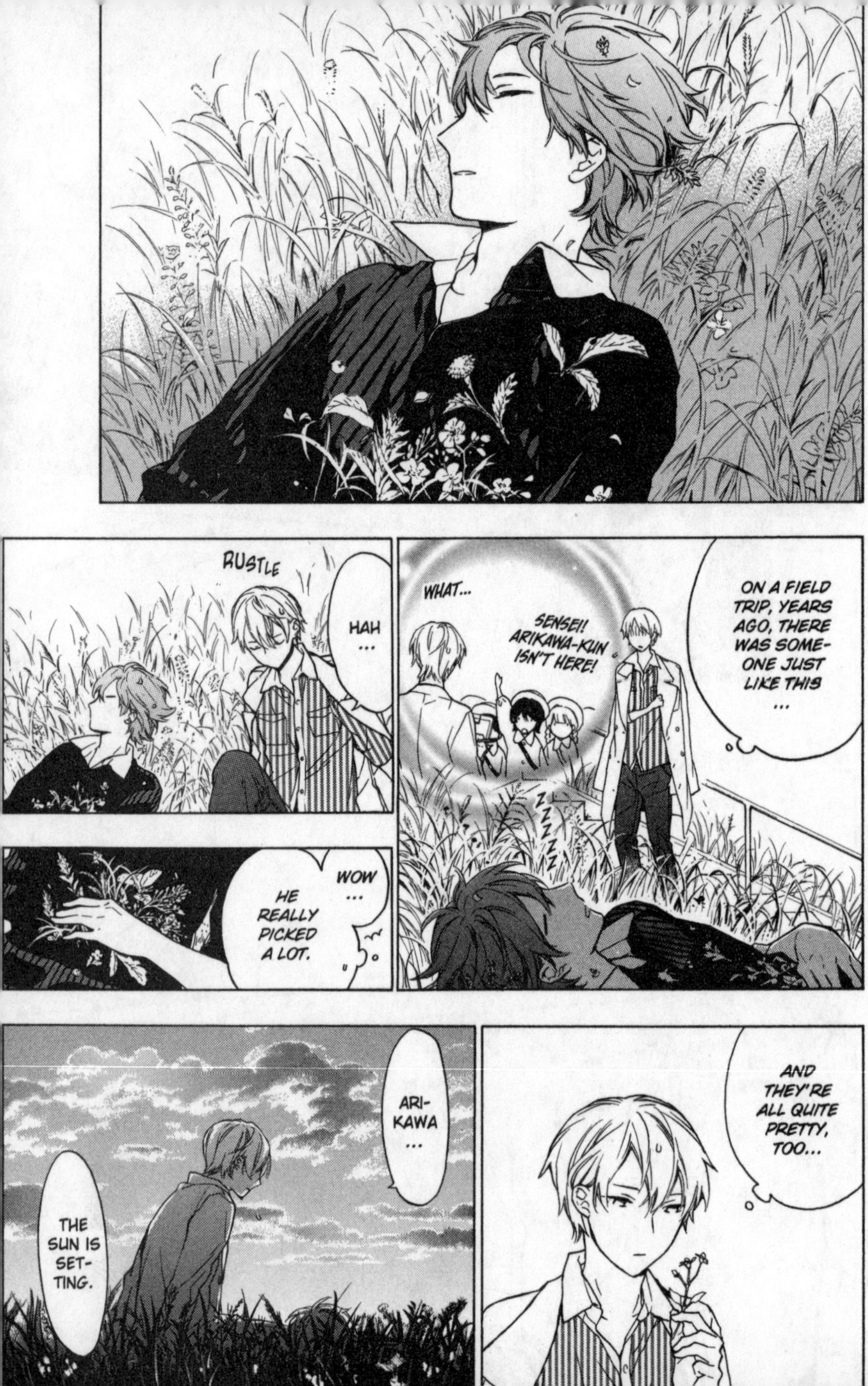
ON A FIELD TRIP, YEARS AGO, THERE WAS SOME-ONE JUST LIKE THIS ...
WHAT...
SENSEI! ARIKAWA-KUN ISN'T HERE!
ZZZZZ
RUSTLE
HAH ...
WOW ... HE REALLY PICKED A LOT.
AND THEY'RE ALL QUITE PRETTY, TOO...
ARI-KAWA ...
THE SUN IS SET-TING.

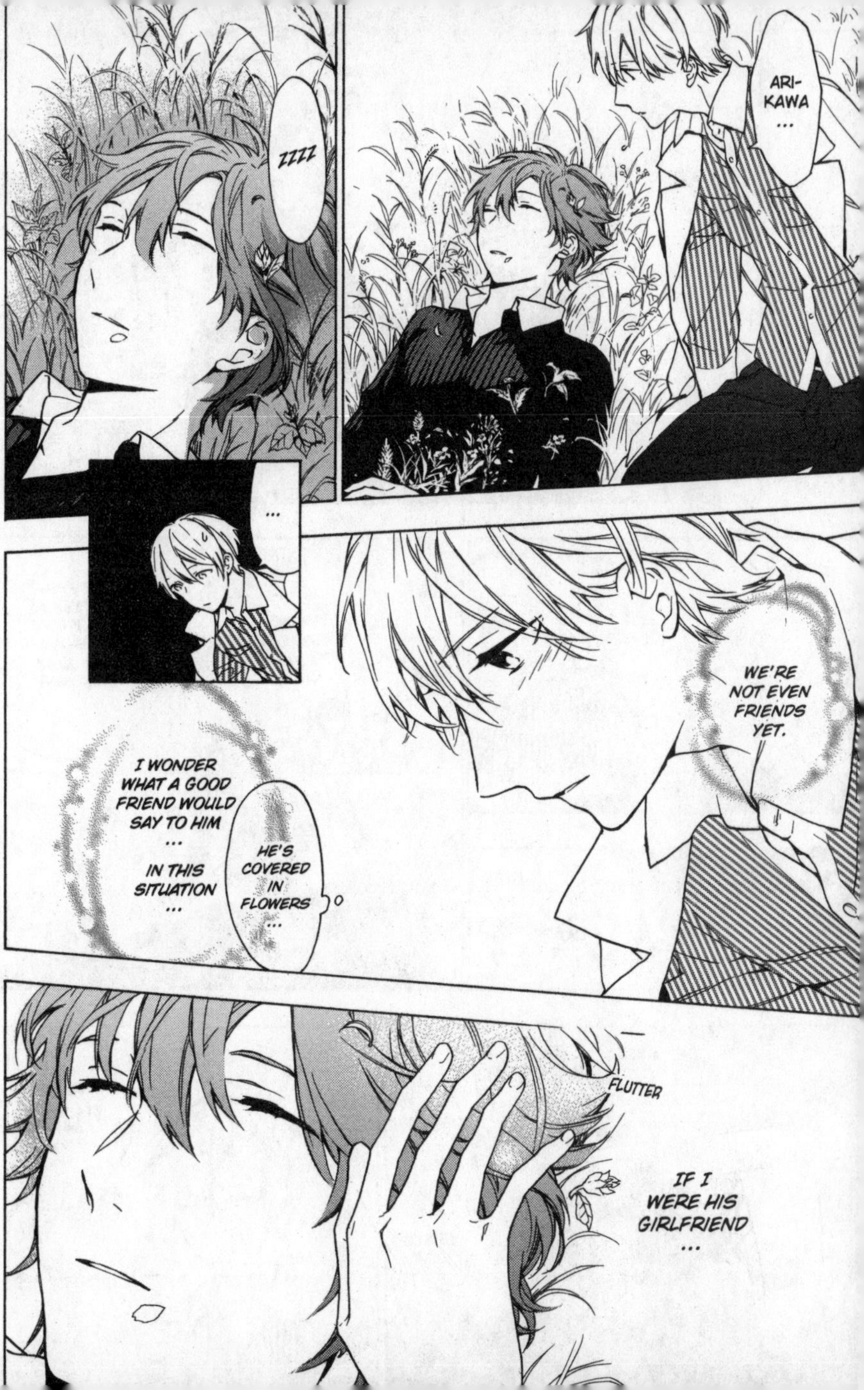
ARI-KAWA ...
ZZZZ
...
WE'RE NOT EVEN FRIENDS YET.
HE'S COVERED IN FLOWERS ...
I WONDER WHAT A GOOD FRIEND WOULD SAY TO HIM ... IN THIS SITUATION ...
FLUTTER
IF I WERE HIS GIRLFRIEND ...

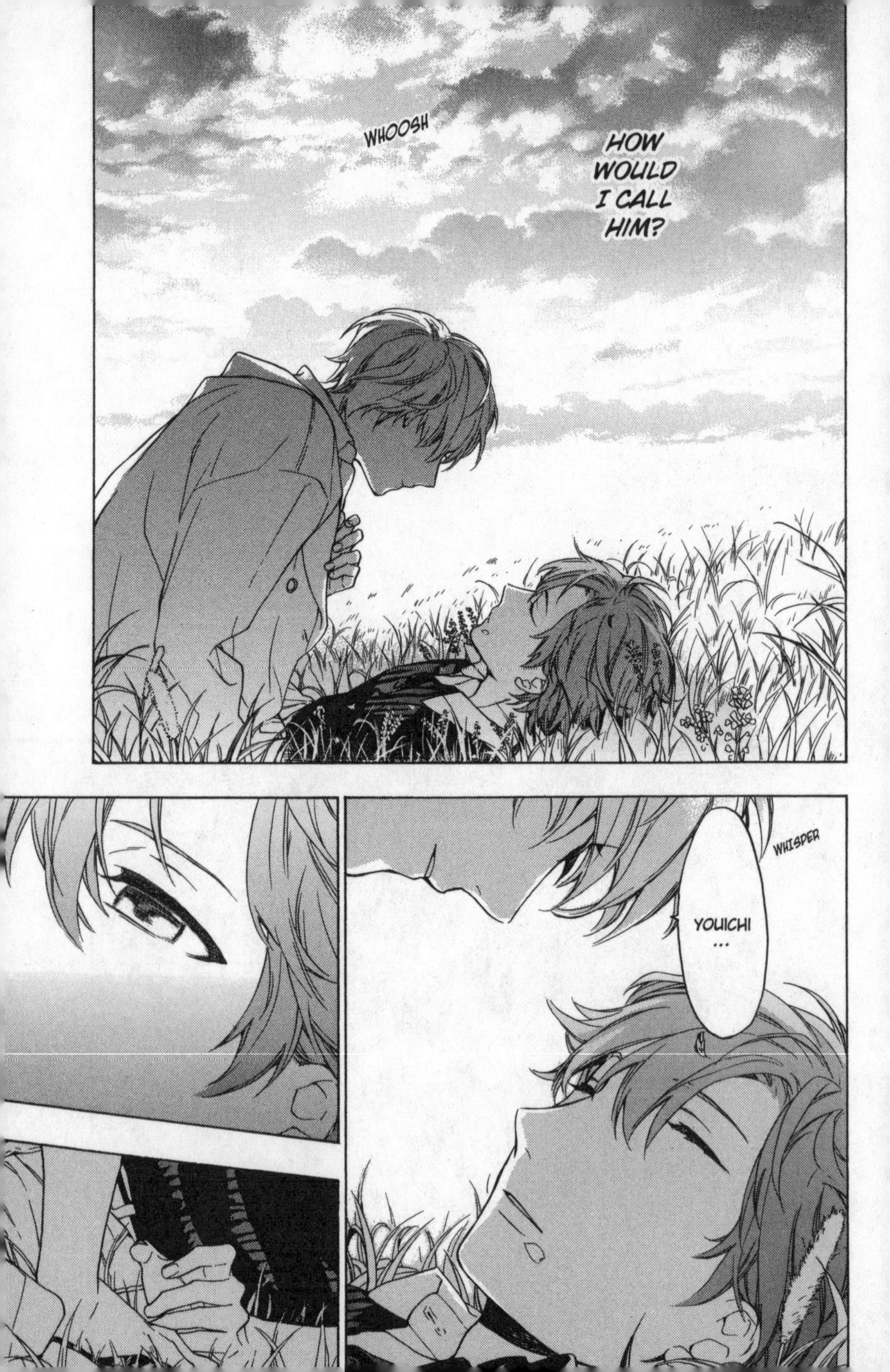
HOW WOULD I CALL HIM?
WHOOSH
WHISPER
YOUICHI ...

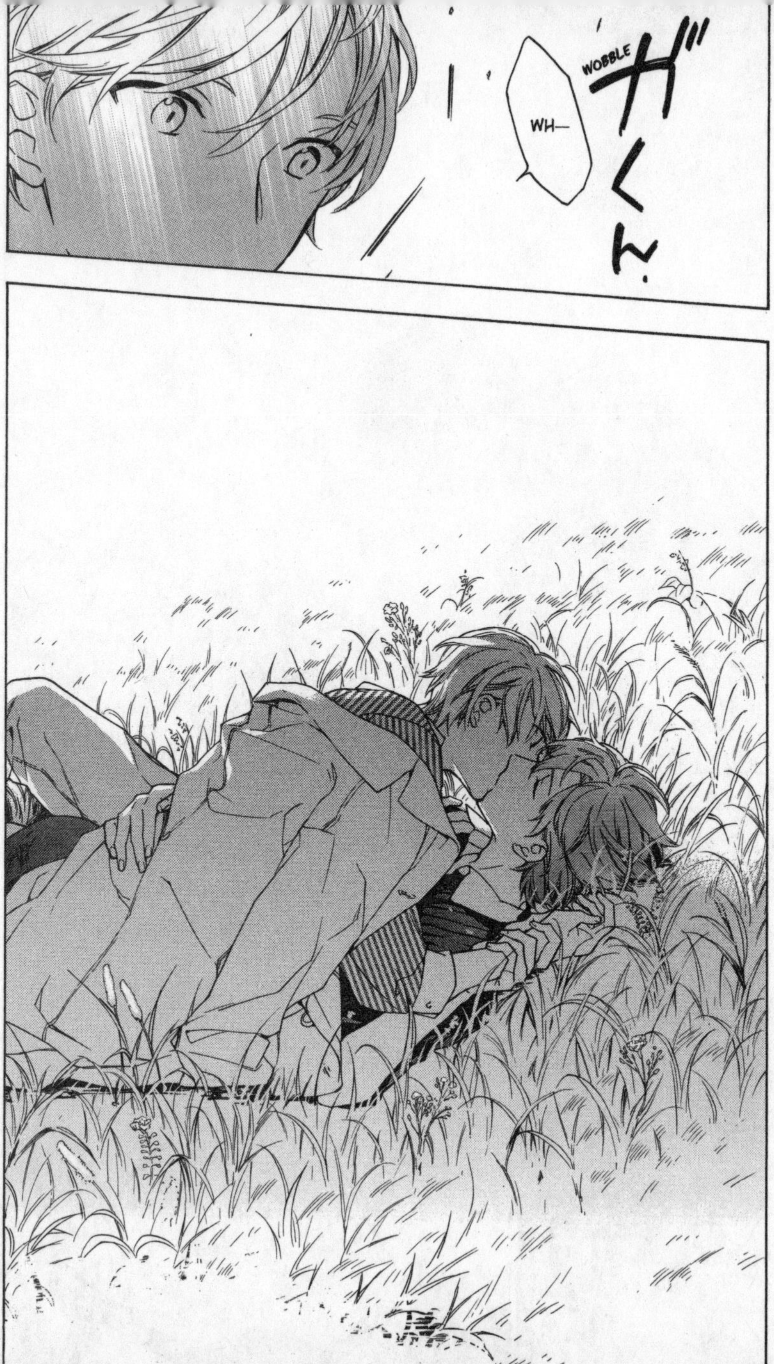
WOBBLE
ガくん
WH—

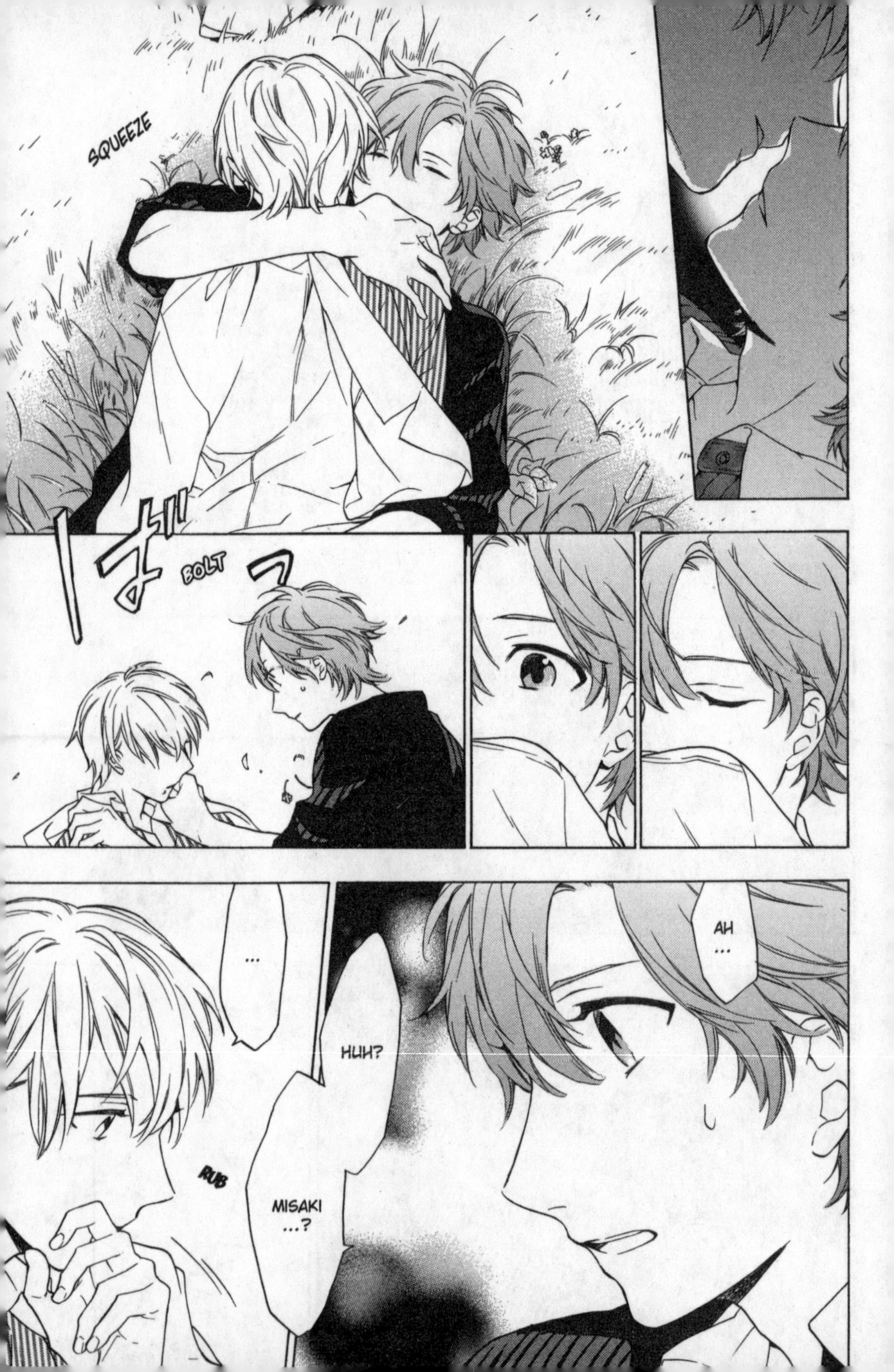
SQUEEZE
ばっ
BOLT
AH ...
...
HUH?
RUB
MISAKI ...?

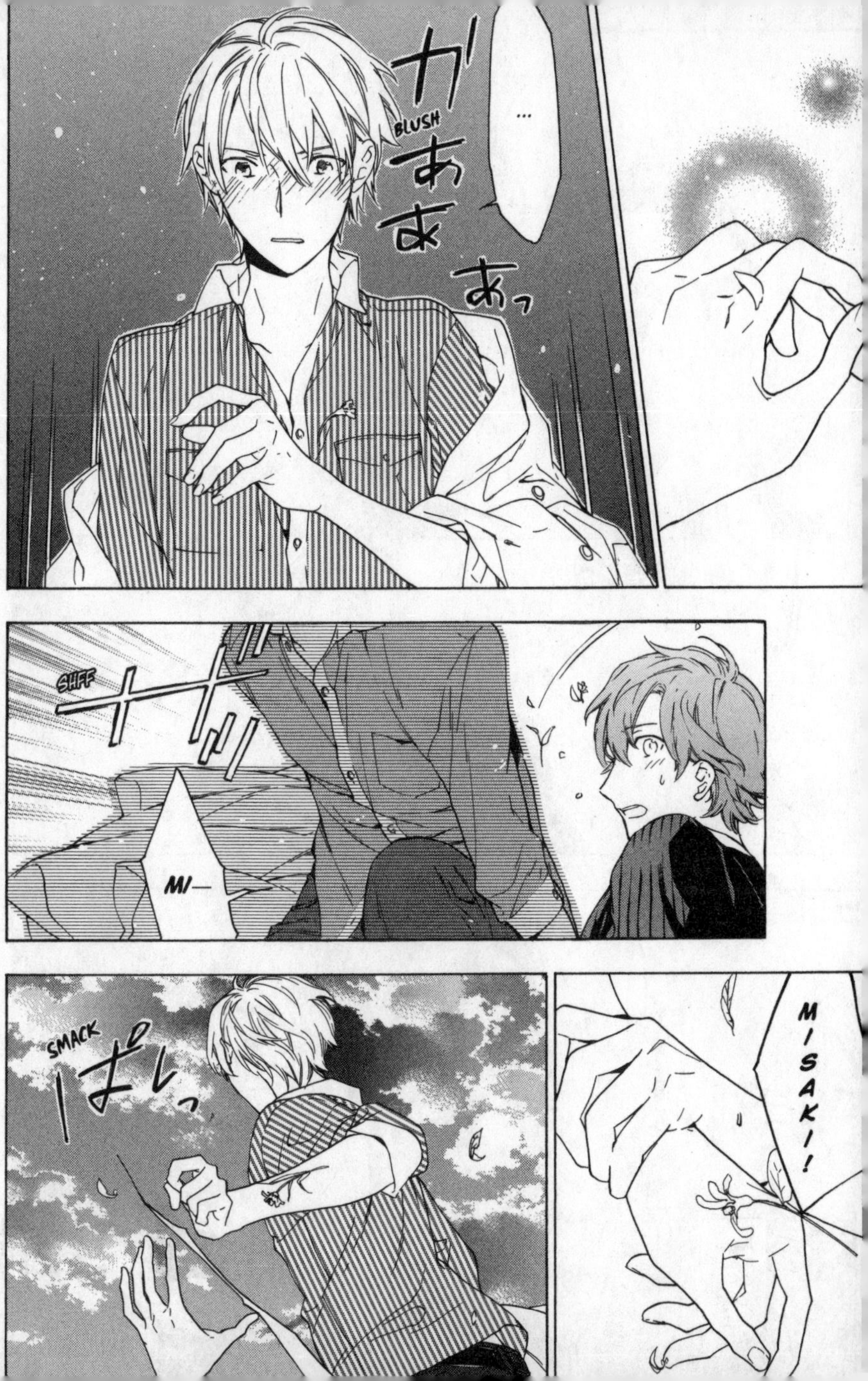
…
BLUSH
SHFF
MI—
MISAKI!
SMACK

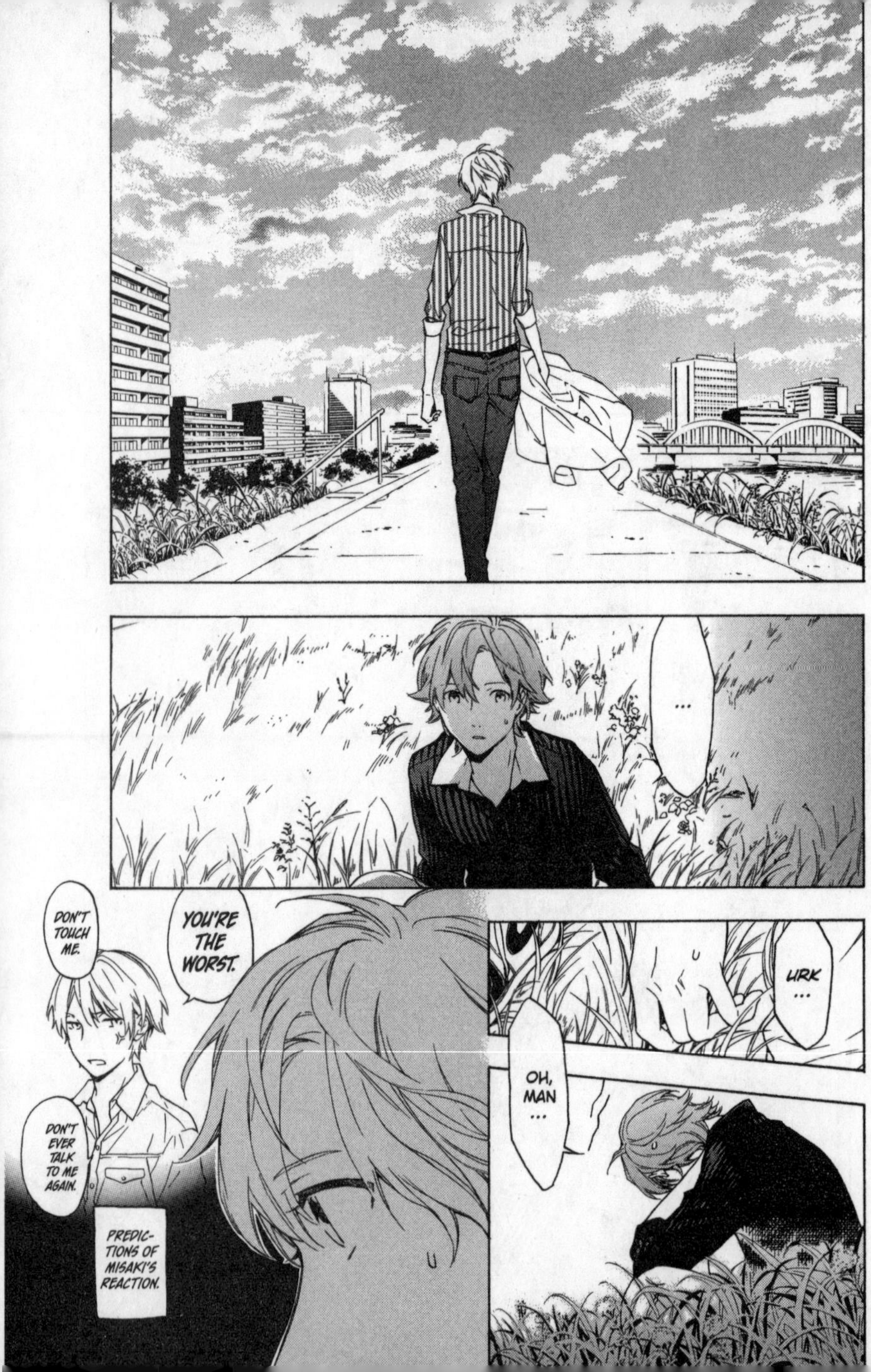
...
URK ...
OH, MAN ...
YOU'RE THE WORST.
DON'T TOUCH ME.
DON'T EVER TALK TO ME AGAIN.
PREDICTIONS OF MISAKI'S REACTION.

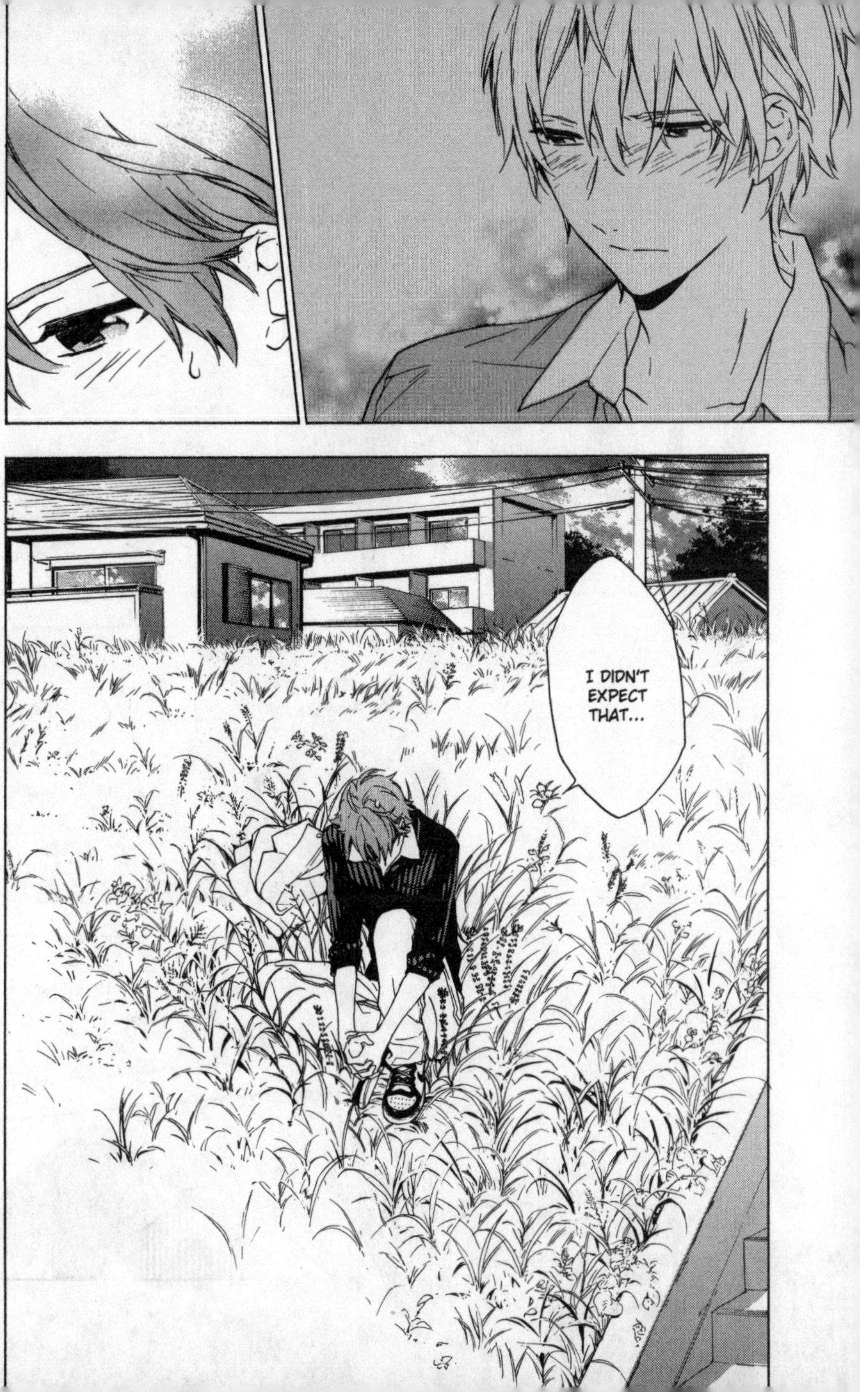
I DIDN'T EXPECT THAT...

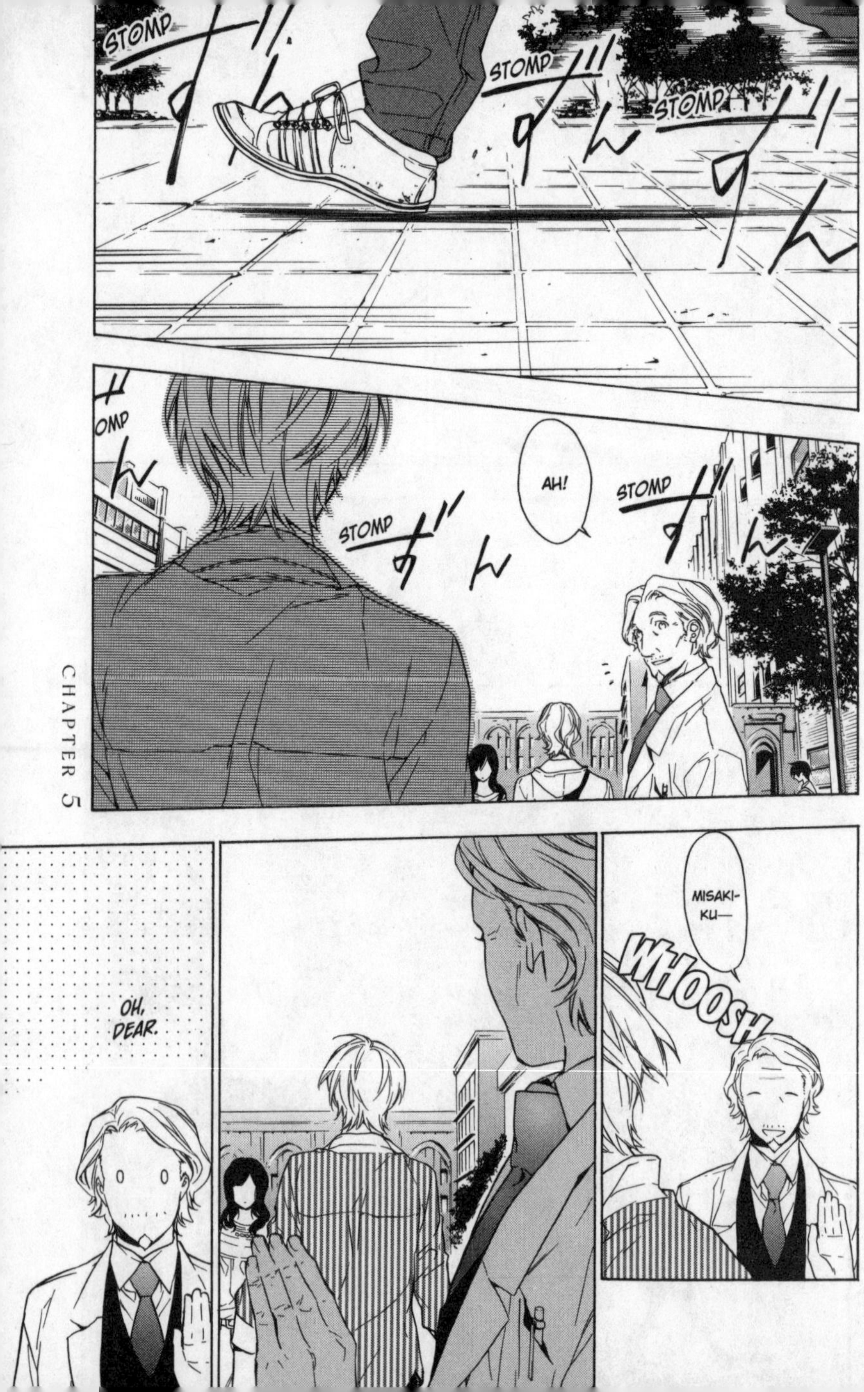
STOMP
STOMP
STOMP
STOMP
AH!
STOMP
OMP
MISAKI-KU—
WHOOSH
OH, DEAR.

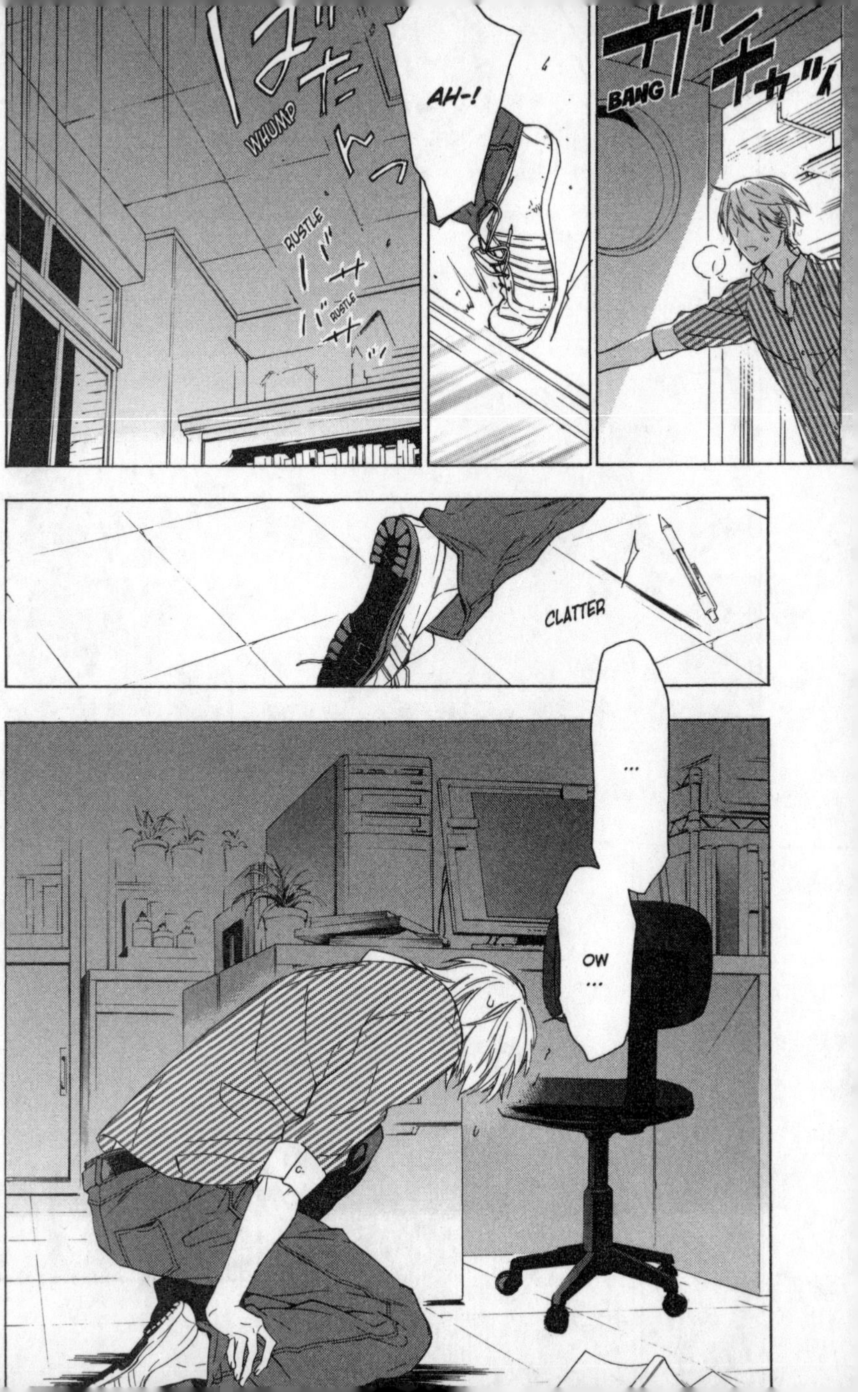
ガチャッ
BANG
AH-!
ばたんっ
WHUMP
バサ
RUSTLE
バサッ
RUSTLE
CLATTER
...
OW ...

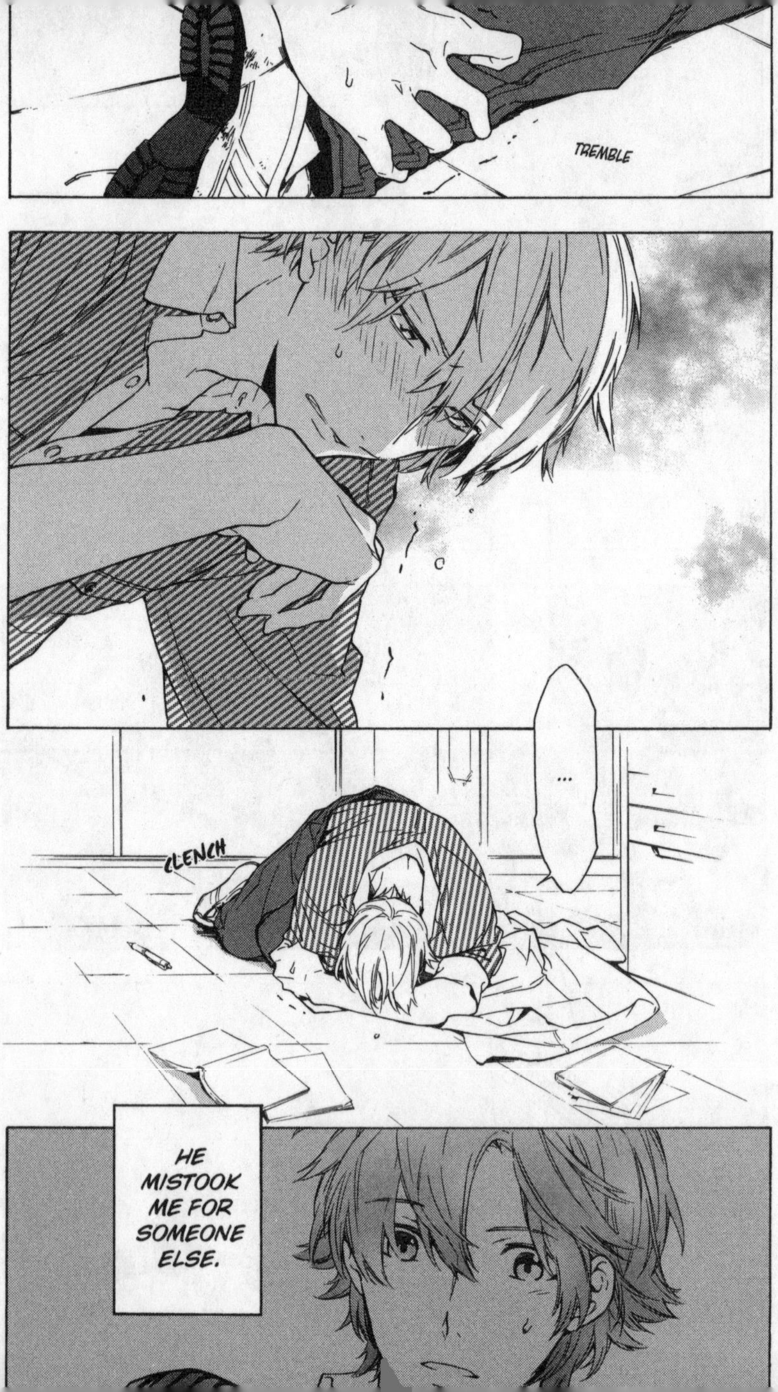
TREMBLE
...
CLENCH
HE MISTOOK ME FOR SOMEONE ELSE.

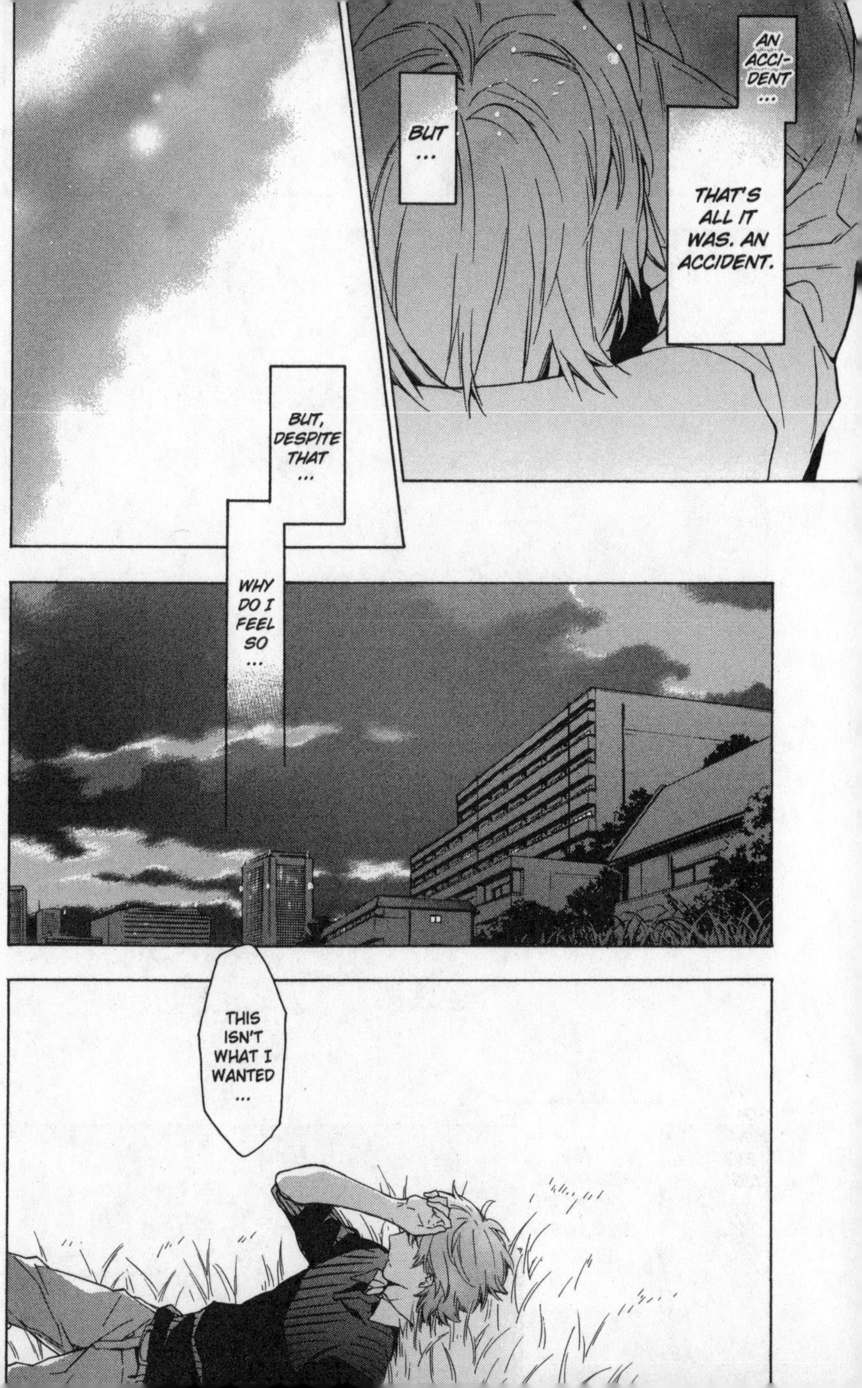
AN ACCI-DENT …
THAT'S ALL IT WAS. AN ACCIDENT.
BUT …
BUT, DESPITE THAT …
WHY DO I FEEL SO …
THIS ISN'T WHAT I WANTED …

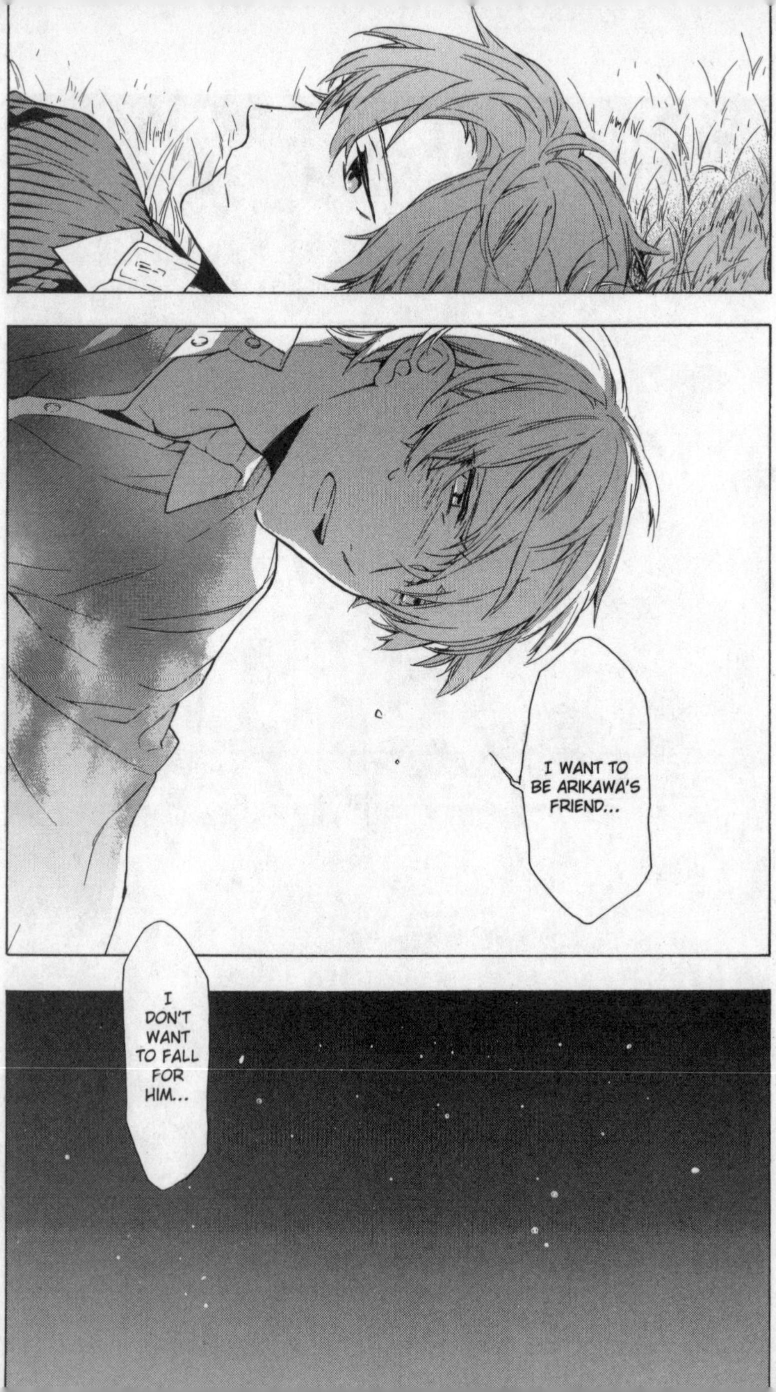
I WANT TO BE ARIKAWA'S FRIEND...
I DON'T WANT TO FALL FOR HIM...

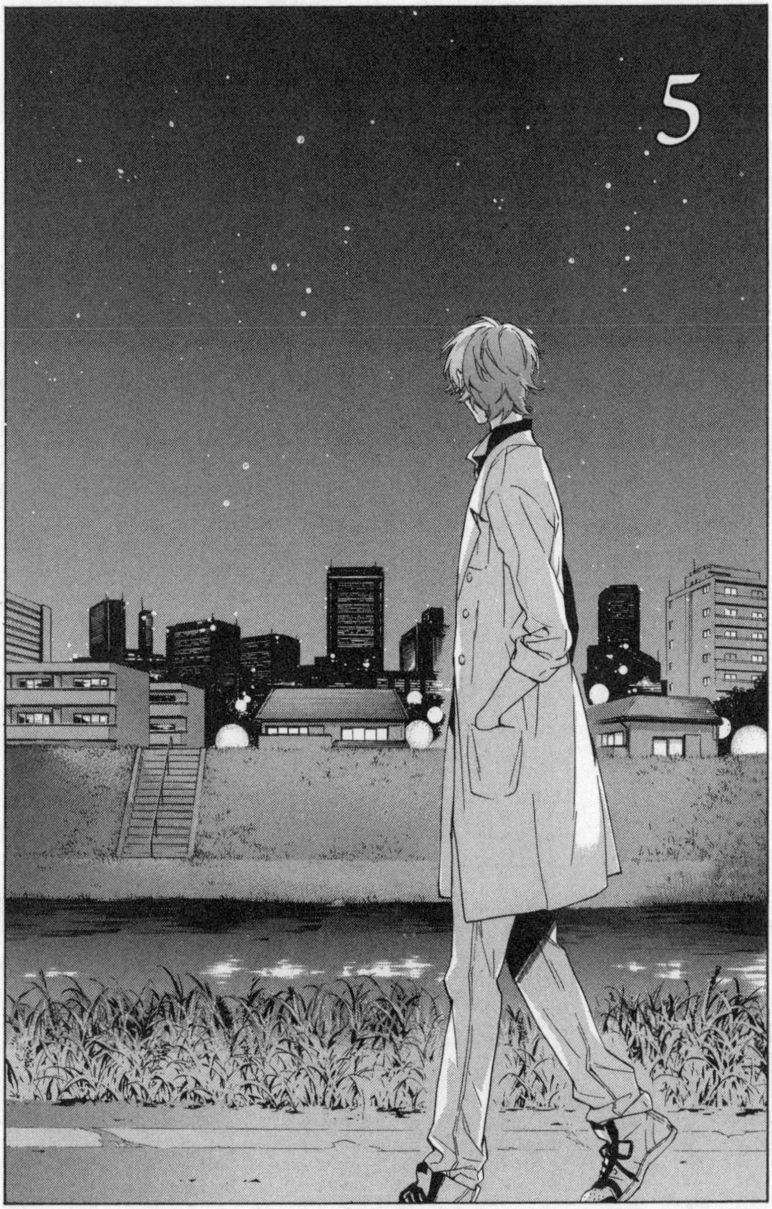
5

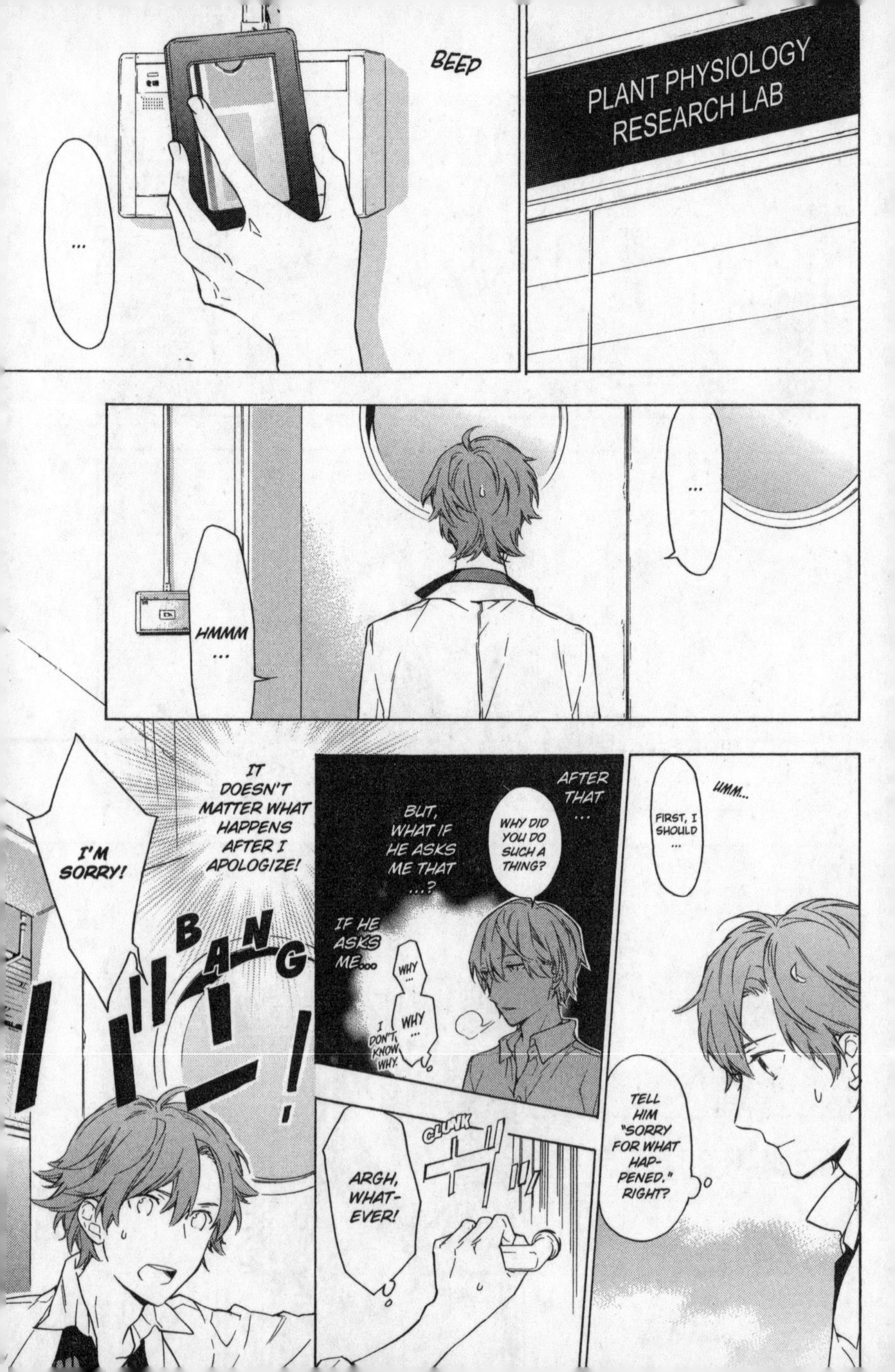
PLANT PHYSIOLOGY RESEARCH LAB
BEEP
...
...
HMMM ...
UMM...
FIRST, I SHOULD ...
TELL HIM "SORRY FOR WHAT HAP-PENED." RIGHT?
AFTER THAT ...
WHY DID YOU DO SUCH A THING?
BUT, WHAT IF HE ASKS ME THAT ...?
IF HE ASKS ME...
WHY ...
WHY ...
I DON'T KNOW WHY.
CLUNK
ARGH, WHAT-EVER!
IT DOESN'T MATTER WHAT HAPPENS AFTER I APOLOGIZE!
I'M SORRY!
BANG

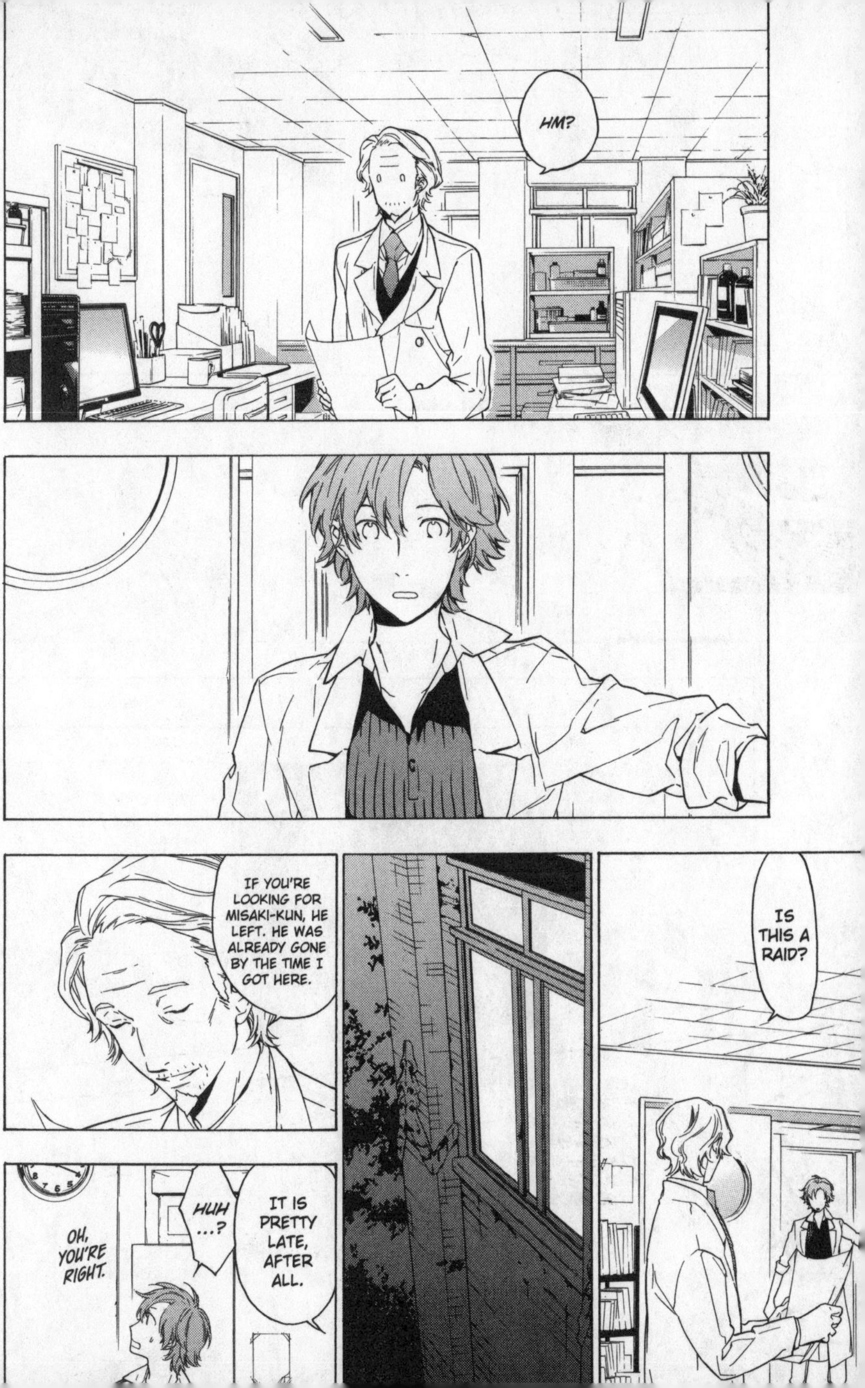
HM?
IS THIS A RAID?
IF YOU'RE LOOKING FOR MISAKI-KUN, HE LEFT. HE WAS ALREADY GONE BY THE TIME I GOT HERE.
IT IS PRETTY LATE, AFTER ALL.
HUH ...?
OH, YOU'RE RIGHT.

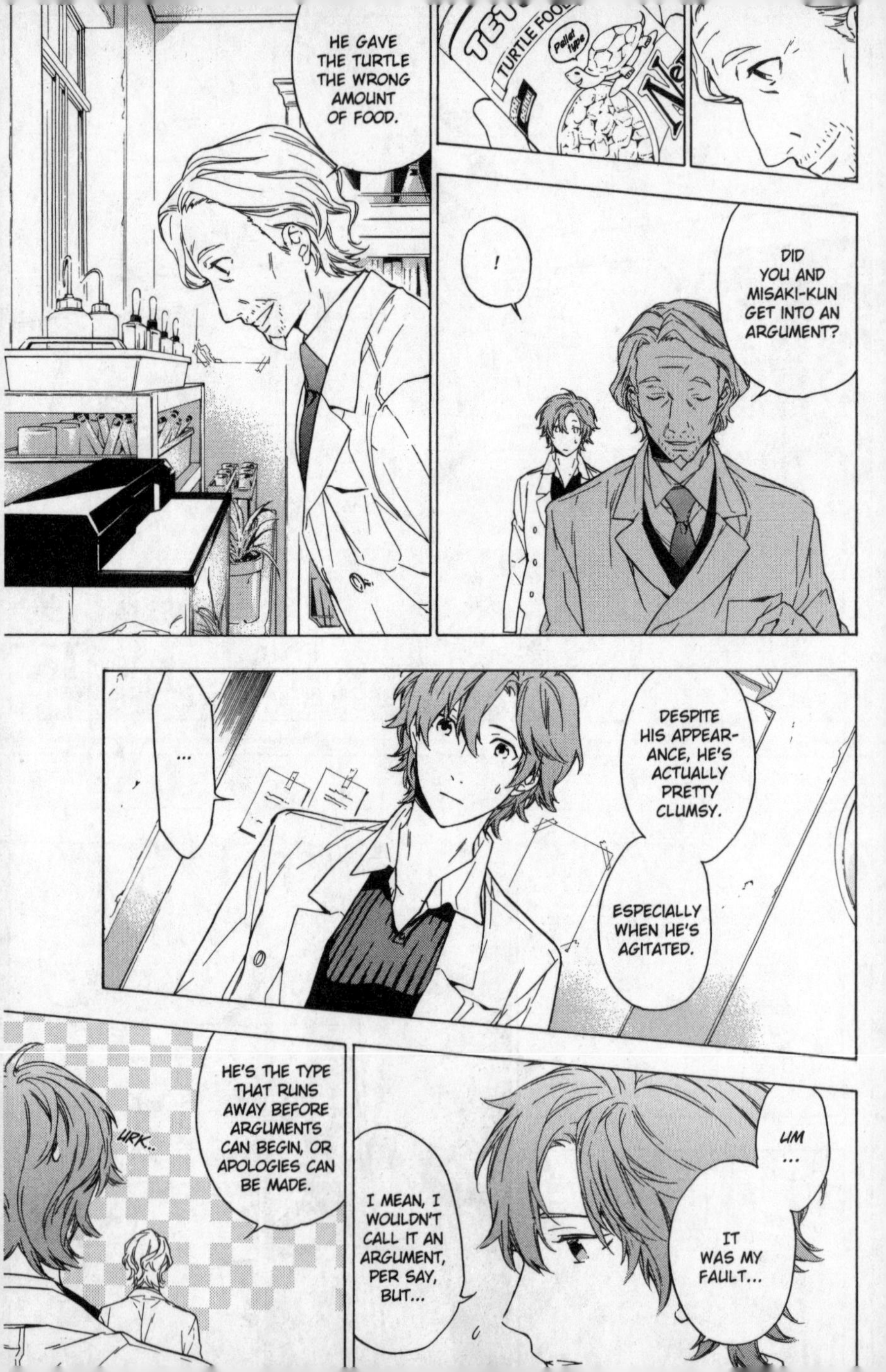
TURTLE FOOD
Pellet type
DID YOU AND MISAKI-KUN GET INTO AN ARGUMENT?
!
HE GAVE THE TURTLE THE WRONG AMOUNT OF FOOD.
DESPITE HIS APPEARANCE, HE'S ACTUALLY PRETTY CLUMSY.
ESPECIALLY WHEN HE'S AGITATED.
...
UM ...
IT WAS MY FAULT...
I MEAN, I WOULDN'T CALL IT AN ARGUMENT, PER SAY, BUT...
HE'S THE TYPE THAT RUNS AWAY BEFORE ARGUMENTS CAN BEGIN, OR APOLOGIES CAN BE MADE.
URK..

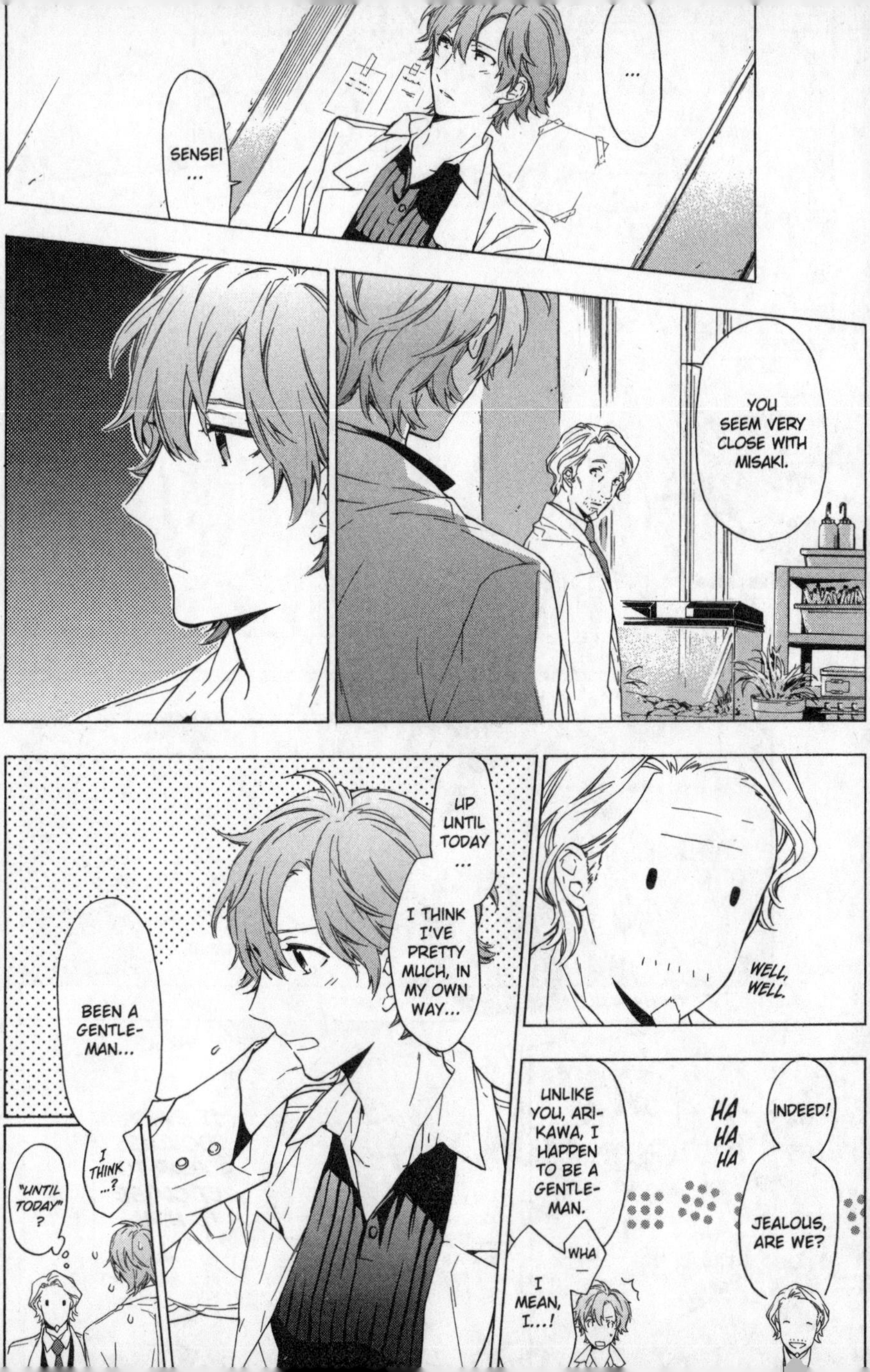
...
SENSEI ...
YOU SEEM VERY CLOSE WITH MISAKI.
WELL, WELL.
UP UNTIL TODAY ...
I THINK I'VE PRETTY MUCH, IN MY OWN WAY...
BEEN A GENTLE-MAN...
I THINK ...?
HA HA HA
INDEED!
JEALOUS, ARE WE?
UNLIKE YOU, ARI-KAWA, I HAPPEN TO BE A GENTLE-MAN.
WHA —
I MEAN, I...!
"UNTIL TODAY"?

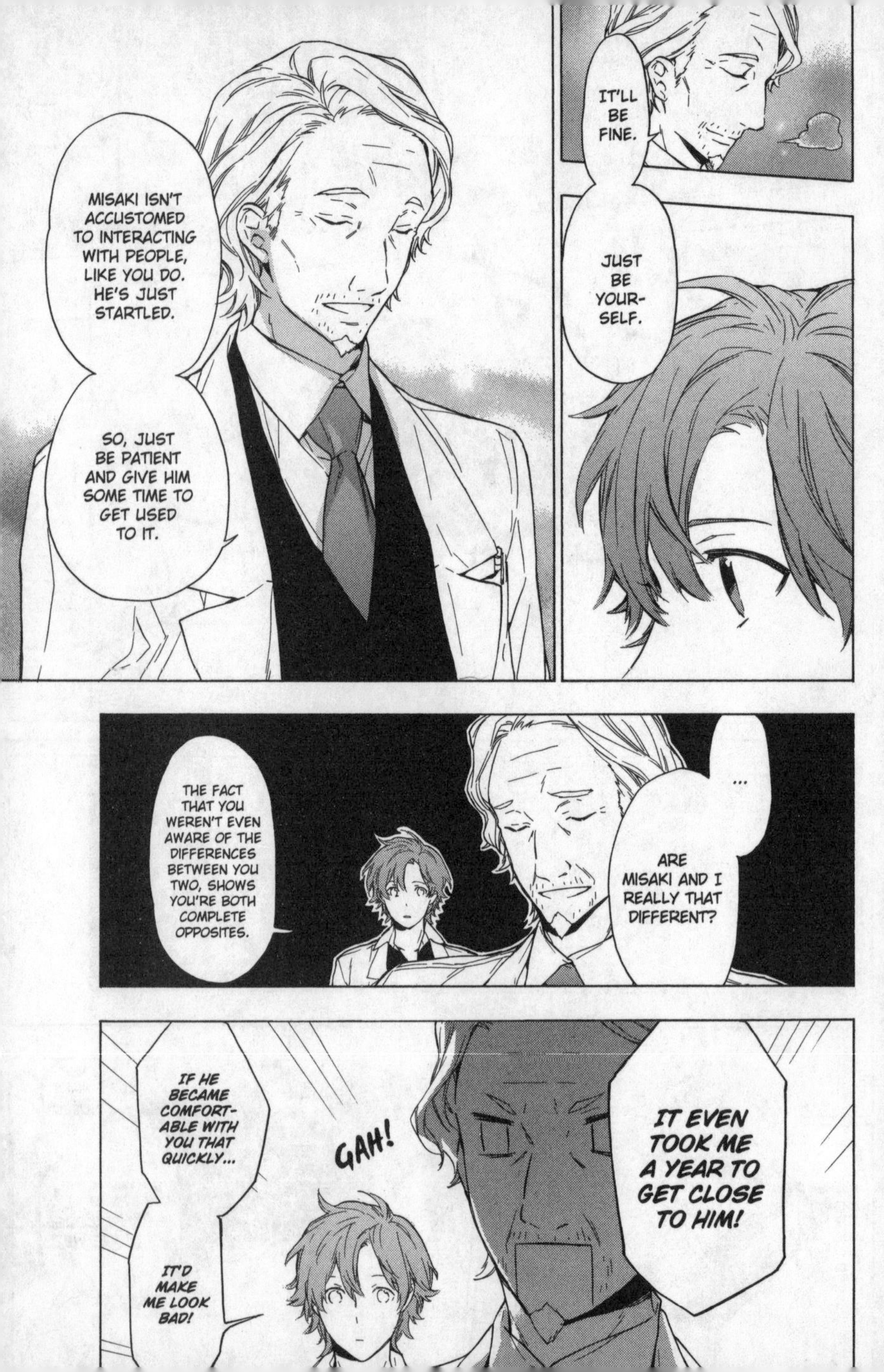

IT'LL BE FINE.
JUST BE YOURSELF.
MISAKI ISN'T ACCUSTOMED TO INTERACTING WITH PEOPLE, LIKE YOU DO. HE'S JUST STARTLED.
SO, JUST BE PATIENT AND GIVE HIM SOME TIME TO GET USED TO IT.
...
ARE MISAKI AND I REALLY THAT DIFFERENT?
THE FACT THAT YOU WEREN'T EVEN AWARE OF THE DIFFERENCES BETWEEN YOU TWO, SHOWS YOU'RE BOTH COMPLETE OPPOSITES.
IT EVEN TOOK ME A YEAR TO GET CLOSE TO HIM!
GAH!
IF HE BECAME COMFORTABLE WITH YOU THAT QUICKLY...
IT'D MAKE ME LOOK BAD!

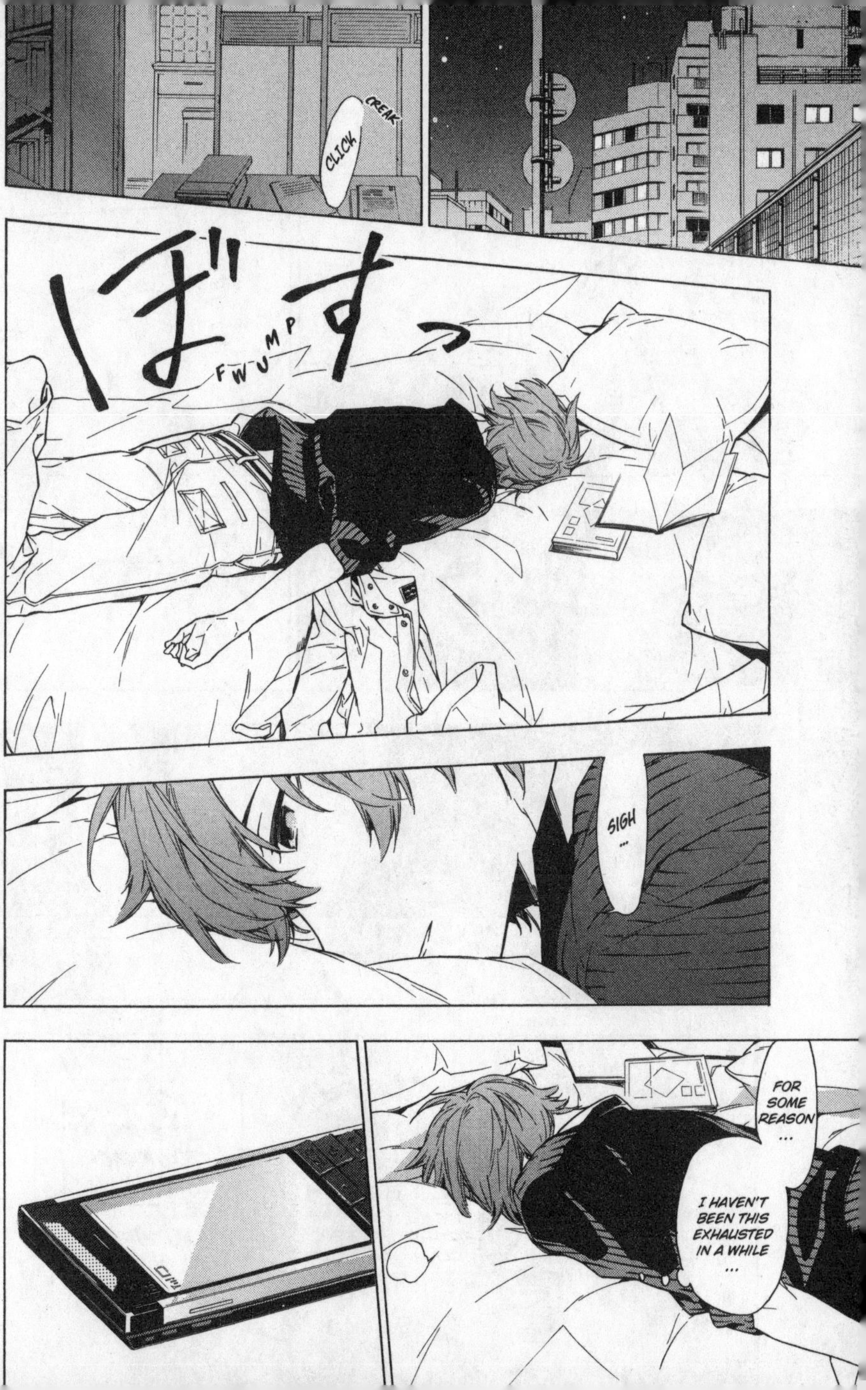
CREAK
CLICK
ぼすっ
FWUMP
SIGH
...
FOR SOME REASON
...
I HAVEN'T BEEN THIS EXHAUSTED IN A WHILE
...

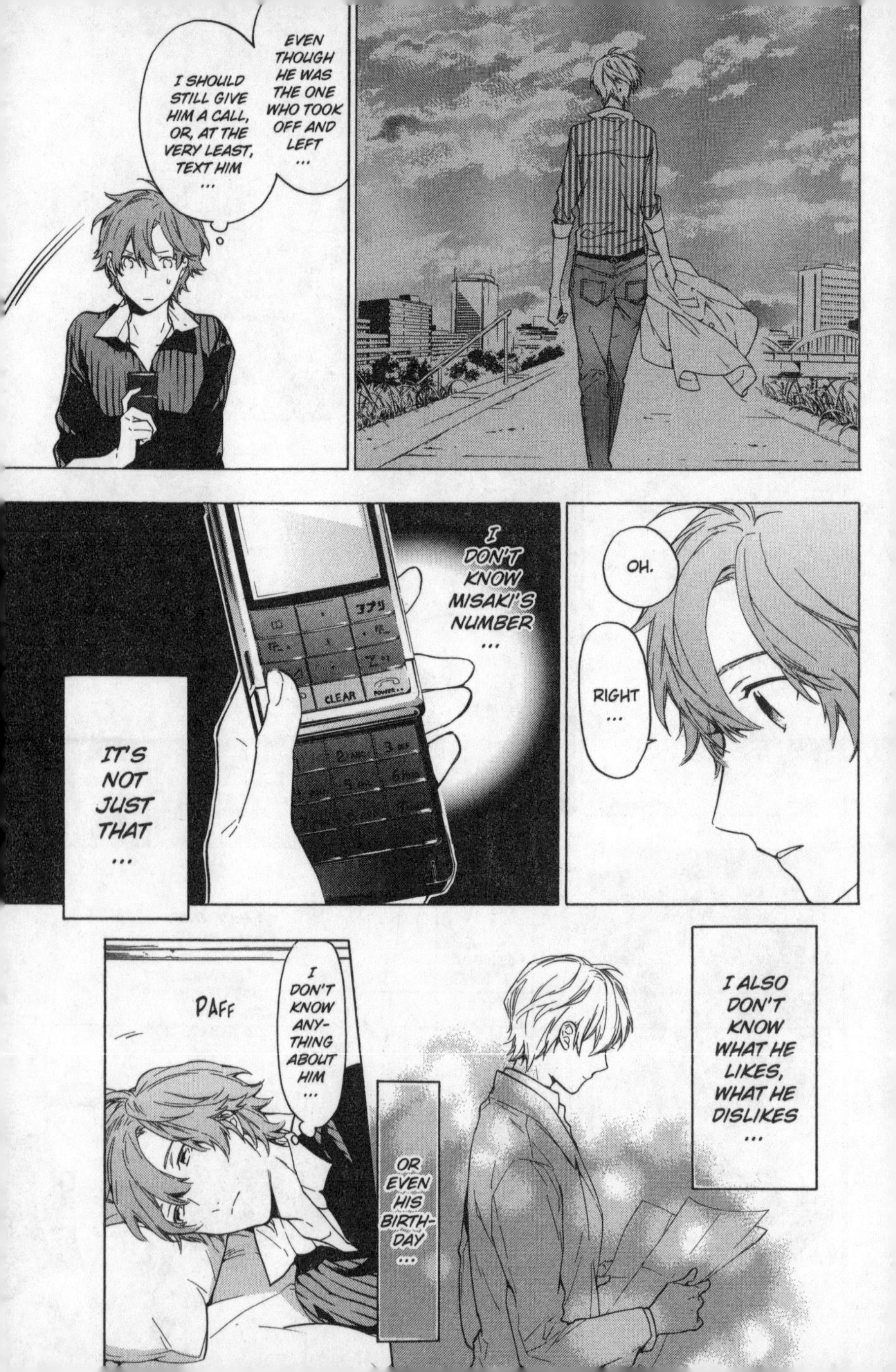
EVEN THOUGH HE WAS THE ONE WHO TOOK OFF AND LEFT ...
I SHOULD STILL GIVE HIM A CALL, OR, AT THE VERY LEAST, TEXT HIM ...
OH.
RIGHT ...
I DON'T KNOW MISAKI'S NUMBER ...
IT'S NOT JUST THAT ...
I ALSO DON'T KNOW WHAT HE LIKES, WHAT HE DISLIKES ...
OR EVEN HIS BIRTHDAY ...
I DON'T KNOW ANYTHING ABOUT HIM ...
PAFF

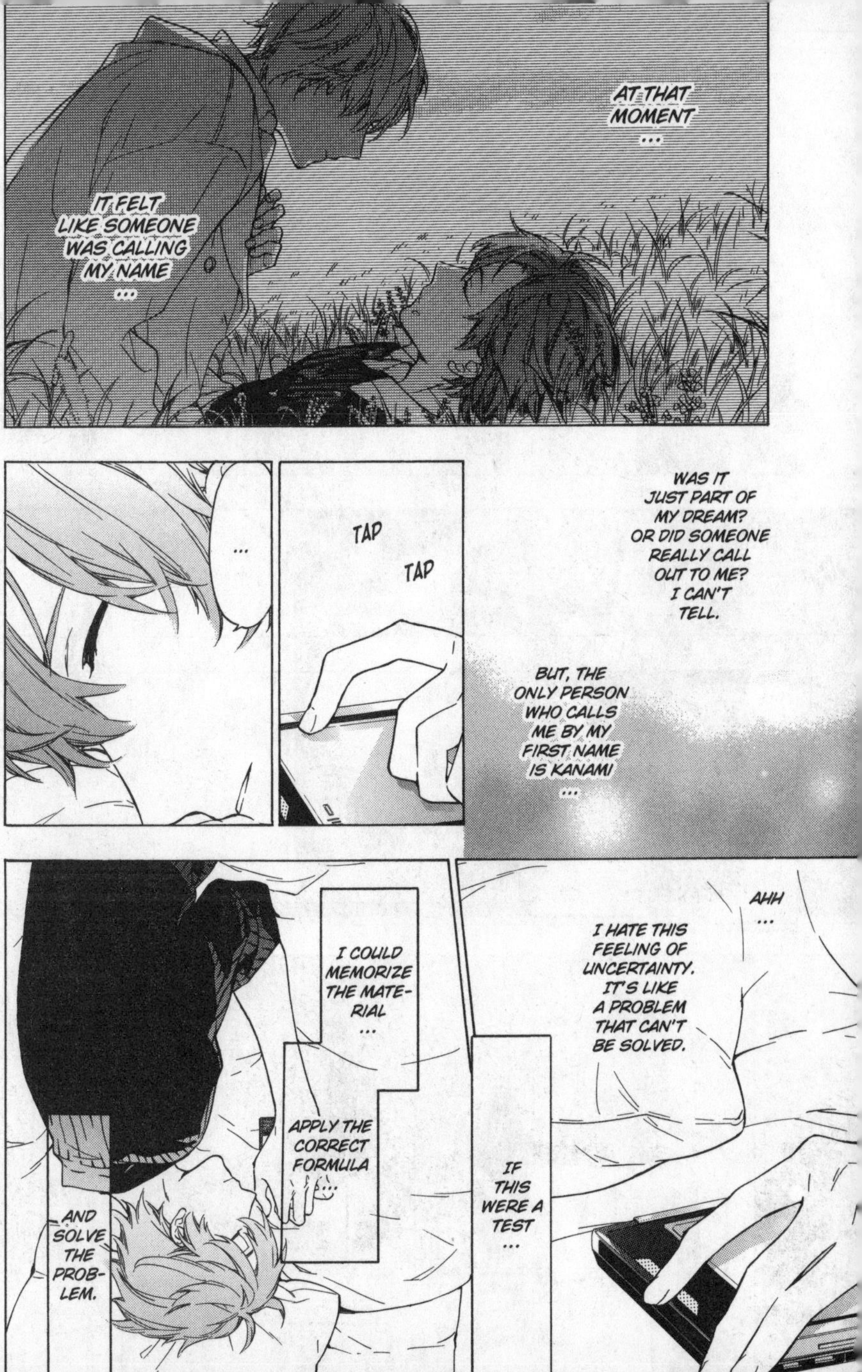
AT THAT MOMENT ...
IT FELT LIKE SOMEONE WAS CALLING MY NAME ...
WAS IT JUST PART OF MY DREAM? OR DID SOMEONE REALLY CALL OUT TO ME? I CAN'T TELL.
BUT, THE ONLY PERSON WHO CALLS ME BY MY FIRST NAME IS KANAMI ...
TAP
TAP
...
AHH ...
I HATE THIS FEELING OF UNCERTAINTY. IT'S LIKE A PROBLEM THAT CAN'T BE SOLVED.
IF THIS WERE A TEST ...
I COULD MEMORIZE THE MATE-RIAL ...
APPLY THE CORRECT FORMULA ...
AND SOLVE THE PROB-LEM.

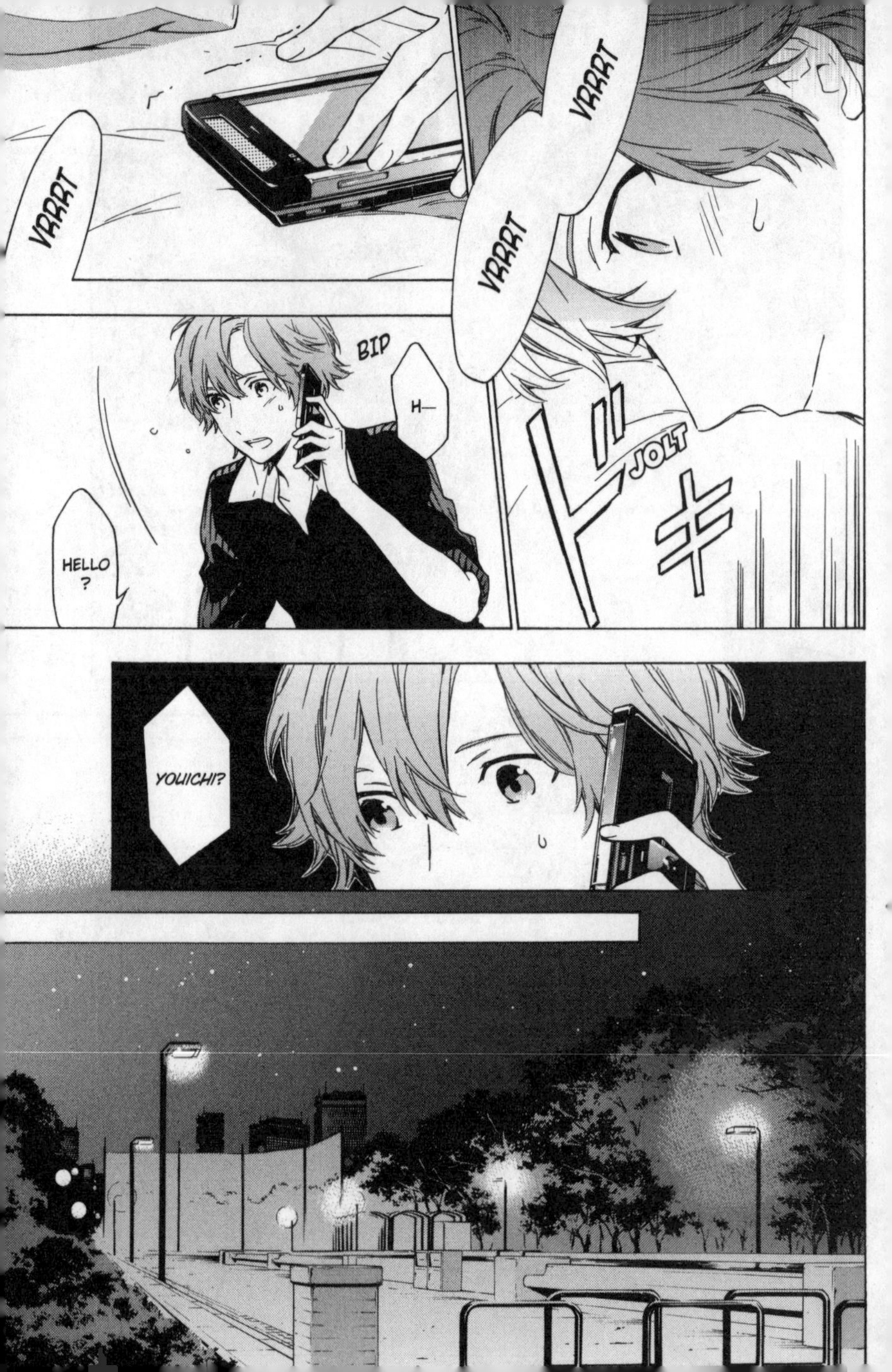
VRRRT
VRRRT
JOLT
ドキ
VRRRT
BIP
H—
HELLO?
YOUICHI?

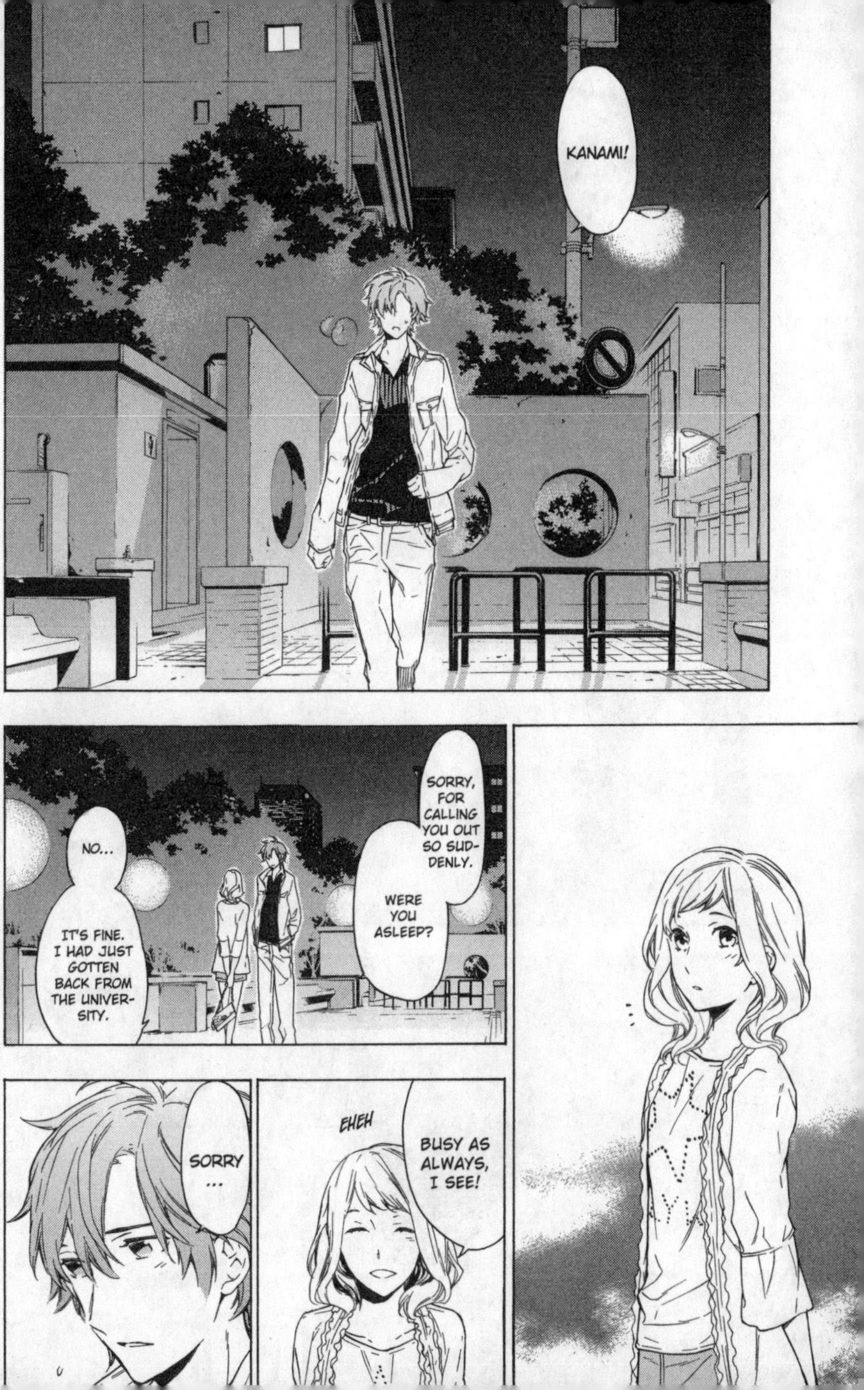
KANAMI!
SORRY, FOR CALLING YOU OUT SO SUDDENLY.
WERE YOU ASLEEP?
NO...
IT'S FINE. I HAD JUST GOTTEN BACK FROM THE UNIVERSITY.
EHEH
BUSY AS ALWAYS, I SEE!
SORRY ...

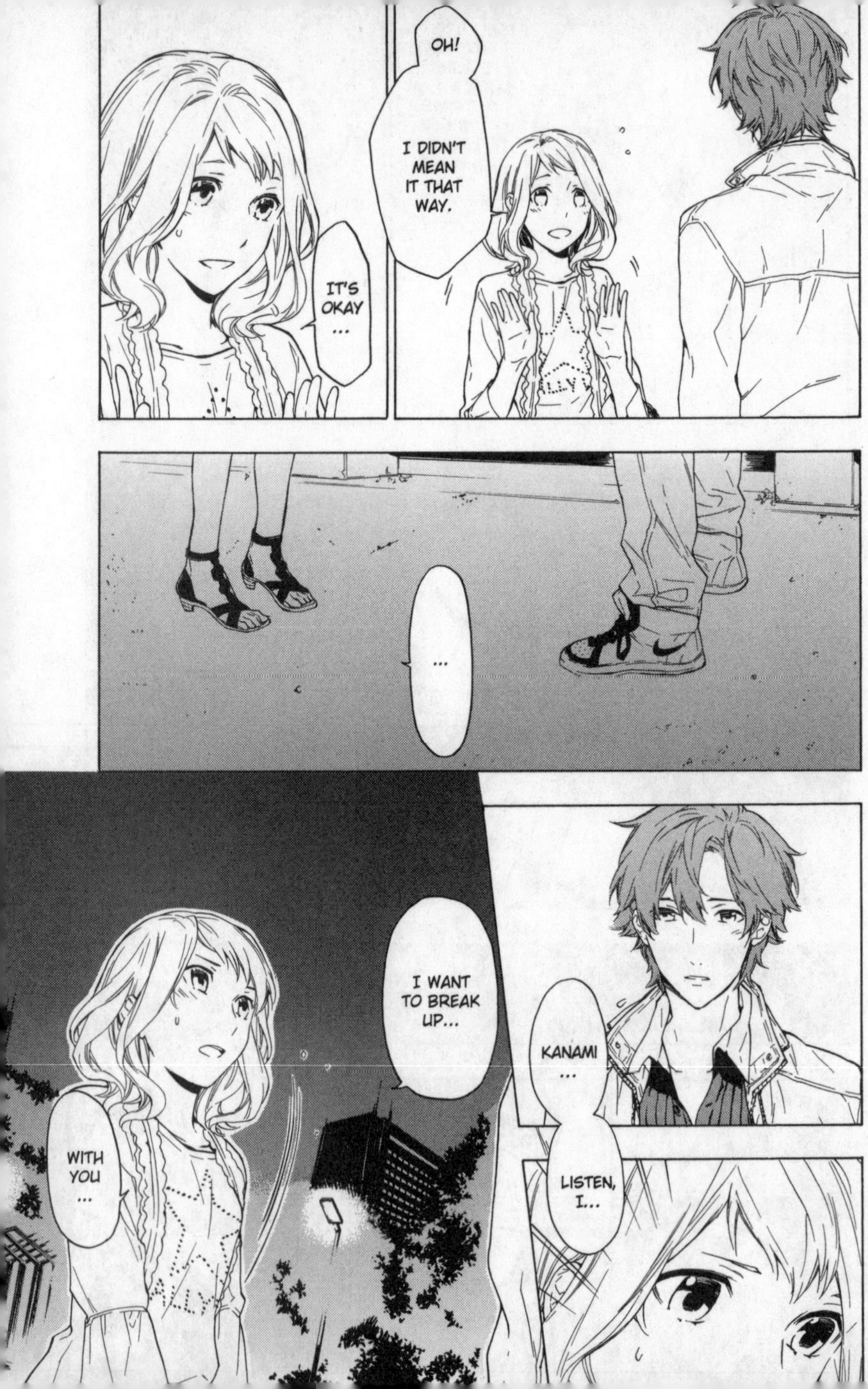
OH!
I DIDN'T MEAN IT THAT WAY.
IT'S OKAY ...
...
KANAMI ...
LISTEN, I...
I WANT TO BREAK UP...
WITH YOU ...

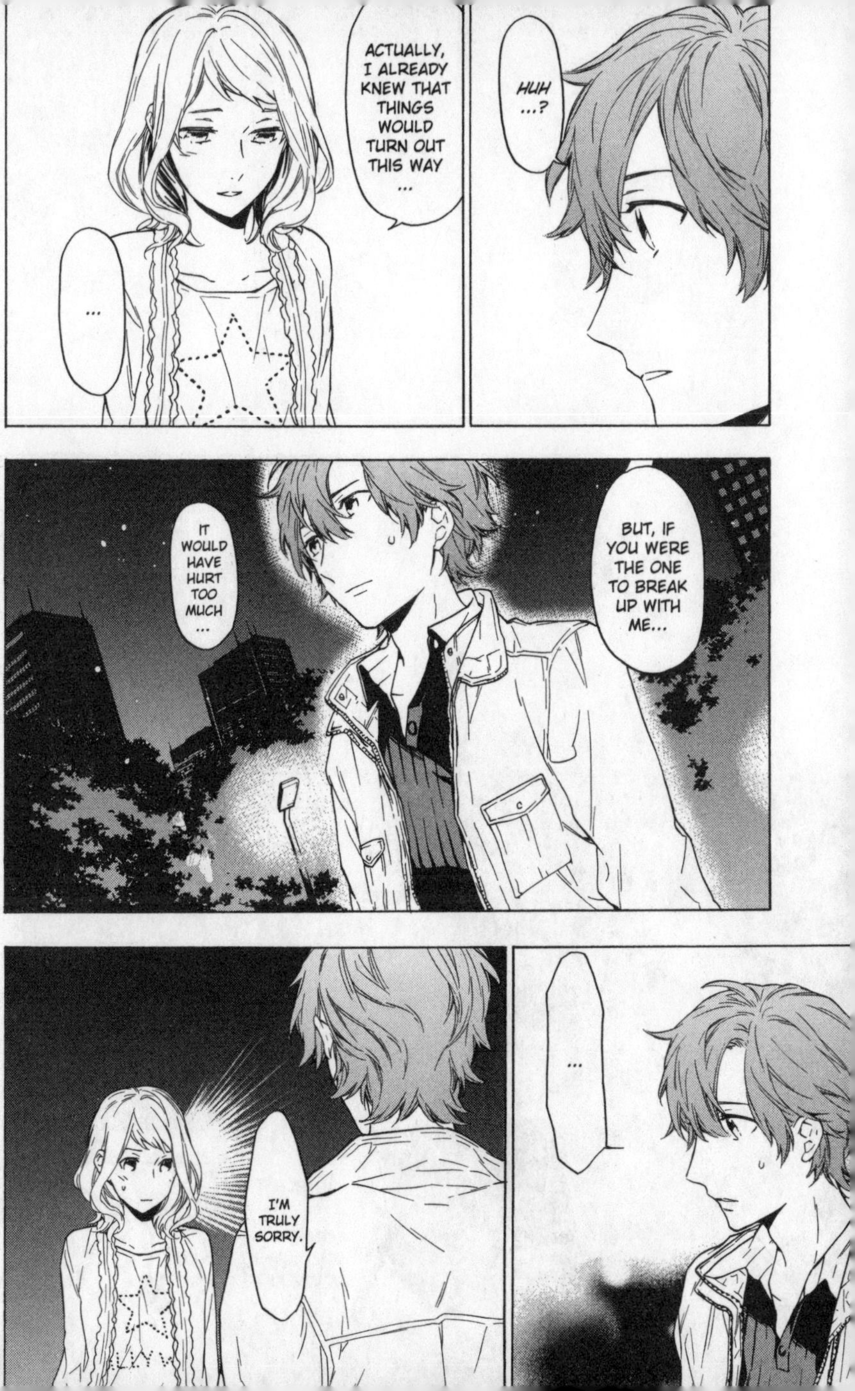
HUH ...?
ACTUALLY, I ALREADY KNEW THAT THINGS WOULD TURN OUT THIS WAY ...
...
BUT, IF YOU WERE THE ONE TO BREAK UP WITH ME...
IT WOULD HAVE HURT TOO MUCH ...
...
I'M TRULY SORRY.

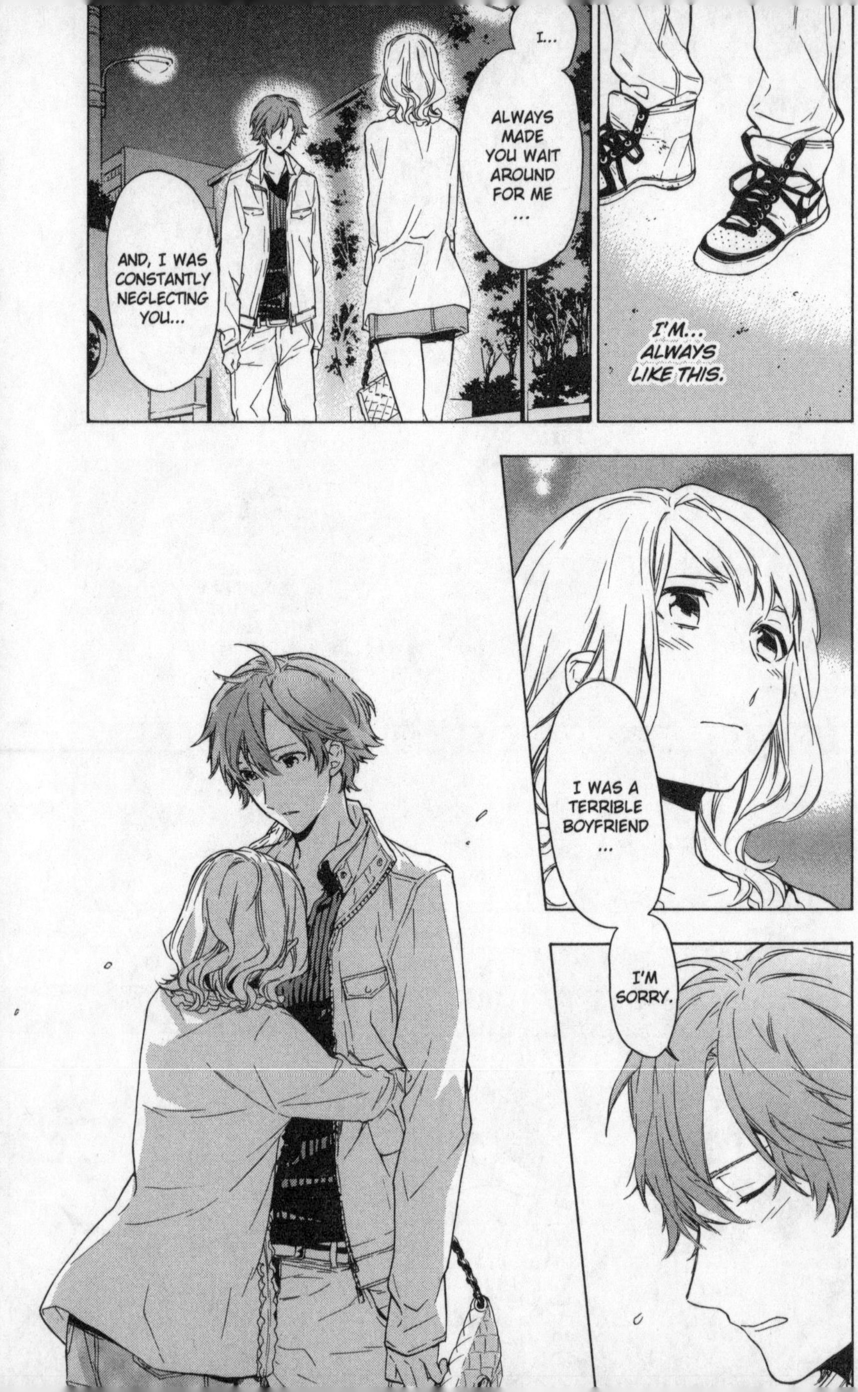
I'M... ALWAYS LIKE THIS.
I...
ALWAYS MADE YOU WAIT AROUND FOR ME ...
AND, I WAS CONSTANTLY NEGLECTING YOU...
I WAS A TERRIBLE BOYFRIEND ...
I'M SORRY.

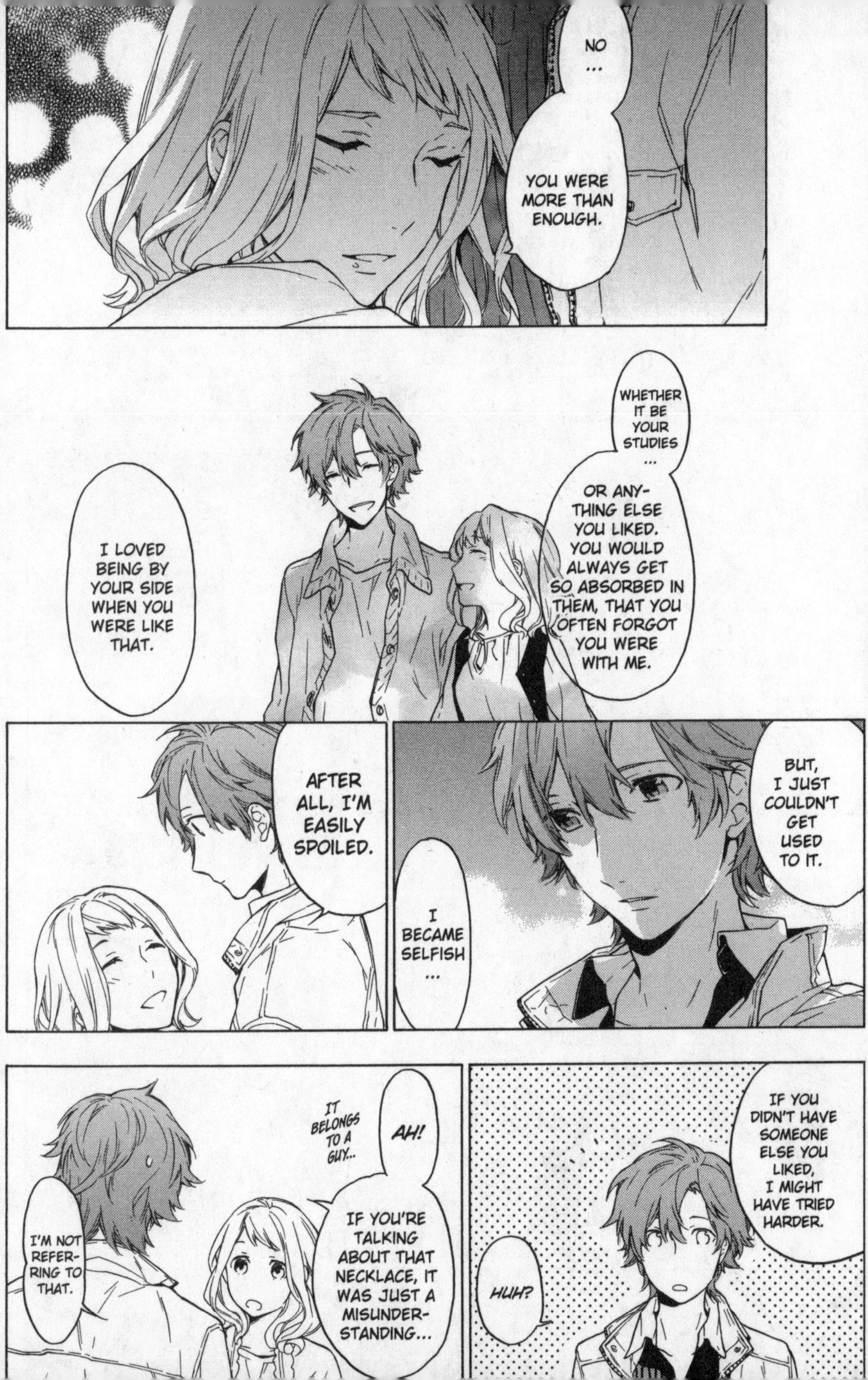
NO ...
YOU WERE MORE THAN ENOUGH.
WHETHER IT BE YOUR STUDIES ...
OR ANYTHING ELSE YOU LIKED. YOU WOULD ALWAYS GET SO ABSORBED IN THEM, THAT YOU OFTEN FORGOT YOU WERE WITH ME.
I LOVED BEING BY YOUR SIDE WHEN YOU WERE LIKE THAT.
BUT, I JUST COULDN'T GET USED TO IT.
I BECAME SELFISH ...
AFTER ALL, I'M EASILY SPOILED.
IF YOU DIDN'T HAVE SOMEONE ELSE YOU LIKED, I MIGHT HAVE TRIED HARDER.
HUH?
AH!
IT BELONGS TO A GUY...
IF YOU'RE TALKING ABOUT THAT NECKLACE, IT WAS JUST A MISUNDERSTANDING...
I'M NOT REFERRING TO THAT.

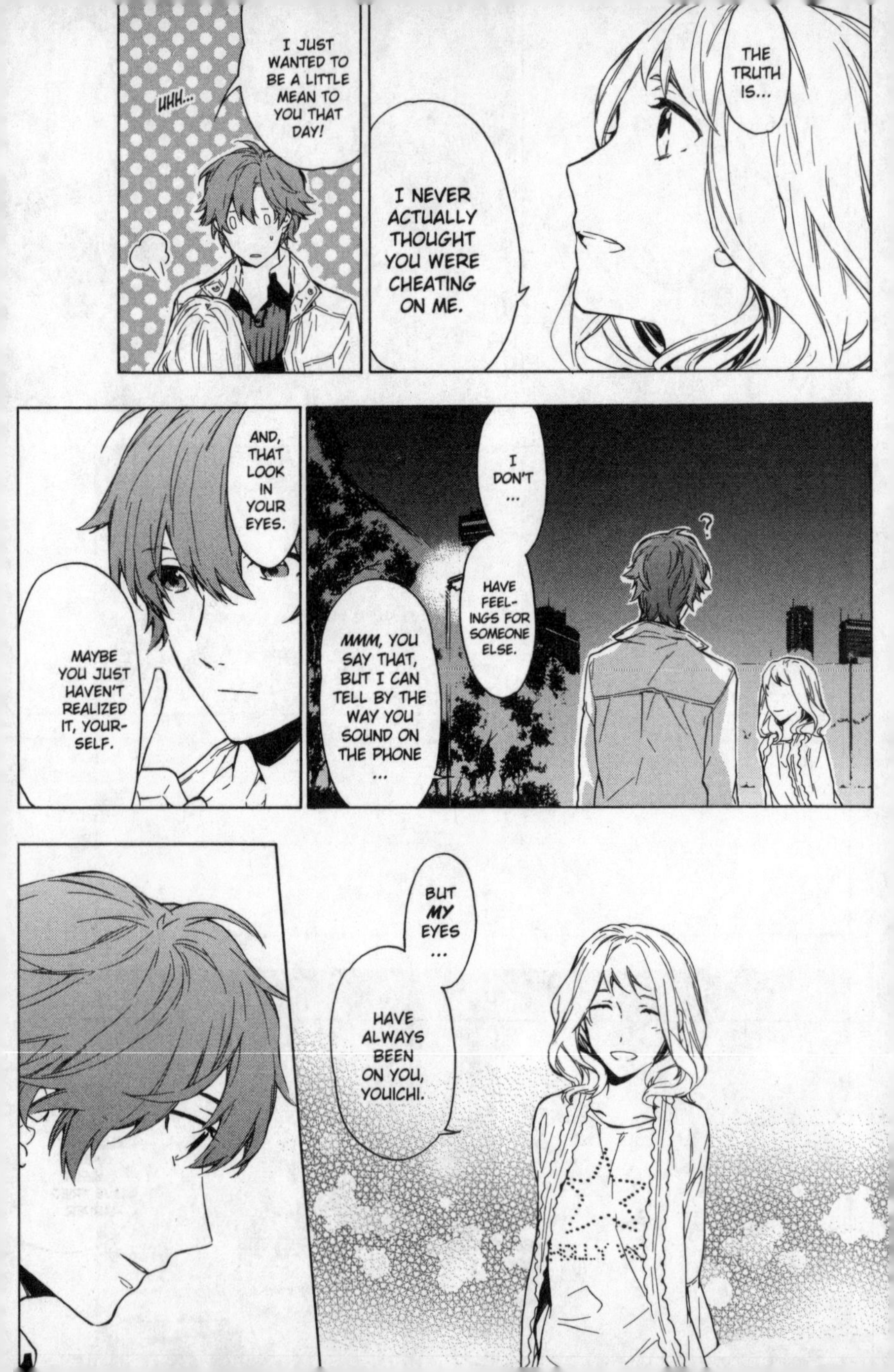
THE TRUTH IS...
I NEVER ACTUALLY THOUGHT YOU WERE CHEATING ON ME.
I JUST WANTED TO BE A LITTLE MEAN TO YOU THAT DAY!
UHH...
I DON'T ...
HAVE FEEL-INGS FOR SOMEONE ELSE.
MMM, YOU SAY THAT, BUT I CAN TELL BY THE WAY YOU SOUND ON THE PHONE ...
AND, THAT LOOK IN YOUR EYES.
MAYBE YOU JUST HAVEN'T REALIZED IT, YOUR-SELF.
BUT MY EYES ...
HAVE ALWAYS BEEN ON YOU, YOUICHI.

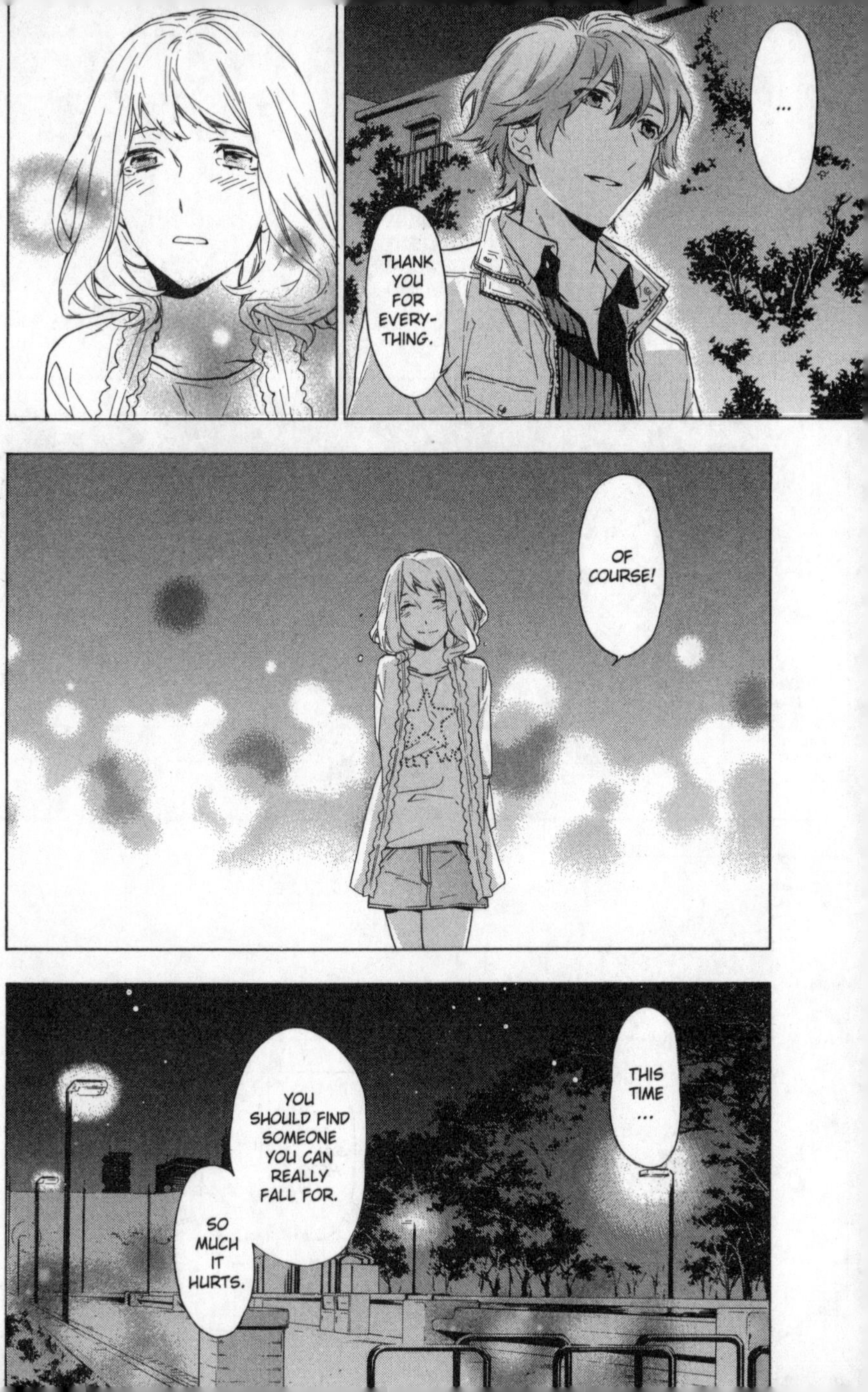
...
THANK YOU FOR EVERY-THING.
OF COURSE!
THIS TIME ...
YOU SHOULD FIND SOMEONE YOU CAN REALLY FALL FOR.
SO MUCH IT HURTS.

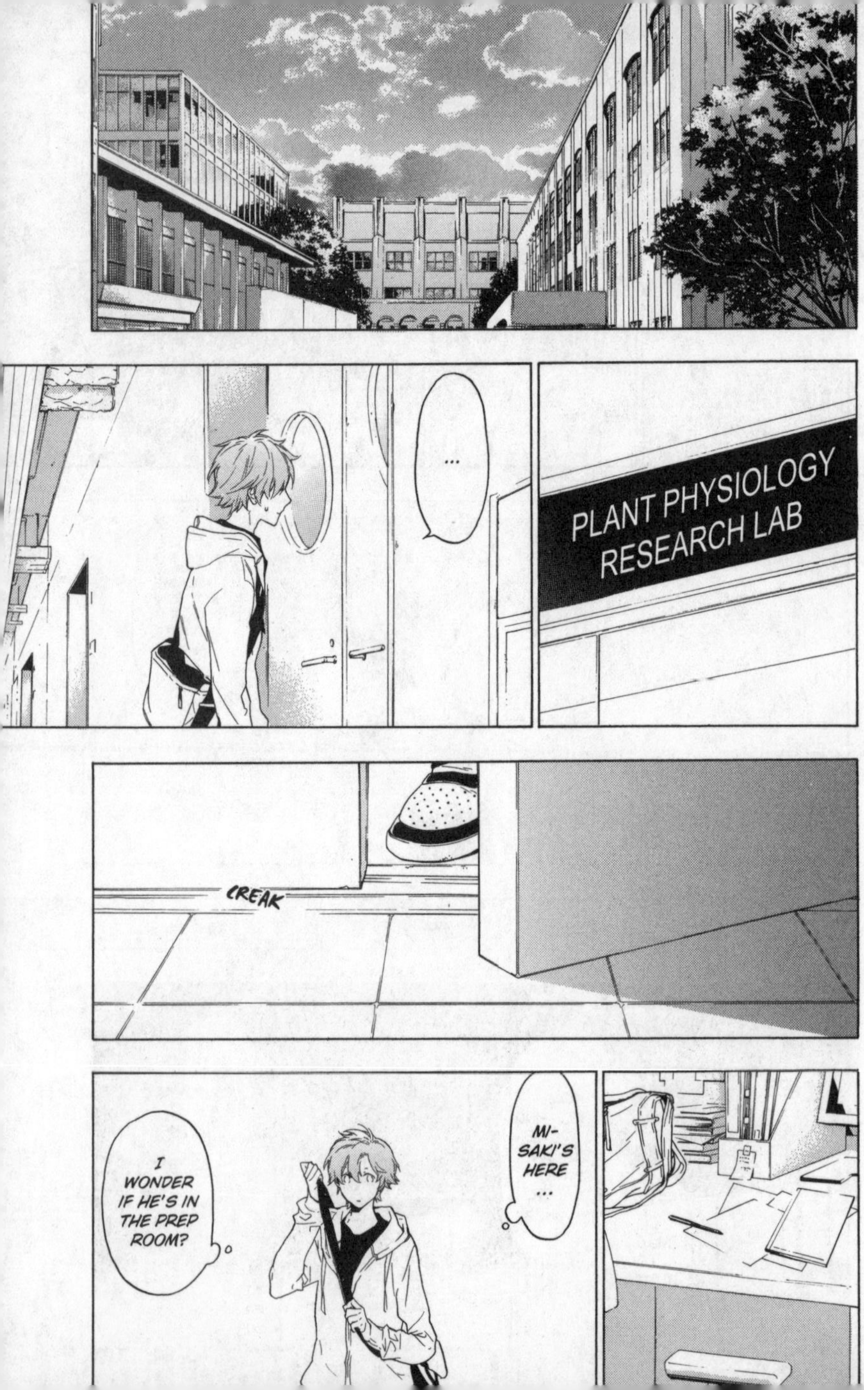
PLANT PHYSIOLOGY RESEARCH LAB
...
CREAK
MI-SAKI'S HERE ...
I WONDER IF HE'S IN THE PREP ROOM?

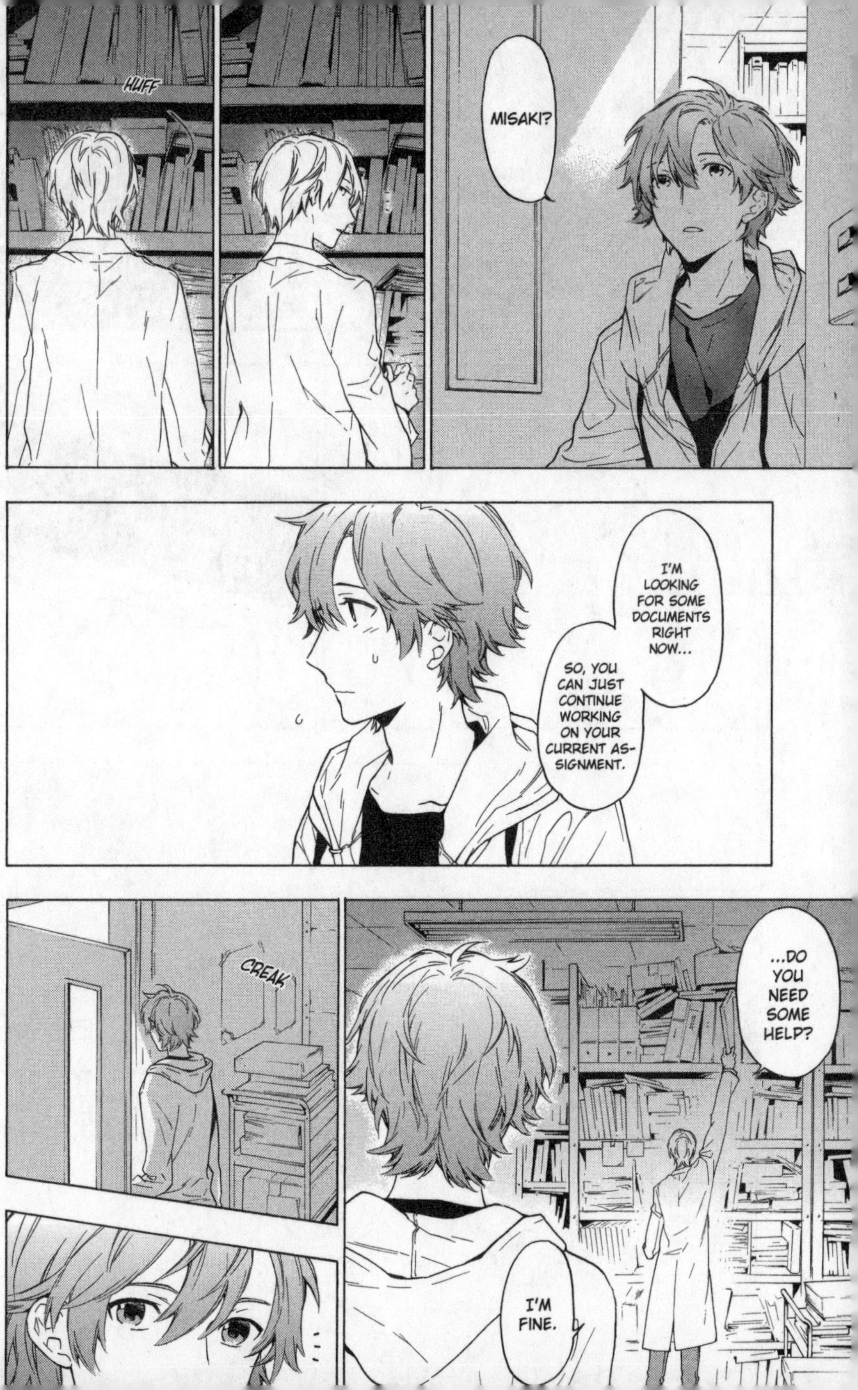
MISAKI?
HUFF
I'M LOOKING FOR SOME DOCUMENTS RIGHT NOW...
SO, YOU CAN JUST CONTINUE WORKING ON YOUR CURRENT AS-SIGNMENT.
...DO YOU NEED SOME HELP?
I'M FINE.
CREAK

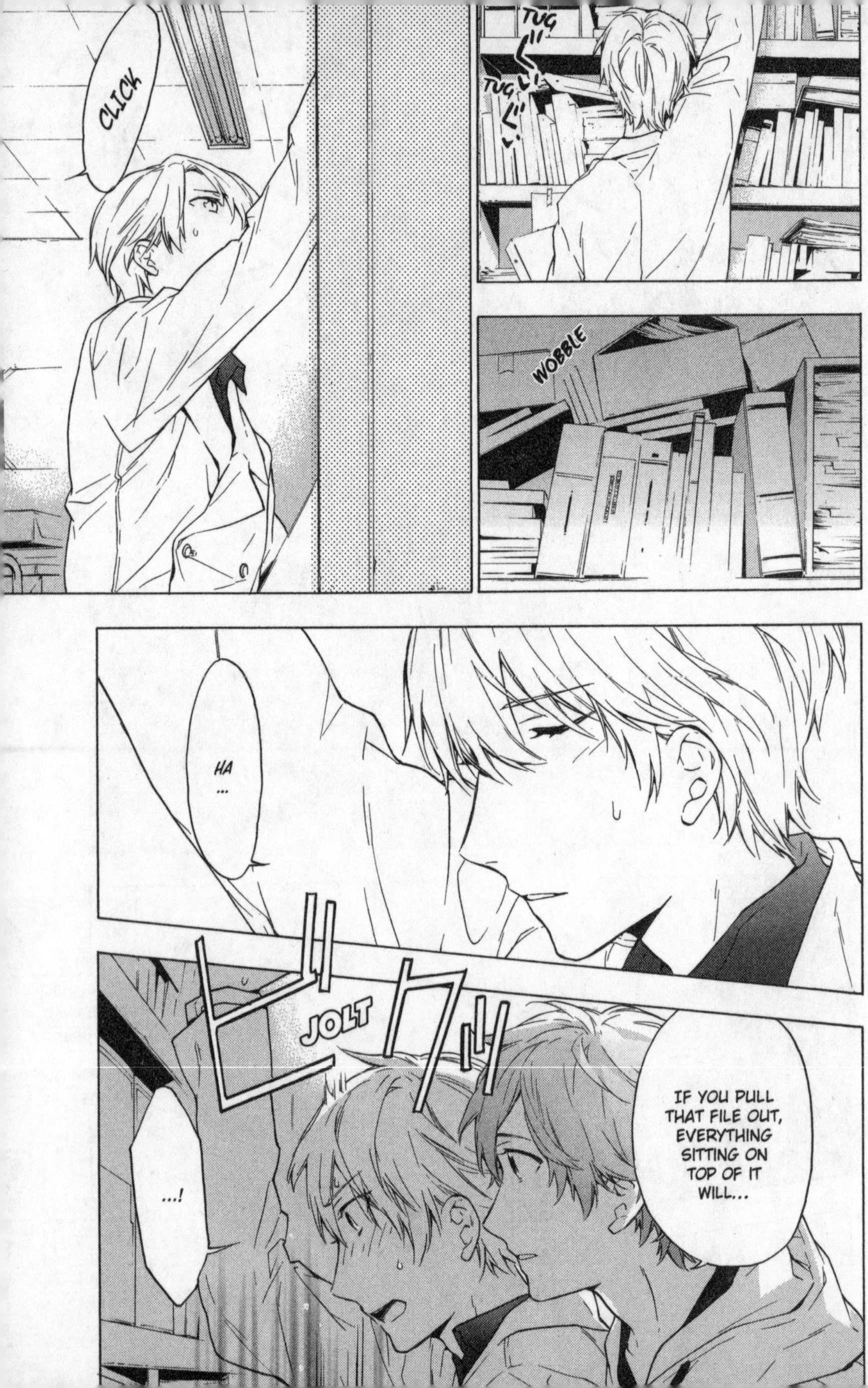
TUG
TUG
WOBBLE
CLICK
HA ...
JOLT
IF YOU PULL THAT FILE OUT, EVERYTHING SITTING ON TOP OF IT WILL...
...!

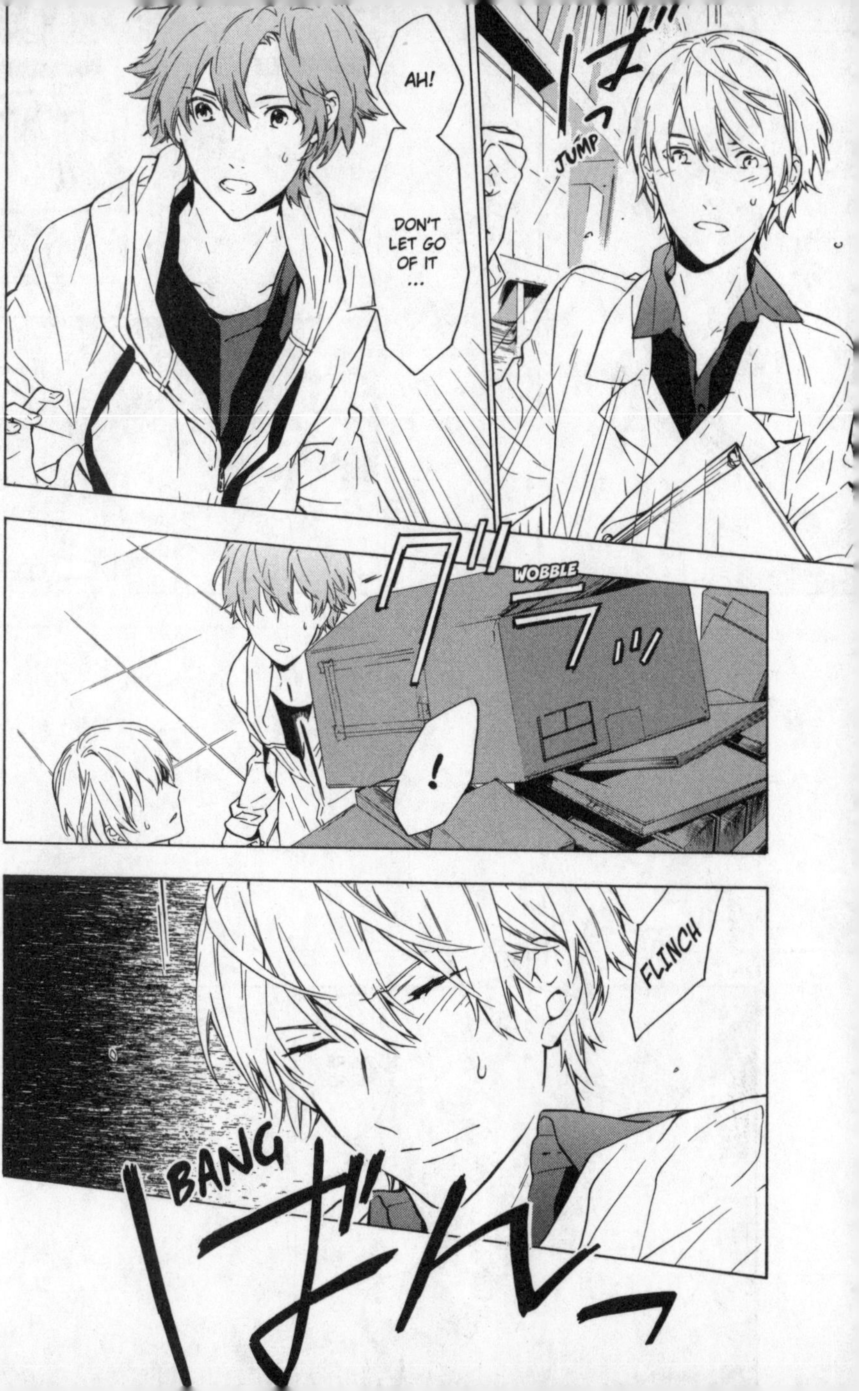
JUMP
AH!
DON'T LET GO OF IT ...
WOBBLE
!
FLINCH
BANG

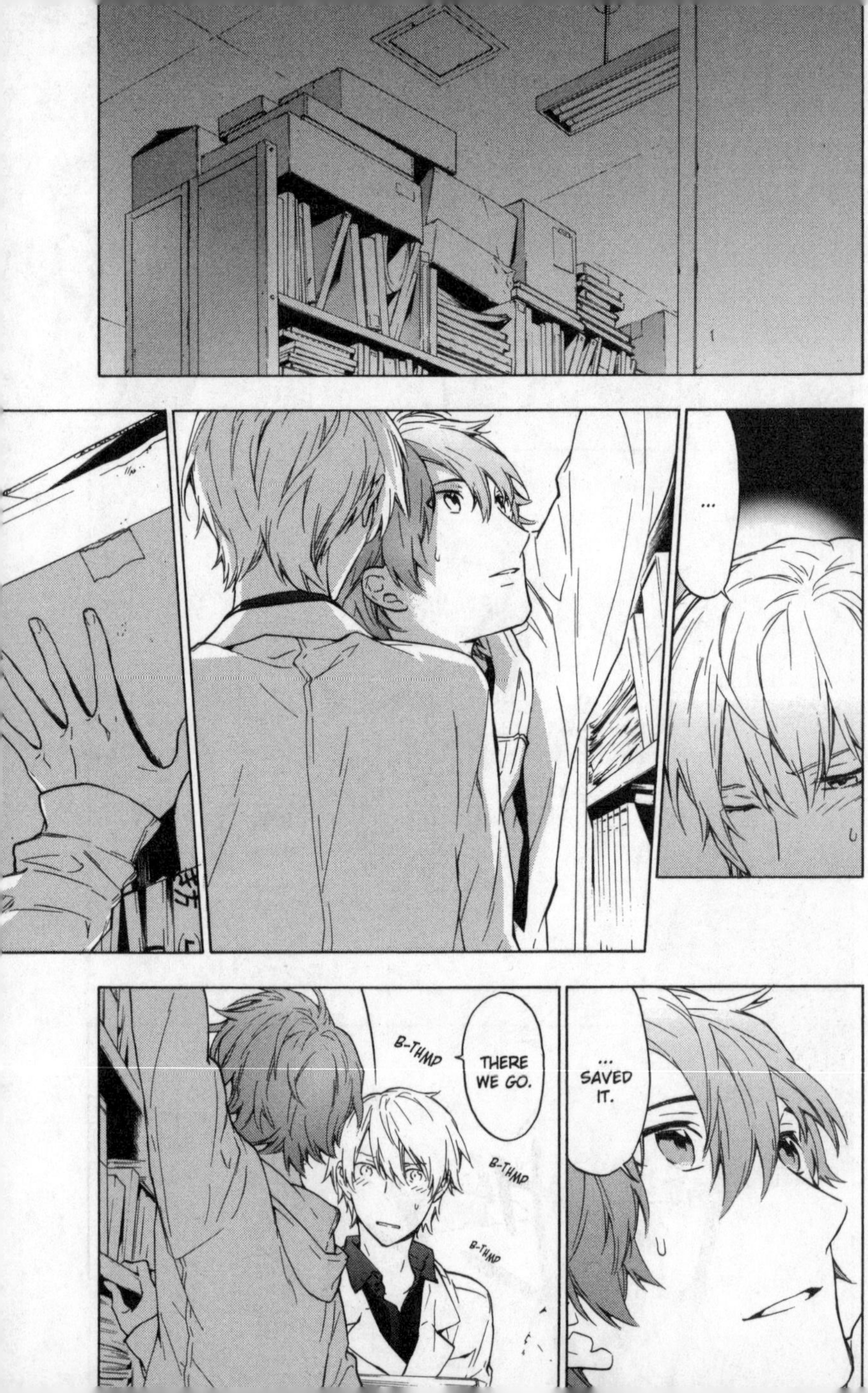
...
... SAVED IT.
THERE WE GO.
B-THUMP
B-THUMP
B-THUMP

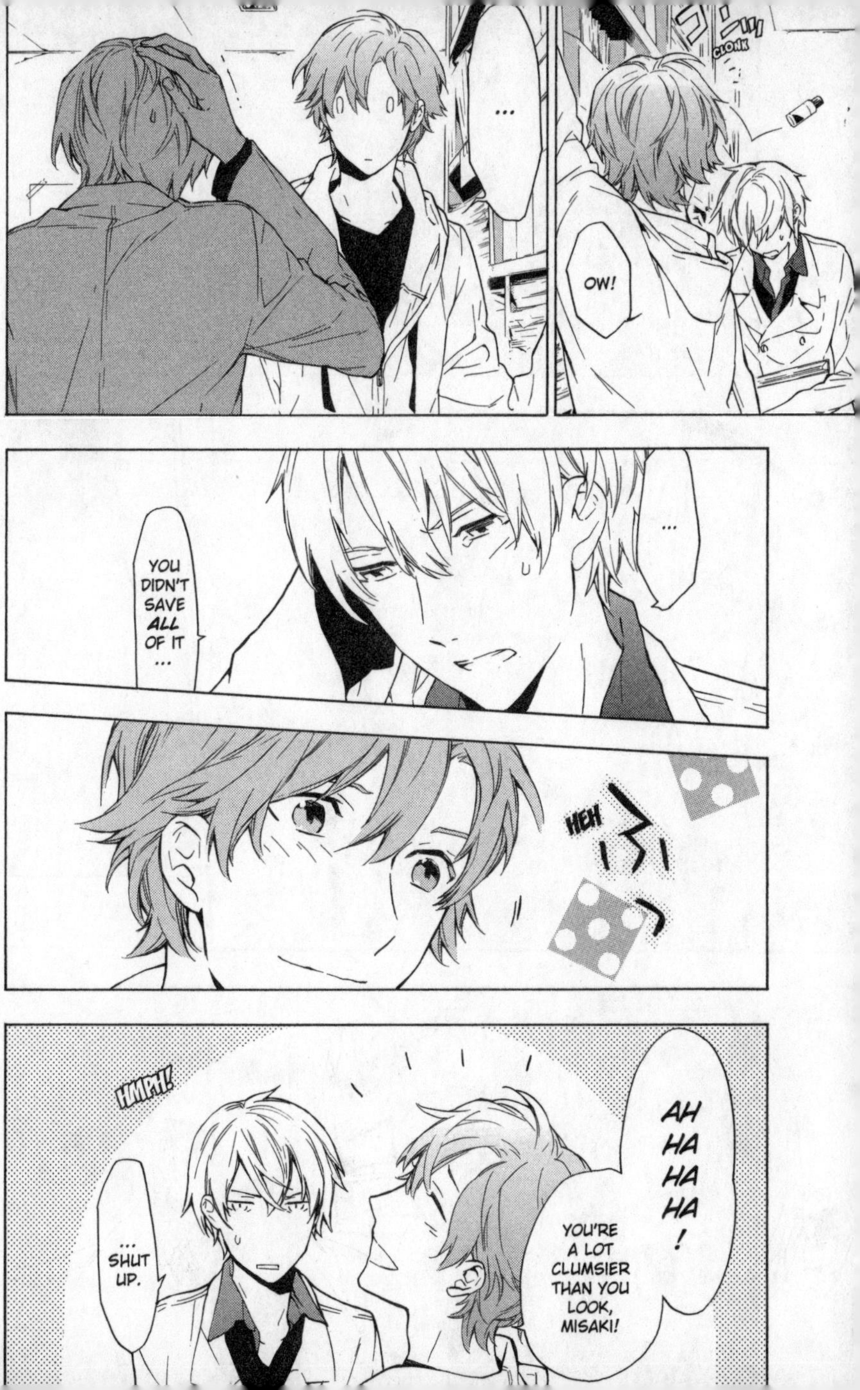
CLONK
OW!
...
...
YOU DIDN'T SAVE ALL OF IT ...
HEH
AH HA HA HA!
YOU'RE A LOT CLUMSIER THAN YOU LOOK, MISAKI!
HMPH!
... SHUT UP.

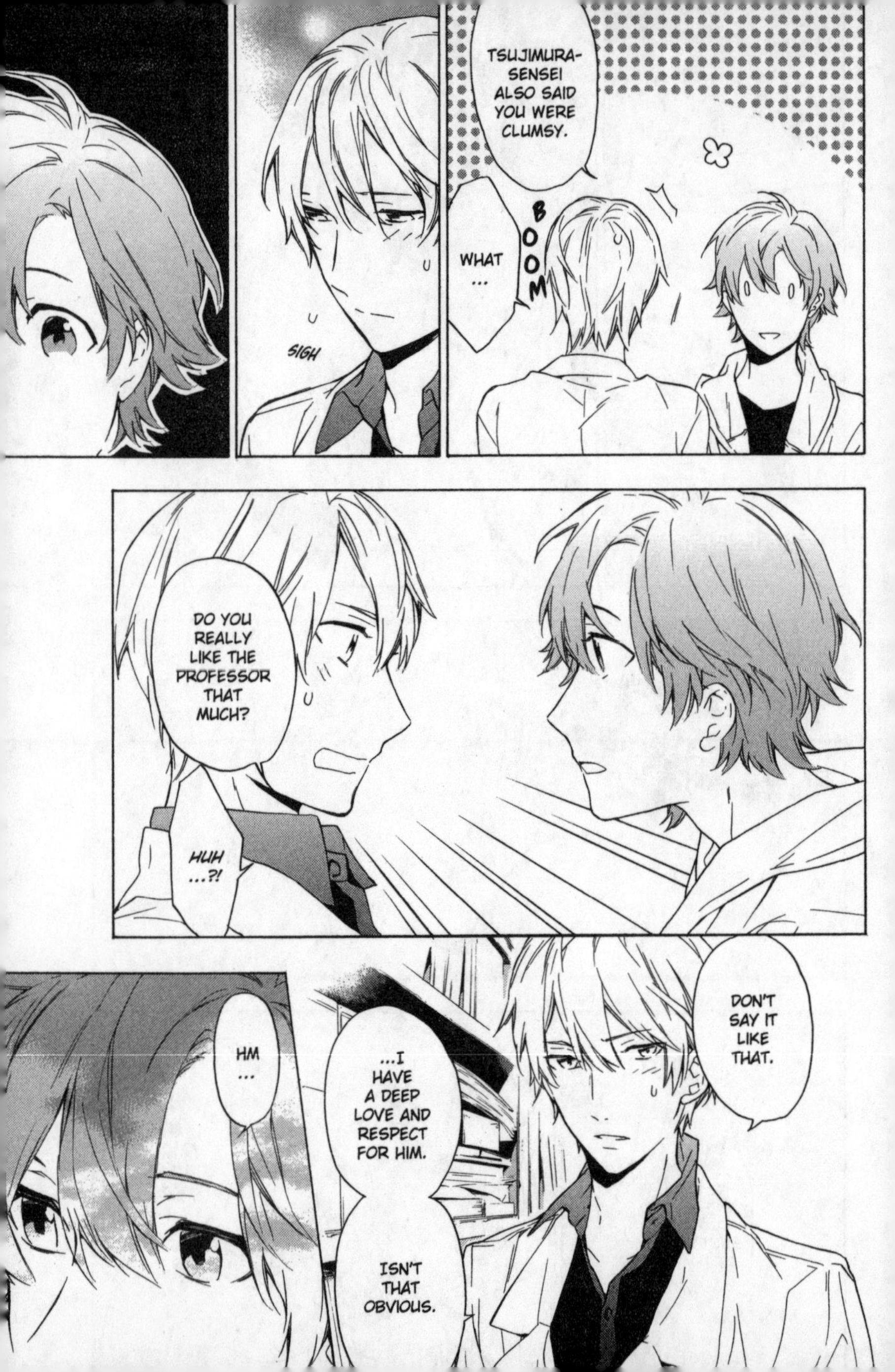
TSUJIMURA-SENSEI ALSO SAID YOU WERE CLUMSY.
BOOM
WHAT ...
SIGH
DO YOU REALLY LIKE THE PROFESSOR THAT MUCH?
HUH ...?!
DON'T SAY IT LIKE THAT.
...I HAVE A DEEP LOVE AND RESPECT FOR HIM.
ISN'T THAT OBVIOUS.
HM ...

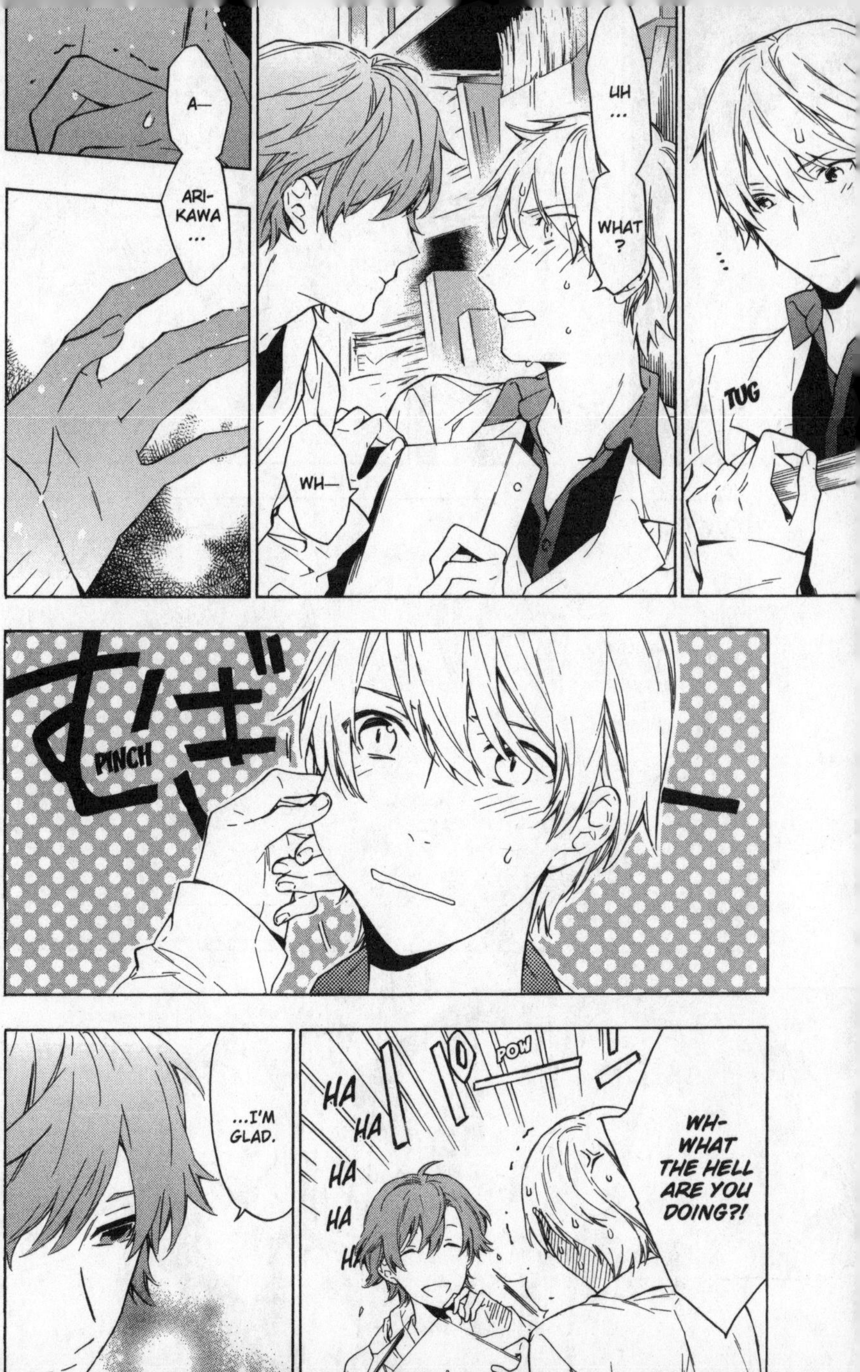
...
TUG
UH ... WHAT?
WH—
A—
ARI-KAWA ...
むぎ
PINCH
POW
HA HA HA HA HA
WH-WHAT THE HELL ARE YOU DOING?!
...I'M GLAD.

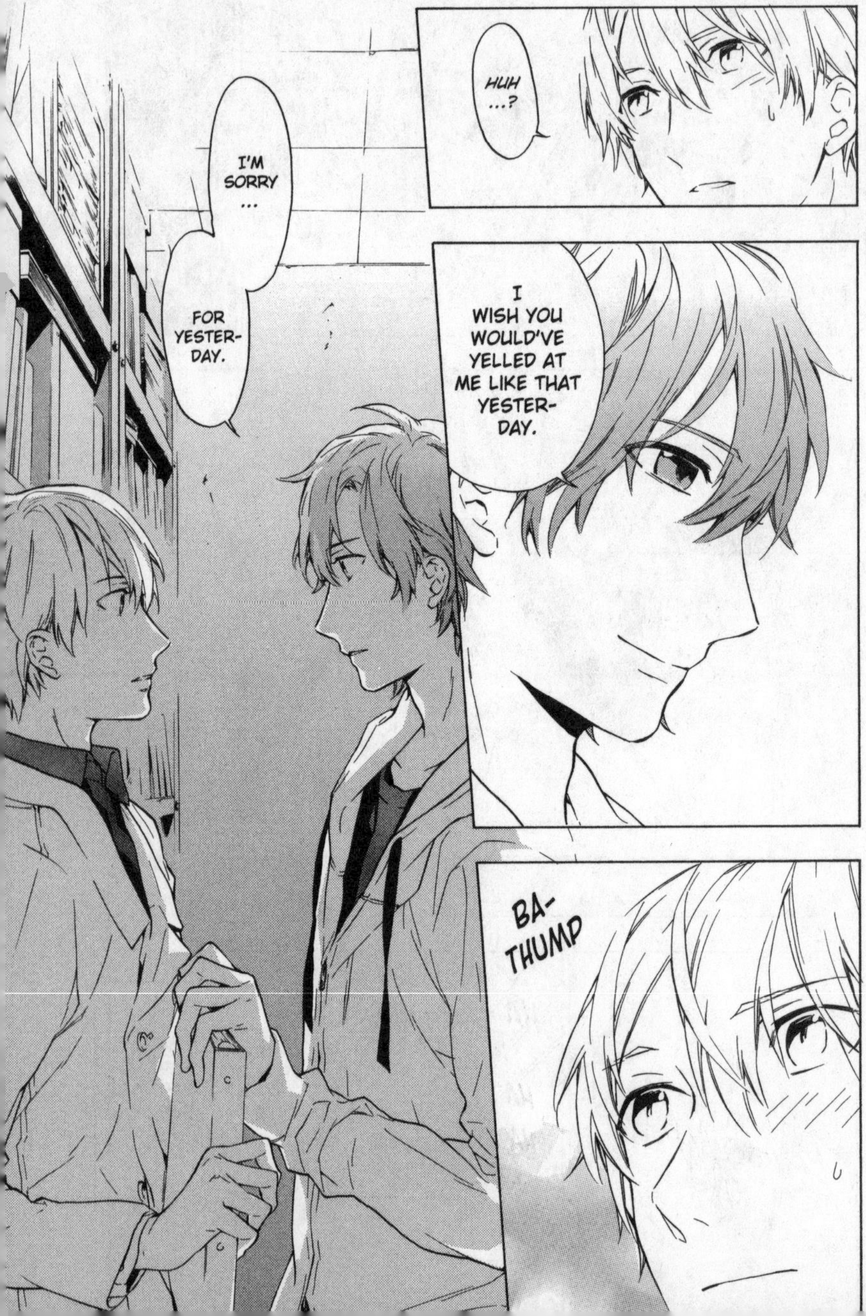
HUH ...?
I WISH YOU WOULD'VE YELLED AT ME LIKE THAT YESTER-DAY.
BA-THUMP
I'M SORRY ...
FOR YESTER-DAY.

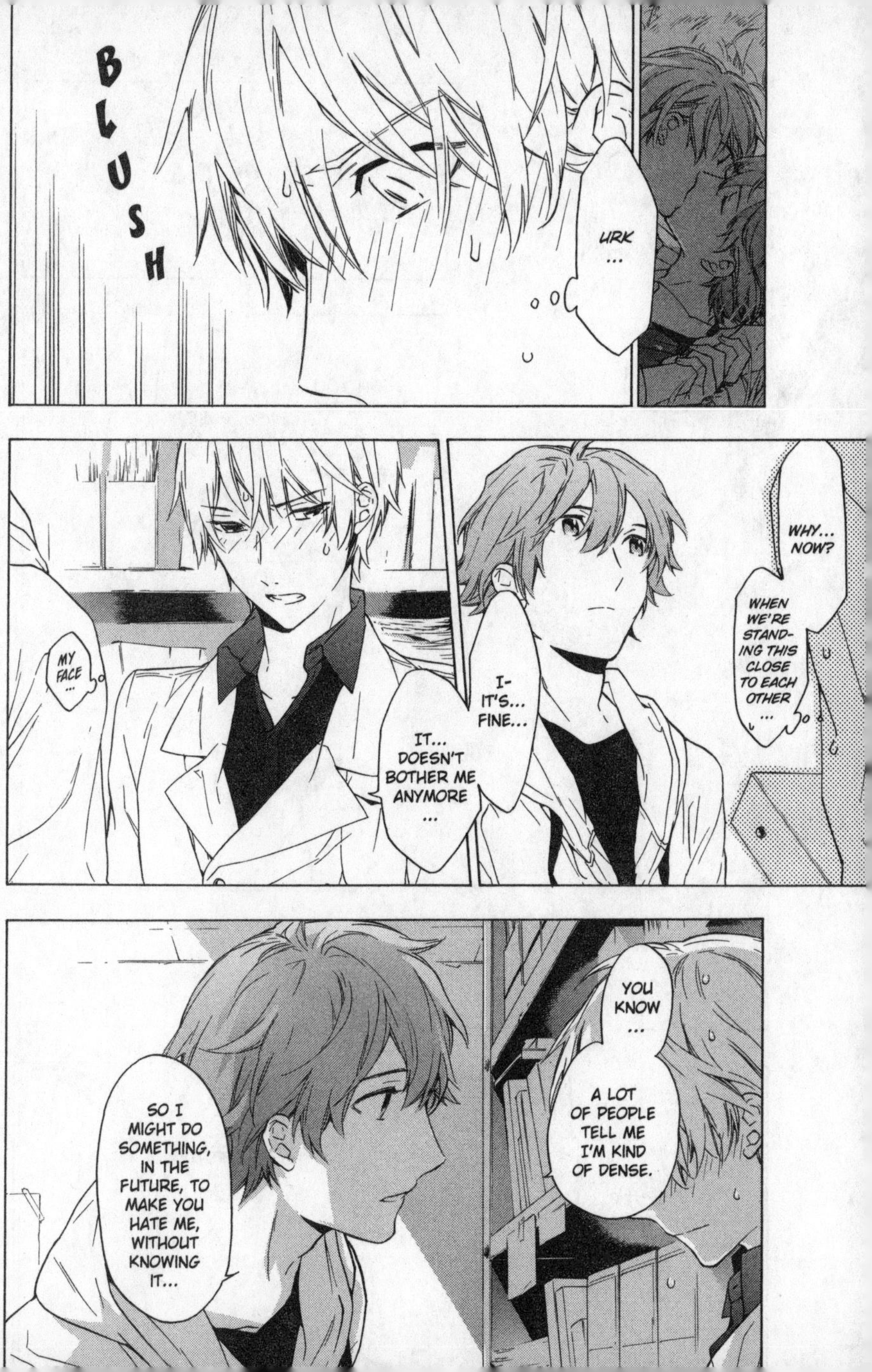
URK ...
BLUSH
WHY... NOW?
WHEN WE'RE STANDING THIS CLOSE TO EACH OTHER ...
I- IT'S... FINE...
IT... DOESN'T BOTHER ME ANYMORE ...
MY FACE ...
YOU KNOW ...
A LOT OF PEOPLE TELL ME I'M KIND OF DENSE.
SO I MIGHT DO SOMETHING, IN THE FUTURE, TO MAKE YOU HATE ME, WITHOUT KNOWING IT...

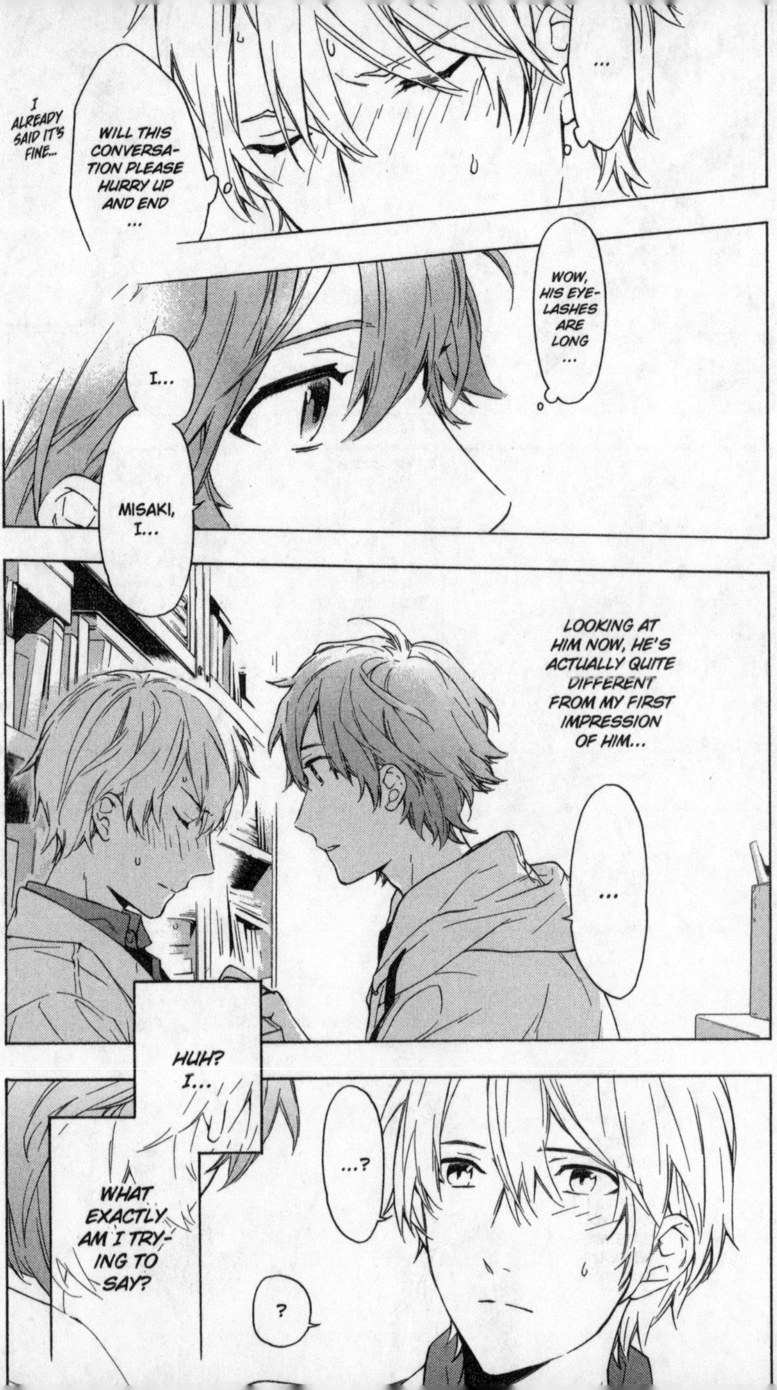
...
WILL THIS CONVERSATION PLEASE HURRY UP AND END ...
I ALREADY SAID IT'S FINE...
WOW, HIS EYELASHES ARE LONG ...
I...
MISAKI, I...
LOOKING AT HIM NOW, HE'S ACTUALLY QUITE DIFFERENT FROM MY FIRST IMPRESSION OF HIM...
...
HUH? I...
...?
WHAT EXACTLY AM I TRYING TO SAY?
?

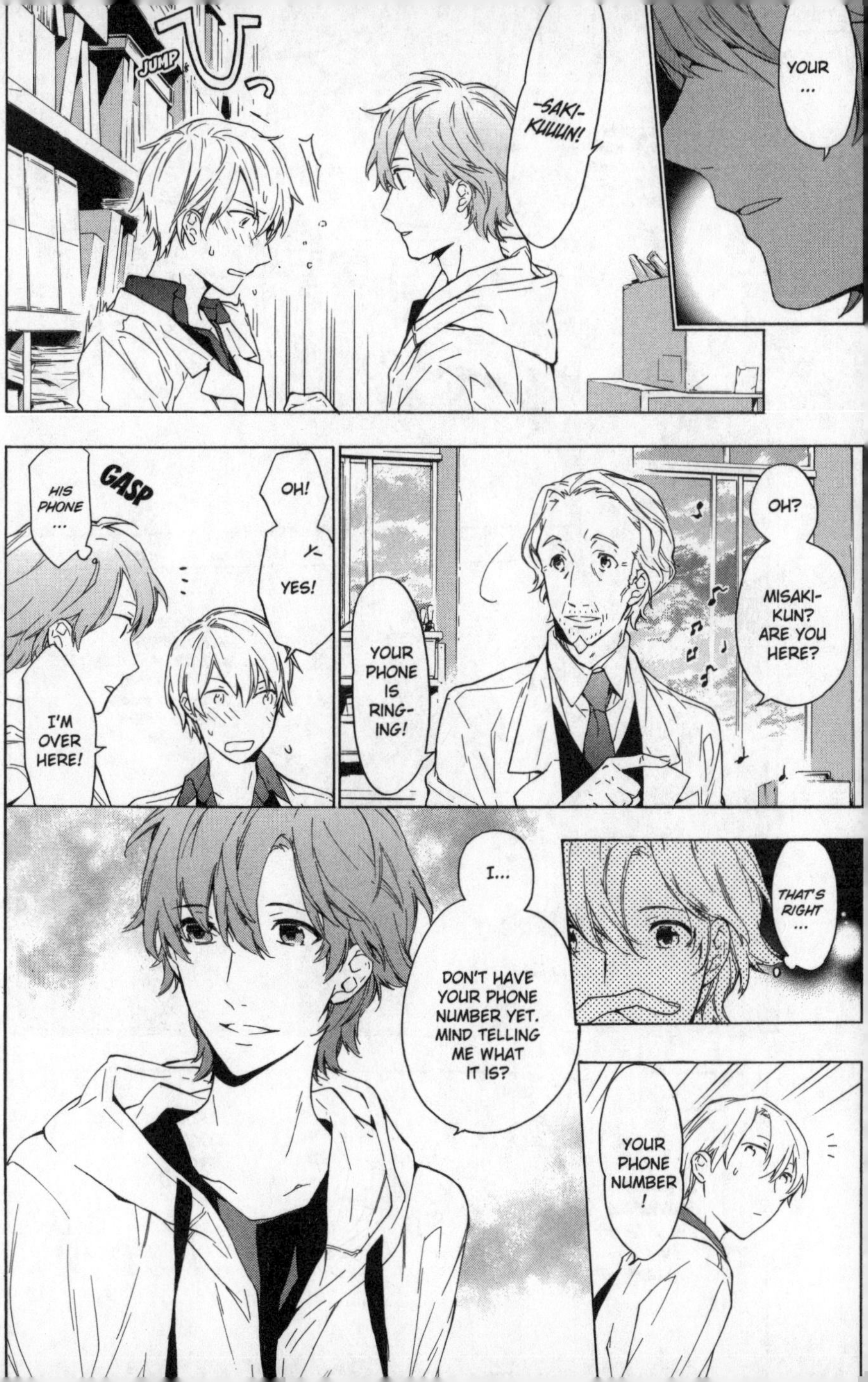
YOUR ...
-SAKI-KUUUN!
JUMP
OH?
MISAKI-KUN? ARE YOU HERE?
YOUR PHONE IS RING-ING!
OH!
YES!
GASP
HIS PHONE ...
I'M OVER HERE!
THAT'S RIGHT ...
YOUR PHONE NUMBER !
I...
DON'T HAVE YOUR PHONE NUMBER YET. MIND TELLING ME WHAT IT IS?

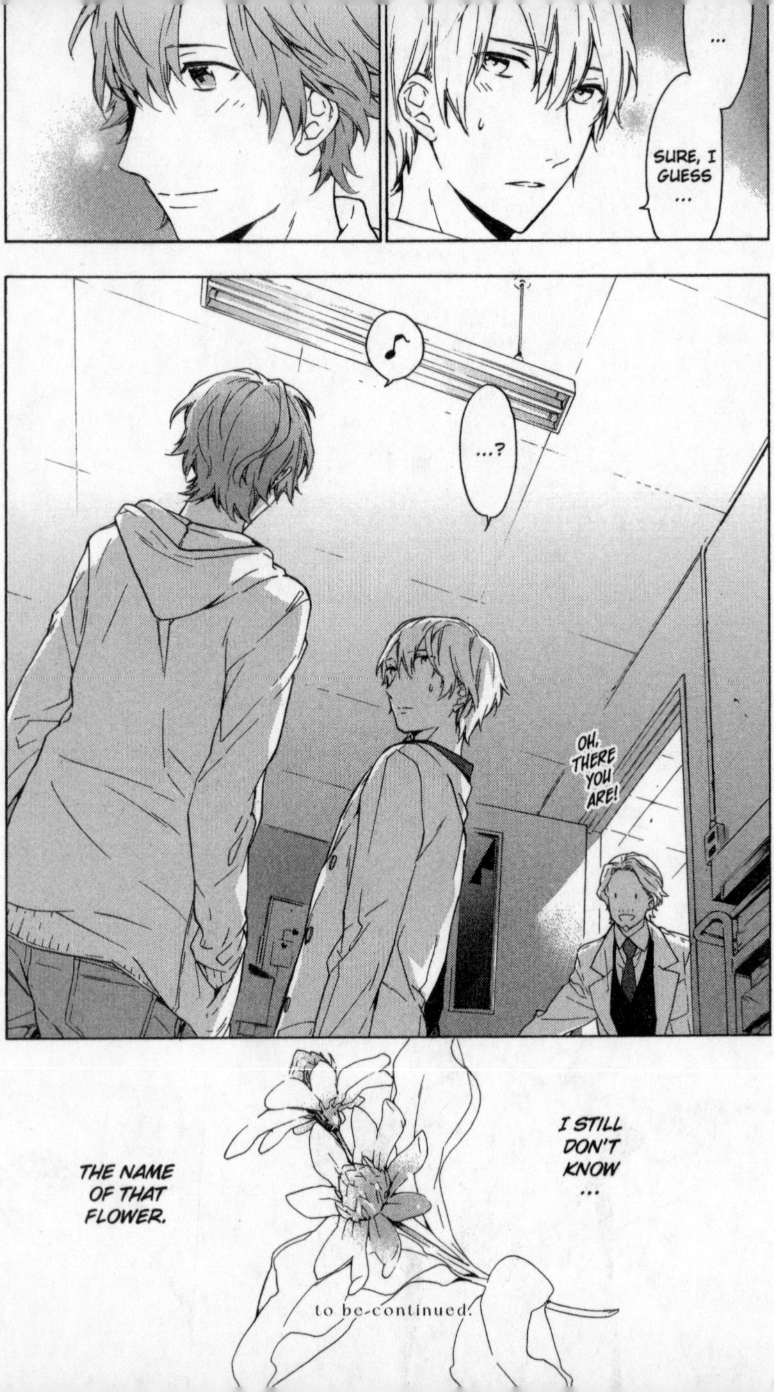
...
SURE, I GUESS ...
♪
...?
OH, THERE YOU ARE!
I STILL DON'T KNOW ...
THE NAME OF THAT FLOWER.
to be continued.

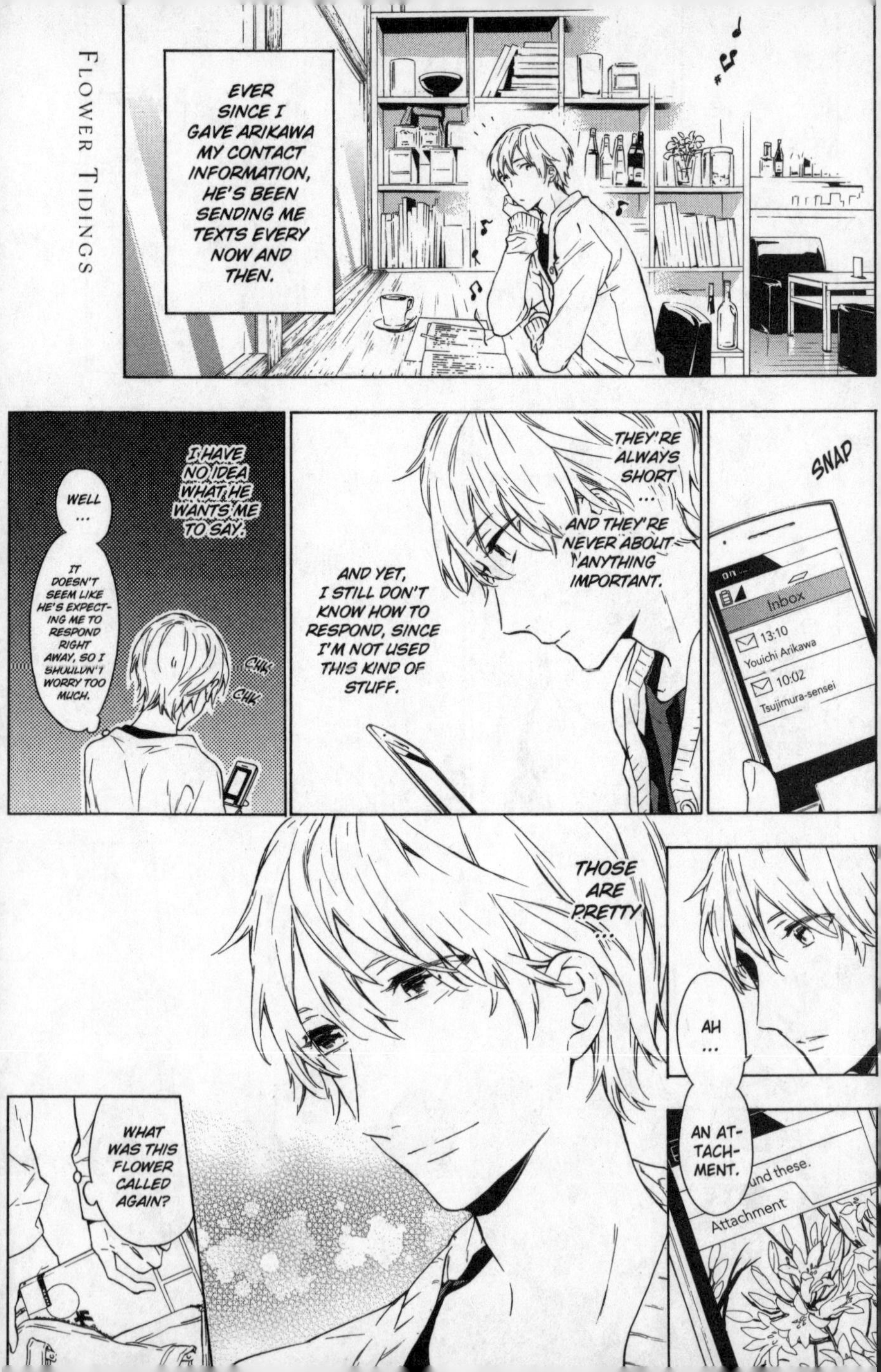
EVER SINCE I GAVE ARIKAWA MY CONTACT INFORMATION, HE'S BEEN SENDING ME TEXTS EVERY NOW AND THEN.
SNAP
Inbox
13:10
Youichi Arikawa
10:02
Tsujimura-sensei
THEY'RE ALWAYS SHORT ...
AND THEY'RE NEVER ABOUT ANYTHING IMPORTANT.
AND YET, I STILL DON'T KNOW HOW TO RESPOND, SINCE I'M NOT USED THIS KIND OF STUFF.
I HAVE NO IDEA WHAT HE WANTS ME TO SAY.
WELL ...
IT DOESN'T SEEM LIKE HE'S EXPECTING ME TO RESPOND RIGHT AWAY, SO I SHOULDN'T WORRY TOO MUCH.
CHK
CHK
AH ...
AN AT-TACH-MENT.
und these.
Attachment
THOSE ARE PRETTY ...
WHAT WAS THIS FLOWER CALLED AGAIN?

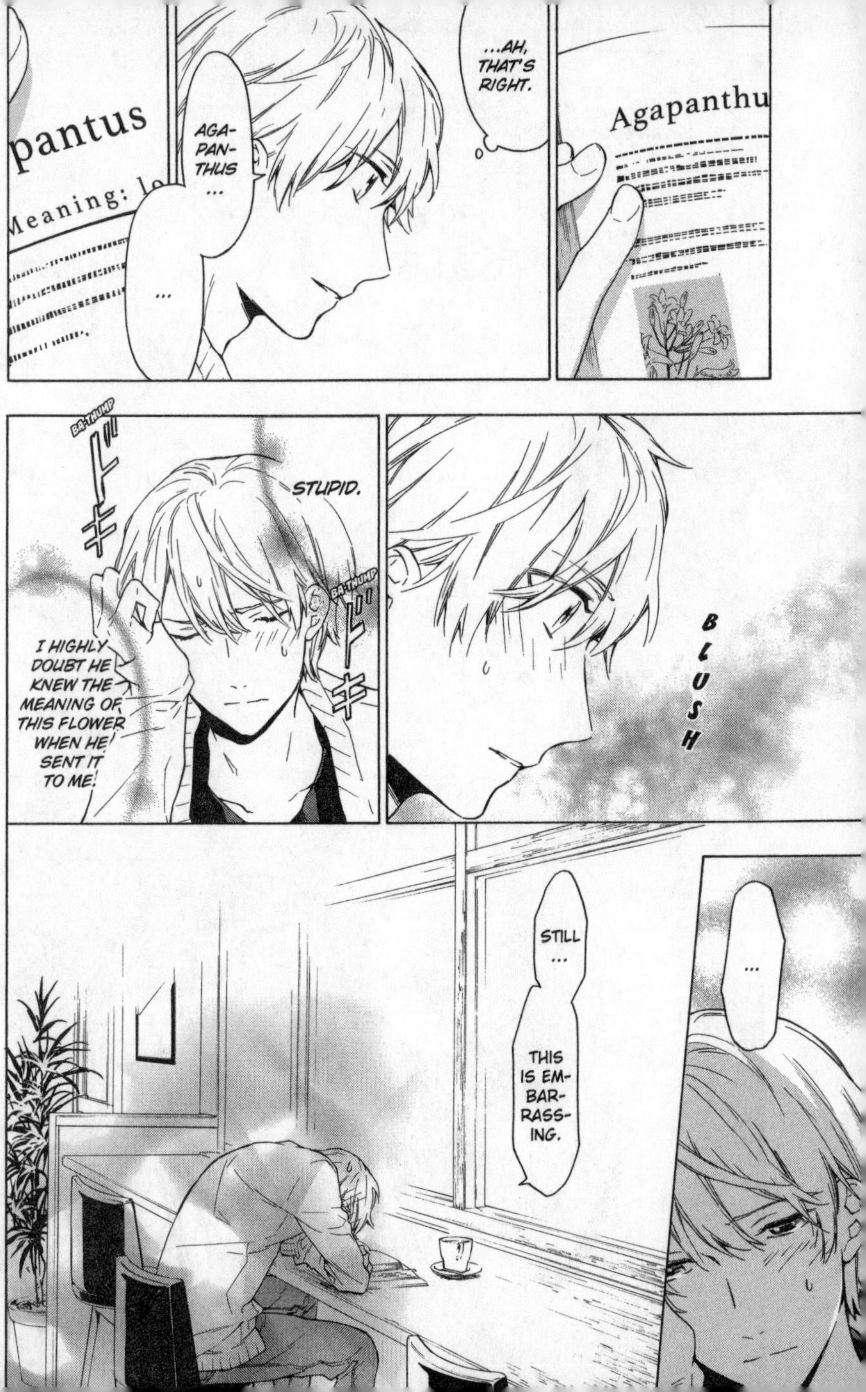
Agapanthu
...AH, THAT'S RIGHT.
pantus
AGAPANTHUS...
Meaning: lo
...
BLUSH
BA-THUMP
STUPID.
BA-THUMP
I HIGHLY DOUBT HE KNEW THE MEANING OF THIS FLOWER WHEN HE SENT IT TO ME!
...
STILL...
THIS IS EMBARRASSING.

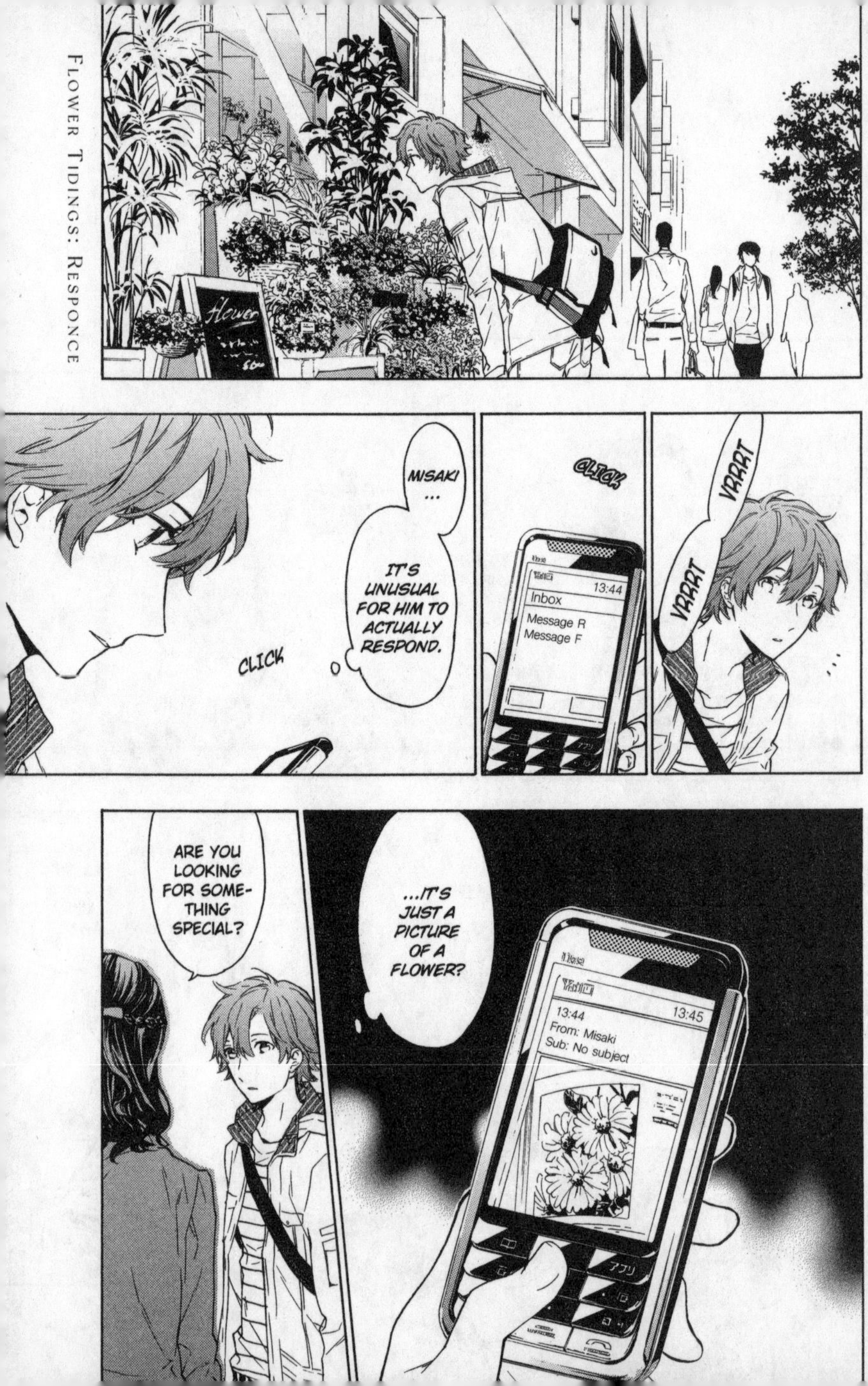
VRRRT
VRRRT
...
CLICK
13:44
Inbox
Message R
Message F
MISAKI ...
IT'S UNUSUAL FOR HIM TO ACTUALLY RESPOND.
CLICK
...IT'S JUST A PICTURE OF A FLOWER?
13:44
13:45
From: Misaki
Sub: No subject
ARE YOU LOOKING FOR SOME-THING SPECIAL?

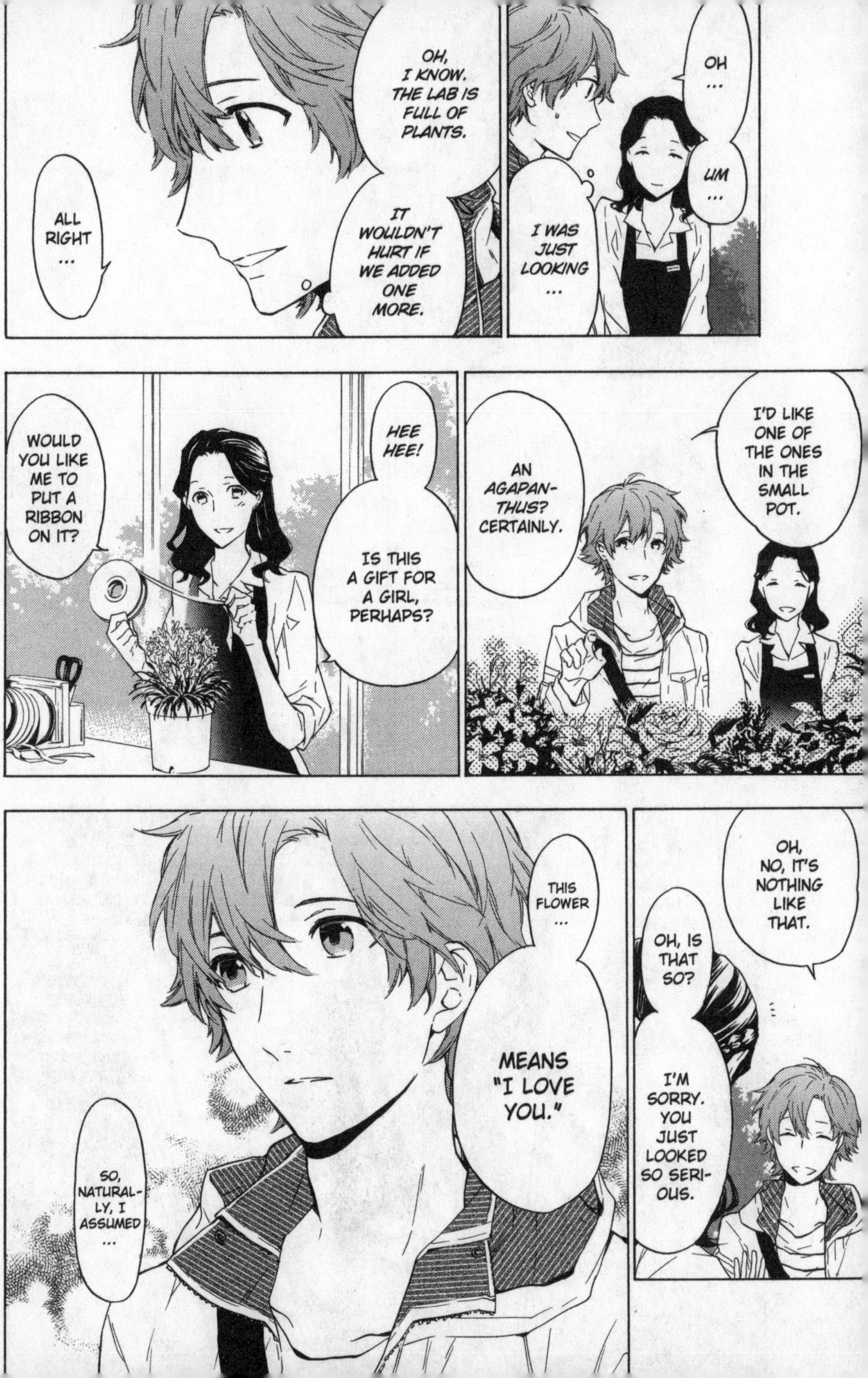
OH ...
UM ...
I WAS JUST LOOKING ...
OH, I KNOW. THE LAB IS FULL OF PLANTS.
IT WOULDN'T HURT IF WE ADDED ONE MORE.
ALL RIGHT ...
I'D LIKE ONE OF THE ONES IN THE SMALL POT.
AN AGAPANTHUS? CERTAINLY.
HEE HEE!
IS THIS A GIFT FOR A GIRL, PERHAPS?
WOULD YOU LIKE ME TO PUT A RIBBON ON IT?
OH, NO, IT'S NOTHING LIKE THAT.
OH, IS THAT SO?
I'M SORRY. YOU JUST LOOKED SO SERI-OUS.
THIS FLOWER ...
MEANS "I LOVE YOU."
SO, NATURAL-LY, I ASSUMED ...

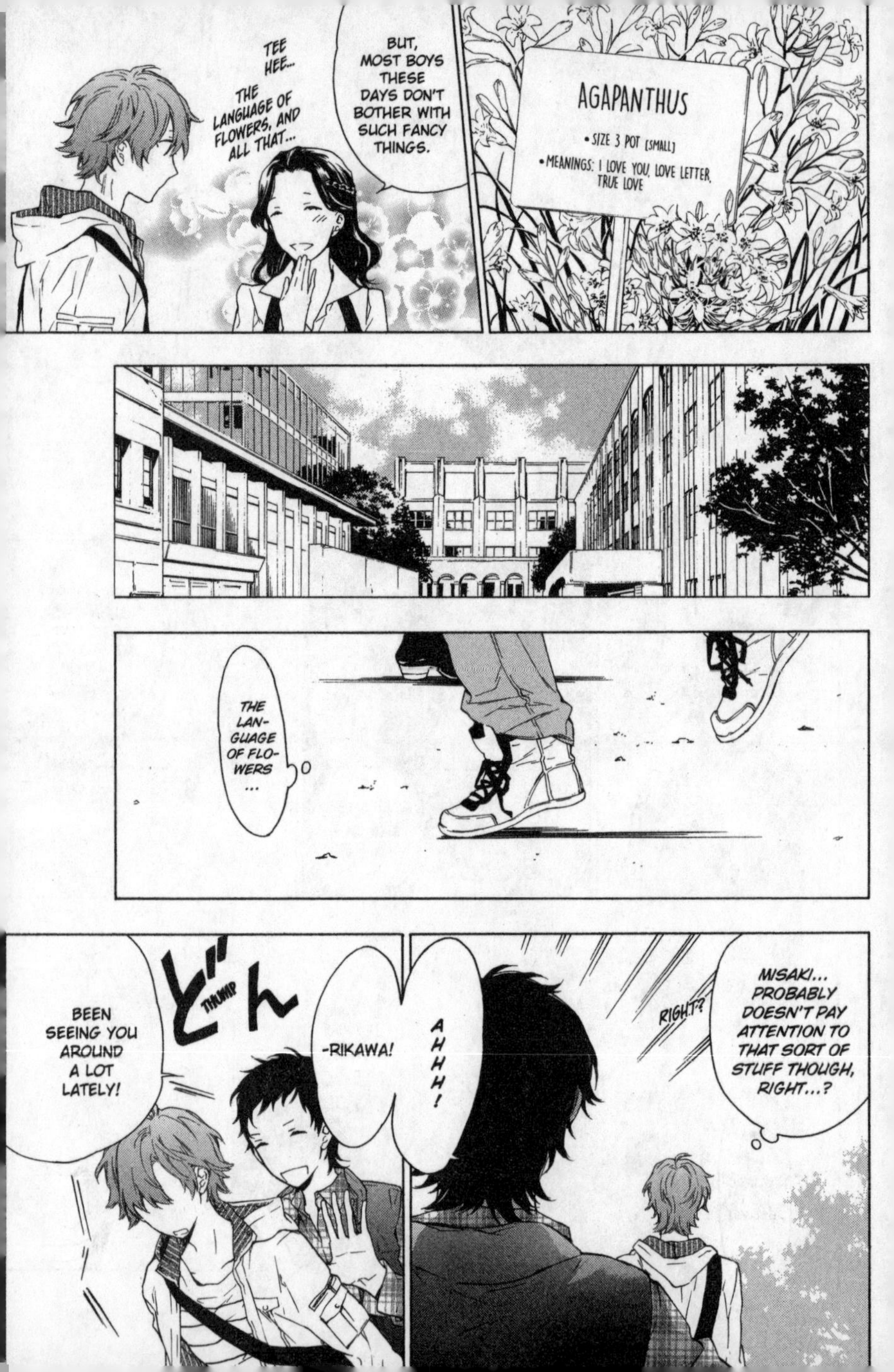
AGAPANTHUS
• SIZE 3 POT [SMALL]
• MEANINGS: I LOVE YOU, LOVE LETTER, TRUE LOVE
BUT, MOST BOYS THESE DAYS DON'T BOTHER WITH SUCH FANCY THINGS.
TEE HEE...
THE LANGUAGE OF FLOWERS, AND ALL THAT...
THE LANGUAGE OF FLOWERS...
MISAKI... PROBABLY DOESN'T PAY ATTENTION TO THAT SORT OF STUFF THOUGH, RIGHT...?
RIGHT?
AHHH!
-RIKAWA!
THUMP
BEEN SEEING YOU AROUND A LOT LATELY!

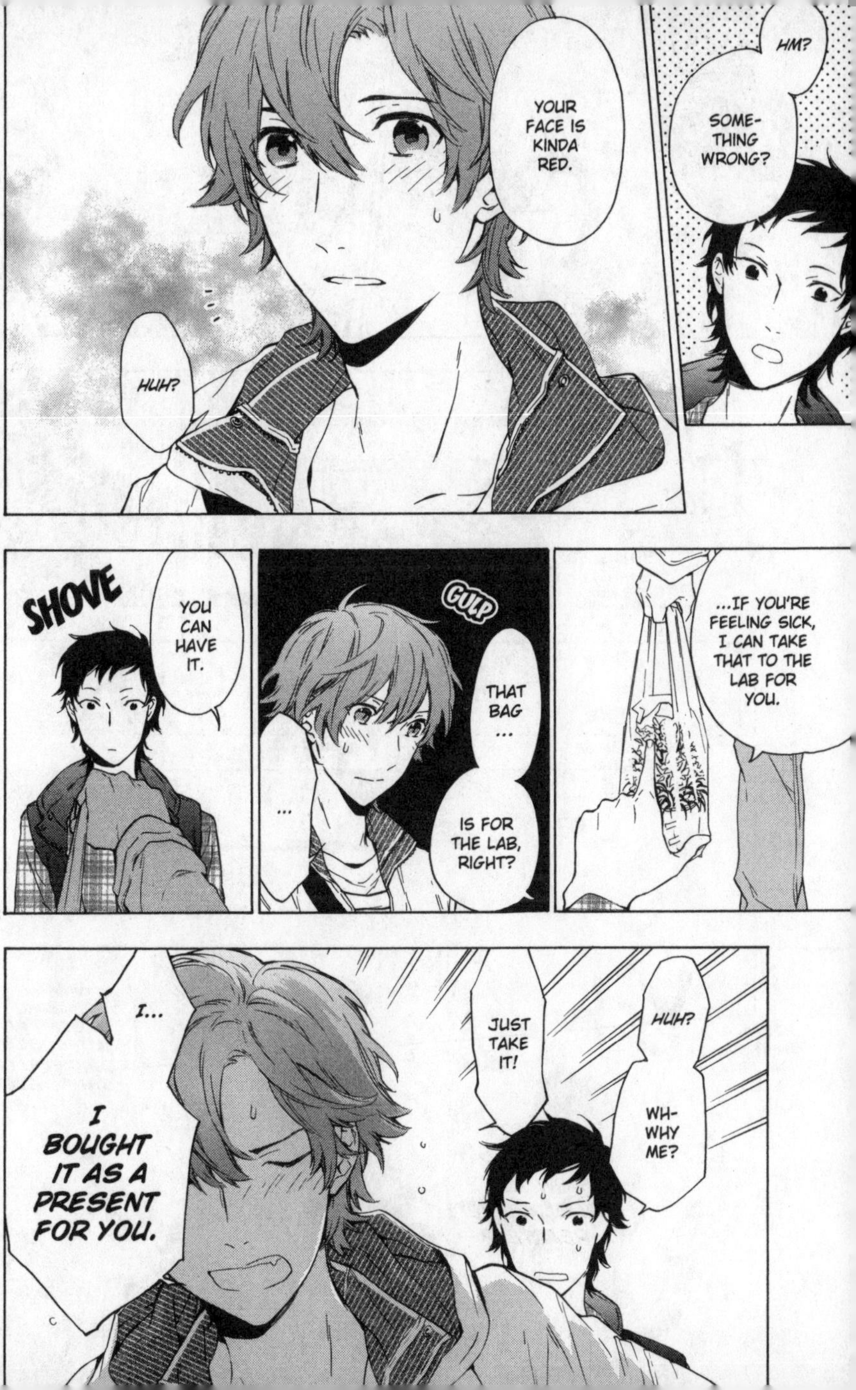
HM?
SOME-THING WRONG?
YOUR FACE IS KINDA RED.
...
HUH?
...IF YOU'RE FEELING SICK, I CAN TAKE THAT TO THE LAB FOR YOU.
GULP
THAT BAG ...
IS FOR THE LAB, RIGHT?
...
YOU CAN HAVE IT.
SHOVE
HUH?
WH-WHY ME?
JUST TAKE IT!
I...
I BOUGHT IT AS A PRESENT FOR YOU.

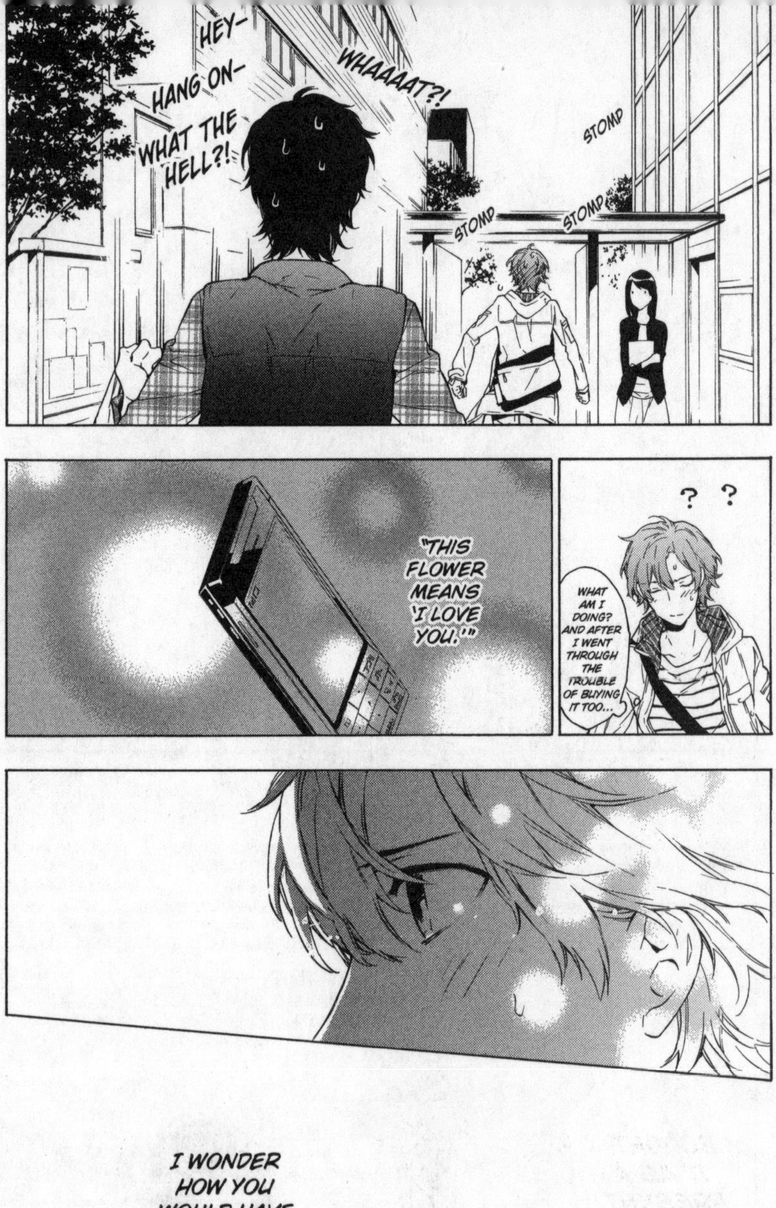
STOMP
STOMP
STOMP
WHAAAAT?!
HEY-
HANG ON-
WHAT THE HELL?!
? ?
WHAT AM I DOING? AND AFTER I WENT THROUGH THE TROUBLE OF BUYING IT TOO...
"THIS FLOWER MEANS 'I LOVE YOU.'"
I WONDER HOW YOU WOULD HAVE REACTED?

Only the Flower Knows

花 の み ぞ 知 る

1

RIHITO TAKARAI

Graphic Design: J F
Production Manager: J F
Publisher: Hikaru Sasahara

Translating: Ailie B.
Lettering: Ana Vegara
Editing: Yuto

Only the Flower Knows - 花のみぞ知る © Rihito Takarai. All rights reserved. Original Japanese edition published in 2011 by Taiyoh Tosho Publishing Co., Ltd. All other material © 2020 by DIGITAL MANGA, Inc. All rights reserved. No portion of this publication may be reproduced or transmitted in any form or by any means without written permission from the copyright holders. Any likeness of characters, places, and situations featured in this publication to actual persons (living or deceased), events, places, and situations is purely coincidental. All characters depicted in sexually explicit scenes in this publication are at least the age of consent or older. The JUNÉ logo is © of DIGITAL MANGA, Inc.

English Edition Published by
DIGITAL MANGA PUBLISHING
A division of DIGITAL MANGA, Inc.
1447 W 178th Street, Suite 302
Gardena, CA 90248

www.junemanga.com

First Edition: January 2022
ISBN-10: 1-56970-394-9
ISBN-13: 978-1-56970-394-6

1 3 5 7 9 10 8 6 4 2

Printed in Canada

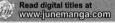

Read digital titles at
www.junemanga.com

Become our fan on Facebook
June Manga

Follow us on Twitter
@JuneManga

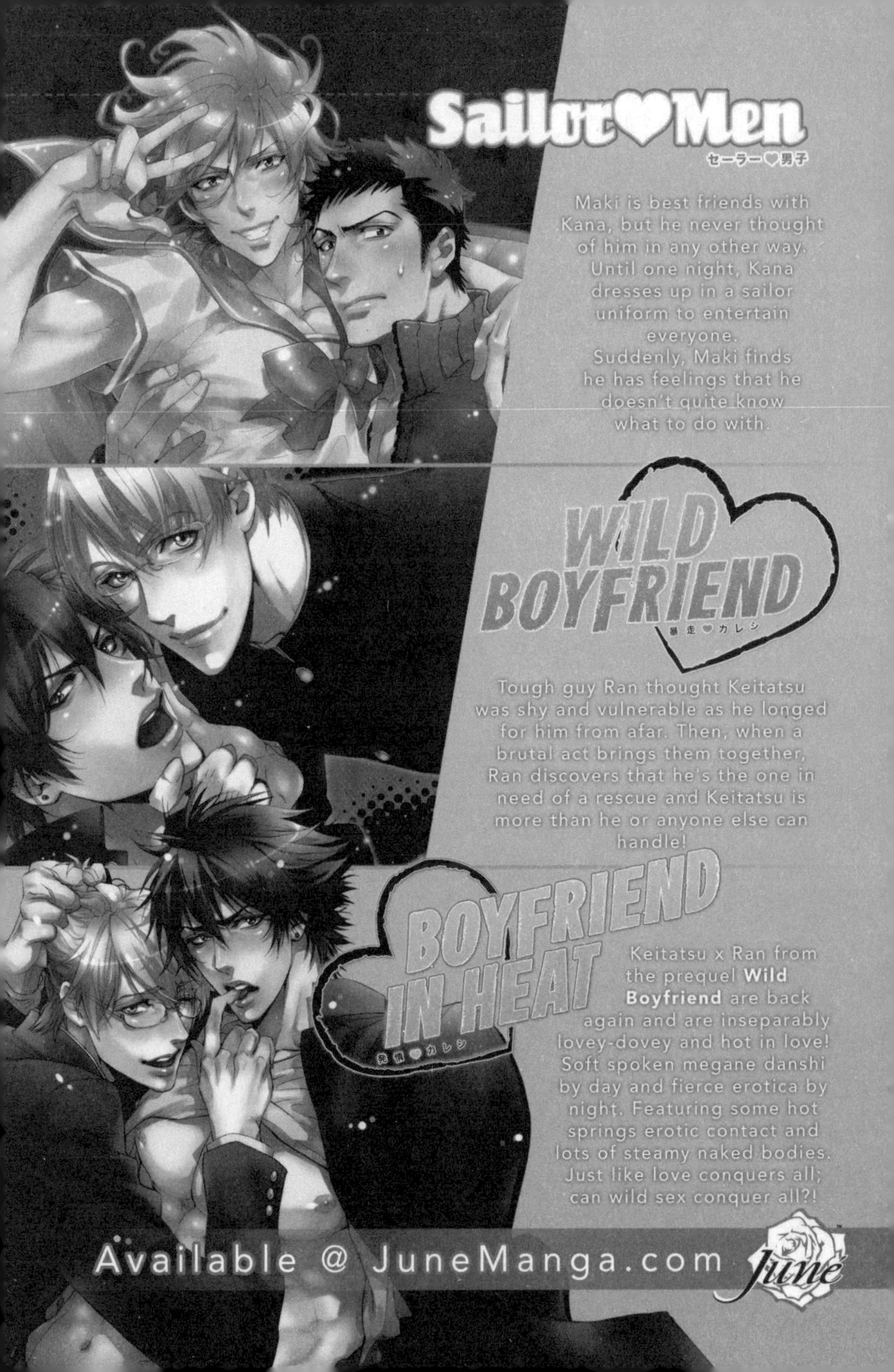
Sailor♥Men
セーラー♥男子
Maki is best friends with Kana, but he never thought of him in any other way. Until one night, Kana dresses up in a sailor uniform to entertain everyone. Suddenly, Maki finds he has feelings that he doesn't quite know what to do with.
WILD BOYFRIEND
暴走♥カレシ
Tough guy Ran thought Keitatsu was shy and vulnerable as he longed for him from afar. Then, when a brutal act brings them together, Ran discovers that he's the one in need of a rescue and Keitatsu is more than he or anyone else can handle!
BOYFRIEND IN HEAT
発情♥カレシ
Keitatsu x Ran from the prequel **Wild Boyfriend** are back again and are inseparably lovey-dovey and hot in love! Soft spoken megane danshi by day and fierce erotica by night. Featuring some hot springs erotic contact and lots of steamy naked bodies. Just like love conquers all; can wild sex conquer all?!
Available @ JuneManga.com
June

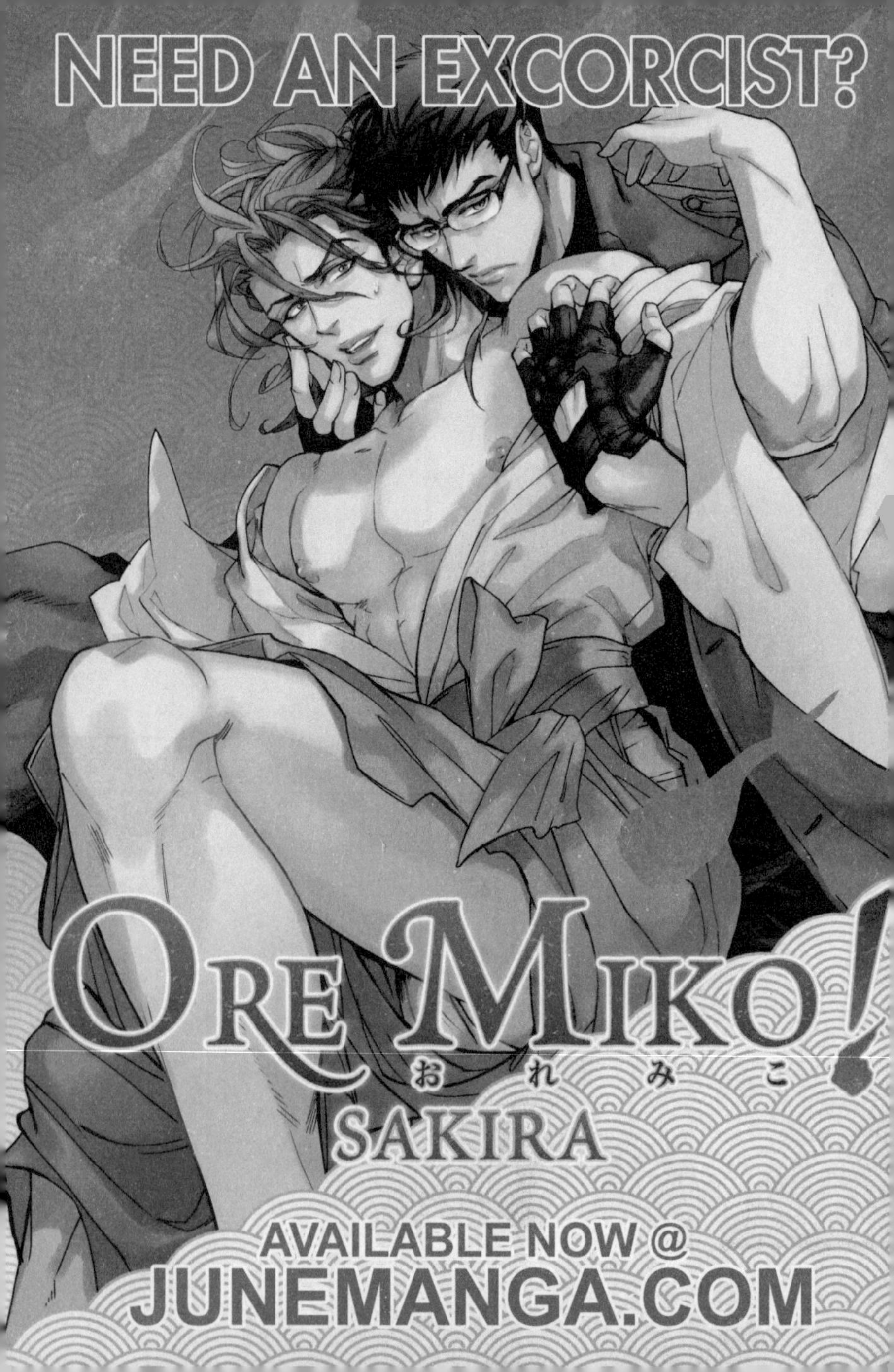
NEED AN EXCORCIST?
ORE MIKO!
おれみこ
SAKIRA
AVAILABLE NOW @
JUNEMANGA.COM

Available @ JuneManga.com

THE
TYRANT
FALLS
in LOVE
恋する暴君

HINAKO
TAKANAGA

The Tyrant Falls in Love v. 11   The Tyrant Falls in Love v. 10

© Hinako Takanaga

June

SAKIRA'S LATEST BARA TITLE IS AVAILABLE NOW

Teach Me,
教えて ♥ カテキョ
Tutor

June

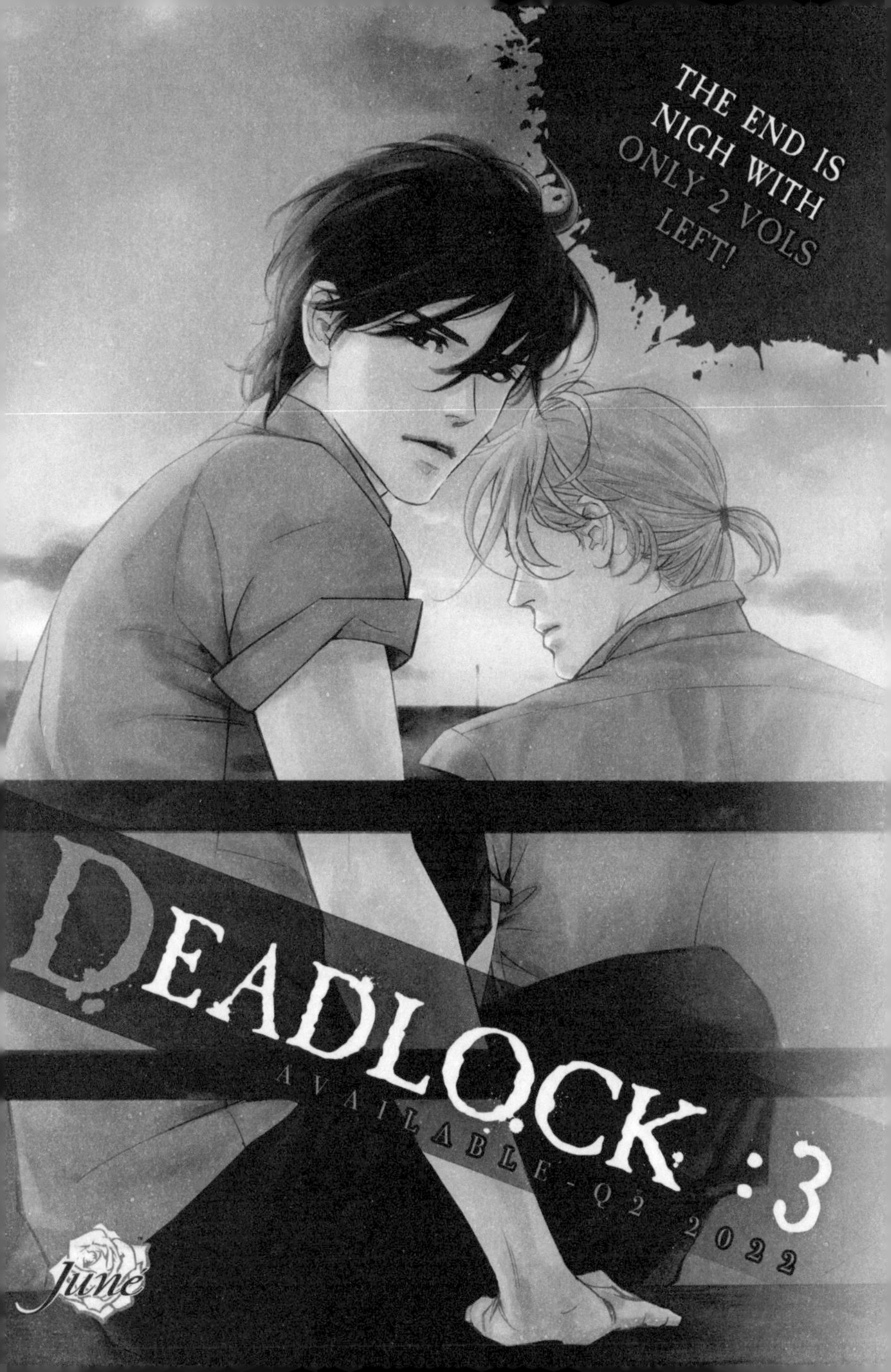
THE END IS NIGH WITH ONLY 2 VOLS LEFT!
DEADLOCK :3
AVAILABLE Q2 2022
June

Stay up to date on all June and 801 related news!

follow us online at...

f June Manga

y @JuneManga

t coming soon

ST

**This is the back of the book.
Please start the book from the
other side...**

Native manga readers read manga
from right to left to keep the manga
true to its original vision. To
enjoy, turn the book over and
start from the other side and read
right to left, top to bottom.

Follow the diagram to see how
it's done!

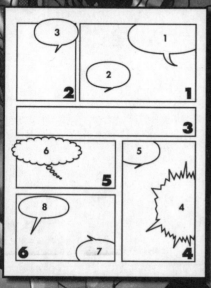

NATIVE MANGA

READ RIGHT
TO LEFT

If you see the
logo above,
you'll know that this
book is published in
its original native
format.